Communicating for Results

Fifth Edition

A Guide for Business and the Professions

Cheryl Hamilton
with Cordell Parker

Wadsworth Publishing Company

I(T)P® An International Thomson Publishing Company

Belmont, CA • Albany, NY • Bonn • Boston • Cincinnati • Detroit
Johannesburg • London • Madrid • Melbourne • Mexico City • New York
Paris • San Francisco • Singapore • Tokyo • Toronto • Washington

To Erin and Katherine

Communications Studies Editor: Randall Adams
Project Development Editor: Lewis DeSimone
Editorial Assistant: Michael Gillespie
Marketing Manager: Mike Dew
Project Editor: Vicki Friedberg
Print Buyer: Barbara Britton
Permissions Editor: Robert M. Kauser
Art Editor: Laura Murray

Cover Design and Illustration: Andrew Ogus/Book Design
Photo Researcher: Karen Wollins
Copy Editor: Jennifer Gordon
Illustrator: Precision Graphics
Compositor: Thompson Type
Printer: Quebecor Printing/Fairfield

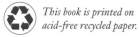 *This book is printed on acid-free recycled paper.*

Printed in the United States of America
    3 4 5 6 7 8 9 10

For more information, contact Wadsworth Publishing Company, 10 Davis Drive, Belmont, CA 94002, or electronically at http://www.thomson.com/wadsworth.html

International Thomson Publishing Europe
Berkshire House 168-173
High Holborn
London, WC1V 7AA, England

Thomas Nelson Australia
102 Dodds Street
South Melbourne 3205
Victoria, Australia

Nelson Canada
1120 Birchmount Road
Scarborough, Ontario
Canada M1K 5G4

International Thomson Publishing GmbH
Königswinterer Strasse 418
53227 Bonn, Germany

International Thomson Editores
Campos Eliseos 385, Piso 7
Col. Polanco
11560 México D.F. México

International Thomson Publishing Asia
221 Henderson Road
#05-10 Henderson Building
Singapore 0315

International Thomson Publishing Japan
Hirakawacho Kyowa Building, 3F
2-2-1 Hirakawacho
Chiyoda-ku, Tokyo 102, Japan

International Thomson Publishing Southern Africa
Building 18, Constantia Park
240 Old Pretoria Road
Halfway House, 1685 South Africa

Library of Congress Cataloging-in-Publication Data
Hamilton, Cheryl.
    Communicating for results : a guide for business and the
professions / Cheryl Hamilton with Cordell Parker. — 5th ed.
        p.   cm.
    Includes bibliographical references and index.
    ISBN 0-534-22968-9
    1. Communication in management.   I. Parker, Cordell.   II. Title.
HD30.3.H35   1996
658.4'5—dc20   96-9485

Brief Contents

AWARENESS CHECKS

CONTENTS

. . . .

Chapter 13 ■ Persuasive Presentations: Individual or Team   406

PREFACE

Communication skills are a major concern for any organization. Managers and employees who are skilled communicators have fewer misunderstandings, make fewer mistakes, create less waste, and deal with disagreements more effectively. Thus, they are more productive. And in this time of global marketing, downsizing, and technological advances, these communication skills are essential.

Communicating for Results is directed at those who are interested in self-improvement. It is designed to introduce needed communication skills to students with very little work experience, to improve the communication skills of entry-level managers and employees, and to serve as a reference for experienced professionals who wish to refresh or update their communication skills.

We emphasize various communication skills—interpersonal and organizational, interviewing and group, and public. Interpersonal and organizational skills include decreasing misunderstandings with others, understanding organizational theory, giving clear instructions, improving listening, interpreting and using nonverbal communication, and improving communication and relationships with bosses, employees, and customers. Interviewing and group skills include conducting or participating in interviews of various types, preparing conventional and electronic resumes, knowing what questions are unlawful in preemployment interviews, conducting and participating in conferences, making decisions in small groups, and handling conflict. Public communication skills include giving individual or team presentations to employees, managers, and groups inside or outside the organization, using effective organization and delivery techniques, and preparing professional visual aids.

Although the chapters in this book may be read in any order, they are organized so that each chapter builds on the skills taught in those preceding it. The skills are discussed practically and lend themselves to immediate application. In other words, what is read today can be applied at work tomorrow. Activities at the end of each chapter (Checkpoints) suggest ways for the reader to practice new skills and techniques. We suggest the

Instructor's Manual for additional application activities, test questions, and more.

We hope readers will find this book valuable and that they will add it to their personal libraries, since *Communicating for Results* is not only skills-oriented but also includes the theoretical basis for each skill.

Features of the New Edition

The fifth edition has the same number of chapters in the same order as the previous edition, but we have fine-tuned them for clarity and reading smoothness, updated references, and added new examples. Because of the global nature of today's business, we have added many international and intercultural examples. Chapter 1, The Communication Process, has a new section on ethics, a topic that we expand in the discussion of persuasive speaking in Chapter 13. Chapter 8, on employment interviewing, has been completely revised and includes a new section on creating electronic resumes. We have updated the three chapters on speaking with information on using and preparing visual aids and organizing persuasive presentations. We have added recent research on speaker anxiety to the section on confidence building in Chapter 6, as well as do-it-yourself suggestions for managing different types of anxiety.

In addition, there are several other new or revised sections:

- New section on the stages of listening
- New information on using E-mail effectively
- Revised section on gender and communication
- New photographs and art
- New section on transformational leadership
- New section on the role of diversity in problem solving
- New examples and practice quizzes

Acknowledgments

For their helpful reviews and suggestions, we would like to thank the following people: Ruth D. Anderson, North Carolina State University; Michael Laurie Bishow, Indiana-Purdue University; Cam Brammer, Marshall University; Pat Brett, Emory University; Larry M. Caillouet, Western Kentucky University; Joan T. Cooling, University of Northern Iowa; Margie Culbertson, University of Texas, Austin; Ann Cunningham, Bergen Community College; Janis Edwards, Georgia State University; Dave Elkins, Tarleton State University; Vella Neil Evans, University of Utah; Lawrence Hugenberg, Youngstown State University; James A. Johnson,

State University of New York at Geneseo; J. Daniel Joyce, Houston Community College; Sandra M. Ketrow, University of Rhode Island; Donovan J. Ochs, University of Iowa; Steven Ralston, East Tennessee State University; Edwin N. Rowley, Indiana State University; Robert Sampson, University of Wisconsin; Paul Scovell, Salisbury State College; Gary Shulman, Miami University; Gary F. Soldow, Baruch College/City University of New York; Robert A. Stewart, Texas Tech University; Bobbi Stringer, Tarrant County Junior College–NW; Susan Timm, Northern Illinois University; Tyler Tindall, Midland College; Rona Vrooman, Old Dominion University; Lionel Walsh, Virginia Commonwealth University; John L. Williams, California State University; and Thomas Wirkus, University of Wisconsin.

The staff at Wadsworth Publishing Company and the project team have been extremely helpful. In particular we'd like to thank Todd Armstrong, Lewis DeSimone, Vicki Friedberg, Michael Gillespie, Laura Murray, Steve Bolinger, Andrew Ogus, Bob Kauser, Barbara Britton, Jennifer Gordon, and Karen Stough.

We would also like to give special thanks to Patrice Wheeler for producing the new multimedia presentation ancillary that instructors are raving over; Charles Conrad, Texas A&M University, for his help and advice on the organizational chapter; Edward T. Hall for his suggestions on the three levels of culture; and the communication and business students from our many classes and seminars for their helpful advice.

Cheryl Hamilton
Cordell Parker
Ft. Worth, Texas

1

The Communication Process: An Introduction

P eople who understand how communication functions in an organization, who have developed a wide repertory of written and oral communicative skills, and who have learned when and how to use those skills seem to have more successful careers and contribute more fully to their organizations than people who have not done so.[1]

CHARLES CONRAD,
Texas A&M University

While millions of horrified viewers watched on live television, on January 28, 1986, the space shuttle *Challenger* exploded less than two minutes after lift-off. All seven crew members perished. In retrospect, it was clear the launch should have been cancelled. Was it just as clear before the fact? Consider the following:

On the evening before the launch, a teleconference took place between representatives of Morton Thiokol (manufacturer of the booster rocket), the Marshall Space Flight Center (MSFC), and the Kennedy Space Center. Morton Thiokol engineers expressed concern over the integrity of the O-ring seals at temperatures below 53 degrees (temperatures at the launch site were below freezing). The Thiokol senior engineer concluded the data supported a no-launch decision. The director of space engineering at MSFC indicated he was "appalled" by the Thiokol recommendation but would not launch over the contractor's objections. At that point the MSFC chief of solid rockets gave his view, concluding that the data presented were inconclusive.

Based on NASA's rule that contractors and they themselves had to prove it was safe to fly, the statements that the data were inconclusive should have stopped the launch. However, a Thiokol vice president who was also on the line requested an off-line caucus to reevaluate the data. During the caucus, two engineers attempted to make themselves heard as management representatives began a discussion. Their attempts were met with cold stares as management representatives struggled to compile data that would support a launch decision. Returning to the teleconference, the Thiokol VP read the launch support rationale and recommended that the launch proceed.[2] [The final launch decision was made by top NASA management without knowledge of the no-go recommendation of the Thiokol engineers.]

IMPORTANCE OF BUSINESS AND PROFESSIONAL COMMUNICATION

Sometimes it is easy to forget that organizations are made up of people like us and that the everyday decisions we make can affect the organization, customers, other workers, and our own destiny in the organization. Indeed, sometimes, as in the incident just described, our decisions can affect the very survival of other people. Communication skills are important because it is through communication that we gain and offer the information we and our coworkers (as well as management) need to make successful decisions at work.

The success of an organization depends on the communication skills of all its employees.[3] In a survey, eighty-four personnel officers from different organizations were asked, "In assessing an individual's chance of success in your company, how important do you think communication skills are, relative to other kinds of abilities?" Communication skills were rated "extremely important" by 85 percent of the respondents, and 95 per-

Business and professional organizations depend on the communication skills of all their employees. (© *Tom McCarthy/The Picture Cube, Inc.*)

cent reported that communication skills were considered when they hired employees.[4]

Another survey, described in *The Endicott Report*, asked 170 businesses to list their most common reason for not hiring an applicant. "Inability to communicate" and "poor communication skills" were mentioned more frequently than other reasons.[5]

The best way to improve communication is, first, to understand exactly what it is. To help you improve your communication skills, this chapter will introduce the communication process and the major causes of our communication errors; Chapter 2 will deal more specifically with communication in the organizational setting.

Communication Defined

. . . .

When people in business and the professions are asked to define *communication*, they often respond by saying something like this: "Communication is the process of transferring thoughts and ideas from one person to another." On the surface, this definition sounds good, it acknowledges that communication is a process (which means that it is a continual happening), and it includes the idea of communicating our thoughts and ideas to others (which is a necessary occurrence in business). However, the words *transferring* and *from one person to another* inaccurately imply that communication is like pouring liquid from a pitcher. The definition implies a simple, one-way action where person A takes knowledge from his or her

Figure 1.1 A basic model of communication.

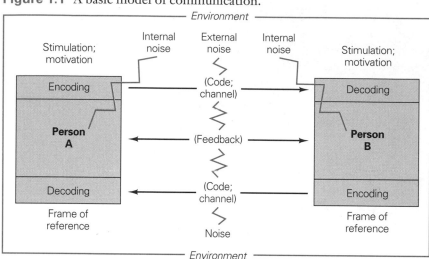

head and simply pours (transfers) it into the head of person B. Obviously, communication is not so simple. Person B may refuse to accept A's ideas and may, instead, wish to present his or her own ideas (give feedback). Or person B may completely misinterpret A's message. As one communication scholar notes, "Communication does not consist of the transmission of meaning. Meanings are not transferable. Only messages are transmittable, and meanings are not in the message, they are in the message-user."[6]

A more accurate definition of communication can be found by looking at its original meaning. *The Oxford English Dictionary* lists the Latin root of *communicate* as *communicare*, which means "to make common to many, share."[7] According to this definition, when people communicate, they express their ideas and feelings in a way that is *understandable* (common) to each of them. They attempt to share information with each other. Each person has a direct effect on the other and on subsequent communication. Therefore, **communication** is the process of people sharing thoughts, ideas, and feelings with each other in commonly understandable ways.

THE BASIC MODEL OF COMMUNICATION

Whether you are communicating with only one person, with a small group, or with many people, the same basic process occurs and the same misunderstandings can arise. Successful business and professional communicators owe a large part of their success to their ability to minimize potential misunderstandings. This ability results from knowing the elements of the communication process and the role that each element plays. The model in Figure 1.1 will help you to visualize these basic elements: person A/person B, stimulus and motivation, encoding and decoding, code, channel, feedback, environment, and noise.

Person A/Person B

Person A in the model could be the sender (the source of the message) or the receiver (the interpreter of the message). Person B also could be either the sender or the receiver. Actually, during most of their communication, they will both send and receive simultaneously. Think, for example, of conversations between supervisors and employees. When supervisors initiate conversation, they are the senders and the employees are the receivers. However, when the employees respond, the supervisors become the receivers and the employees are the senders. When conversations really get rolling, it is very difficult to determine at any one moment who are senders and who are receivers. However, to simplify our discussion of the model, we will continue to use the terms *sender* and *receiver*.

Stimulus and Motivation

Two things must happen before the sender even wants to send a message. First, the sender must be **stimulated.** Some type of stimulus triggers a thought, which in turn triggers the desire to communicate. A stimulus can be either internal or external. For example, a supervisor in the technical publications department of a company is assigned to brief a group of newly hired personnel. While discussing the basic procedures used by the company in lettering charts and signs, the supervisor suddenly remembers that the media equipment needed for the next day's briefing has not yet been ordered. He tells the new workers to take a 5-minute break, hurries to the office, and calls the media secretary. The supervisor's communication with the secretary was triggered by an internal stimulus.

An external stimulus can also trigger the desire to communicate. Meetings and professional gatherings that are filled with awkward silences are missing the necessary external stimuli that are needed to start relaxed communication. For example, a sales representative promoting a new book at a convention is very careful to arrange for such appropriate stimuli as cocktails, soft drinks and juices, appetizers, soft music, and the author of the book—all in a suite with a breathtaking view of the city. When the guests arrive, they are faced with a variety of stimuli to ensure conversation. Carefully planned business meetings might include such external stimuli as coffee, a progress chart, or an outside consultant.

It is important to remember, however, that a stimulus alone is not enough to trigger communication. The second requirement to send a message is sufficient **motivation.** Think of the times a manager or leader has asked a question, and some of the people present were fairly sure they knew the answer (were stimulated) but did not respond. Why didn't they respond? Probably because they were not sufficiently motivated—that is, they saw no personal benefit in answering. Or perhaps they saw greater benefit in not answering: Some may have feared being ridiculed by the leader or group for an incorrect answer. Maybe others were trying to impress someone in the group and didn't want to risk appearing unprofessional. In contrast, if the people suspected that their promotions could be influenced by the amount of their participation, they might be motivated to answer the question.

The importance of these two steps—stimulation and motivation—cannot be overlooked. Customers will rarely listen carefully to a sales presentation if the stimulus is absent, and they certainly won't buy unless they can see how they will benefit (motivation). The key to being a good salesperson lies in knowing how to stimulate and motivate the customer. Good speakers are also aware of these two steps. In the introduction of an oral presentation, a good business speaker first gets the listeners' attention (stimulation to listen) and then shows them how this particular presentation will be of value to them personally (motivation to continue to listen).

Encoding and Decoding

After being stimulated and motivated to communicate, the sender must decide how best to convey a message to the specific receiver. The process of putting a message into the form in which it is to be communicated is called **encoding.** For example, when a manager finds it necessary to reprimand an employee, encoding becomes very important. Before (or almost simultaneously with) encoding the message, the manager may consider such topics as: What type of words should be used—mild or firm? What volume should be used—loud or soft? Would a frown or a smile achieve the best result? What specific examples would help the employee understand? Because senders encode messages before communicating them, the sender is often referred to as the *encoder.*

When the encoder's message is picked up, the receiver tries to make sense out of it, that is, to decode it. **Decoding** is the process the receiver goes through in trying to interpret the exact meaning of a message. Everyone tends to read between the lines in an effort to interpret what the sender means by the message. When an employee is reprimanded by a supervisor, the employee may consider such questions as: How serious a mistake have I made? Is the boss serious or just joking? Am I going to be fired or lose my promotion? Because receivers decode messages, they are often referred to as *decoders*.

Frame of Reference

Although encoding and decoding may seem to be fairly simple processes, they are often responsible for major communication breakdowns. As a sender, you use your own background and experience to encode messages. But receivers use *their* own background and experiences to decode those messages. Unless the backgrounds and experiences—the **frames of reference**—of both sender and receiver are identical, problems may develop in accurately encoding and decoding messages. For example:

- General Motors had no success in selling the Chevy Nova in Mexico. Nova means "No ɡo" in Spanish!
- The "I'm a Pepper" commercial that was so successful in the United States was changed in England when Dr. Pepper's management realized that *pepper* is British slang for prostitution.
- Doctors and psychologists have found that patients may not volunteer needed information because they are uncertain what is expected of them.[8] For example, when you go to a doctor, do you volunteer your symptoms or wait to be asked?
- In investigating the explosion of the space shuttle *Challenger*, the Rogers Commission found that technical personnel had listed the O-ring factor as "closed" in their safety review reports. Management thought this meant that the problem was solved when, in fact, the technicians meant that further safety testing was required.

Each person's frame of reference includes educational background, race, sex, where the person grew up, what his or her parents were like, attitudes, personality, all past experiences, and much more. Think of your frame of reference as an invisible window.[9] Everything you see, touch, taste, smell, and hear must take place through your particular window. Some windows have a large frame that gives a broad view of what is going on outside them; others have a small frame that limits what can be observed. Some windows have thin or clear glass in their frames, which allows for accurate viewing; others have glass so thick or tinted that images are distorted. People whose windows have rose-tinted glass may judge everything as good in spite of obvious evils, while people with dark-tinted windows may think the world is doomed regardless of the good things happening around them.

Is it possible, then, for any two people to have exactly the same frame of reference? The answer is no. Even identical twins have different personalities and therefore react differently to the same experiences.

Managers and employees certainly have different frames of reference. Managers in one study were asked to rank a list of morale factors that their employees might consider important on the job. These managers selected appreciation of work done, a feeling of being "in on things," and sympathetic help on personal problems as eighth, ninth, and tenth in importance to employees. Their subordinates, however, listed the same three factors as first, second, and third.[10] In another study, conducted at a public utility, supervisors and workers were asked how often the supervisor obtained workers' ideas in solving job-related problems. Seventy-six percent of the supervisors said they always or almost always involved subordinates. Only 16 percent of the workers agreed that this was true.[11]

If everyone's frame of reference is not identical, then we must take into account the probability that people will encounter difficulties in communicating. Consider the following examples that illustrate encoding and/or decoding breakdown caused by differences in frames of reference. Remember, when you read these examples, you are doing so from your own frame of reference.

EXAMPLE 1

In exchange for some U.S.-controlled land in West Germany, the German government agreed to construct a new facility at another military installation controlled by the U.S. Army. After the preliminary drawings were completed, a meeting was held with the German and American engineers and one translator. When a German engineer asked a question, the translator repeated the question in English; the American's answer was then translated back into German.

A German asked a question about the maximum distance allowed between two points that he had indicated in the drawing. The question was translated, and an American engineer quickly raised his hand with his index finger pointing upward and answered, "1 meter." The translator, thinking no translation was necessary, remained silent. The German engineers wrote "2 meters" in their notes; the Americans wrote 1 meter. (The Germans, when using fingers to show a number, begin counting with the thumb as number one; therefore, the index finger, being the second finger from the thumb, represents the number two.)

EXAMPLE 2

A college professor was a member of a particular credit union. Needing a quick loan one day, she filled out all the necessary application forms and waited while the employee typed the request into the computer terminal. When the answer was received, the employee told the professor, "I'm very sorry, but we can't give you a loan."

"Why not?" asked the professor, who knew her credit was good.

"I don't know why, but the computer says we can't."

"What does the computer say?" asked the professor.

The words the computer had typed out were NO LOAN THIS MEMBER. Urged by the professor, the employee referred the matter to the manager and discovered that "No loan this member" meant that the professor did not have a loan. If she had already had a loan with the credit union, the computer would have responded with ONE LOAN THIS MEMBER.

EXAMPLE 3

A merchant ordered 350 turkeys for the Thanksgiving holiday season. A few weeks before Thanksgiving his sales dropped sharply. Afraid that he would not be able to sell all of the turkeys, he phoned the distributor and said, "Cut my order in half!" When his order arrived, it contained 350 turkeys, each cut in half!

EXAMPLE 4

A new employee at a large company walked up to a paper shredder and stood before it looking confused. "Need some help?" the senior secretary asked. "Yes, how does this thing work?" "It's simple," she said as she took the fat report from her colleague's hand and fed it into the shredder. "See?" "I see," he said, "but how many copies does it make?"[12]

EXAMPLE 5

On final approach, just short of touchdown, the pilot of a military plane determined that the runway was too short to land and that the landing must be aborted. He yelled to his engineer, "Takeoff power." The engineer reached up and turned off the engines, and the plane crashed off the end of the runway. The pilot had wanted the engineer to give him extra power for takeoff!

These examples of communication breakdown might not have occurred if the senders had attempted to put their messages into the frames of reference of the receivers or if the receivers had attempted to decode the messages from the senders' frames of reference. Each communicator needs to remember that *the message that counts is the one received*. It does not matter what you really said, what you thought you said, or what you meant to say. As a sender, you need to be concerned with what your receiver thought you said. Therefore, the burden of communication lies with you as sender. You will not improve communication by placing blame and complaining, "That's not what I said! Don't you ever listen to me?" Senders must try to phrase messages so that receivers will understand them. Of course, the only way to judge the reception of your message is to ask the receivers to paraphrase (that is, summarize in their own words) what they think you meant.

A Communication Fallacy ■   After reading examples of communication breakdown, some business and professional people tend to say (or think), "These examples do not apply to the more technical business world. We couldn't afford to make such ridiculous mistakes!" The second part of that statement is true: Communication errors are often expensive. But is the business world exempt from them? Is it possible that 100 percent communication—when the sent messages and the received messages are identical—can be achieved in the business setting or is this a communication fallacy?

To answer this question, we must first decide whether 100 percent communication is *ever* possible. In other words, are the sent messages and the received messages ever identical? For just a moment, let's move outside the business world and consider an example most people have observed firsthand. Imagine that a couple who have been married for fifty years are attending a social gathering. The husband and wife are on opposite sides of the room when one guest begins to tell the same joke he has told at every party for the past ten years. The husband and wife look at each other from across the room and grimace. Obviously, both of them are showing disgust at the joke-telling guest, so general understanding has occurred between them. Is it 100 percent? No, because their intensity of feeling differs. The woman may be finding the joker so repulsive that she wishes to leave, while the man regards him as disgusting but tolerable. Also, the exact thoughts behind the husband's and the wife's grimaces differ. The woman's grimace may mean, "How embarrassing for the hostess! How can she stand it when he makes a fool of himself at her party?" The man's grimace may mean, "The poor guy! How can he stand to make such a fool of himself?" In order for 100 percent communication to occur, husband and wife would have to have identical frames of reference. Obviously, they do not.

Now consider two business examples:

EXAMPLE 1

Imagine that a supervisor is sitting at her desk working on a prototype for a new production item. She has been working on the prototype for several days and is angry about all the work required. She reaches for her jeweler's screwdriver but finds it missing. Wilson, a technician who works for the supervisor, walks by at that moment. "Wilson, bring me a set of jeweler's screwdrivers," shouts the angry supervisor. Looking rather surprised, Wilson walks to the tool crib, picks up a set of jeweler's screwdrivers, and hands them to the supervisor.

Is this an example of 100 percent communication? The supervisor probably thinks so because she got what she requested. But she has forgotten
that her tone of voice and facial expression also communicated something
to Wilson. Although the supervisor may feel good about the communication, Wilson may be thinking, "What have I done wrong? She only picks
on us when we've done something she doesn't like" or "I guess she doesn't
like the way I handled the Smith job."

EXAMPLE 2

A foreman told a machine operator as he was passing, "Better clean up
around here." Ten minutes later, the foreman's assistant phoned: "Say,
boss, isn't that bearing Sipert is working on due up in engineering
pronto?"
    "You bet your sweet life it is. Why?"
    "He says you told him to drop it and sweep the place up. I thought
I'd better make sure."
    "Listen," the foreman flared into the phone, "get him right back on
that job. It's got to be ready in twenty minutes."
    What [the foreman] had in mind was for Sipert to gather up the oily
waste, which was a fire and accident hazard. This would not have taken
more than a couple of minutes, and there would have been plenty of time
to finish the bearing.[13]

If no two individuals have the same frame of reference, how can a
person ever communicate 100 percent with anyone on any topic, even in
the business setting? Perhaps you can reach 80 to 95 percent when communicating horizontally with other people in the same position or rank,
but upward and downward communication gets progressively worse the
higher or lower on the corporate ladder you proceed. One company researched 100 businesses and discovered that, of a message communicated
downward through five levels of management, only 20 percent reaches the
workers for whom it is intended (see Figure 1.2).[14] Because of individual
frames of reference, a message progressing up or down the various levels
(chain of command) is

- *Leveled.* Some details are lost.
- *Condensed.* The message becomes shorter and simpler.
- *Sharpened.* Some details are highlighted, thereby becoming more
  important.
- *Assimilated.* Ambiguities are clarified and interpreted to conform to
  past messages and future expectations from individual frames of
  reference.
- *Embellished.* Details are added.

Figure 1.2 Amount of message received when communicated downward through five levels of management.

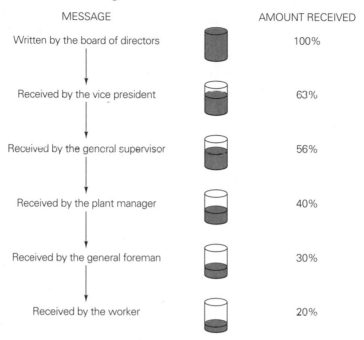

MESSAGE		AMOUNT RECEIVED
Written by the board of directors		100%
Received by the vice president		63%
Received by the general supervisor		56%
Received by the plant manager		40%
Received by the general foreman		30%
Received by the worker		20%

Although business communicators should strive for the best communication possible, they will probably be better communicators if they agree that 100 percent communication is a communication fallacy. The realization that effective communication is very difficult changes one's attitude toward communication. For example, when a secretary fails to type a letter exactly as the boss intended, the boss who expects to be able to communicate 100 percent feels perfectly justified in criticizing the secretary for not following instructions. After all, the boss had told the secretary what to do. When a subordinate fails to follow the exact orders of a manager, the manager who assumes 100 percent communication feels justified in blaming the subordinate, deciding not to grant the scheduled promotion or maybe even firing the employee. After all, managers don't have time to pamper employees.

People who believe that 100 percent communication is easily attainable spend a great deal of time accusing other people or justifying their own actions. Such defensive behavior is emotionally exhausting and counterproductive. *The effective communicator, in contrast, knows that 100 percent communication is highly unlikely and prepares for possible misunderstanding ahead of time.* By anticipating and recognizing potential areas of misunder-standing, the effective communicator is able to prevent many errors from happening.

Code

Another element of the basic communication model is the code. The **code** is not the message but the symbols that carry the message. There are three basic communication codes:

- *Language (verbal code).* Either spoken or written words used to com-municate thoughts and emotions.
- *Paralanguage (vocal code).* The vocal elements that go along with spo-ken language, including tone of voice, pitch, rate, volume, and em-phasis. (Although many texts list paralanguage as a subcategory of nonverbal communication, we have elected to separate them in order to emphasize the importance of each.)
- *Nonverbal (visual code).* All intentional and unintentional means other than writing or speaking by which a person sends a message, includ-ing facial expressions, eye contact, gestures, appearance, posture, size and location of office, and arrival time at meetings.

Many businesspeople think that the only important code is the lan-guage code. Researchers, however, have found that language is not as im-portant to the meaning of a message as either the nonverbal or the para-language codes. R. L. Birdwhistell reports that "probably no more than 30–35 percent of the social meaning of a conversation or an interaction is carried by the words."[15] This leaves 60–65 percent of meaning conveyed by the nonverbal and paralanguage codes. Analyzing the results from twenty-three studies, J. S. Philpott's findings support Birdwhistell's asser-tion. Philpott found that the verbal code accounted for 31 percent of the variance in meanings, while the vocal and visual codes accounted for the remaining variance (see Figure 1.3).[16] Many other studies have found that when adults attempt to determine the meaning of a statement, they rely more heavily on visual and vocal cues than they do on what is ac-tually said.[17] This seems to be true regardless of whether the situation involves first impressions, attitudes, job interviews, or boss–employee conversations.[18]

The difference among the codes can be illustrated in the following example. You arrive home after a hard day at work. You walk in, slam the door, plop down on your recliner, and let out a long sigh. When asked, "How was your day?" you reply, "Oh, it was fine!" In this instance, to

Figure 1.3 When interpreting a message, listeners rely more heavily on the visual and vocal codes (what they see and how you speak) than on the verbal code (what you say).

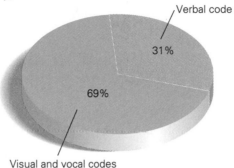

which code would the questioner pay more attention—the nonverbal slamming of the door, the loud sigh (paralanguage), or the actual words spoken (language)?

To communicate effectively, the sender must communicate the same message by all three codes. However, many people either deliberately or unknowingly send conflicting messages. Whenever there is a conflict among the messages received, people tend to believe more of what they see than what they hear. Grouping language and paralanguage together as verbal, M. Argyle found "that with initially equated signals the nonverbal messages outweighed the verbal ones at least 5 to 1, and where they were in conflict the verbal messages were virtually disregarded."[19] The flight attendants' reassuring words (language code) on a nearly disastrous Eastern Airlines flight were probably ignored by the passengers, who could see the fear on their faces (nonverbal code) and could hear the fear in the voice of the captain (paralanguage code). One passenger reported, "The worst part was when the captain told us that the ditching was imminent. . . . He had a real quivering voice, and it scared the hell out of everyone."[20]

To further illustrate the problem of conflicting messages, consider this example. A supervisor was pleased at the way her employees had completed a very difficult and important project. She called a special meeting of the employees just to praise them. Five minutes before the meeting, however, she received a call from her boss telling her that she was wanted in the office of the vice president to discuss a problem relating to her department's budget. She was still concentrating on the phone call as she walked into the meeting. Her employees noticed her strained smile and abstracted manner and began to feel nervous. Maybe, they thought, they weren't going to be praised after all.

"I can't tell you how pleased I am with the way you handled last week's project," the supervisor began. "You worked together as a team and I'm proud of all of you. Well, take a few minutes for coffee and donuts before getting to work." Then, instead of casually joining her employees for coffee as she usually did, the supervisor hurried from the room.

The employees were confused. Was she pleased with them or not? Her language said she *was* pleased. Yet her paralanguage (tone of voice and rushed delivery) seemed to indicate displeasure. Her strained smile, abstracted manner, and failure to stay for coffee all communicated nonverbally that she was displeased. Most employees would probably ignore what was actually said and interpret the conflicting messages to mean that the supervisor was unhappy. Actually, all the supervisor meant was, "I'm pleased." She was completely unaware that she was sending conflicting messages. Like many people, she incorrectly assumed that the only message being sent was the verbalized (language) message.

Channel

In many instances, the success of your message may depend on the channel you select. A **channel** is the medium selected to carry the message. Some examples of communication channels are face-to-face discussion, memos, magazines, newsletters, radio, telephone, and television.

In a business meeting, where participants are using the face-to-face communication channel, all three codes—nonverbal, language, and paralanguage—carry messages. Television also carries all three codes. Because radio and telephone communication lack the nonverbal code, depriving the listener of visual clues to the meaning, these channels involve a greater chance of communication breakdown. Memos are even more limited because they contain only the language code (although we attempt to add paralanguage by underlining, drawing an arrow, or circling in red pen).

In deciding which channel is most appropriate for communication with your superior, subordinate, or colleague, consider these items:[21]

- *The importance of the message.* Important messages usually require the face-to-face channel.
- *The needs and abilities of the receiver.* Some people are able to work from memos and phone conversations; others are better at interpreting messages and are happier in face-to-face situations.
- *The amount and speed of the feedback required.* Complicated messages and messages needing immediate feedback require the face-to-face channel, in which all codes are present.

- *The necessity of a permanent record.* Memos and written instructions can be used to verify a conversation and to serve as a permanent record of what was said.
- *The cost of the channel.* In the business world, time and energy spent equal cost. For example, it costs less to fax, more to speak on the phone long distance, and much more to bring employees to a central place for a face-to-face meeting.
- *The formality or informality desired.* Although face-to-face communication can be quite formal, it is normally considered less formal than a newsletter or a memo.

The channel selected is also very important when communicating with the public. When selling merchandise or ideas, the organization should select the channel that (1) is the least expensive but (2) reaches the target audience with (3) the appropriate codes needed to sell the item or idea. For example, suppose your company is planning to sell a new brand of laundry detergent. In deciding which channel to use for marketing, you would first want to identify the target audience—in this instance, probably homemakers. You would then decide which codes would be needed to sell the item. For example, do they need to see the item's size or packaging or would hearing about it be enough? Finally, you would decide which channel would be as inexpensive as possible and still contain the necessary codes to reach the target audience.

One supervisor found out the importance of the channel the hard way. During the lunch hour, he received a call from a person representing a key account, who wanted to know if it was possible to get a special shipment of parts by 5:00 that afternoon. "No problem," assured the supervisor. "We can ship them to you by a special flight in plenty of time." "I'm counting on you," replied the caller. "If we don't get that shipment by 5:00, we will lose a big account!" The supervisor was scheduled to attend a very important meeting in 5 minutes, so he wrote a detailed memo and dropped it on the shipping foreman's desk on his way to the meeting. The supervisor was involved in this important meeting for most of the afternoon and soon forgot about the noon phone call. Two days later, he received a letter from the key account representative stating that they not only had failed to receive the parts by 5:00 but also had never received the parts at all. As a result, they were canceling all current orders and taking their business elsewhere!

What did the supervisor do wrong? First, he chose a poor channel for such an important message, and second, he failed to follow up the memo to make sure its meaning was clear to the foreman. When using a channel other than a face-to-face meeting, a sender must be sure to follow through by checking to see that the message has been received, understood, and carried out correctly.

Memos and Word Choice ■   The extensive use of memos indicates the importance that business and professional people incorrectly place on this channel of communication. Indeed, many people keep copies of the memos they send so that they can "prove" what they said if the receivers fail to follow instructions correctly. However, memos can be used effectively when they follow up a face-to-face meeting, list the decisions reached during a meeting, or summarize the areas discussed. Those who receive this type of memo have less difficulty in decoding the message accurately because they were present at the meeting and their frames of reference are more closely attuned to the sender's.

However, when memos must be used to send important or new information, the sender should take extreme care in the selection of language. Researchers have found that the tone of a written statement determines how the reader perceives the author of the message and even the organization for whom the author works. For example, one study found that when flexible-sounding words (such as *asked, hesitate, agreeable,* and *offering*) were used, readers judged the organization to be concerned with employees, fair to women and minorities, involved with community problems, generous in determining employee salaries, open in communication with the union, and liked by employees. However, when strict-sounding words (*required, willing, forceful,* and *pushing*) were used, the readers judged the organization to be exactly the opposite.[22]

One company always substitutes the word *issue* for *problem*, feeling that people who don't wish to discuss "problems" will feel comfortable with "issues." Here are some similar examples of corporate language selection:

> J. C. Penney, Physio-Control, and Quad/Graphics never refer to their people as "employees." At Penney, you're an associate. At Physio-Control, . . . [an] Eli Lilly unit that makes medical electronic products, you're a team member. And at Quad/Graphics . . . [a] Wisconsin-based printer, you're a partner.[23]

Feedback

When people observe their own behavior and resolve to do better next time, when people ask friends to give an opinion on how well they handled a certain situation, or when managers suggest ways in which employees can improve their performance, feedback is being employed. **Feedback** refers to the verbal and visual responses to messages. Feedback can be a self-monitoring response that allows individuals to modify their behavior until it meets their expectations. Feedback is also the only way a person can know whether messages sent are interpreted as intended. Without feedback, all that one can do is assume that the messages have been received correctly.

Advantages of Feedback ■ Supervisors who encourage their employees to give feedback (to ask questions and make comments) find that feedback improves the accuracy of employee understanding and employee productivity.[24] Misunderstandings often occur because employees honestly think they have understood the boss' instructions well enough that feedback is unnecessary. The few seconds that it would take to verify the assignment could save both time and money (mistakes are expensive).

Another advantage is that feedback increases employee satisfaction with the job. People like to feel that their ideas and opinions are of value. When given the opportunity to ask questions or make suggestions, employees tend to feel more a part of the organization and are willing to take on responsibility for accurate communication.

Difficulties with Feedback ■ Despite the advantages of feedback, however, many managers and employees avoid its use for several reasons.[25] First of all, feedback causes people to feel under attack psychologically. Even the most experienced manager or employee can become defensive when feedback seems negative or overwhelming. Sometimes, feedback indicates that the message was not communicated very well. Actually, however, people should worry when they don't receive *any* feedback— the receivers may be either so confused that they don't know what to ask or so confident of their understanding that they ignore the need for verification.

Another difficulty is that feedback is time-consuming. It *does* take time to make sure that everyone understands, but it takes more time (and money) to redo tasks that could have been accomplished correctly the first time. One consulting firm uses this slogan in its seminars: "If you don't have time to do the job correctly, when will you find time to do the job a second time?"

In addition, feedback is difficult to elicit. Many people seek feedback by asking, "Are there any questions?" or "Are you sure you understand?" Then they can't understand why no one ever has any questions. Asking others if they understand pressures them to say, "No, I don't have any questions" or "Yes, I do understand," even when the opposite may be true. When employees are afraid of appearing stupid in front of the manager, they will pretend to understand whether they do or not. Instead of asking employees *if* they understand, managers should ask them *what* they understand. Communication is further improved when employees are asked to paraphrase the instructions they have received. Paraphrasing allows managers to determine which part of the instructions, if any, are unclear.

Another reason people are reluctant to give feedback is that they may have reacted negatively to comments received from others in the past, or others may have reacted badly to what they said. It takes only a few negative verbal or nonverbal reactions to convince people that it is simply too dangerous to say what they think or to admit that they don't understand.

Effective Use of Feedback ■   To improve your use of feedback, try adopting the following suggestions.[26] When receiving feedback from others, follow these guidelines:

- *Tell people you want feedback.* When people feel that their opinions and observations may be used against them or that your feelings may be easily hurt, they withhold feedback. Therefore, let them know that you consider feedback (including personal opinions, questions, and disagreement) not only useful but necessary.
- *Identify the areas in which you want feedback.* If you want personal feedback, you might say, "I am trying to improve my delivery and am interested in how confident I appeared in today's meeting." If you want only feedback pertaining to the clarity of your organization, then specify that topic.
- If you are a manager, *set aside time for regularly scheduled feedback sessions.* Such sessions show employees that you value feedback and tend to make it easier for them to ask questions and express opinions.
- *Use silence to encourage feedback.* Too many people ask a question, wait 2 or 3 seconds, and then begin talking again. It takes more than 2 or 3 seconds for most people to organize and verbalize their responses. If you remain silent for at least a full 10 seconds, you will probably get more responses.
- *Watch for nonverbal responses.* Because nonverbal code carries a significant amount of the meaning of a message, it is an excellent source of feedback.
- *Ask questions.* Do not assume that you understand the meaning of the feedback you receive from others. When in doubt, ask for clarification.
- *Paraphrase.* Even when you feel sure you understand a person's feedback, it is a good idea to paraphrase, summarizing the statement in your own words. For example, if your boss says, "This rush job has top priority," you could paraphrase by saying, "Then this rush job is more important than the rush job I'm working on now. Is that

correct?" As the need for message accuracy increases, the need for paraphrasing increases.

- *Use statements that encourage feedback.* People usually adjust their feedback by monitoring the listener's verbal and nonverbal reactions. If you want a person's honest opinion, you must encourage it by purposely saying such things as "Really?" "Interesting." "So, you feel that . . ."
- *Reward feedback.* If you are a manager, you can reward feedback by complimenting the person, preferably in front of his or her colleagues. Some companies have a "Best Idea of the Month" contest and put the winners' names on a placard or give each of them a company pen with their name engraved on it. As an employee, you can sincerely thank people for their comments and perhaps write them a thank-you note.
- *Follow up.* Individual conversations and group meetings often require oral or written follow-up to ensure that successful communications occurred and to encourage implementation of any decisions reached.

When giving feedback to others, follow these guidelines:

- *Direct feedback toward behavior rather than toward the person.* A common mistake is to criticize the person rather than the behavior. Telling a secretary, "You are a poor excuse for a secretary" is an attack on the secretary rather than on the offensive behavior and causes a defensive, emotional response. Your feedback is much more likely to be received positively if you mention the action or behavior that is unacceptable and focus on what can be done to avoid it in the future.
- *Use language that is descriptive instead of evaluative.* Descriptive feedback is tactfully honest and objective, whereas evaluative feedback is judgmental and accusatory. Evaluative feedback: "Where is your sales report? You know it is due on my desk no later than 9:00 each morning. You're obviously not reliable anymore." Descriptive feedback: "When you don't turn your sales reports in on time, I'm unable to complete the departmental sales report on time. This makes me look bad and the department look bad. You've been late twice this month. Is there something I can do to help you get those reports in on time?" Evaluative, judgmental words cause defensiveness and hurt feelings; words that simply describe the situation nonjudgmentally are more likely to result in cooperation.
- *Recognize that feedback involves sharing ideas, not giving advice.* It is not always sensible to give advice to other people. If your advice does not

work, you will be blamed. One of the best ways to improve a relationship is by openly sharing opinions and ideas. Suppose a manager who is having trouble with some employees comes to you and asks, "What am I doing wrong?" Instead of giving advice, share a personal experience with the manager. For example, you might describe a similar problem you had and how you handled it. It is then up to the manager to decide what to do.

- *Include only as much information as the person can handle at one time.* Suppose during a performance appraisal you give an employee a list of twenty items that need improvement. Is this type of feedback beneficial? *You* may feel better now that you have dumped your feelings, but how can anyone improve on twenty things at the same time? When giving feedback, include only two or three suggestions at a time—a number the person can reasonably handle.

- *Remember that effective feedback is immediate and well timed.* Immediate feedback is obviously more valuable than delayed feedback. After a foul-up in shipping, instead of waiting for two weeks to discuss the problem with the responsible employee, discuss the error immediately, or at least within a day or two. Immediate feedback allows the person to correct actions or behaviors while they are still fresh in mind. But feedback should also be well timed, and sometimes this means that it can't be immediate. If you point out an employee's mistakes in front of a group of coworkers, such feedback is likely to be resented. And if, after quitting time, you confront an employee anxious to get home, your suggestions may be received absentmindedly. This type of feedback should be given in a private, relaxed atmosphere. Unfortunately, many people tend to give feedback in anger and don't stop to consider the consequences.

Environment

The effective communicator plans and controls the environment as much as possible. The **environment** includes the "time, place, physical and social surroundings"[27] in which the communicators find themselves. For example, the mood of a meeting, and consequently the success of its communication, depends on the *time* at which the meeting is scheduled—8:00 a.m., 2:00 p.m., or 30 minutes before quitting time. The best time depends on the people involved, their expectations, and the purpose and expected length of the meeting. The *location* of a meeting can also greatly affect the communication of the participants. For this reason, many business deals take place outside the office, such as at restaurants or on golf courses, where pressures are not felt so keenly. Communication is also affected by the *physical environment*. Such conditions as the size of the room, the brightness of the lights, the room temperature, the comfort and arrangement of the chairs, the shape of the table, and the noise level can alter the type and success of communication. *Social environment* refers to the relationships of the people present. For example, employees at a party feel and act differently when supervisors are present than when they are not.

An organization's social and work environment is often referred to as its **climate.** An organization's climate, which is determined by the prevailing atmosphere and attitudes of its members, can have a powerful effect on communication. Climate is so important to communication that we will expound on it in Chapters 2, 3, and 5.

Noise

Anything that interferes with communication by distorting or blocking the message is noise. *External noise* includes distractions in the environment, such as the speaker's poor grammar, papers being shuffled, phones ringing, people talking, cold air in the room, or lights that are too bright or too dim. *Internal noise* refers to conditions of the receiver, such as a headache, daydreaming, lack of sleep, preoccupation with other problems, or lack of knowledge on the topic. Any of these noises can distort or block communication.

The effect of noise on communication is demonstrated by the following example. Suppose you are very upset about not receiving the same raise as the other people in your office. You write a memo to your boss requesting a private interview. Two days after sending the memo, and getting no response, you and your boss unexpectedly run into each other in a busy workroom. The boss, thinking that this time is as good as any other, motions you to sit down and says, "So, what did you want to talk to me about?" How successful can this grievance interview be with phones ringing, machines running, and interested people walking in and out? These external noises are fairly obvious. Less obvious, but equally distracting, are the internal noises. We can only guess at the internal noise the boss is experiencing—preoccupation with other problems, a perception of you as a satisfied employee, and so on. However, your internal distractions seem fairly clear. You are in an unhappy emotional state, feeling mistreated and abused. You will probably interpret this new action by the boss—interviewing you on the spur of the moment in such a noisy public place—as further proof of disrespect and unfair treatment. The chance that the two of you will arrive at a mutually agreeable solution is being influenced by both external and internal noise.

As a communicator, you need to be aware of potential noise and its effect on a message. When possible, you should select an environment that is relatively noise-free. If unexpected noise does occur, you should either postpone the message until the noise ends or eliminate the noise. If all else fails, simply acknowledge the problem and continue as best you can.

AWARENESS CHECK: COMMUNICATOR QUIZ

How skilled a communicator are you? To check your communication effectiveness, take the following quiz.

Directions: For each of these statements about your communication select one of the following: (A) rarely, (B) sometimes, or (C) usually.

_____ 1. Do you knowingly stimulate and motivate the receiver of the message?

_____ 2. Do you try to encode ideas so they will fit into the frame of reference of the receiver?

_____ 3. Do you try to decode messages using the sender's frame of reference?

_____ 4. Do you try to send each message by the nonverbal, paralanguage, and language codes?

_____ 5. Do you try to improve your communication success by controlling the environment?

_____ 6. Do you let the importance of the message and the ability and skill of the receiver determine the channel you select?

_____ 7. Do you realize that 100 percent communication is unlikely and therefore plan for ways to avoid possible misunderstandings?

_____ 8. When you communicate, do you remember that the only message that counts is the one received?

_____ 9. Do you avoid becoming defensive or placing blame when communication breakdown occurs?

_____ 10. Do you view feedback as absolutely necessary for successful communication, and therefore both give and receive feedback on a regular basis?

(continued)

Number of times you answered "rarely"_____

Number of times you answered "sometimes"_____

Number of times you answered "usually"_____

ANSWERS

If you answered "sometimes" or "rarely" on fewer than three questions, you perceive yourself to be a good communicator. If you answered "sometimes" or "rarely" on three to six questions, you are an average communicator. If you answered "sometimes" or "rarely" on seven or more questions, you need immediate improvement of your communication skills. Begin by rereading Chapter 1.

COMMUNICATION NETWORKS

Earlier we stated that the success of an organization depends on the communication skills of all its employees. With this in mind, we've discussed the basic elements involved in the communication process and pinpointed some major causes of communication error. Next let's look at the formal and informal networks found in organizations and see what effect they have on communication success. A **network** represents the way in which communication flows in an organization (see Figure 1.4).

Formal Communication Network

In the formal communication network, messages flow along the official paths prescribed by the organization's chain of command. Formal messages flow downward, upward, and horizontally (see Figure 1.5).

Downward Communication ■ Formal messages that flow from managers and supervisors to subordinates are called *downward communication*. The importance of downward communication is illustrated by the following example:

> The computer operators in the data processing department of a large insurance firm were told to do an analysis of premium and claims payment at the end of each day. The task was unpleasant, because of frequent errors in the submitted data that required correction. Completing the run often held the operators past closing time. Periodically, the operators would delay finishing the computer run until the next morning, which brought admonitions from management and excuses from the computer operators. During one of these failures the exasperated manager said, "Don't you realize how crucial this run is?" An operator replied, "Not really. You only told us that it was important and to do the job."

Figure 1.4 Organization chart showing formal (black lines) and informal (colored lines) paths of communication.

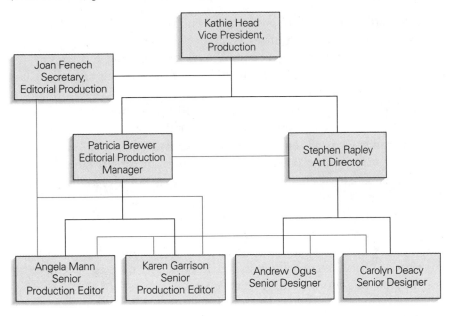

Figure 1.5 Formal messages flow upward, downward, and horizontally.

The operators had never been told that the information not only reported the company's cash flow position, but was used the next morning as the basis for short-term investments. Not having that information, even periodically, had resulted in the company's losing millions of dollars of investment potential over the years.[28]

Obviously, downward communication is not always adequate. For employees to be truly productive, they must receive more than job instructions. They need to know how their particular job fits into the overall picture of the organization.

In downward communication, the following types of messages flow from management to subordinates:[29]

- *Job instructions.* "Before pushing lever number 3, make sure that both levers 1 and 2 are securely locked into position."
- *Job rationale* (why a specific task is important and how it relates to other tasks in the organization). "If any of these panels are more than 1/1000 of an inch over- or undersized, the assembly crews will not be able to get the perfect fit needed and will return the panels to us. And as you know, once a panel has been formed, it cannot be resized, so any returned panels end up as scrap!"
- *Policy and procedures* (rules and regulations of the organization). "All unused sick leaves will be converted into cash bonuses at the end of every year."
- *Employee performance appraisal.* "You did a great job on the Walter project, Marion."
- *Motivational appeals* (to motivate and increase organizational commitment). "If everyone will put in a little extra effort, we can become the number one producer of X components."

Which of these five types of messages do you least often receive (as a subordinate) or send (as a boss)? For many people, the answer would be job rationale messages. Imagine working for two bosses at the same time. Boss A comes in and says, "I don't care what you are working on. Drop it and get on this!" Five minutes later, Boss B comes in and tells you, "Drop everything and get on this rush job now!" Neither boss gives any rationale, so which job is really the most crucial? Telling an employee that a certain job is important is not the same as telling the employee *why* the job is important or why it must be completed by a certain time.

Lack of this type of downward communication often makes employees feel unimportant, that no one would even notice if they failed to show up for work one day. Feeling this way, they are less likely to be satisfied with the job and less likely to give it their best. They develop a "get by" attitude. Gerald Goldhaber found:

> Information about personal job-related matters (e.g., how to do my job, my pay and benefits, etc.) is needed to *prevent dissatisfaction* but it will *NOT* create satisfaction. Information about organization-wide concerns (policies, plans, decision-making, failures, etc.) is needed to *create satisfaction.*[30]

Although it is certainly possible to get information overload (receiving too much information at one time), one researcher found that employees with information *overload* were not dissatisfied with their jobs; however, all the employees who experienced information *underload* were dissatisfied.[31]

Matters are further complicated by our expectations. In other words, how we expect a person to respond influences our communication with that person. Analyzing 120 managers' messages, Linda McCallister found that "while the managers overwhelmingly endorsed a non-directive style of communication, they expected compliance from the subordinate only when a directive/autocratic style of communication was utilized."[32] In other words, the messages managers use in downward communication with subordinates may be determined more by expectations of employee needs and reactions than by actual employee needs and reactions.

Another problem with downward communication is that it is often in written form. Although written English is approximately 60 percent redundant, thus helping readers interpret messages,[33] there are several problems. Because written messages take time to prepare, they are usually brief and may omit needed details (supervisors often assume that subordinates know more than they really do). Again, for the sake of brevity, memos normally do not include the job rationale. And, as we discussed earlier in this chapter, frame of reference differences between supervisors and subordinates make interpretation of messages very difficult; we often wrongly assume that others see things as we do.

Upward Communication ■   Formal messages also flow upward from subordinates to supervisors and managers. Without *upward communication*, management would never know how their downward messages were received and interpreted by the employees and would miss out on valuable ideas; also, workers would not get the chance to participate in the company.[34]

The following types of messages are valuable when upwardly communicated:[35]

- *What employees are doing*, such as highlights of their work, achievements, progress, and future job plans.
- *Outlines of unsolved work problems*, when employees need help to resolve the problems.
- *Suggestions or ideas for improvements* within the department or in the company as a whole.
- *How employees think and feel* about their jobs, their associates, and their company.

Of course, walking the thin line between telling the boss too much and not telling enough presents a real dilemma to some employees. A management consultant with twenty years' experience offers these guide-lines on what to communicate to the boss:[36]

- Alert your boss in advance to potential bad news in areas for which you are responsible.
- Inform your superior, without delay, of problems that may affect his or her job or reputation with the boss or peers.
- Involve your supervisor in decisions that will have a major impact on a significant number of your employees, other resources, or goals.
- Advise your boss of substantive decisions you've made that may come to his or her attention.
- Consult the person you report to on problems when you think his or her knowledge or expertise can help.
- Keep your superior aware of your department's significant achievements.
- Tell your boss of any major mistakes you've made, and the corrective action you've taken, before he or she hears of them from others.
- Secure approval from the person above you before undertaking actions that may require his or her intervention.
- Solicit your supervisor's ideas concerning your long-range plans for increasing your department's productivity.
- Respect your boss' lack of time, and spare him or her the details of your daily problems and accomplishments.

Obviously, for upward communication to be effective, it must be accurate. Unfortunately, many subordinates tend to conceal or distort upward communication to protect themselves and to make messages more acceptable to superiors. The desire to conceal bad news is referred to by researchers as the "MUM effect."[37] In other words, "if a subordinate believes that disclosure of his feelings, opinions, or difficulties may lead a superior to block or hinder the attainment of a personal goal, he will conceal or distort them."[38] For example, suppose you and several other employees are discussing the merits of a new product with the boss. Because the boss is obviously pleased with the idea, everyone concentrates on positive comments. However, you can see a drawback to the product that could be disastrous. Should you mention it or keep quiet? Chances are that you will keep your observation to yourself if you feel that the boss might view your comment as evidence of a negative attitude and hold it against you in some way. However, if the boss has indicated a desire to look at possible drawbacks, you will probably voice your opinion.

Upward messages are also more likely to be distorted when subordinates have significantly less power and status, when trust between parties is weak, and when subordinates desire upward mobility or recognition.[39] Employees who desire upward mobility or recognition should recognize that upward communication is more likely to be utilized by management if it is positive, is timely, supports current policy, is sent directly to the person(s) who can act on it, and is seen as a commonsense idea.[40]

Horizontal Communication ■ In *horizontal communication*, messages flow laterally between persons of the same rank or position. Horizontal communication is especially important in an organization for the following purposes:[41]

- *To coordinate tasks* when several employees or departments are each working on part of an important project.
- *To solve problems*, such as how to reduce waste or how to increase the number of items assembled each hour.
- *To share information*, such as an easier way to perform a task or the results of a new survey.
- *To resolve conflict*, such as jealousy or disagreements between coworkers.

Horizontal communication is receiving much more attention in today's organizations. In their best-seller *Re-inventing the Corporation*, John Naisbitt and Patricia Aburdene state,

> The top-down authoritarian management style is yielding to a networking style of management, where people learn from one another horizontally, where everyone is a resource for everyone else, and where each person gets support and assistance from many different directions.[42]

Informal Communication Network

If you have ever been congratulated on some award or promotion before any formal announcement was made officially, you have experienced the informal communication network. Not all messages flow along the official paths prescribed by the organization's chain of command. Many messages flow along an informal network commonly called the *grapevine*. Informal networks exist due to weaknesses in formal networks. According to Conrad,

> Formal communication networks allow people to handle predictable, routine situations. Because they tend to be filled with written rather than oral messages, they effectively transmit broad kinds of information.

But, . . . communicating through formal channels is a laborious process that involves a high probability of distortion. Formal channels are inefficient means of meeting unanticipated communication needs, for managing crises, for dealing with complex or detailed problems, or sharing personal information.[43]

Characteristics of the Informal Network ■ Although many people view the grapevine as unimportant, research indicates the opposite. For example, all organizations have informal networks, but the type of information the grapevine carries depends on the health of the organization. If an organization's managers are fairly open with the employees and send all necessary information through formal channels, the grapevine usually carries only personal interest items, such as whom the company Romeo is chasing now or who just got divorced. However, when the formal communication channels fail to do the job, the grapevine begins to carry information about the organization. In other words, "The grapevine busies itself with official matters only when the formal channels of communication fail to deliver, are not understood, or are not accepted by the people for whom the messages are intended."[44]

Researchers have also found that although some entirely false rumors are spread through the grapevine, generally information carried by the grapevine is 75 to 95 percent accurate.[45] Keep in mind that grapevine information can be confirmed while rumors cannot. Informal grapevine messages may even be more accurate than formal ones—status, power, and rank differences are temporarily set aside. In a recent study, middle managers reported that they often found informal networks to be a better source of organizational information than formal networks.[46]

Information carried by the grapevine travels fast, and both men and women participate equally in passing such information along.[47] It is not uncommon for top management, who reached an important decision late at night, to arrive at work early the next morning only to find that the decision is common knowledge.

Managers who listen carefully to the informal communication network find it a useful source of information about employee concerns and problems. Some managers actually leak new ideas or proposals to the grapevine to test worker response. If an idea is greeted with hostility, they drop it or revise it; if the idea is received positively, they introduce it through official channels.

In his study of bureaucratic organizations, Peter Blau found two main advantages to users of informal communication networks: (1) We can get advice and information without formally having to admit we need it, and (2) we can "think out loud" about problems, thus increasing our self-confidence and problem-solving ability.[48]

COMMUNICATION AND ETHICS

So far we have discussed the basic elements involved in the communication process, identified some major causes of communication errors, and examined the effects that formal and informal networks have on an organization's communication. Before leaving this chapter, we also need to take a careful look at the crucial role ethics plays in communication success. One author defines ethics this way:

> Ethics . . . are the standards by which behaviors are evaluated as to their morality—their rightness or wrongness. When applied to communication, ethics are the moral principles that guide our judgments about the good and bad, right and wrong of communication.[49]

According to Gallup poll surveys, the American public has lost faith in the honesty and ethics of most professional people, including business professionals.[50] Since 1976 pollsters have asked, "How would you rate the honesty and ethical standards of people in these different fields—very high, high, average, low, or very low?" Table 1.1 includes the percentage of respondents from 1990 through 1994 who rated each profession as having "high" or "very high" ethical standards. Note that in 1994, only dentists, college teachers, clergy, and pharmacists scored 50 percent or better—with no one scoring higher than 62 percent. Business executives scored in the middle with 22 percent, while those in the Senate, state offices, and Congress scored at the bottom—only higher than persons selling cars or insurance. Apparently, the American public has little faith in the honesty and ethics of professionals.

Pick up almost any newspaper to see reports of unethical practices in organizations, ranging from industrial espionage and sabotage, bribery and coercion, deceptive advertising, tax evasion, stock manipulation, and overpricing of products to withholding of relevant information from the public and discriminatory employment practices.[51] To avoid such unethical practices, Gary Kreps recommends that organizations follow three basic principles:[52]

- *Avoid intentional deception.* Honesty is the best policy.
- *Avoid communication that harms others.* Do unto others as you would have them do unto you.
- *Avoid treating members unfairly.* Equal treatment for all.

According to Tom Peters in *Thriving on Chaos*, organizations that follow principles similar to those listed above are more likely to succeed. He

Table 1.1 Percentage of Respondents Rating Each Profession as Having "High" or "Very High" Ethical Standards

Profession	Rating				
	1990	1991	1992	1993	1994
Druggists, pharmacists	62%	60%	66%	65%	62%
Clergy	55	57	54	53	54
Dentists	52	50	50	50	51
College teachers	51	45	50	52	50
Engineers	50	45	48	49	49
Medical doctors	52	54	52	51	47
Policemen	49	43	42	50	46
Funeral directors	35	35	35	34	30
Public opinion pollsters	NA	NA	NA	NA	27
Bankers	32	30	27	28	27
Business executives	25	21	18	20	22
TV reporters/commentators	32	29	31	28	22
Journalists	30	26	27	26	20
Local officeholders	21	19	15	19	18
Building contractors	20	20	19	20	17
Newspaper reporters	24	24	25	22	17
Lawyers	22	22	18	16	17
Stockbrokers	14	14	13	13	15
Real estate agents	16	17	14	15	14
Labor union leaders	15	13	14	14	14
State officeholders	17	14	11	14	12
Advertising practitioners	12	12	10	8	12
Senators	24	19	13	18	12
Insurance salesmen	13	14	9	10	9
Congressmen	20	19	11	14	9
Car salesmen	6	8	5	6	6

Source: Leslie McAneny and David W. Moore, "Congress and Media Sink in Public Esteem," *The Gallup Poll Monthly* 349 (October 1994), p. 4.

writes that "without doubt, honesty has always been the best policy. The best firms on this score have long had the best track records overall."[53] One of these "best" firms, Johnson & Johnson, is well known for its code of ethics,[54] called The Credo, which covers physicians, customers, employees, communities, and stockholders. The Credo begins with the following words: "We believe our first reponsibility is to the doctors, nurses and patients, to mothers and fathers and all others who use our products and services."[55] Johnson & Johnson's top management credit this code of ethics with the action they took during the Tylenol scare of 1982.[56] When it was discovered that seven people had died after taking Extra Strength Tylenol, the company pulled all Tylenol capsules off the shelves, urged people not to use any Tylenol they had at home, and offered a $100,000 reward for information leading to a resolution of the case (it was later found that the deaths were due to tampering). According to Greenberg and Baron, "Company officials credited the statement [the opening lines of The Credo] with helping them decide what to do at a time when there was no time to gather all the information and weigh all the options."[57] The decision was obviously a difficult one—management knew the costs would run high. Not only did the company experience a loss of revenue (31 million bottles of Tylenol were removed from store shelves), many loyal customers switched brands. Fortunately, when Tylenol "reintroduced the product in tamper-proof packages," the company "very shortly thereafter regained 95 percent of the market share it had before the crisis."[58]

Texas Instruments is another company with a strong code of ethics.[59] They have a 1-800-ethics hot line, available from anywhere in the United States, and they provide their employees with an ethics wallet card:

SIDE 1 ETHICS QUICK TEST

- Is the action *legal*?
- Does it comply with our *values*?
- If you do it, will you feel *bad*?
- How will it look in the *newspaper*?
- If you know it's *wrong*, don't do it.
- If you're not sure, *ask*.
- Keep asking until you get an *answer*.

SIDE 2 WHERE TO GO FOR ETHICS ANSWERS

- Talk with your supervisor.
- Contact the Personnel Department.
- Use the Open Door.
- Call the legal department.
- Contact the Ethics Office.[60]

Ethics training programs are being implemented in many companies.[61] Being aware of the company code of ethics isn't enough; employees need to know how to use it in their day-to-day decision making. As Richard Daft warns, "Formal ethics codes and training programs are worthless if leaders do not set and live up to high standards of ethical conduct."[62] He summarizes a report from the chief executives of 100 large companies who stated that, in their opinion, "the single most important factor in ethical decision making was the role of top management in providing commitment, leadership, and example for ethical values."[63]

A commitment to ethics must be made by all employees at all levels of the organization if it is to work. As an employee, watch out for the following ethics traps that tempt business and professional communicators regularly:[64]

- *The trap of necessity.* "I really have no choice. If I suddenly stop charging as much, someone is sure to investigate."
- *The trap of relative filth.* "What I'm doing isn't nearly as bad as what others have done."
- *The trap of rationalization.* "It's all right if I call in sick. They don't pay me what I'm worth anyway."
- *The trap of self-deception.* "So what if I claim my experience is more varied than it really is. No one will ever find out."
- *The trap of the end justifies the means.* "If I exaggerate the uses of this product just a bit, I will be able to double my sales and get a promotion."

Being an ethical communicator is a responsibility we all share. In addition, there are some very practical reasons for being ethical:

1. If people lose faith in you, or in your company, failure is inevitable.
2. People like to deal with honest people—being ethical is good business.
3. Unethical behavior weighs heavily on your conscience and can make it very difficult for you to feel good about yourself.

SUMMARY

Now that you have read this chapter, has your frame of reference on communication changed? Effective communication involves more than just talking or listening—communication is hard work. Whether you are new to the business or professional world or have already launched your career, perfecting your communication skills will help ensure your success.

Organizations are looking for employees who can communicate. They are looking for employees who prepare carefully, execute effectively, and follow up their communications. For example, effective communicators check out the frame of reference of those with whom they communicate and try to encode their messages specifically for each person's understanding; they realize that 100 percent communication is unlikely to occur and plan ways to avoid misunderstanding. Effective communicators also realize the importance of using all three codes (language, paralanguage, and nonverbal) when communicating. They attempt to select the best environment and channel for their communication and use feedback effectively. Even when communication seems successful, they follow up to make sure instead of assuming all is well. When communication misunderstanding occurs, they remember that the message to be concerned with is the one that is received and do not become defensive or assign blame for the problem. In addition, effective communicators use both formal and informal communication networks with ease, realizing that sometimes the grapevine is more effective than the formal networks (upward, downward, or horizontal communication). And, of course, effective communicators ensure that their communication with colleagues, bosses, and customers is ethical at all times. Finally, effective communicators know that misunderstandings are going to occur—no one is perfect. However, when problems do occur, they will analyze them carefully so that the same problems won't happen again.

CHECKPOINT

Before continuing to the next chapter, check your understanding of Chapter 1 by completing the following exercises:

1. Select a person with whom you have had several misunderstandings or disagreements. Make a detailed list of the person's likes, dislikes, background, abilities, and so on until you have a fairly good idea of his or her frame of reference. Then make a similar list for yourself. Compare the two lists to determine frame of reference differences that could account for the misunderstandings or disagreements.

2. To determine whether your feedback to others is evaluative (rather than descriptive), analyze others' responses to your questions. For example, when you and your date, spouse, or close friend are trying to decide where to eat, does the conversation sound something like this?

   You: Where would you like to eat?

   Other: Oh, anywhere is fine. I don't care.

   You: Now come on. I decided last time. Tell me where you would like to eat.

   Other: Really! Any place you like is fine with me!

   And so on. The result may be that you eat in a place neither of you likes or become angry and don't go out at all. If this type of conversation about what to eat or what movie to see occurs often, the chances are that you are evaluative. People send double messages (say one thing but mean another) when they fear that an honest opinion will be criticized. For example,

Other: O.K. Let's eat at Pizza Place.

You: Not again! I might have known you would pick Pizza Place! You know I don't like that place.

3. Share the examples of communication breakdown included in this chapter with a few of your fellow workers. Ask them to give you additional examples they especially like.

4. What type of information does the grapevine in your institution or organization carry? What does this say about the health of the organization?

5. Select a community, government, university, or business organization in which you have an interest. What type of communication is used the most: downward, upward, or horizontal? What communication problems or successes have resulted from such use?

6. Break into groups to create a situation involving an ethical dilemma. Exchange dilemmas and discuss ethical ways to handle each situation.

NOTES

1. Excerpt from p. 3 of Charles Conrad, *Strategic Organizational Communication: Toward the Twenty-First Century,* 3rd ed. Copyright © 1994 by Harcourt Brace. Reprinted by permission of the publisher.
2. John M. Ivancevich and Michael T. Matteson, *Organizational Behavior and Management,* 4th ed. (Chicago: Irwin, 1996), p. 535; based in part on Robert D. Marx, Charles I. Stubbart, Virginia Traub, and Michael Cavanaugh, "The NASA Space Shuttle Disaster: A Case Study," *Journal of Management Case Studies* (Winter 1987), pp. 299–318; and G. Whyte, "Decision Failures: Why They Occur and How to Prevent Them," *Academy of Management Executive* (August 1991), pp. 23–31.
3. J. Fulk, "Social Construction of Communication Technology," *Academy of Management Journal* 36 (1993), pp. 921–950.
4. J. Belohlov, P. Popp, and M. Porte, "Communication: A View from the Inside of Business," *Journal of Business Communication* 11 (1974), pp. 53–59.
5. F. S. Endicott, *The Endicott Report: Trends in the Employment of College and University Graduates in Business and Industry 1980* (Evanston, IL: Placement Center, Northwestern University, 1979).
6. David Berlo, *The Process of Communication* (New York: Holt, Rinehart & Winston, 1960), p. 175.
7. *The Oxford English Dictionary,* 2nd ed., vol. II (Oxford: Clarendon, 1961), p. 699.
8. Fraser N. Watts, "Strategies of Clinical Listening," *British Journal of Medical Psychology* 56 (June 1983), p. 115.
9. The window analogy was first presented by William V. Haney in an article entitled "Perception and Communication." In William V. Haney, *Communication and Organizational Behavior,* 3rd ed. (Homewood, IL: Irwin, 1973), pp. 55–101.
10. Ernest G. Bormann, William S. Howell, Ralph G. Nichols, and George L. Shapiro, *Interpersonal Communication in the Modern Organization* (Englewood Cliffs, NJ: Prentice-Hall, 1969), p. 190.
11. R. Likert, *New Patterns in Management* (New York: McGraw-Hill, 1961).
12. Kermit Moore, "Learning to Listen," *American Way* (March 1984), p. 41.
13. From *The Foreman's Letter,* National Foreman's Institute, Inc., February 8, 1950, p. 3, in William V. Haney, *Communication and Organizational Behavior,* 3rd ed. (Homewood, IL: Irwin, 1973), p. 246.
14. Ray Killian, *Managing by Design . . . for Executive Effectiveness* (New York: American Management Association, 1968), p. 255.

15. R. L. Birdwhistell, *Kinesics and Context: Essays on Body Motion Communication* (Philadelphia: University of Pennsylvania Press, 1970), p. 158.

16. J. S. Philpott, "The Relative Contribution to Meaning of Verbal and Nonverbal Channels of Communication: A Meta-Analysis" (unpublished master's thesis, University of Nebraska, 1983); reported by Judee K. Burgoon, "Nonverbal Signals," in *Handbook of Interpersonal Communication*, Mark L. Knapp and Gerald R. Miller, eds. (Beverly Hills: Sage, 1985), p. 346.

17. T. A. Seay and M. K. Altekruse, "Verbal and Nonverbal Behavior in Judgments of Facilitative Conditions," *Journal of Counseling Psychology* 26 (1979), pp. 108–119; D. T. Tepper and R. F. Haase, "Verbal and Nonverbal Communication of Facilitative Conditions," *Journal of Counseling Psychology* 25 (1978), pp. 35–44; D. Archer and R. M. Akert, "Words and Everything Else: Verbal and Nonverbal Cues in Social Interpretation," *Journal of Personality and Social Psychology* 35 (1977), pp. 443–449; A. G. Gitter, H. Black, and J. E. Fishman, "Effect of Race, Sex, Nonverbal Communication and Verbal Communication on Perception of Leadership," *Sociology and Social Research* 60 (1975), pp. 46–57; G. L. Zahn, "Cognitive Integration of Verbal and Vocal Information in Spoken Sentences," *Journal of Experimental Social Psychology* 9 (1973), pp. 320–334.

18. Burgoon in Knapp and Miller, pp. 346–347.

19. M. Argyle, "The Syntaxes of Bodily Communication," *International Journal of Psycholinguistics* 2 (1973), p. 78; see also Timothy Hegstrom, "Message Impact: What Percentage Is Nonverbal?" *Western Journal of Speech Communication* 43 (1979), pp. 134–142.

20. Michael A. Lerner, "A Dead Stick at 23,000 Feet," *Newsweek*, May 16, 1983, p. 40.

21. Paul R. Timm, *Managerial Communication: A Finger on the Pulse*, 2nd ed. (Englewood Cliffs, NJ: Prentice-Hall, 1986), pp. 57–60.

22. Raymond W. Kulhavy and Neil H. Schwartz, "Tone of Communication and Climate Perceptions," *Journal of Business Communications* 18 (Fall 1980), p. 23.

23. Milton Moskowitz, "Lessons from the Best Companies to Work For," *California Management Review* 27 (Winter 1985), p. 43.

24. Phillip Clampitt and Cal Downs, "Communication and Productivity," paper presented at a meeting of the Speech Communication Association, Washington, DC, November 1983.

25. Adapted from Bormann et al., pp. 148–149; also from the film *Meanings Are in People* by David K. Berlo, produced by BNA Incorporated, 1965.

26. Adapted from Bormann et al., pp. 151–154, and G. F. J. Lehner, "Giving and Receiving Personal Feedback," in *Proceedings: Grass Valley Training Laboratory 4*, Robert Morton and A. Wright, eds. (Sacramento: Aerojet-General Corporation, 1963).

27. James N. Holm, *Business and Professional Communication* (Boston: American Press, 1981), p. 22.

28. David L. Bradford and Allan R. Cohen, *Managing for Excellence: The Guide to Developing High Performance in Contemporary Organizations* (New York: Wiley, 1984), p. 122.

29. Daniel Katz and Robert L. Kahn, *The Social Psychology of Organizations* (New York: Wiley, 1966), p. 239.

30. Excerpt from p. 157 of Gerald M. Goldhaber, *Organizational Communication*, 6th ed. © 1993 by Brown & Benchmark. All rights reserved. Reprinted by permission of the publisher.

31. C. A. O'Reilly, "Individuals and Information Overload in Organizations: Is More Necessarily Better?" *Academy of Management Journal* 23 (1980), pp. 684–696.

32. Linda McCallister, "Predicted Employee Compliance to Downward Communication Styles," *Journal of Business Communication* 20, No. 1 (1983), p. 67.

33. Marshall Sashkin and William C. Morris, *Organizational Behavior: Concepts and Experiences* (Reston, VA: Reston, 1984), p. 118.

34. Earl Planty and William Machaver, "Upward Communications: A Project in Executive Development," in *Readings in Interpersonal and Organizational Communication*, 3rd ed., Richard C. Huseman, Cal M. Logue, and Dwight L. Freshley, eds. (Boston: Holbrook Press, 1977), p. 167.

35. Planty and Machaver, p. 167.

36. Robert P. Hagen, "What and When to Tell the Boss," *The Executive Female* 7 (July–August 1984), p. 41.

37. F. Lee, "Being Polite and Keeping MUM: How Bad News Is Communicated in Organizational Hierarchies," *Journal of Applied Social Psychology* 23 (1993), pp. 1124–1149.

38. Gary Gemmill, "Managing Upward Communication," *Personnel Journal* 49 (February 1970), p. 107.

39. Sashkin and Morris, pp. 50–51.

40. J. W. Koehler and G. Huber, *Effects of Upward Communication on Managerial Decision-Making* (New Orleans: International Communication Association, 1974).
41. Goldhaber, p. 163.
42. John Naisbitt and Patricia Aburdene, *Re-inventing the Corporation* (New York: Warner, 1985), p. 62.
43. Conrad, p. 215.
44. Eugene Walton, "How Effective Is the Grapevine?" *Personnel* 28 (1961), p. 46.
45. Walton, pp. 45–49; also see Keith Davis, *Human Behavior at Work*, 5th ed. (New York: McGraw-Hill, 1977), pp. 277–286.
46. J. Harcourt, V. Richerson, and M. J. Waitterk, "A National Study of Middle Managers' Assessment of Organization Communication Quality," *Journal of Business Communication* 28 (1991), pp. 348–365.
47. Everett M. Rogers and Rekha Agarwala-Rogers, *Communication in Organizations* (New York: Free Press, 1976), pp. 100–101.
48. Peter M. Blau, *On the Nature of Organizations* (New York: Wiley, 1974), p. 7.
49. Pamela Shockley-Zalabak, *Fundamentals of Organizational Communication* (New York: Longman, 1988), p. 326.
50. Leslie McAneny and David W. Moore, "Congress and Media Sink in Public Esteem," *The Gallup Poll Monthly* 349 (October 1994), pp. 2–4; for more information see "A Crisis of Confidence" in James A. Jaska and Michael S. Pritchard, *Communication Ethics: Methods of Analysis*, 2nd ed. (Belmont, CA: Wadsworth, 1994), pp. 35–62.
51. Gary L. Kreps in *Organizational Communication*, 2nd ed. (New York: Longman, 1990), pp. 258–259.
52. Kreps, pp. 250–251.
53. Thomas J. Peters, *Thriving on Chaos: A Handbook for a Management Revolution* (New York: Knopf, 1987), p. 519.
54. Francis J. Aguilar, *Managing Corporate Ethics* (New York: Oxford University Press, 1994), p. 66.
55. Aguilar, p. 66.
56. The following information on Johnson & Johnson and Tylenol came from Jerald Greenberg and Robert A. Baron, *Behavior in Organizations*, 5th ed. (Englewood Cliffs, NJ: Prentice-Hall, 1995), pp. 546–547.
57. Greenberg and Baron, pp. 546–547.
58. Greenberg and Baron, p. 547.
59. Aguilar, p. 132.
60. Aguilar, p. 132.
61. Susan J. Harrington, "What Corporate America Is Teaching About Ethics," *Academy of Management Executive* 5 (February 1991), pp. 21–30.
62. Richard L. Daft, *Organization Theory & Design*, 5th ed. (Minneapolis/St. Paul: West, 1995), p. 346; see also James Weber, "Institutionalizing Ethics into Business Organizations: A Model and Research Agenda," *Business Ethics Quarterly* 3 (1993), pp. 419–436.
63. Daft, p. 346.
64. Alison Bell, "What Price Ethics?" *Entrepreneurial Woman* 68 (January–February 1991), p. 68.

2 Theories of Organization

Organizations are . . . much more than means for providing goods and services. They create the settings in which most of us spend our lives. In this respect, they have profound influence on our behavior.[1]

JOHN M. IVANCEVICH,
MICHAEL T. MATTESON,
Organizational Behavior and Management

Not until the beginning of the twentieth century did anyone pay much attention to the workings of an organization, regardless of whether the organization was corporate, nonprofit, educational, governmental, or service-oriented. Since that time, theorists have searched for a "best way" to do things.[2] Each has presented a theoretical solution for curing organizational ills. Some of these theories became passing fads; others have had lasting effects on organizational structures and management. We can get a good feel for communication problems unique to organizations by looking at the four main organization models still in use today: the traditional or classical model, the human relations model, the human resources model, and the systems/contingency model.[3]

The four models we shall review are theories of organization rather than theories of communication. However, understanding the organization theories sheds light on how communication works differently in each model. For example, managers from each model view employees quite differently and thus their expectations of and communication with employees also differ. As you read about each model, you will notice that within the formal communication network, each model places different emphasis on the flow of messages (whether downward, upward, or horizontal); some models pay attention to the grapevine (the informal communication network) and some ignore its existence completely.

To get a feel for the differences in each of the four organization models, let's listen as a manager representing each model discusses basic management techniques. Which of these managers seems to be describing an organization for which you have worked or a company with which you are familiar?

TRADITIONAL MANAGER

Always remember to let employees know who's boss. If you are too friendly and get involved with their personal problems, they will take advantage of you and respect you less. To keep employee respect, you must take control. For example, lateness should never be tolerated.

To feel secure, employees need and want structure. Let them know where they fit in the company's organizational chart and clarify the expected chain of command. Tell them exactly how you want things done. Don't waste time asking for their opinions. Oh, sure, some may grumble at first, but if you let them know that they are being watched, and conduct time and motion studies to let them know how they stand, they'll appreciate you.

As I've indicated, for productive employees, structure and control are essential. Employees are basically lazy, and they will goof off if you let them. If structure and control are not enough, money is a certain motivator. For a bonus, employees will do almost anything.

HUMAN RELATIONS MANAGER

I totally disagree with the traditional manager! Employees are more productive if they feel appreciated and content. You can't treat people like machines. Pushing a control, structure, or money button does not result in a more productive employee. Employees need and want TLC [tender loving care]. If you are nice to people, they will bend over backwards for you when you ask them.

Social and psychological needs of employees should be an important management concern. We view our organization as "one happy family." Managers should call their employees by first names, be friendly, joke and laugh with them, and express sympathy with their personal problems. We show that we really care by celebrating birthdays and sponsoring company picnics and athletic events. Managers can gauge the happiness of employees by listening carefully to the grapevine [informal communication network]. When problems and conflicts do occur, smooth over them or even ignore them if possible, because conflict can damage the friendly atmosphere and hamper employee productivity.

HUMAN RESOURCES MANAGER

Both of the previous managers have an inaccurate view of employees and of the employee–management relationship. First of all, employees aren't lazy and they don't have to be bribed or manipulated with bonuses or with TLC. Employees want to work and will motivate themselves if they are allowed to participate in decision making and are committed to the goals of the organization.

Second, successful organizations like a team-oriented approach to employee–management relationships. Open communication and feedback should flow freely up and down the organization. The organization's climate should be supportive, flexible, and trusting. Therefore, it is the role of the manager to be a facilitator, to allow employees to take an active role in problem solving and in developing their potential. Employees must be allowed to make mistakes if you want them to be creative.

Long-term employee motivation comes from a feeling of self-worth, personal satisfaction, and achievement. If given a chance, employees will exhibit self-control and self-direction compatible with the goals of the organization.

SYSTEMS/CONTINGENCY MANAGER

Regardless of what other managers may say, there is no single best way to manage. Any of the other three organization models could be successful depending on any number of internal and external factors. In deciding which manager style would be the most effective in a particular situation, a manager might consider such internal factors as employee needs, expectations, and abilities; the complexity of employee jobs and the level of satisfaction available from each job; as well as the manager's own friendliness and comfort when using various communication approaches.

A manager should also consider such external factors as customer expectations, local and national economy, and competition from other organizations.

In addition, managers and employees must be aware that every part of the organization is interdependent on every other part, and that any one department or even one person's actions can affect the entire organization. Therefore, communication and feedback within and between departments are extremely important. In large organizations where change is a regular occurrence, effective communication is a must.

Each manager obviously approaches problems and relates to employees quite differently. Therefore, the four organization models clearly make a difference to the kind of communication that goes on in an organization. Each model has its "best way" to do things; each model has both strengths and weaknesses. However, although each model is currently in use by various organizations, not all fare equally well in today's diverse, global market. The influx of women and minorities into the workplace, the global competition for customers, and the emerging information age (illustrated by the rapid growth of the Internet) are making constant change the norm. As Michael Hammer and James Champy note in their book *Reengineering the Corporation*, "In today's environment, nothing is constant or predictable—not market growth, customer demand, product life cycles, the rate of technological change, or the nature of competition."[4] Organizations that succeed in today's changing marketplace may well be those that capitalize on diversity, are flexible, are fast at problem solving and operation start-up, encourage and reward innovation, and make use of new information-age technology.[5] As you read about their differences, consider which models are more likely to succeed in today's changing environment. Understanding these differences should help you select your future working environment more effectively and communicate more successfully with others in that environment.

THE TRADITIONAL OR CLASSICAL MODEL

Early in the twentieth century, large organizations were new and had no role models (the military was the only large organization). A manager could not go to a library or bookstore and find self-help books on management. Therefore, companies were managed by hunch or intuition, and their attempts to motivate and control employees were inefficient and often inhumane. When managers' decisions (made with little planning and inadequate information) reaped less than desirable results, the managers blamed employees.

Two groups of organization theorists whom we now call traditionalists emerged: the so-called scientific managers who wanted to improve organizations "from the bottom up" (meaning they were concerned with employee problems) and the bureaucratic theorists who felt improvements should occur "from the top down" (meaning they were concerned with management problems). Both groups were interested in creating "efficient and productive organizations in which people were treated fairly and equitably."[6]

Traditional Model and Scientific Managers

Frederick Taylor, an American, was responsible for the popularity of the scientific management approach. As a manager, Taylor observed firsthand many of the organizational problems of the day.[7] For example, worker and manager roles were not clearly defined; hostilities existed between workers and management; decision making was haphazard because it was based on too little information; and production was inefficient because of poorly motivated workers, poorly designed job procedures, minimal work standards, and inept employee placement (employees were often overqualified or underqualified for their jobs).

Taylor's "best way" involved applying four scientific principles to the problems of production and management:

- *Scientific design of each task.* With the help of subordinates, managers were to find the shortest and easiest way to perform each task. For example, in the 1890s, Taylor conducted time–motion studies on shoveling at Bethlehem Steel Company.[8] Traditionally, the workers had provided their own shovels, so a wide variety existed. From careful experimentation, Taylor found that maximum shoveling efficiency was obtained with a shovel load of 21 pounds. When workers were issued shovels with a 21-pound capacity, given instructions on the most productive and least fatiguing way to shovel, and given a pay incentive for superior performance, the results were amazing:

  The average volume of material moved per day soared from sixteen to fifty-nine tons. Handling cost plummeted from 7.3 cents to 3.2 cents per ton (even after deducting the total cost of the experiment and incentive pay that boosted the average shovel pay from $1.15 to $1.88 per day). Bethlehem was able to reduce its yard crew from more than 400 to 140 employees.[9]

- *Scientific selection of workers.* For each task, management was to determine the necessary characteristics for an individual to successfully perform that task and then hire only workers with those characteristics.
- *Adequate training and rewards for productivity.* Once management had determined the most productive method to complete a task and had

THE TRADITIONAL OR CLASSICAL MODEL IN BRIEF

Key Theorists	Landmark Books
Frederick Taylor	*Scientific Management* (1911)
Henri Fayol	*General and Industrial Management* (1949)
Max Weber	*The Theory of Social and Economic Organization* (1947)

Bias of Theory

Concern with management and supervision

View of Communication

Limited communication; restricted to downward use by managers.

hired the appropriate workers, employees were trained to use this method and were carefully timed to see how much they could produce without exerting themselves. This level became a production standard on which their pay was based. Believing that workers could be motivated to higher efficiency if they were given the opportunity to make more money, Taylor advocated that a piece-rate incentive or bonus be offered to workers for producing above the standard rate. However, if workers earned too much, management would reduce the piece-rate amount to keep wages in line. Viewing this as punishment, workers began to produce at a minimum acceptable level.

■ *Division of both labor and responsibilities.* Problems and errors were no longer to be blamed on employees. Management and labor were to be team members and share the responsibility and the monetary rewards for increased efficiency.

In his book *Scientific Management*, Taylor summed up his principles:

> Science, not rule of thumb. Harmony, not discord. Cooperation, not individualism. Maximum output, in place of restricted output. The development of each man to his greatest efficiency and prosperity.[10]

Unfortunately, managers tended to implement Taylor's techniques without much consideration for employees. For example, managers viewed

Figure 2.1 Pyramidal organization chart.

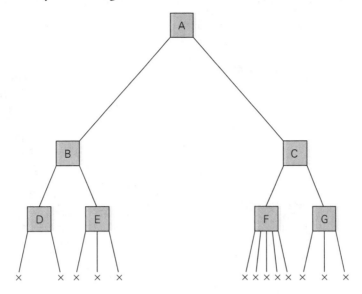

the savings from time–motion studies (such as those conducted at Bethlehem Steel) as miraculous, while generally ignoring the cost to employees faced with loss of livelihood. Taylor's rewards for productivity also had problems. Without the concern for workers that Taylor felt and without the necessary employee and manager cooperation, his techniques often became manipulative and dehumanizing.[11]

Traditional Model and Bureaucratic Theorists

Henri Fayol, a Frenchman, and Max Weber, a German, were Taylor's contemporaries. Whereas Taylor sought to improve organizational efficiency by redesigning employee tasks, the bureaucratic theorists were interested in improving the efficiency of the manager through structure and control. **Organizational structure,** the formal patterns of relationships and roles needed to get tasks accomplished (who works with whom and who reports to whom), was the foundation of bureaucratic theory. Fayol and Weber believed that organizations must have a clear division of labor. The **division of labor** is the way an organization parcels out the work to be done (who does what). Division of labor works best when the organization has clear lines of authority, or chain of command. The **chain of command** is the communication structure of an organization and is shown by the pyramidal organization chart introduced by the bureaucratic theorists (see Figure 2.1).

Figure 2.2 Fayol's bridge.

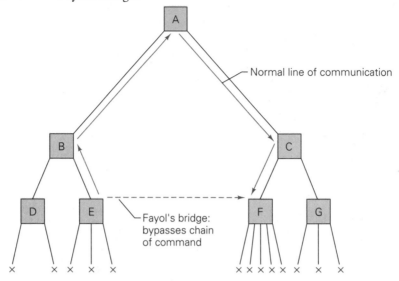

The burcaucratic theorists discussed the role of communication as it flowed up and down the chain of command and noted the restrictions placed on communication by the organizational structure. Fayol's "best way" was an innovative suggestion that direct, horizontal communication between persons of different departments be allowed in legitimate crisis situations. If person E needed information from person F that would arrive too late to use if obtained through the formal chain of command, then person E could contact person F directly.[12] This method of bypassing the chain of command became known as Fayol's bridge (Figure 2.2).

The bureaucratic theorists also believed in a small **span of control,** meaning the number of employees that a manager can effectively supervise. They said that each person should have only one supervisor and each supervisor should oversee no more than five or six people. Span of control determines the shape of an organization. "If most managers throughout the organization have a small span, the overall shape of the organization will be tall. If the typical span is great, then the overall shape of the organization will be flat."[13] Figure 2.3 illustrates the tall and flat organization structures.

The decentralized flat organization, used throughout most of history, has several advantages over the tall structure: Complex problems are handled more efficiently, problems are handled faster, communication is less distorted (because messages pass through fewer people), and employee morale and satisfaction are fairly high (because employees make more of their own decisions).[14]

Figure 2.3 Tall and flat organizations.

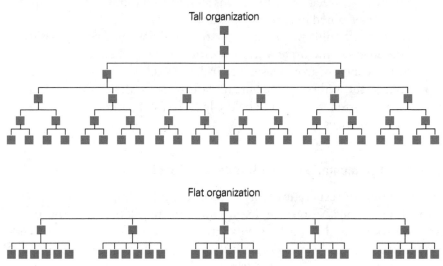

The centralized tall organization, often used by large companies, has contrasting characteristics. These include greater efficiency in handling uncomplicated tasks, lower employee morale and satisfaction, and slower communication.[15]

Organizations that depend heavily on formal communication networks (as tall organizations do) are faced with a dilemma. On the one hand, effective decision making depends on timely, accurate, and complete information traveling upward from subordinates. On the other hand, if *all* information reached the top decision makers, information overload would hamper their decisions. For example, one author estimates that top decision makers would receive an unmanageable 4,096 messages per day in a 7-level hierarchy, with each supervisor having 4 subordinates and all employees producing 1 message per day to be sent to the top. Obviously, some messages need to be screened out or shortened, but doing so can create another problem. For example, in the above example, if each person screened out only one-half of the upward-bound messages received from those lower in the chain of command, 98.4 percent of the information would never reach the top of the hierarchy![16] Thus, the problem is how to get the information you need through the formal communication networks without flooding them.

Weber's "best way" was to formalize the bureaucracy, which he considered the best organization structure for the times.[17] Some of his most enduring ideas, which typify the thinking of the bureaucratic theorists, are summarized here:

- The policies and rules of an organization should be specified in written form. All decisions and actions should be put in writing, even those determined in oral conversations.
- Managers should "maintain impersonal and detached relationships" with others in the organization in order "to keep their personal feelings or concerns from biasing their decisions."
- Because the authority of a bureaucratic organization is limited, the formal written rules should be the legal basis of authority and control over employees.

Current Implementation of the Traditional Model

Scientific and bureaucratic theorists have certainly left their mark on modern organizations. For example, automation, merit pay, and the time–motion studies and reward systems introduced by Taylor are used to enhance productivity in many organizations today. Furthermore, practically every organization uses "some degree of bureaucratic control."[18] For example, Weber's organization charts, division of labor, chain of command, and span of control are all now in common use. In fact, "The bureaucratic organization, with its tight hierarchy, controlled and formal communication, and legal, written rules of action, still is the dominant model for governmental agencies, educational institutions, and many private firms."[19] Many nonprofit organizations also prefer a bureaucratic structure.[20]

If you have ever worked for the federal government, you know that Weber's bureaucracy still exists, especially when it comes to paperwork: In 1976, the Internal Revenue Service had 2,335 different forms. At a recent check, the agency had reduced the paperwork 31 percent to only 1,611 forms.[21] In 1988, the U.S. Department of Energy prepared an environmental impact study in conjunction with the site selection for the Superconducting Super Collider (a project that is no longer being funded by Congress). Each copy of the report contained 8,000 pages and weighed 25 pounds!

UPS (United Parcel Service) is an example of a large, successful bureaucracy—UPS even has more business than the U.S. Postal Service:

> There are safety rules for drivers, loaders, clerks, and managers. Strict dress codes are enforced—no beards, hair cannot touch the collar, no sideburns, mustaches must be trimmed evenly and cannot go below the corner of the mouth, and so on. Rules specify the cleanliness of buildings and property. All sixty thousand UPS delivery trucks must be washed inside and out at the end of every day. Each manager is given bound copies of policy books with the expectation that they will be used regularly. Jobs are broken down into a complex division of labor, including those of drivers, loaders, clerks, washers, sorters, and maintenance per-

sonnel. Each task is calibrated according to productivity standards. The hierarchy of authority is clearly defined and has eight levels, extending from a washer at the local UPS plant up to the president of the national organization. Drivers often are expected to make fifteen deliveries or pickups an hour, no matter what. . . . [At the same time, UPS] has never become impersonal to employees. Everyone is on a first-name basis. No one, not even the chairman, has a private secretary. Top executives started at the bottom, and they still do their own photocopying.[22]

Communication in the Traditional Organization

Communication in traditional organizations is very rational, task-oriented, formal, and usually written. It is mainly downward and used by supervisors and managers to clarify orders, rules, and tasks. The social side of communication is relatively unimportant. Traditional managers feel that employees are happier and more productive when they know what topics are appropriate to discuss, what behaviors are expected, and with whom they are free to communicate. Formally structured roles are an effective way for employees to know what is expected. In the traditional model, roles exist separately from the employees who fill them. Each position has its own place in the chain of command and its own set of expected behaviors. According to traditional managers, an employee's behavior and communication is determined by his or her position. Decision making is the responsibility of management. Because communication is mainly downward and minimal, employees may feel the need to supplement it with information from the grapevine.

Criticisms of the Traditional Organization

In Taylor and Weber's time, management tended to implement the new traditional techniques without changing their basic attitudes toward employees.[23] In fact, management so distorted Taylor's concepts that "workers and union representatives forced an end to most of the incentive systems Taylor and his successors had inspired."[24] Even Weber's concept of impersonal (meaning objective) communication was used by management as support for treating employees as nonpersons. Thus, workers felt abused by management and a new organizational model was sought.

Currently, traditional organizations are criticized for their lack of flexibility and their slowness at problem solving and operation start-up. Recall the painfully slow disaster relief efforts of FEMA (Federal Emergency Management Agency) following Hurricane Andrew in 1992.[25] The very characteristics that make traditional organizations (like FEMA) what they are—formalized rules and procedures, centralized decision making, and vertical complexity—may be responsible for their sluggish performance.[26]

As a result, many companies have chosen to **downsize**—reduce the levels of authority. For example, GM (General Motors) has twenty-two levels of management between the CEO (chief executive officer) at the top and the factory employees at the bottom; Toyota, with a higher profit margin, has only seven levels.[27] The extent of American downsizing is illustrated by a single year: In 1990, approximately 1 million managers lost their jobs due to downsizing.[28]

Sears is an example of a giant bureaucracy that, until recently, moved too slowly to keep up with faster, sleeker discount chains. For example,

> When Sears decided to reduce inventories on men's apparel from a twenty-two to an eight weeks' supply, items were boxed up but never returned to suppliers. Disagreement over who did what meant that the apparel sat in boxes until the next selling season. Or consider the power battles between headquarters buyers and store managers. Store managers may simply ignore new merchandise or a new promotion if it doesn't suit them. One senior executive tried to institute a bedding department with flashy quilts and sheets for yuppie tastes. The plan stalled through several layers of approval. Twelve stores agreed to participate as a test, but after huge delays, only four stores were left. Now the bedding idea is collecting dust along with the boxed men's apparel. As a former senior executive pointed out, the processes of how decisions were made took up so much time at Sears that there was little time to focus on what—or if—decisions were ever actually made.[29]

THE HUMAN RELATIONS MODEL

In addition to worker and labor union rejection of the traditional organization, by the time of the Great Depression, many organizations had their own reasons to welcome the human relations movement. Engineering and business schools were turning out large numbers of educated, professional white-collar workers—workers so valuable that companies suddenly became concerned with the employee. At about the same time, one of the key ideas of scientific management—that employee productivity could be improved solely by economic motivation—was apparently disproved by a group of research studies conducted at the Western Electric Hawthorne plant in Cicero, Illinois.

One of these studies was designed to determine at what brightness level the workers would be the most productive.[30] Surprisingly, productivity increased no matter what the researchers did. When lighting was increased from 24 to 46, then to 70 footcandles, productivity increased both times; when lighting was decreased to 10, then to 3 footcandles, productivity still increased. Productivity dropped only when the room became so

THE HUMAN RELATIONS MODEL IN BRIEF

Key Theorists   **Landmark Books**
Elton Mayo   *The Human Problems of an Industrial Civilization* (1933); *The Social Problems of an Industrial Civilization* (1960)

Chester Barnard   *The Functions of the Executive* (1938)

Bias of Theory
Concern with social and psychological needs of employees

View of Communication
Downward supportive communication important; informal communication acknowledged

dark that the workers could not see. It even increased in the control group where the light level remained constant! These results were so unexpected that the Hawthorne executives contacted Harvard University.

Human Relations and Elton Mayo

The Hawthorne studies, conducted by Elton Mayo and his Harvard University colleagues between 1927 and 1932, substantiated the earlier findings at the Hawthorne plant that changes in task conditions (for example, lighting) had no effect on productivity. In addition, the studies reached two radical conclusions:

■ Workers involved in friendly, relaxed, and congenial work groups with supervisors who listen to them, are concerned about their needs, and are supportive are more productive than other workers, even when other working conditions are not favorable.
■ Workers' satisfaction with the social and interpersonal relationships they have with their peers significantly influences their productivity, and workers feel substantial pressure from their peers to conform to the norms of their work group.[31]

These conclusions served as the foundation of the human relations movement. In short, Mayo's "best way" was the concept that individual-centered tender loving care by supervisors and upper management would lead to greater work productivity. He replaced the "economic man" of the scientific managers with the "social man."

Human Relations and Chester Barnard

Chester Barnard, a contemporary of Mayo's and past president of the New Jersey Bell Telephone Company, was another important figure in the human relations school. Barnard's "best way" emphasized the importance of communication to organizational success. "The first executive function," he wrote, "is to develop and maintain a system of communication."[32] He also acknowledged the existence and importance of informal communication, pointing out that informal groups within an organization establish individual norms and codes of conduct and provide cohesion, communication, and satisfaction to workers. Like Mayo, Barnard recognized that economic motives were not the only employee motivators.

Despite Barnard's opinion of the importance of communication, he still viewed it much as the scientific managers did—as one-way communication to be used by managers for command functions. Indeed, he urged the use of clearly established, formal communication channels and recommended that bypassing them not be allowed.[33]

Current Implementation of the Human Relations Model

An open, trusting climate may be easier to implement and maintain in small, family-run organizations. A good example of the human relations model is provided by a well-known computer company, which in its infancy required no clocking in or out. In fact, employees could determine their own working hours. They were encouraged to take a break at the recreation club across the street whenever stress built up. The owner often would order out for pizza or chicken, and everyone would eat together. It was not uncommon to hear laughter and discussion at all times of the day. In other words, everyone had a good time. However, productivity remained high, with employees often staying until well after midnight working on some new software or hardware application to add to the company's success.

Other organizations have not been as successful using the human relations approach to management. Take, for example, a major league baseball team.

The owner of this team paid his players higher salaries than any other team in baseball. Curfews were relaxed and almost never enforced. Star players were practically their own boss, and if a conflict between a star and an average player arose, the latter was usually traded quickly, with no attempt made to resolve the conflict. As a result of this human relations approach, the members of the team reported to the press that they were extremely satisfied with the management. Word spread around the league, and this team was soon labeled "the country club of baseball." The team hardly ever finished out of the second division (which in baseball is very unimpressive).[34]

Communication in the Human Relations Organization

Although managers in human relations organizations provide a friendly, relaxed work environment, they still view communication as a command tool for use by management. Therefore, communication in the human relations organization is basically downward, although it is also supportive. Human relations managers are concerned with the social and psychological needs of employees mainly because they believe that employees who are treated with tender loving care are more satisfied and therefore more productive. Managers seek feedback from employees and use the grapevine (informal network) to gauge employee satisfaction. Employees are allowed to make routine decisions, and as we shall see in Chapter 10, employees who are involved in a decision are much more likely to abide by it (even if they aren't completely happy with it) than employees who were not involved in the decision. However, even though the human relations model produces a friendly, social environment, managers and employees rarely work together as a team.

Criticisms of the Human Relations Organization

Whereas traditional managers are criticized for their mechanical and inhumane treatment of subordinates, human relations managers are criticized for putting *too much* emphasis on subordinates. In some cases, managers apply the techniques of the human relations theorists without heeding the underlying principles. They become friendly with employees, allow them to participate in minor decision making, and use other relational techniques not because they believe in them, but in an attempt to increase worker compliance with authority—in other words, to manipulate workers. Critics also question whether friendly, open, and supportive supervisors really do improve subordinates' satisfaction and whether satisfied workers really do produce more. Research has found that the bond between productivity and job satisfaction is quite complex and that improved job satisfaction does not necessarily lead to improved performance.[35]

More important than the criticisms are the costs and the problems encountered by organizations attempting to implement the human

THE HUMAN RESOURCES MODEL IN BRIEF

Key Theorists	Landmark Books and Articles
Douglas McGregor	*The Human Side of Enterprise* (1960)
Rensis Likert	*New Patterns of Management* (1961); *The Human Organization* (1967)
Robert Blake and Jane Mouton	*The Managerial Grid* (1964)
Raymond Miles	"Keeping Informed—Human Relations or Human Resources?" *Harvard Business Review* (1965); *Theories of Management* (1975)

Bias of Theory

Equal emphasis on workers and management—a team orientation

View of Communication

Openness and trust in superior–subordinate communication very important

relations model. Although some organizations are successful at producing a satisfying and productive work environment, for most organizations these conditions are difficult to create and difficult to sustain. An open, trusting climate may not be possible if management is skeptical and subordinates don't want to take the risk involved in openness.

THE HUMAN RESOURCES MODEL

The human resources model grew out of the criticisms and problems of the human relations school, and by the late 1960s, it had practically replaced the earlier model.

There is no clear-cut line between the human relations and human resources models, just a gradual changeover. Douglas McGregor and Rensis Likert helped bring about the transition by comparing traditional management with the human relations model and combining the best of both. Therefore, the human resources model (1) focused on both increased employee satisfaction and improved organizational decision making and

Table 2.1 Comparison of Human Relations and Human Resources Models

Human Relations	*Human Resources*
People wish to be liked and respected.	Most people desire a sense of accomplishment.
If their needs are met, employees will produce for the organization.	Most employees have untapped resources and are capable of more than most jobs allow.
Managers should convince workers that they are valuable team members.	Managers should tap and guide each employee's hidden talents and creativity to harmonize with organizational goals.
Managers should allow employee participation in routine decision making.	Managers should allow (and encourage) employee participation in routine *and* important decision-making situations.
Sharing information with employees will increase their satisfaction, which will improve morale and reduce resistance to authority, thus improving productivity.	Employee satisfaction is a by-product of improved performance.

Source: Adapted from Raymond Miles, "Keeping Informed—Human Relations or Human Resources?" *Harvard Business Review* 43 (July–August 1965), pp. 148–163.

(2) emphasized both relational communication (open, supportive, friendly) and command communication.

Raymond Miles may have been the first to use the term *human resources*. In a 1965 article entitled "Keeping Informed—Human Relations or Human Resources?" he compared the two models.[36] Table 2.1 lists some of the basic differences. As the table indicates, the human resources model takes a more positive view of employee potential. Managers are encouraged to trust their employees and permit them to participate in important decisions and in their own development.

Let's take a brief look at some of the better-known human resource theorists and their "best ways."

Human Resources and McGregor's Theory Y

Douglas McGregor was very critical of the businesses that he saw following the traditional model. He felt that traditional beliefs inspired employee fear and distrust and significantly decreased employee performance. According to McGregor, when managers believe in the traditional model

(McGregor called this Theory X), the following communication behaviors occur:[37]

- Most messages flow downward from managers to subordinates. Information is often inadequate for employee needs.
- Upward communication is extremely limited (thus, the informal grapevine is very important to employees).
- Subordinates fear and distrust management.
- Most decisions made by top management are based on inadequate information.

At the same time McGregor was criticizing the traditional model of management, he wasn't completely satisfied with the human relations model because he felt it did not do enough to encourage employee potential. Therefore, he developed a series of assumptions he called Theory Y, which he felt would produce the best managers and inspire employee trust and openness. The following communication behaviors are common when managers adopt Theory Y (or human resources) beliefs:

- Messages travel up, down, and across the organization.
- Decision making is spread throughout the organization. Even important decisions involve input from employees at all levels.
- Because feedback is encouraged in an upward direction—and management listens—no supplemental upward system is required.
- Frequent, honest interaction with employees takes place in an atmosphere of confidence and trust.
- The flow of messages downward is usually sufficient to satisfy the needs of employees.
- Decision making is based on messages from all levels of the organization, and thus the accuracy and quality of the decisions are improved.[38]

See Table 2.2 for a comparison of McGregor's Theory X and Theory Y. McGregor based his theories on Abraham Maslow's hierarchy of needs (discussed in Chapter 13). Theory X deals only with the physiological and safety needs of the hierarchy; Theory Y covers all five levels of needs (physiological, safety, social, esteem, and self-actualization).

Human Resources and Likert's Four Systems

Rensis Likert was another theorist who helped formulate the human resources model. He identified four management styles he called the Four Systems. System 1 (Exploitive/Authoritative) is similar to Theory X, and System 4 (Participative) resembles Theory Y. The other two systems (Be-

Table 2.2 Beliefs of Theory X and Theory Y Managers

Theory X (Traditional)	*Theory Y (Human Resources)*
1. The average person has an inherent dislike of work and will avoid it if possible.	1. The use of physical and mental energy in work is as natural as play or rest.
2. Most people will not strive to achieve organizational objectives unless they are coerced, controlled, directed, and threatened with punishment.	2. External control and threats are not the only ways to motivate workers to meet organizational objectives. A person who is committed to the objectives will exercise self-direction and self-control.
3. The average person prefers to be directed, wishes to avoid responsibility, has relatively little ambition, and wants security above all else.	3. Commitment to objectives is both a motivator and a function of the rewards of achievement.
	4. Under proper conditions, workers learn not only to accept but also to seek responsibility.
	5. The capacity to exercise a relatively high degree of ingenuity and creativity is widely distributed in the population.
	6. The intellectual potentialities of most people are only partially utilized in modern organizations.

Source: Norma Carr-Ruffino, *The Promotable Woman: Becoming a Successful Manager,* rev. ed. (Belmont, CA: Wadsworth, 1985), p. 274. Reprinted by permission.

nevolent/Authoritative and Consultative) fit between 1 and 4. *Likert considered System 4 the ideal model for an organization.* He and his colleagues from the University of Michigan found from their research that organizations high in System 4 characteristics also have high productivity. System 4 has three key elements: (1) supportive relationships based on trust, (2) group decision making and group supervision, and (3) high performance goals.[39] In System 4 organizations, communication is both formal and informal with upward, downward, and horizontal communication used often and regularly.

Human Resources and Blake and Mouton's Managerial Grid

According to Robert Blake and Jane Mouton, managerial effectiveness depends on two main attitudes: concern for production and concern for

Figure 2.4 The managerial grid. *(Source: Robert R. Blake and Jane S. Mouton, "Managerial Facades," Advanced Management Journal (July 1966), p. 31. Reprinted by permission.)*

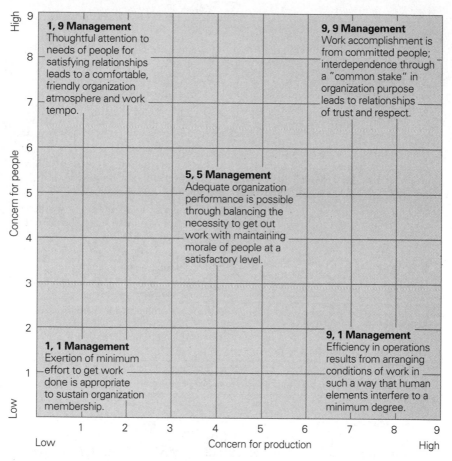

people. By combining concern for production (the primary focus of the traditional organization) and concern for people (the focus of the human relations organization), Blake and Mouton helped clarify the human resources model. A person's management style—that is, a manager's attitude toward the relative importance of people and production—can be plotted on the managerial grid (see Figure 2.4). According to the grid, an organization is most effective when its managers use the 9,9 (or team) approach to leadership, expressing a high concern for both people and results. This approach is similar to other human resources models in that it requires that employees be given the chance to participate in decision making and

Companies following the human resources model involve their employees in decision making. (© *Bruce Ayres/Tony Stone Images.*)

that a climate of trust and respect exist between managers and their subordinates.

Current Implementation of the Human Resources Model

The current application of the human resources model has a variety of names: quality control circle (QCC) or simply quality circle (QC), productivity groups, platform teams, self-management teams, TQM (total quality management), quality improvement teams, employee participation groups, high performance teams, or simply teams. Although the name and procedures may vary somewhat, essentially these are groups of employees who participate in generating ideas and decision making. Nonprofit organizations, businesses, educational groups, and governmental agencies are just a few of the organizations that use participative employee involvement groups. For example, Lockheed attributed $2,844,000 in documented savings to QCs over a period of two years; Honeywell's QCs reduced the costs of an assembly shop by 40 percent;[40] Oregon State University has fifteen successful TQM teams in operation;[41] and Chrysler Corporation credits its "comeback from near-insolvency to become the world's most successful automaker" to its use of "platform teams—autonomous groups made up of all the professionals needed to design and produce a new car."[42]

Although quality circles and employee teams have been very successful in some companies, other companies have experienced a high failure rate. Larry Smeltzer and Ben Kedia suggest that the following characteristics are necessary for team success:[43]

1. Horizontal communication between departments and flexibility within departments
2. Managers willing to listen to employees
3. Managers flexible enough to allow employee participation in problem solving
4. Organizations open to change
5. Management response to suggestions within 72 hours
6. Cooperation between management and the unions
7. Support for employees' teams from top and middle management.

Successful teams also must be comprised of members willing to work with one another, as well as with other teams.[44]

Communication in the Human Resources Organization

As the previous discussion of quality circles and employee teams indicates, the human resources organization takes a team-oriented or participative approach to employee–management relationships. Employees are not just *allowed* to participate in minor decision making; they are *expected* to take an active role in all decisions, big and small. To facilitate creative ideas and decisions, information and feedback flow freely up and down the organization, and the working environment is supportive, flexible, and trusting. Clearly, then, for the information flow required in the human resources model, employees at all levels need to have the communication skills discussed in Chapter 1.

Criticisms of the Human Resources Organization

McGregor was criticized for polarizing his management styles because such extremes may not be realistic. Likert's System 4 gives more management choices but still doesn't allow for overlapping of systems. His idea that there is one best method for all situations may also be unrealistic. By using a grid approach, Blake and Mouton allow for more combination of management styles; however, they limit the important variables to two: concern for people and concern for results. Many organizations have attempted to implement human resources values and techniques. Some have been successful, others have not. As with the human relations model, successful managers need to be trained, implementation costs are high, and the necessary open, trusting climate is difficult to maintain.

THE SYSTEMS/CONTINGENCY MODEL

Although all the organizational theorists we have discussed so far have presented what they felt was the "best way," each theory has fallen short in one or more areas. Current theories and the systems/contingency model contend that there is no best way. Joan Woodward's research supports this view. She decided to test important management principles to see whether successful companies applied these principles more often than less successful companies. She found no relationship between the use of any management principles and organizational effectiveness.[45] Upon reexamination of her data, however, she found that the effectiveness of certain management principles depended on the type of industry.

> In other words, there seemed to be a best method of organizing to fit each type of technology. Firms that stayed close to this best approach for their technical system were most effective.[46]

Thus, it would seem that no organizational model will fit all organizations. Our look at systems theory and contingency theory may help explain why this is true.

Systems Theory

Systems theory as it applies to organizations grew out of general systems theory, which was introduced by German biologist Ludwig von Bertalanfy.[47] To summarize:

> The central principle of general systems theory rests on the idea that the whole is more than the sum of its parts; each part must be considered as it interacts with, changes, and is changed by every other part within the system. The parts, or subsystems, of any given system are assumed to be interdependent, and it is primarily through communication that this interdependence is facilitated.[48]

To illustrate how one part of a system can affect the whole, imagine that you are traveling from Houston, Texas, to Santa Barbara, California, to attend a family reunion. A surprise thunderstorm delays your plane's departure, and you arrive in Los Angeles 3 hours behind schedule. Because the flight is so late, there are no available gates for your flight. You sit on

THE SYSTEMS/CONTINGENCY MODEL IN BRIEF

Key Theorists	Landmark Books and Articles
Joan Woodward	*Industrial Organization: Theory and Practice* (1965)
Daniel Katz and Robert Kahn	*The Social Psychology of Organizations* (1966)
Fred Fiedler	*A Theory of Leadership Effectiveness* (1967)
Robert House	"A Path–Goal Theory of Leader Behavior," *Administrative Science Quarterly* (1971)

Bias of Theory

Concern with the organization as a whole

View of Communication

All types of communication are essential because even one person can affect the entire organization.

the plane 45 minutes before a gate becomes available. Upon deplaning, you discover that the last commuter flight for Santa Barbara departed 30 minutes earlier. By the time you stand in line to rent a car and drive the 91 miles to your aunt's house through heavy evening traffic, the reunion is over and most of the relatives have gone. You missed the event for which you came. Not only are *you* disappointed, but so are many family members from all over the country.

Applying the systems approach to organizations, Daniel Katz and Robert Kahn referred to organizations as open systems.[49] An **open system** has flexible boundaries that allow communication to flow easily in and out of the organization. In open organizations, the "people who maintain communication with outsiders" are referred to as **boundary spanners:** They provide useful outside information to insiders, they "screen" outsiders for insiders, they control the dissemination of information, and they convince outsiders that the organization is interested in them.[50]

The strengths of systems theory are that (1) it recognizes the interdependence of all parts of an organization (what affects one part affects all parts), (2) it acknowledges both formal and informal communication as central to the success of an organization, and (3) it integrates the biases of both the traditional and the human relations models and gives them equal weight. In other words, "Questions of job duty, chain of command, span of control, and decision making are equal in importance to questions of attitude, morale, behavior, role, and personality."[51]

Contingency Theory

Like systems theory, contingency theory has evolved from the framework of general systems theory. Whereas systems theory is fairly mature, contingency theory is still being developed. There are several versions of contingency theory, but all have the same basic belief: "No one type of organizational structure or leadership style is most appropriate for all situations."[52]

One of the best-known models is Fred Fiedler's contingency theory. From his research with bomber crews, high school basketball teams, foundry workers, and management groups, Fiedler came to the conclusion that "which management style will be the most effective in a particular situation depends on the degree to which the group situation enables the manager to exert influence."[53]

Fiedler analyzes such contingent variables as leader–follower relations, position power, and task structure. For example, he found that a task orientation was most effective in either situation A or C:[54]

SITUATION A

- Manager well liked
- Manager powerful
- Tasks well defined

SITUATION C

- Manager disliked
- Manager has little power
- Tasks poorly defined

However, a human relations orientation is more effective in situation B, in which the manager has moderate influence:

SITUATION B

- Manager moderately liked
- Manager has some power
- Tasks moderately defined

Research by Fiedler and his colleagues shows that managers can be trained to identify and modify various situations to better fit their own communication and leadership styles.[55]

Another type of contingency theory is Robert House's *path–goal theory*, which asserts that the overall job satisfaction and performance levels of employees are contingent on three things: (1) employee satisfaction with the job, (2) the uncertainty and difficulty of the job, and (3) the communication style of the supervisor.[56]

Instead of employees adapting to fit management style, House suggests that leadership can adapt to fit the given situation.[57] Leadership that provides direction and structure is needed in situations in which the task is uncertain, the procedure to complete the task is ambiguous, or the employee is new or uncertain of the task. Supportive, considerate leadership is needed in situations in which the task is highly structured, dull, and unsatisfying or in which employees are uncertain of themselves although capable of doing the job. Neither directive nor supportive leadership will be effective unless employees perceive the leader as helping them achieve desired goals. Successful leaders make the path to these goals clear and attainable.

Current Implementation of the Contingency Model

Theory Z, developed by William Ouchi, is one of the latest applications of contingency theory.[58] According to Ouchi, successful organizations are those that have a culture that reflects the values of their employees. In other words, instead of a company imposing its preferred management style on employees, a Theory Z company adapts its management style to the existing employee culture. In his book *Theory Z*, he cites Hewlett-Packard, Dayton-Hudson Corporation, Rockwell International, Intel, and Eli Lilly as examples of organizations with Theory Z cultures.[59] **Culture** can be defined as the "pattern of beliefs and expectations shared by the organization's members—which produce norms that shape the behavior of individuals and groups in the organization."[60]

In the past, many American workers valued individual decision making and responsibility, employee specialization, short-term employment, and rapid promotions, and they did not expect to get much social satisfaction from the job; church, community, and family groups provided for social needs. For these employees, Ouchi says, "type A" firms (similar to McGregor's Theory X or the classical organization model) were appropriate and reasonably successful. However, employee values and needs seem to have changed. Due perhaps to the mobility and urbanization of Americans, social needs are no longer being met by nonwork organizations. Many of us have moved away from our families and close friends; often we don't even know our neighbors and have few, if any, close relationships outside of the work environment. In these instances, Ouchi feels that type A organizations are inappropriate. He recommends Theory Z, which combines the best qualities of type A with the successful Japanese approach. Theory Z organizations have the following characteristics:[61]

- Individual advancement and achievement, but with less competitiveness and more cooperative effort
- Collective decision making but with the ultimate responsibility assigned to a single person
- Close personal relationships
- Trust
- Emphasis on interpersonal skills
- Respect and value of employees
- Long-term employment
- Community feeling at work

Noting that type Z organizations are not appropriate in all situations, Charles Conrad states,

> Our culture is not homogeneous—there are many subcultures that value community more than individuality and there are some areas in which nonwork organizations still fulfill employees' need for community. In these areas, type A organizations still are appropriate; attempts to impose a type Z organization on employees would be resisted.[62]

In a speech entitled "Employee Involvement," the senior vice president of operations for Miller Brewing Company spoke from a contingency systems orientation:

> We know that "Employee Involvement" is not a "corporate program" to be implemented "as is" at every Miller facility. We also know that how EI is implemented—the methods used and the timing—are going to vary with each different circumstance. Each of our plants is different. Each has its own culture, its own history, its own traditional way of doing things.
> What works in New York might not work at our Fort Worth can plant. The methods used at Albany, Georgia might not be the same methods that will work out in Irwindale, California or in Milwaukee. On the other hand, some might work with just a slight modification or alteration. And we encourage the sharing of ideas and projects in order to stimulate ideas that will work.[63]

The U.S. Marine Corps, Disney World, and Southwest Airlines are examples of other organizations with strong cultures. Because a culture is an attitude shared by employees, it is not always easy to identify. Evidence of a culture at Disney World is seen through "shared things (wearing the Walt Disney uniform . . .), shared sayings (a good 'Mickey' is a compliment for doing a good job), shared behavior (smiling at customers and being polite), and shared feelings (taking pride in working at Disney)."[64]

Communication in the Contingency Organization

The contingency model asserts that there is no single best way to manage, and there is no single best way to communicate. Both management styles and communication processes are influenced by the situation and any number of internal and external factors. Employees' needs and abilities, manager personality and communication skills, customer expectations, economy, and many other variables play a role in communication choice. Communication flexibility, a must in the contingency organization, is valued even more than in the human resources organization.

Criticisms of the Systems/Contingency Organization

Because these models are still in the construction stage, it may be too soon to criticize. Nevertheless, Conrad notes that each model contains specific contingency factors, although none contains all the important factors. He further states that contingency models will be more helpful when they "simultaneously consider the external pressures which stem from an organization's relationship to its environment *and* the internal pressures that are created by its subsystems."[65]

SUMMARY

To get a feel for the complexity and the unique communication problems of organizations you are familiar with or have worked for, it's important to know which organization model they follow: traditional or classical, human relations, human resources, or systems/contingency. The traditional model is made up of two groups of theorists: the scientific managers, who urge the scientific design of each task and the scientific selection of workers, and the bureaucratic theorists, who want to improve the efficiency of managers by formalizing the official chain of command, insisting that all decisions and actions be put in writing, and recommending a detached relationship with employees. The human relations model emphasizes employee–boss relationships and believes that giving employees tender loving care will result in greater productivity. The human resources model, represented by Theory Y, focuses on employee–manager teamwork, built on both employee satisfaction and management control. And finally, the systems/contingency model tries to select the management style that best meets the needs, expectations, and culture of the employees.

Communication in the traditional organization is mainly downward. In the human relations organization communication is also primarily downward but supportive. In the human resources and contingency models, communication flows in all directions. Communication, feedback, and company expectations differ significantly from model to model. We hope you can now feel more comfortable identifying and selecting your work environment and communicating in any environments in which you find yourself.

Checkpoint

Before continuing to the next chapter, check your understanding of Chapter 2 by completing the following exercises:

1. Does the primary burden of effective communication within an organization rest with management? Why or why not?
2. Think back to a job you have held in the last five years. Consider your attitude toward the management of the firm for which you worked and answer the questions below:

   a. **Always   Sometimes   Rarely**
   Management tried its best to treat employees fairly.
   b. **Always   Sometimes   Rarely**
   Management was usually concerned about the employees' personal problems.
   c. **Always   Sometimes   Rarely**
   Management did everything possible to make our customers happy.

   Now assume that everyone else in the organization had the same attitude as you. What would be the effects of these attitudes on the overall operation of the organization?
3. If you are employed or involved in volunteer work, what type of organization model does your organization seem to follow? How do you and other workers feel about it? If you could change this organization in any way, what changes would you implement?
4. Conduct an interview with one or more employees from an organization that interests you (such as a community, government, university, or business organization). What type of organizational model do they seem to follow? Is it effective, in your opinion?

NOTES

· ·

1. John M. Ivancevich and Michael T. Matteson, *Organizational Behavior and Management*, 4th ed. (Chicago: Irwin, 1996), p. 5.
2. Marshall Sashkin and William C. Morris, *Organizational Behavior: Concepts and Experiences* (Reston, VA: Reston, 1984), chap. 15.
3. The material in this section is largely based on the first edition of Charles Conrad, *Strategic Organizational Communication* (New York: Holt, Rinehart & Winston, 1990). The authors wish to express their appreciation to Professor Conrad for his assistance.
4. Michael Hammer and James Champy, *Reengineering the Corporation: A Manifesto for Business Revolution* (New York: HarperBusiness, 1993), p. 17.
5. Ivancevich and Matteson, pp. 10–12.
6. Excerpt from p. 146 of Charles Conrad, *Strategic Organizational Communication: Toward the Twenty-First Century*, 3rd ed. Copyright © 1994 by Harcourt Brace. Reprinted by permission of the publisher.
7. Frederick W. Taylor, *Scientific Management* (New York: Harper & Row, 1911), p. 90.
8. Everett M. Rogers and Rekha Agarwala-Rogers, *Communication in Organizations* (New York: Free Press, 1976), p. 32.
9. Jerry W. Koehler, Karl W. Anatol, and Ronald L. Applbaum, *Organizational Communication: Behavioral Perspectives* (New York: Holt, Rinehart & Winston, 1976), p. 12.
10. Taylor, p. 140.
11. Conrad, p. 143.
12. Henri Fayol, *General and Industrial Management* (London: Sir Isaac Pitman and Sons, 1949).
13. Excerpt from p. 41 of Gerald M. Goldhaber, *Organizational Communication*, 6th ed. Copyright © 1993 by Brown & Benchmark. All rights reserved. Reprinted by permission of the publisher.
14. R. Carzo, Jr., and J. N. Yanouzas, "Effects of Flat and Tall Organization Structures," *Administrative Science Quarterly* 14 (1969), pp. 178–191.
15. Carzo and Yanouzas, pp. 178–191.
16. Anthony Downs, *Inside Bureaucracy* (Boston: Little, Brown, 1967), p. 117.
17. Max Weber, *The Theory of Social and Economic Organization* (New York: Oxford University Press, 1947).
18. Richard L. Daft, *Organization Theory and Design*, 5th ed. (Minneapolis/St. Paul: West, 1995), p. 315.
19. Conrad, p. 163.
20. Daft, p. 315.
21. Goldhaber, pp. 37–38.
22. Daft, p. 169.
23. Edwin Locke, "The Ideas of Frederick W. Taylor: An 'Evaluation,'" *Academy of Management Review* 7 (1982), pp. 14–24.
24. Raymond Miles, *Theories of Management* (New York: McGraw-Hill, 1975); adapted by Charles Conrad (1st ed.), p. 74.
25. Bob Davis, "Federal Relief Agency Is Slowed by Infighting, Patronage, Regulations," *Wall Street Journal*, August 31, 1992, pp. A1, A12.
26. Daft, pp. 163–171.
27. J. B. Treece, "Will GM Learn from Its Own Role Models?" *Business Week*, April 9, 1990, pp. 62–64.
28. Jerald Greenberg and Robert A. Baron, *Behavior in Organizations*, 5th ed. (Englewood Cliffs, NJ: Prentice-Hall, 1995), p. 582. [Original source: C. F. Hendricks, *The Rightsizing Remedy* (Homewood, IL: Business One Irwin, 1992)]
29. Daft, p. 169.
30. Fritz J. Roethlisberger and William J. Dickson, *Management and the Worker* (Cambridge, MA: Harvard University Press, 1939).
31. Conrad, p. 202.
32. Chester I. Barnard, *The Functions of the Executive* (Cambridge, MA: Harvard University Press, 1938), p. 226.
33. Barnard, pp. 175–181.
34. Goldhaber, p. 45.
35. Richard Franke and James Kaul, "The Hawthorne Experiments," *American Sociological Review* 43 (1978), pp. 623–643; Nancy A. Euske and Karlene H. Roberts, "Evolving Perspec-

tives in Organization Theory: Communication Implications," in *Handbook of Organizational Communication*, Fredric M. Jablin, Linda Putnam, Karlene H. Roberts, and Lyman W. Porter, eds. (Newbury Park, CA: Sage, 1987), p. 45.

36. Raymond Miles, "Keeping Informed—Human Relations or Human Resources?" *Harvard Business Review* 43 (July–August 1965), pp. 148–163.
37. Goldhaber, p. 78.
38. Goldhaber, p. 79.
39. Rensis Likert, *New Patterns of Management* (New York: McGraw-Hill, 1961), p. 47.
40. Joel E. Ross and William C. Ross, *Japanese Quality Circles and Productivity* (Reston, VA: Reston, 1982), p. 16; Phillip C. Thompson, *Quality Circles: How to Make Them Work in America* (New York: AMACOM, 1982), pp. 11–12.
41. L. Edwin Coate, "TQM at Oregon State University," *Journal for Quality and Participation* (December 1990), pp. 90–101; Daft, p. 191.
42. Daft, p. 191.
43. Larry R. Smeltzer and Ben L. Kedia, "Knowing the Ropes: Organizational Requirements for Quality Circles," *Business Horizons* 28 (July–August 1985), pp. 32–34.
44. Greenberg and Baron, pp. 314–316.
45. Joan Woodward, *Industrial Organization: Theory and Practice* (London: Oxford University Press, 1965).
46. Sashkin and Morris, p. 348.
47. Ludwig von Bertalanfy, *General Systems Theory* (New York: Braziller, 1968).
48. Patricia H. Andrews and John E. Baird, Jr., *Communication for Business and the Professions*, 6th ed. (Dubuque, IA: Brown & Benchmark, 1995), p. 17.
49. Daniel Katz and Robert L. Kahn, *The Social Psychology of Organizations* (New York: Wiley, 1966), pp. 16–17.
50. Conrad, pp. 131–133; for a discussion of boundary spanners, see Howard Aldrich and D. Herker, "Boundary Spanning Roles and Organizational Structures," *Academy of Management Review* 2 (1977), pp. 217–230.
51. Goldhaber, p. 47.
52. Rogers and Agarwala-Rogers, p. 45.
53. Reported in Norma Carr-Ruffino, *The Promotable Woman: Becoming a Successful Manager*, rev. ed. (Belmont, CA: Wadsworth, 1985), p. 277.
54. Fred Fiedler, *A Theory of Leadership Effectiveness* (New York: McGraw-Hill, 1967).
55. Fred Fiedler, M. Chemers, and L. Mahar, *Improving Leadership Effectiveness* (New York: Wiley, 1976).
56. Conrad, p. 227.
57. Robert House, "A Path–Goal Theory of Leader Behavior," *Administrative Science Quarterly* 16 (1971), pp. 321–339; Robert House and T. Mitchell, "Path–Goal Theory of Leadership," *Journal of Contemporary Business* 3 (1974), pp. 81–98.
58. William G. Ouchi, *Theory Z: How American Business Can Meet the Japanese Challenge* (Reading, MA: Addison-Wesley, 1981).
59. Ouchi, pp. 225–260.
60. Howard Schwartz and Stanley Davis, "Matching Corporate Culture and Business Strategy," *Organizational Dynamics* 10 (Summer 1981), pp. 30–48.
61. Ouchi, pp. 71–76, 195–218.
62. Conrad, p. 19.
63. Allen A. Schumer, "Employee Involvement: The Quality Circle Process," *Vital Speeches* 54 (July 1, 1988), pp. 563–566.
64. Ivancevich and Matteson, p. 83.
65. Conrad, p. 230.

3 Improving Interpersonal Relationships

Put simply, good interpersonal relationships at work are no longer a luxury but a *bona fide* qualification for effective job performance.[1]

ERIC M. EISENBERG,
H. L. GOODALL, JR.,
Organizational Communication

Interpersonal relationships are extremely important to an organization's success. Organizations that desire high productivity and that want to be known for providing quality customer service must depend on their employees. Employees who develop and maintain strong interpersonal relationships with their bosses, coworkers, and customers have a different outlook on their jobs than do those who have poor relationships. Positive relationships produce confidence and trust in employees and encourage them to freely communicate their opinions and feelings; poor relationships inspire suspicion and lead to distorted communication. Both productivity and customer service are topics that appear regularly in business journals and are concerns of such popular books as *A Passion for Excellence*, *Reengineering the Corporation*, *When Giants Learn to Dance*, and *Busting Bureaucracy*.[2] Research has shown that productivity and customer service are directly related to the quality of relationships in the organization. When employees feel they are valued, listened to, and cared about, and have a sense of shared responsibility, their attitudes are positive and their performance is distinguished.

INTERPERSONAL RELATIONSHIPS AND ORGANIZATIONAL SUCCESS

Regardless of the status you hold in your organization, the organization's success is influenced by the quality of your relationships with your coworkers. The quality of the relationships employees form with those around them (including the boss) affects (1) their job satisfaction, (2) their ability to "gain the information and support they need in order to perform their job" and their willingness to provide similar information and support to coworkers, and (3) their ability to understand messages from the boss as well as their willingness to carry them out.[3]

The quality of a supervisor's relationships is equally important. One management consultant lists the following managerial characteristics as important to "high-quality boss [and] subordinate" relationships:

- A boss who praises subordinates
- A boss who understands a subordinate's job
- A boss who can be trusted
- A boss who is warm and friendly
- A boss who is honest
- A boss with whom subordinates are free to disagree[4]

Just as the quality of relationships among members affects the organization, so too does the climate of the organization determine the quality of the relationships formed by its members. According to W. Charles Redding,

> A member of any organization is, in large measure, the kind of communicator that the organization compels him to be. In other words, the very fact of holding a position in an organization determines many of the ways in which a person speaks, listens, writes, and reads.[5]

For example, imagine the types of relationships you would form in a defensive climate that makes you feel that you are

- Being judged (even praise creates discomfort if it is excessively strong or too public)
- Being manipulated or controlled too tightly or inappropriately
- Being tricked, especially into believing that you are having an important impact on decisions or playing an important role in the organization when you are not
- Being subject to cold, impersonal, uncaring treatment
- Being treated as an inferior, relatively useless person
- Being "preached at" by a "smug" or "know-it-all" supervisor[6]

Even a trusting, sharing, hard-working person can become angry and uncaring in a company in which most of the managers and employees are hostile and suspicious, and generally dislike one another. *Everyone's communication style is affected by the work environment.* In fact, our lives at work may very well influence our lives at home.[7] Thus, you need to be careful in selecting the organization for which you work because its atmosphere and attitudes can directly affect your communication style, your relationships, and your communication behavior. At the same time, the organization needs to be careful in deciding whether to hire you: The way you relate to people can affect the organization's communication success and even its climate.

DEVELOPING AND MAINTAINING RELATIONSHIPS[8]

The strong, lasting relationships that we develop with people at work (or anyplace, for that matter) fulfill one or more needs that we have. As long as the relationship continues to mutually fulfill some need for each partner, it will survive; if not, the relationship will deteriorate. In developing and maintaining relationships, keep two important concepts in mind: clear expectations and the reciprocal quality of interpersonal relationships.

Clear Expectations

Every partner in a relationship has certain expectations of other partners. Your boss has certain expectations of you and other employees; you have expectations of your boss and coworkers; your coworkers have expectations of you, the boss, and one another. Actually, the climate found in an organization is often "a measure of whether or not people's expectations of what it should be like to work in an organization are being met."[9] When our expectations are not fulfilled, we often react with frustration, anger, suspicion, and withdrawal of our trust. Some people tend to hold these feelings inside; others retaliate. Each time our expectations are not met, a strain is placed on the relationship. We probably assume that the person who disappointed us is being purposefully uncooperative or just stupid. Unless the violated expectations are uncovered and behavior is changed, or the expectations are revised in some way, the relationship will begin to deteriorate. Take, for example, a new marriage: He refuses to help around the house as the wife expected; she wants to establish a career before starting a family, which the husband did not expect. Business relationships operate in the same way: The employee expects a warm, social working environment; the supervisor expects employees to complete their tasks without talking to one another and to socialize only at break time. Chances are that neither the employees nor the supervisor will fulfill the others' expectations.

One key to developing and maintaining effective relationships is to make our expectations of one another clear. Think about your relationships. Have you made it your business to learn about the expectations of your boss, fellow worker, family, instructor, or friend? Have you made clear what expectations of yours they must meet in order to please you? According to Gary Kreps, most of our "expectations remain unspoken until they are violated."[10] We *assume* that others know what is expected of them without being told. For example, one supervisor assumes that all employees know they are expected to take an active role in office decisions and becomes upset when a new employee seems to want others to make all the decisions. At the same time, another supervisor for the same company assumes that all employees know they are expected to clear any decisions with their supervisor and becomes extremely upset when a new employee solves a problem without getting prior supervisor approval. Not only do most expectations remain unspoken until violated, but also our expectations "continually change, making the potential for the fulfillment of these expectations less likely."[11]

Reciprocal Quality of Interpersonal Relationships

Interpersonal relationships have a reciprocal quality about them. For example, if a coworker does something especially nice for you, such as help with a difficult task, you will most likely reciprocate and do something nice for the coworker. No one actually said, "If you help me, I'll help you," but because of the reciprocal quality of relationships, "people communicate with others in accord with the way they perceive these others communicating with them."[12] If you share some work-related knowledge with me that makes my job easier, I will share some knowledge I have with you. If you treat me with trust and respect, I'll treat you in the same manner. As long as we continue to reciprocate, the relationship will grow. However, if you do considerably more for me than I can do for you, the reciprocal quality of our relationship is out of balance and the relationship will deteriorate or at least stagnate until the balance is restored.[13]

In a relationship, when our expectations of another person are reciprocated, a *self-fulfilling prophecy* is likely to occur. For example, if manager A believes that subordinate B is dishonest and untrustworthy, the manager is likely to communicate these suspicions to the subordinate through verbal and nonverbal behaviors, such as unwarranted questioning, staring, and unfriendly facial expressions. The more the subordinate detects these untrusting behaviors, the more he or she will feel uncomfortable with the manager. Subordinate B may be hesitant to disclose full and honest information to manager A because the subordinate does not trust the manager. Because the subordinate is not providing full and honest information to the manager, the manager's expectations about the subordinate are fulfilled.[14]

The power of reciprocated expectations or self-fulfilling prophecies is frightening. A friend of ours experimented with three of her college classes to see if she could cause a self-fulfilling prophecy. When she graded the first exam, the average grade was the same for three of her business and professional communication courses. When she returned the student papers to the first class, she praised them for their high grades and intelligent, thoughtful answers. While returning the papers to the second class, the professor neither praised nor criticized the class. However, while returning the papers to the third class, the professor severely reprimanded the students for having the lowest grades she had ever seen and for giving careless, undeveloped answers. No further mention was made of the exam grades and class continued as usual. The results of the second exam were surprising. The grades from the class that had been praised were much better than on the first exam; the class that was neither praised nor criticized remained the same; and the grades from the class that had been severely criticized were much worse than on the first exam. Feeling bad

Figure 3.1 Relationship between trust and performance. *(Source: W. Haney, Communication and Organizational Behavior: Text and Cases, 5th ed. Copyright © 1986, p. 14. Reprinted by permission of Richard D. Irwin, Inc., Homewood, IL.)*

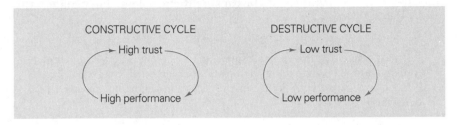

about what had happened, the professor told the classes what she had done. No one believed her! The improved class said that they made better grades because they were better students. The class with the poor grades said that she was just trying to make them feel better—they knew that they were truly poor students.

Although we need to be aware that our expectations of others and even of ourselves can lead to negative self-fulfilling prophecies, we can also predict and achieve positive results. Therefore, *another key to establishing and maintaining relationships is to use the reciprocal nature of relationships to elicit interpersonal cooperation and trust.* Trust may well be one of the most important determiners of manager–employee relationships. Research has determined that if employees trust their managers, they are much more likely to be open in their communications.

After interviewing 1,220 supervisors from 14 organizations, W. Haney determined that there are both constructive and destructive "trust cycles" (Figure 3.1). In the constructive cycle, high trust on the part of a supervisor stimulates high worker performance, which in turn reinforces high trust (a positive self-fulfilling prophecy). However, in the destructive cycle, low trust on the part of the supervisor contributes to low worker performance, which then reinforces the supervisor's low trust (a negative self-fulfilling prophecy).

To improve trust, either the supervisor or the worker can initiate a break from the destructive cycle. Using the reciprocal nature of relationships, the supervisor can react to a low-producing employee with increased trust and responsibility, hoping to motivate better performance; or the employee can react to low trust with increased productivity, hoping to persuade the supervisor that he or she is deserving of trust. Although both methods involve a risk, the destructive cycle will continue unless someone moves first to break it.

In *Managing for Excellence*, David Bradford and Allan Cohen suggest that instead of automatically attributing an employee's low productivity to a defect or negative personality trait, which could cause a negative self-fulfilling prophecy, the supervisor should check to see if something in the employee's work situation could be causing the problem. They suggest the supervisor take this view:

> Let me assume that this difficult subordinate is really a very competent, well-intentioned person. How then could such a nice, able person behave in such a negative way? What in the situation might be causing this behavior?[15]

Such a view makes it easier "to move from an initial rejection position into a direct data-collection mode."[16] Trust requires that we give everyone the benefit of the doubt. And it has a definite influence on the type of interpersonal relationships established and maintained in an organization.

COMMUNICATION STYLES AND BUSINESS RELATIONSHIPS

Strong interpersonal relationships are not only the heart of a successful organization, but also the foundation of our own business successes. In order to make relationships work, we need to be aware of people's expectations and of the reciprocal nature of relationships. However, there is another critical factor that affects our relationships with bosses, coworkers, and customers: the communication style that each of us uses. Each of us has a communication style that we feel the most comfortable using. Many professions and businesses also seem to have preferred communication styles. Imagine a boss who has a communication style that is completely different from most of the employees, or two coworkers with quite different communication styles, or a customer with a communication style that significantly differs from the salesperson or the sales company. What type of relationships are likely to develop? What are the chances that their expectations are clear to one another and that these expectations will lead to positive self-fulfilling prophecies? Obviously, our communication styles have a direct effect on our interpersonal relationships. *We are able to communicate more successfully and establish more meaningful work relationships with people if we not only understand their styles but also can attune our style to theirs.*

In the next few sections, we will look at four styles that managers, employees, and customers typically use when communicating: the closed style, the blind style, the hidden style, and the open style. Few people are ever completely closed, completely blind, completely hidden, or completely open. Although a person may have some characteristics of all four

Figure 3.2 Feedback and disclosure continuums.

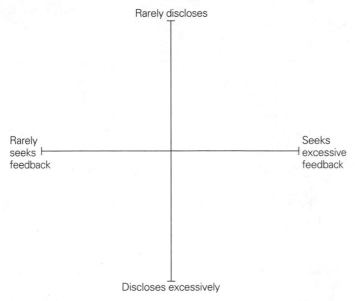

styles, most people have one or sometimes two dominant styles they typically use when things are going well, and another style (or styles) they use under stress. None of these styles is totally good or totally bad; each has its "best" and "worst" side.

The styles vary in the amount of feedback obtained and disclosure volunteered to others (see Figure 3.2). **Feedback** (response from others in the form of facts, opinions, and feelings) can vary on the feedback continuum from complete avoidance of feedback to excessive use of feedback. Either end of the continuum can inhibit effective communication. For example, we all know people who seldom ask for the opinions or advice of others, either because they don't feel they need it or because feedback makes them uncomfortable. In the same manner, **disclosure** (voluntarily sharing information, opinions, and feelings with others) can vary from very little disclosure to excessive disclosure. Either too much or too little disclosure can hamper successful communication. We've all met people who volunteer very few ideas or opinions and other people who seem to volunteer everything! Disclosure does not have to be personal. Fritz Steele, author of *The Open Organization: The Impact of Secrecy and Disclosure on People and Organizations*, explains disclosure this way:

> Disclosure can be of ideas, information from other sources, feelings, or any other topics we can pass on to another person. Individuals can dis-

close opinions, descriptions of past behaviors, future intentions, feelings, or anything else that can be conceptualized or acted out. Organizations can also disclose, that is, make information available, and in different degrees to different people.[17]

We present this classification system involving the four styles not as a method for stereotyping people but as a practical way of understanding other people's frames of reference so that you can improve your relationships and communication with them. We use the terms *manager, supervisor,* and *boss* to refer to any level of supervision from the lowest to the highest. Both *customer* and *client* may refer to a single individual, a group, or a large corporation. As you read the following sections, remember that the descriptions of these styles are not perfect or even complete; rather, the sections describe tendencies. As such, we hope you will find them helpful in your daily business and professional communication.*

> **NOTE:** Before reading further in this chapter, we urge you to complete the Survey of Communication Styles found in Appendix A. The survey will help you to determine your own communication style tendencies and will make the following discussion more meaningful.

If you complete the Survey of Communication Styles, you will see in both the Employee Tendency Indicator and the Manager Tendency Indicator surveys that your largest total represents the style that you typically use when things are running smoothly; the next largest total or totals (you may have two scores that are only one or two points apart) represent the style or styles you use under stress. For example, a person might usually communicate in an open manner but under stress begin communicating in a hidden manner. As we have indicated, there is no perfect style. Each style has a good side and a bad side. Which style is the most effective in a particular situation depends on several factors: Which styles can you use comfortably? Which style or styles are preferred or expected by your boss? your company? your employees? your customers? Knowing the best and worst of each style can help you better assess your preferred style's strengths and weaknesses.

---

*The manager, employee, and customer styles presented in this section are a composite of Luft and Ingham's "JoHari window" concept,[18] Hall's "interpersonal styles and managerial impacts,"[19] Lefton's "dimensional models of subordinate and superior appraisal behaviors,"[20] Likert's "management systems approach,"[21] and Bradford and Cohen's "manager-as-conductor" and "manager-as-developer" middle manager styles.[22] The result, although it does not contradict these authors' concepts, is our own product and, therefore, does not parallel any of the other five approaches exactly.

Figure 3.3 The closed communication style.

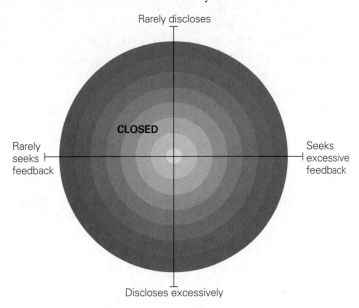

The Closed Style

If you had the choice of a job in which your desk would be in a room with five or six other people that you would work with each day or a job in which your desk would be in a back room all alone and you would work with a machine that only one person could operate at a time, which one would you choose? If you have closed tendencies, you probably selected the job in which your desk is in the back room and you work alone. Closed communicators are usually productive, hard workers who simply feel more comfortable working with things than with people. For example, if you are a closed person, you would probably be very productive working in an out-of-the-way place at your own computer terminal or making widgets on your own machine, but would feel apprehensive working in a complaint booth at a department store.

As Figure 3.3 indicates, closed communicators tend to fall on the low disclosure, low feedback ends of the two continuums. In other words, closed persons seek very little feedback from others and disclose very little information to others. In fact, people with a very closed style not only feel uncomfortable around people, they actually fear them. In their experience, people are unpredictable and it is safer just to stay away from them (rather like a turtle that retreats completely into its shell each time someone approaches).

Because closed persons find it very difficult to communicate their expectations to others, they are often disappointed by those around them. As a result, relationships with closed persons are difficult. Closed persons are often anxious about many things such as looking like a fool, getting blamed for something, or maybe even losing their job. As a result, they spend much of their energy in safety seeking. Avoiding decisions is one safety procedure. However, when decisions have to be made, closed persons use other safe procedures such as "going by the book," following tradition, and treating everyone alike. Don't forget that closed people can be quite productive as long as only minimal interaction with others is required.

Closed Managers ■   Feeling more comfortable with things than people, closed managers are usually very organized people who enjoy such things as inventory control, ordering supplies, and detail work that other managers may dislike. Their employees don't have to worry whether needed supplies will arrive on schedule as some employees do.

However, as you might expect, closed managers are less successful dealing with employees and employee problems. Employees who need encouragement rarely receive it; those who need firm guidance fail to get it; and those who need the freedom to be creative rarely find the closed manager willing to risk the unknown. In their quest for safety, closed managers tend to stay as far away from employees as possible. They keep a low profile and want their employees to do the same. The decisions that closed managers make are designed to lower their risk and enhance their feelings of safety. As a result, they tend to treat all employees the same—all will receive the same appraisal, the same raise, and so on. Managers with extremely closed styles prefer not to give employee appraisals at all. If appraisals are required by their organization, they give very brief and superficial evaluations. They prefer that no records be kept (too risky); if the company insists, the records will be middle-of-the-road, noncommittal notes that could describe anyone.

Other safety-seeking strategies used by closed managers are: (1) Never initiate upward communication. If it is required, say little and keep it vague. (2) Do not try to motivate employees, because nothing works anyway. (3) Ignore employee conflicts—eventually someone else will solve them or they will go away by themselves. If a problem comes to the attention of upper managers, who insist that something be done, the closed managers will usually go by the book. Complaining employees are shown the company policy and procedures manual and told, "Hey! It's not my fault. I didn't make the rules. If we don't follow them, we'll all get fired."

Employees who are highly trained and motivated view closed managers as laissez-faire leaders and may appreciate being left alone to make their own decisions. Also, other closed employees, who feel safer when not

REMEMBER, CLOSED COMMUNICATORS . . .

At Their BEST Are
- Productive as long as they can work in an environment free of interpersonal demands.
- Seen as reserved.
- Considered similar to the laissez-faire leader, who lets employees do whatever they want.

At Their WORST Are
- Likely to spend most of their energy looking for security; therefore, productivity is fairly low.
- Seen as difficult to get to know and unresponsive to needs of others.
- Thought to be aloof and noncommunicative.

required to communicate, appreciate a closed boss. However, creative employees and employees who need guidance often become frustrated and sometimes hostile toward the closed manager.

Closed Employees ■   This type of employee rarely offers opinions and seldom seeks feedback from others. Because closed employees believe that the only way to get through life is to keep your mouth shut, they rarely participate in team activities. When forced to state their views, their comments are very cautious, and they usually take a neutral position. Preferring to work alone, they may be very productive as long as they are not required to interact regularly with others. They passively accept any criticism the boss gives. The boss who expects employees to actively participate in group meetings and decision making will be disappointed in the closed employee. As with the closed manager, the closed employee's behavior is motivated by a need for security. Therefore, asking their opinion in meetings does not make it easier for them to participate; instead, it increases their anxiety.

Closed Customers ■   Like the closed manager and closed employee, the customer with an extremely closed style tends to have a low self-image and a fear of people. Such a fear is illustrated by the man who would rather wear worn-out clothes than go shopping for new ones because shopping requires interaction with salespeople. Closed customers view decision making as a personal threat and may decide not to buy just to avoid having to make a decision. They really want the salesperson to lead them by the hand. If they are pleased with the help and advice the salesperson gives, they will direct their business exclusively to this person. If the product or

Figure 3.4 The blind communication style.

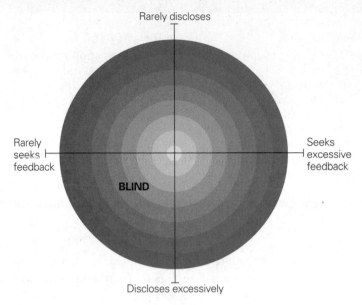

service recommended by the salesperson turns out to be a poor choice, rarely will closed customers openly complain. Instead, they may change stores without letting the store or the salesperson know why. Many closed customers expect to get a raw deal from life; bad products or services just reinforce this belief.

The Blind Style

If you are looking for someone you know you can depend on to get the job done, or someone to train a group of overconfident new-hires, or someone with the self-assurance to trouble-shoot a problem department, or someone who can command authority in a crisis situation, you couldn't do better than to hire a blind communicator. Whereas closed communicators would experience disabling anxiety in these situations, blind communicators thrive in situations in which they can demonstrate their expertise and experience.

As Figure 3.4 indicates, blind communicators tend to fall on the low feedback and high disclosure ends of the two continuums, which causes others to view them as authoritarian. As with closed persons, blind communicators seldom ask for feedback, and yet they are the opposite of closed communicators in several ways. Instead of having a low self-image, blind communicators tend to be very confident (even overly confident) and are not afraid to express their views, expectations, or needs. As a result, people know where they stand with a blind communicator. However, blind communicators don't ask for feedback (ideas or opinions) from others because they don't feel they need it—they already know what's best. Instead of avoiding others, blind-style communicators tend to overuse disclosure, telling others their opinions, how things should be done, what others are doing wrong, and so on, even when their advice may not be wanted (this unasked-for information is more task-oriented than personal).

Blind communicators are often right when they say their ideas are better. They are usually experienced and very knowledgeable on the topic. They fail to recognize, however, that there may be several other acceptable ways to do things. As many blind communicators have discovered the hard way, most people are not interested in the perfect or even the best way to do things and are not impressed by all the hard work that went into such a proposal. If you often feel dismayed by the quality of ideas generated by others and think to yourself "If I want something done right, I've got to do it myself," you are exhibiting some blind tendencies.

Blind Managers ■ As you can see from the above discussion, blind communicators (as well as closed communicators) have both strengths and weaknesses. Feeling comfortable dealing with people and not being afraid to exercise authority or to disclose opinions are desirable management characteristics, especially during a crisis or when organizational change has caused high employee anxiety. In these situations, a person who is willing to take charge creates a needed atmosphere of confidence. However, at other times, authoritarian approaches (similar to those found in the traditional or classical model discussed in Chapter 2) may be less successful.

Managers with very blind styles believe that good managers know more about employees' jobs than employees do. They also expect employees to mess things up unless they are watched very closely. This may be one reason why it is so difficult for them to delegate responsibility; they want employees to *do* the work, but to do it as they themselves have envisioned. Blind-style managers can be very critical and demanding of employees. Mistakes or failures are seldom tolerated. However, when people are not allowed to give feedback, to try things their way, or to make mistakes, they can't develop their potential. Therefore, even though blind managers are good trainers, they don't allow their employees the freedom to develop to the point where they can take over for the boss. If the manager is promoted or leaves the company, the organization usually finds that there is no one ready to step into the vacated position.

At the same time that blind managers overuse disclosure, they underutilize feedback. There are several reasons why blind managers don't seem to want much feedback from employees. First, because they think they know more than their employees, they see no reason to ask for employee ideas or opinions. Second, blind managers often believe that employees must be treated firmly and impersonally. Asking for employee opinions might encourage employees to interact on a more personal level or to take advantage of the situation.

A problem with the blind management style is that employees whose ideas are never sought do not feel part of the organization. Once they are trained and ready to make decisions on their own, they often react to the blind manager with hostility, resentment, and lower productivity. If the situation becomes bad enough, employees may either force feedback on the blind manager or retaliate by withholding important information.

To further clarify the blind manager's communication style, consider the following coping strategies used by the manager with an extremely blind style. First, the blind manager usually solves any conflicts without asking for employee agreement or input. Second, although blind managers include a brief mention of employee strengths in appraisals, they spend the majority of time on weaknesses. Many blind managers see the job of supervision as one of pointing out weaknesses so that employees can improve themselves. Employees know when they do things well, thinks the manager, so there is little need to mention strengths.

Occasionally, a person who appears to be a blind manager is really a very insecure, closed person who realized early in his or her career that closed behavior was not producing the desired promotion but that authoritarian managers did get promoted. Therefore, these managers—we'll call their style the *neurotic blind style*—hide their insecurity behind authoritarian masks. Their inconsistent criticism of employees includes unrealistic personal attacks accompanied by much anger. They feel threatened by knowledgeable, hard-working employees. To hide these feelings, when they find a minor employee weakness, they blow it out of proportion. It is impossible to please the neurotic blind manager.

Blind Employees ■ Blind employees are usually hard workers who can be very productive and are valued for their knowledge. Management knows that they can depend on blind employees to get the job done! However, blind employees often feel that their ideas are better than those of their bosses and have problems gracefully receiving feedback, criticism, or orders. They are argumentative, even with their managers, and when criticized, tend to retaliate in kind; and they are usually poor listeners. Just the opposite of closed employees, who say practically nothing during office discussions and department meetings, blind employees are quite vocal and often critical. They stimulate the group's thinking but are fairly difficult to handle and often inhibit shy or insecure people from participating.

REMEMBER, BLIND COMMUNICATORS . . .

At Their BEST Are

- Aware of what they want and willing to express their needs and wants. There is never any doubt about where you stand with them.
- Usually very loyal.
- Usually well organized.
- Seen as dependable. Others know the job will get done.
- Very helpful to those who want to learn as long as the help is appreciated.
- Not afraid to exercise authority.

At Their WORST Are

- Unable to delegate effectively.
- Very demanding and impatient.
- Insist their way is the right way. They know what's best.
- Offer advice whether wanted or not.
- Prefer to be in control at all times.
- Stifle growth and creativity of others by making all the decisions.
- Punish failure and mistakes.
- Expect others to mess things up ("If you want things done right, you must do them yourself").
- Often poor listeners.
- Unable to take criticism although very critical of others.

Blind Customers ■ Like blind managers and employees, blind-style customers tend to be overly confident in themselves and quite demanding of others. They have probably done their homework on the product, service, or idea to be purchased and have compared it with others available. They are prepared with questions and expect the salesperson to know or find the answers. Most likely, they will be annoyed by a salesperson's attempts to socialize, preferring to get right to business. Blind customers may be extremely critical of the product, service, or idea—they expect perfection (and will tip well to get it). If the salesperson earns their respect, these customers may ask for opinions; however, they do not appreciate hand holding. They expect to make their own decisions, and they like to feel that they are in control of the situation. Although few customers enjoy waiting, blind customers become impatient and in some situations (such as a 1-hour wait at the dentist's office) they become angry and even cause a scene. Blind customers are usually the first to tell their friends when they are unhappy with a particular organization. Researchers have found that negative word-of-mouth advertising can reduce a company's business.[23]

The Hidden Style

If you had to choose between an efficient, high-productivity office in which people were friendly but not social, or a social environment in which birthdays were celebrated, employees were allowed to talk while working, and everyone was treated as a family member, which would you pick? People with hidden tendencies prefer a social environment and want to be friendly with everyone. As a result, hidden communicators are interested in people, are good listeners, and are generally well liked. It's very important to them that everyone gets along and that conflicts are avoided.

As Figure 3.5 indicates, hidden communicators fall on the low disclosure, high feedback ends of the two continuums. Although they like social environments, they find it difficult to disclose their feelings, opinions, and expectations to others. We all have things we don't wish to share with others, but for a variety of reasons, people with a hidden style find that even when they want to disclose, they can't. For example, a boss may find it impossible to tell her employee that his grammar will keep him from the executive status he so desires or a young person may be too embarrassed to initiate conversation with others; these people are having problems with disclosure. If you listen carefully to others and invite them to tell you how they feel, but tend to keep your opinions and feelings to yourself, you may have some hidden tendencies.

Don't confuse the hidden communicator with the closed communicator. Hidden communicators are not afraid of people as closed communicators are; they don't hide from people as closed communicators often do. They are called "hidden" because they hide their opinions, feelings, and knowledge from others.

Although hidden communicators find it difficult to disclose, they disguise their lack of disclosure by inviting and carefully listening to feedback from others. We can better understand why they do this by looking at the two seemingly conflicting factors that motivate hidden communicators: mistrust of people and/or desire for social acceptance. Hidden persons have a tendency not to trust others and feel more comfortable when they know what people are up to; they get feedback from them for that purpose. Similarly, hidden persons desire to be socially accepted, and they get feedback from others to determine how they are doing in their quest for acceptance.

Figure 3.5 The hidden communication style.

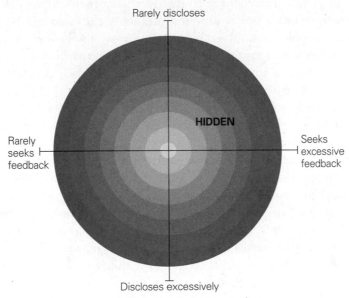

Relationships with hidden persons are basically one-way; hidden persons do most of the listening, while others do most of the sharing. Often, when people realize this, they withdraw their trust or at least stop confiding in the hidden friend.

Hidden Managers ■ Hidden managers operate from the human relations model discussed in Chapter 2. As such, they are good listeners and take pains to create a social, enjoyable working environment. They take time to understand employee problems, which makes them popular with employees. Although they are always interested in receiving feedback, they rarely disclose their feelings or opinions to others, especially if they think their opinions may differ from those of the majority. To disguise the fact that they are not sharing their opinions, the hidden manager often seeks feedback from others and thus creates the appearance of being open. The manager who says, "Come into my office anytime," but really hopes you won't is probably a hidden manager. Hidden managers also create the facade of being open in important meetings when important decisions are to be made. They participate as much as other managers, but they usually speak up only after the majority opinion is clear or the top bosses' views are known. Usually, hidden managers initiate upward communication only when the information is positive, and they edit requested reports carefully to exclude comments that might be disturbing to upper management.

Managers with extremely hidden styles who are motivated by a basic mistrust of people use feedback to discover what their employees are up to. When these hidden managers find problems, they may not be able to disclose the problems to the employees and may simply keep their reactions to themselves. This does not mean, however, that they have forgotten any problems or who caused them. Most likely their decisions about promotions will be based on those hidden feelings.

When managers with hidden styles are motivated by their desire for social acceptance, they use feedback as a way to determine how well they are liked or accepted. Believing that the only way to run an office is to maintain peace and harmony, they smooth over any conflict by minimizing its importance. Hidden managers feel that keeping people happy is more important than productivity. After all, employee complaints can get you fired; low productivity usually doesn't. During performance appraisals, this type of manager tends to list only strengths, even though the employee has weaknesses that need to be addressed. This may not be so much a deliberate oversight as it is the manager's inability to disclose. However, once employees discover that the hidden manager is not the open communicator they first perceived, they tend to become suspicious and to partially withdraw their trust.

Hidden Employees ■ Hidden employees are usually well liked and fun to be around. As with hidden managers, hidden employees try to appear open by willingly listening to feedback from others, by disclosing themselves only on impersonal, safe topics, and by agreeing with others on more important issues. In their search for social acceptance and security, hidden employees often appear overly friendly and eager to please ("yes" persons). They fear conflict and disagreement and try to smooth over discord. Hidden employees take a "country club" approach[24] to work, that is, keeping everyone happy (including the boss) is more important than high productivity. During an appraisal, if the boss says something that the hidden employee feels is unfair, the employee may tactfully disagree in a joking manner. Hidden employees tend to handle difficult situations by laughing them off. If this approach doesn't work, and further disagreement could harm the relationship with the boss, the hidden employee will drop the complaint.

Hidden Customers ■ Accurate communication may be difficult between hidden customers and salespersons because these customers are better listeners than speakers. They may not be able to disclose their real needs and expectations and instead may voice what they feel are more socially accepted ones. A salesperson would be wise not to believe the first explana-

REMEMBER, HIDDEN COMMUNICATORS . . .

At Their BEST Are
- Well liked.
- Fun to be around and work with.
- Concerned with people, their joys and problems.
- Sympathetic listeners.
- Often the organizers of social events.
- Busy smoothing over minor conflicts and keeping a happy office.

At Their WORST Are
- Suspicious of the motives of others.
- Not really interested in productivity and quality. Adequate performance may be all they expect.
- "Yes" people. Their desire to be liked may be so great that they give the appearance of agreement even when they really disagree.
- Unable to disclose opinions and ideas that might not be accepted or might cause rejection.
- Not always loyal.
- Seen as manipulative or two-faced.

tion of needs given by a hidden customer but should tactfully probe for the real customer needs.

Hidden customers who are motivated by mistrust of others may be suspicious that the salesperson is hiding something from them or is trying to take advantage of them in some way. Don't be surprised if it takes several sessions or even several sales before they develop any trust. Hidden customers who are motivated by a desire for social acceptance would rather deal with friendly, sociable people than with someone they don't like. This is often true even though an unfriendly salesperson's product is less expensive.

The Open Style

Open communicators tend to use both disclosure and feedback, and are equally interested in people's needs and company productivity. They are motivated by a real like and respect for people. In fact, of the four communication styles, open communicators are the only ones who really appreciate other people (closed communicators are nervous around people,

Figure 3.6 The open communication style.

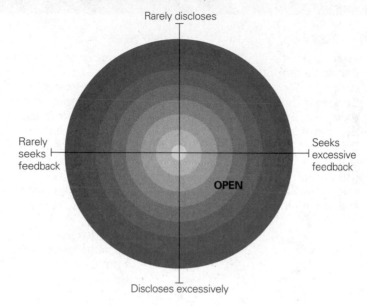

blind communicators tend to view people as relatively unimportant, and hidden communicators don't always trust people). However, as Figure 3.6 indicates, open communicators fall on the high disclosure, high feedback ends of the two continuums. As a result, they may disclose too much too often and may ask for too much feedback. This type of forward communication makes many people very uncomfortable. For example, suppose that you have been working for a company for only one week, but in that week you observe a problem area and have been thinking about possible solutions. If, at the end-of-the-week meeting with all the employees from your department, you mention the observed problem and its possible solution, chances are that you will be perceived as too open. The boss and other employees will be much more likely to accept your ideas if they feel you have been there long enough to really understand the process.

Open Managers ■ Open managers tend to operate from either the human resources or the systems/contingency model discussed in Chapter 2. These managers attempt to use both disclosure and feedback to create an open atmosphere in which people can trust one another. The open manager, who has a high self-image, is motivated by a real liking for people and a desire for effective communication. The open manager is sensitive to the needs of employees and allows them to take active roles in the affairs of the organization. As a result, employees usually develop good, healthy relationships and increase their productivity. However, some employees feel threatened around open managers: They are uncomfortable with these managers' self-disclosure and are apprehensive at their requests for feedback.

Knowing that participation is a motivational tool, the open manager tries to resolve conflict by involving all in reaching a decision each can accept (consensus). If a consensus cannot be reached, the open manager makes the decision (see Chapter 10 for a discussion of conflict).

Please do not assume from what we've said so far that we are advocating the open management style in all situations. *If* the organization's climate is open, and *if* upper management favors the open style, and *if* employees are basically open, then an open management style can stimulate healthy relationships and increase productivity. However, many organizations do not have an open climate. Upper management may not approve of open managers and may fail to promote them. Also, some employees are very uncomfortable around open managers and consider managers' requests for employee input as proof that they cannot make decisions.

Open Employees ■ These employees regularly seek feedback and openly disclose ideas and feelings to the boss and fellow workers. Open employees support their ideas with facts and data, and they normally take responsibility for their own errors. They are motivated by genuinely liking others and are able to concentrate on being the best they can be. They are usually friendly, good listeners, and hard workers.

However, some employees are too open for bosses and employees whose communication styles are less open. In some instances, an open employee is so open that even other open colleagues feel uncomfortable. Obviously, in a closed environment an open employee is less likely to be viewed favorably. Usually, however, if problems arise it is because open employees are too open too soon. In *The Open Organization*, Fritz Steele warns that the order in which we disclose different aspects of ourselves will determine how others react to us. For instance, new members of a group will tend to first show the responsible, concerned side of themselves. When this stance results in their acceptance, then they will feel free to show their less perfect aspects—aspects that would get a nonmember rejected out of hand.[25] In new environments, open employees need to listen and observe others to determine the openness of the climate. Openness is most effective when it produces a gradual sharing with others.

Open Customers ■ Salespeople who know their product and have good self-images should enjoy selling to open customers. These customers are interested in learning about the product, service, or idea (if they don't already know about it), and they are good listeners. They are freer about

REMEMBER, OPEN COMMUNICATORS . . .

At Their BEST Are

- Flexible in meeting the needs of individuals.
- Accepting of instructive criticism.
- Genuine in their liking of others.
- Flexible in using communication styles.
- Careful listeners.
- Seen as trusting, friendly, and dependable.
- Willing to share feelings as well as knowledge.
- Productive.

At Their WORST Are

- Seen as ineffective managers by some blind bosses.
- Frustrated by lack of creative opportunities under nonopen bosses.
- Impatient with time needed to implement organizational changes.
- So open that others feel uncomfortable around them.
- Open at inappropriate times.

sharing honest needs and wants with the salesperson and probably have a realistic idea of how much they want to spend. They are generally friendly, yet businesslike. Most open customers want both the salesperson and themselves to benefit from the sale. Nevertheless, open customers will not hesitate to report manipulative or dishonest treatment to the sales company and to their friends.

Within reason, the more open we are, the better communicators we are likely to be, because we are able to share our frames of reference and expectations with others. This does not mean, however, that open is always the best communication style. An open communicator in a blind environment, for example, will probably be viewed as poor management material and may be passed over for promotion. However, what is too open for one group may be just right for another.

The key to good communication is flexibility of styles. There is a big difference between being closed, blind, hidden, or open because that is all we are capable of being, and deliberately choosing a certain style because it best suits the needs of the individual or group with whom we are dealing.

WHEN AND WHEN NOT TO USE EACH COMMUNICATION STYLE

We have discussed the four basic communication styles at their best and worst and described how managers, employees, and customers tend to use them. In capsule form, this section covers successful and less successful uses of each style.

THE CLOSED STYLE IS SUCCESSFUL WHEN

- Not much interpersonal interaction is required for the job.
- Going by the book is the preferred company stance.
- Subordinates are professionals who need or want little supervision.
- Others in the department are closed or prefer things to people.

THE CLOSED STYLE IS LESS SUCCESSFUL WHEN

- The job requires a high level of interpersonal interaction. The organization is in a high-risk profession with creative, high-strung individuals.
- Subordinates need or want guidance.
- The profession or business is productivity-oriented.

THE BLIND STYLE IS SUCCESSFUL WHEN

- Problems that the blind person is qualified to handle are surfacing in the organization.
- Subordinates lack and, therefore, need the blind manager's expertise.
- Subordinates are closed or hidden. The manager makes all decisions and takes all responsibility.
- A crisis has occurred or ongoing organizational change is occurring and anxious subordinates need security.
- An immediate decision is needed.

THE BLIND STYLE IS LESS SUCCESSFUL WHEN

- The organization has many personnel problems.
- Subordinates are well-trained, professional people who expect to make their own decisions.
- Previously self-sufficient subordinates learn to expect the blind manager to make decisions for them and bail them out of trouble.
- The inability to allow for failure or mistakes stifles creativity and risk taking.

THE HIDDEN STYLE IS SUCCESSFUL WHEN

- A social environment is expected.
- The climate of the organization makes caution necessary.
- Teamwork is a social occasion rarely involving problem solving.
- Adequate performance by subordinates is all that is expected.

■ Members are either so politically or emotionally oriented that maneuvering is necessary to hold the group together.

■ Politics is used as an organizational tool (union/management negotiators usually must ask for more than they expect to get).

THE HIDDEN STYLE IS LESS SUCCESSFUL WHEN

■ The climate is more work-oriented than social.

■ Tasks require a high degree of trust between workers.

■ Complex tasks require team problem solving.

■ Excellent rather than adequate employee performance is sought.

■ A climate of trust exists in the organization.

THE OPEN STYLE IS SUCCESSFUL WHEN

■ Employee involvement in decision making is desired (problems are not seen as property of the boss).

■ Change is expected and employees view change as new opportunity.

■ Tasks are complex.

■ Teamwork is necessary or expected.

■ Tasks require quality work.

THE OPEN STYLE IS LESS SUCCESSFUL WHEN

■ Upper managers operate in a different style and do not view the open style positively.

■ Workers do not view an open manager as a good supervisor.

■ Tasks are extremely simple.

■ Tasks do not require interpersonal interactions.

■ An immediate decision is needed.

■ There is very little trust in the working climate.

AWARENESS CHECK: COMMUNICATOR STYLES

To check your knowledge of the four communicator styles, take the following quiz.

Directions: Identify the communicator style each question describes: (A) closed, (B) blind, (C) hidden, or (D) open.

____ 1. Which style employee prefers not to take any part in office discussions?

____ 2. Which style employee has trouble accepting criticism and is usually argumentative?

____ 3. Which style communicator may make others feel uncomfortable by using too much feedback and too much disclosure?

____ 4. Which style customer prefers to deal with sociable salespeople even at the risk of paying more for the product?

____ 5. Which style persons communicate their expectations to others?

____ 6. Which style communicator is motivated by mistrust of others?

____ 7. Which style communicator uses too little feedback and too much disclosure?

____ 8. Which style communicator is more likely to take responsibility for his or her mistakes?

____ 9. Which style manager would tend to concentrate more on an employee's strengths during an employee appraisal session?

____ 10. Which style communicator prefers working with things over working with people?

ANSWERS

1. A (closed)
2. B (blind)
3. D (open)
4. C (hidden)
5. B and D (blind and open)

6. C (hidden)
7. B (blind)
8. D (open)
9. C (hidden)
10. A (closed)

RELATIONSHIPS WITH PEOPLE OF DIFFERENT STYLES

The chances are that you have a boss, a coworker, or a customer with whom you have some difficulty communicating. Maybe their communication style differs from yours. If so, your expectations are probably different from theirs, which makes relationships difficult to develop and maintain and negative self-fulfilling prophecies more likely. This section offers some advice on how to communicate with people of different styles. Remember, no one person exemplifies any one style perfectly; therefore, our advice should be taken as a guide to understanding, not as the complete answer to communication problems. Again, we have put the information in capsule form for ease of use.

CLOSED COMMUNICATION STYLE

■ How to communicate with *closed managers:*

Carefully. Don't threaten them or increase their insecurity.

Don't ask them questions. Ask other employees or make the decision yourself if you can do so quietly.

Don't make waves.

Downplay new procedures you develop.

Don't expect any outward praise, guidance, criticism, or help from the boss. You should be able to provide these for yourself.

■ How to communicate with *closed employees:*

Put closed employees in environments that feel safe. They work better in situations that do not demand much interaction with others. They want little responsibility and feel safer if you tell them how, what, when, and where.

Explain all policy changes face to face, before the grapevine gets to them.

Make the chain of command clear. To whom are they responsible?

Give them specific directions but avoid criticism.

Occasionally show a mild interest in their family or other personal concerns.

Don't expect their participation in meetings or appraisal interviews.

Be aware that they may be overcritical of themselves.

■ How to communicate with *closed customers:*

Hold their hand and listen to their needs—you could have a customer for life. (However, if something goes wrong with the product and others are pressing them about it, you—the salesperson—will get the blame.)

Try to increase their sense of self-confidence by complimenting them on previous product choices.

Don't expect them to openly express what they really want (you must look for it).

Avoid technical jargon; they may be overwhelmed by it.

The flipchart presentation (see Chapter 12) may give them a sense of security.

Team presentations may increase their feelings of insecurity.

Treat closed customers with respect; don't take advantage of them.

BLIND COMMUNICATION STYLE

■ How to communicate with *blind managers:*

Take their criticism well and expect to learn from them (blind bosses often have extensive knowledge and training).

Meet the blind manager's expectations:

Give proper respect.

Be at work on time each day.

Get projects in on time.

Make projects neat, well supported, and accurate.

Follow appropriate channels even if the boss does not; expect and give loyalty.

Accept that your proposals will be changed by the boss.

Plan to review each stage of an assigned project face to face with the boss.

Because blind bosses often expect you to know more than you do, ask questions to see what information has been left out and to determine whether the boss already has a "correct" solution in mind.

Appeal to the boss' self-confidence: "We need your help." "You've had a lot of experience in this, what do you think?" "Tell me how this should be done."

If the boss is a neurotic blind type (a closed boss pretending to be blind), expect personal attacks on your ego. The insecure neurotic blind boss feels threatened by both logical appeals and well-researched, intelligent proposals. Therefore, your only survival mechanism may be to play dumb.

Remember that if you get on the wrong side of a blind manager, it is very difficult to get off.

Let the blind manager feel in control, in power (blind managers seldom care for quality circles, in which employees take on responsibilities).

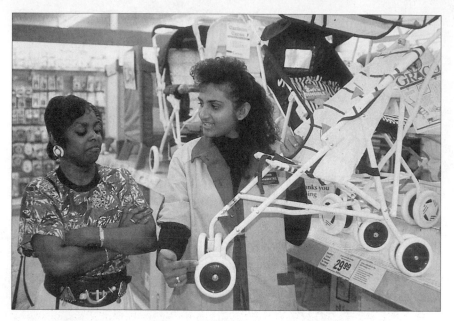

Blind customers are not afraid to show skepticism about your product or your sales presentation. *(© Jeff Isaac Greenberg/Photo Researchers)*

Keep in mind that many blind managers (even those not in your area) will tend to dislike any proposal that failed to get their input or agreement before being made public. Find out who has power to hurt or help your idea, and then get that person behind it before you formally submit it.

■ How to communicate with *blind employees:*

Expect that blind employees are

Very self-assured.

Often argumentative; take criticism poorly; blunt.

Negative toward bosses, especially women bosses.

Usually not team players, but know the rules of the game and can play when it is to their advantage (you may wish to show them that you will reward team involvement).

Respectful of power and have little respect for those without power.

Often hard workers with little respect for those who do a less than competent job.

Try to use the skills of blind employees in productive ways. These employees could well become managers in the future, so they need to know how to deal with people more flexibly.

Let them see that you are in charge but that you do appreciate the skills and knowledge of others.

If possible, let them be in complete charge of a project—you will need to follow up and maintain some control.

■ How to communicate with *blind customers:*

Give them a polished, well-supported sales presentation.

Reading them a canned flipchart presentation will probably insult them.

A team approach, if professional, will probably impress blind customers.

Be prepared for their suggestions on how to improve your selling technique.

Blind customers like to feel in control; let them feel that they negotiated an exceptional deal (they probably did).

Don't keep them waiting.

HIDDEN COMMUNICATION STYLE

■ How to communicate with *hidden managers:*

Expect the following:

If you are too knowledgeable or have come from another area or department, you may be considered a spy.

The boss will probably play politics.

You will not always know where you stand.

The boss is not always loyal.

The boss is well liked, listens well, is sympathetic.

Don't expect the boss to disclose fully. Watch for nonverbal signs that the boss wants to say more. Lead into the topic yourself. ("I'm not sure about last week's presentation. Where do you think I need to improve?")

Show how your work or ideas will bring recognition to the department and thus to the boss who wants social acceptance.

Subtly bring your work to the attention of the boss' colleagues or superiors or get yourself appointed to an important committee or task force. If other important people approve of your work, the boss who wants social acceptance will also approve (at least outwardly).

Assure the boss that you don't want his or her job.

If appropriate, publicly applaud the boss for special accomplishments and occasions (such as a birthday if it fits the social expectations of the department).

Don't be afraid to use tactful confrontation; the boss will often back down.

■ How to communicate with *hidden employees motivated by desire for social acceptance:*

Realize that these employees want to please both you and others because they believe this is the way to success; they feel that the only important things in life are friends and personal relationships.

Motivate them by public praise, criticism given in private, posting their names on a wall chart, asking them to give special talks, and other things that will improve their social standing and acceptance.

Show that you feel positive toward them.

Expect these employees to be "yes" people.

■ How to communicate with *hidden employees motivated by lack of trust:*

Hidden employees are hard to spot because they have learned how to play the game and appear open, are good listeners, and participate in group situations.

It is difficult to get these employees to be team players. Work experience or family training has taught them to express the most acceptable ideas. They want to succeed, but trust few people. Therefore, demonstrate that honest team cooperation is the way to get ahead (by promotions, performance appraisals), and establish a climate in which opinions and disclosures that differ from yours or others' will not be penalized.

Expect your comments to be searched for a double meaning. Be specific; use examples; don't assume meanings are clear.

■ How to communicate with *hidden customers:*

Hidden customers will be more likely to buy if they feel the purchase will improve their social standing and acceptance.

Spend time establishing a friendly feeling before giving your pitch.

Use referral. Hidden customers are more likely to buy if they feel that others they respect are sold on the idea, product, or service. Tell them that so-and-so recommended that you call them or that so-and-so is really happy with the item (the customer may call to verify your statements).

Share some bit of knowledge or a confidence with them to start the sharing, trusting cycle.

Listen carefully and keep your opinions out of the picture (at least until the client's views are known). Because hidden customers want to please, they may say they agree even if they don't. For example, a real estate agent says to client, "I just love formal dining areas, don't you?" Client, who does not like formal dining areas, agrees. Imagine the problem as house after house is rejected for no apparent reason.

OPEN COMMUNICATION STYLE

■ How to communicate with *open managers:*

Be honest and open, but use tact.

Look at all sides of a problem.

Don't hesitate to share job feelings, doubts, concerns.

Share part of your personal life—follow the boss' lead.

Accept shared responsibility and power.

■ How to communicate with *open employees:*

Share confidences—open employees respond well. Examples of topics are your commitment to the company, hopes for recognition, aspirations within the organization, probable length of stay in current department.

Place them in an environment in which some friendships can develop.

Give them constructive criticism; they usually want to improve and are the first to sign up for special courses offered by the company.

Give them challenging tasks; they want to achieve.

Praise them for work well done.

Employees who are too open may talk too much, but don't assume that people can't talk and work at the same time. Some talking employees are actually more productive than nontalkers.

■ How to communicate with *open customers:*

Don't be pushy or manipulative.

Listen carefully to customers' needs and wants. Open customers are usually able to articulate their needs well. Build your persuasive appeals around these needs.

Treat them as equals—don't talk down or defer to them.

Canned flipchart presentations may be tolerated but are normally not impressive.

Open customers are less impressed by show and more impressed by facts. Brief demonstrations can work well.

BECOMING MORE FLEXIBLE IN USE OF STYLES

By now, you should have an idea of your own communication style(s) and have probably determined how appropriate that style is in your work environment. (If you have not yet done so, take the Survey of Communication Styles in Appendix A.) As a result of your self-analysis, you may have found some discrepancies between your style and your work environment—in other words, some communication problems.

Thus, you may be down to two choices: either change your job (remember, we tend to become like the environment in which we spend our time) or adapt your style. The latter is a good choice even if a job change is in order—flexibility may well be your key to effective communication wherever you work. However, we don't recommend that you try a complete style change, at least not all at once. Before making any change, you should get enough feedback to ensure that a change is warranted and then try to start gradually. Adapt some of your responses to mirror those used by a person with a different style. When you feel comfortable with that new behavior, try another one. Communication behavior can be changed, but not without hard work and patience. Few people find it easy to break an old habit. For example, a person with strong blind tendencies can learn to communicate in an open style but will normally retain some blind behaviors, especially in times of stress.

Adapting or changing a style will require changes in your use of feedback, disclosure, or both:

- The person with *blind tendencies* needs to ask for more feedback from others to discover areas needing change.
- The person with *hidden tendencies* effectively uses feedback but neglects to disclose enough. To alter styles, this person must slowly begin to share more information, opinions, and feelings with others.

- Persons who tend to communicate in a *closed style* or who tend to be *too open* need to work equally on both feedback and disclosure—the closed person to use more of each, the overly open person to use less of each.

Using Feedback Effectively

Guidelines for getting and using feedback are covered in Chapter 1. If you wish to improve your effectiveness in using feedback, a quick review of that chapter should prove helpful. Remember when giving feedback to others, it should (1) be directed toward behavior rather than toward the person, (2) be descriptive rather than evaluative, (3) involve sharing ideas rather than giving advice, (4) include only as much information as the person can handle at one time, and (5) be immediate and well timed. Also keep in mind that a sudden and unusual interest in feedback may be viewed with suspicion by those who know you, so move slowly, identify the specific type of feedback you want, and tell them why you want it. Remember also that you must receive any feedback in a positive manner. A negative or defensive response will convince others that being open with you is too dangerous.

Using Disclosure Effectively

For most people, disclosure is more difficult than feedback to use effectively. Many of us have grown up believing such statements as, "It is better to keep silent and be thought a fool than open your mouth and remove all doubt," and "If you want to get ahead in business, keep your mouth shut." Many people who do disclose engage only in small talk or discussion of public information. They are still hidden when it comes to revealing and sharing personal information, feelings, and ideas.

Research described by Lawrence Rosenfeld has found that men normally avoid disclosure because they

- Fear projecting the wrong image
- Fear appearing inconsistent
- Fear losing control over others
- Fear it may threaten their relationships with others

Women normally avoid disclosure because they

- Fear projecting the wrong image
- Fear information may be used against them

- Fear others will view their disclosure as a sign of emotional weakness
- Fear it may hurt their relationships with others

According to Rosenfeld, men's primary concern about disclosure is loss of control; women are more concerned with personal harm and damaged relationships.[26]

It is probably a good idea to be careful in using disclosure. In some climates, all of these fears would probably be justified. However, in open climates, fear should be replaced by mild concern over such things as when to disclose, how much to disclose, with whom to disclose, and so on. The following guidelines should help you decide when and how to use disclosure.[27]

Use Disclosure Only for the Purpose of Establishing and Developing Strong Interpersonal Relationships ■ Research indicates that we are more likely to make disclosures to people we like, and that we tend to like people who disclose with us more than we like those who do not.[28] Therefore, disclosure is necessary for a relationship to develop. If the relationship is weak or dying, self-disclosure may not be considered worth the effort.

Disclosure Should Be Mutually Shared ■ A healthy relationship cannot develop when only one person discloses. All persons involved in the relationship must be willing to trust the others and to share openly with them. There is a reciprocal aspect to disclosure: People seem to view disclosure as rewarding and feel obligated to reciprocate.[29] If one person increases the amount of disclosure, so do the others.[30] The surest way to get others to disclose with you is to disclose with them. Disclosure normally results in trust and respect[31] and people who trust each other are more likely to disclose.[32]

Disclosure Naturally Involves a Certain Amount of Risk ■ When you offer your opinions, ideas, and feelings to coworkers or your boss, you become more vulnerable to attack because they could use such knowledge against you. However, if disclosure has been mutual, all members of the relationship are equally vulnerable.

Disclosure Should Be a Gradual Process ■ In a new group, it is a good idea to avoid any discussion of task problems until the group has a chance to build cohesion.[33] To maintain a good image, you should begin with more conservative disclosures when you are the new member in a group. Relationships do not happen overnight. A truly open relationship may take months or years to develop fully. It would be a mistake to open up suddenly and dump your feelings on someone. The other person would prob-

Figure 3.7 Curvilinear relationship between satisfaction and disclosure.

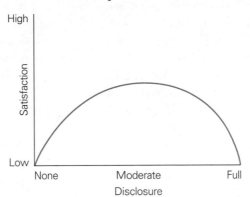

ably wonder what game you were playing. Be cautious. Pay attention to the person's nonverbal reactions—they will tell you if you are moving too fast, too soon, or disclosing inappropriate information. Wait for the other person to reciprocate with a disclosure. Don't forget, however, that someone must be willing to risk the first step. In organizations in which an open climate exists, generally the supervisors or managers should take the first step. When managers are open and supportive, employees tend to follow their lead.

Communicate at a Moderate Level of Disclosure ■ Although some researchers on disclosure advocate full disclosure within relationships, other researchers have found that high disclosure may be perceived by others as inappropriate and that moderate disclosure has more positive outcomes.[34] High levels of disclosure occur in relatively few communication transactions, especially in the business environment.[35] According to Shirley Gilbert, the relationship between disclosure and satisfaction is a curvilinear one (see Figure 3.7). She feels that a moderate level of disclosure is better for maintaining relationships over time.[36]

Summary

The quality of your interpersonal relationships with other members of any business or professional organization will have a direct effect on your ability to communicate and also on the communication ability of your organization. In building and maintaining quality relationships with managers, employees, customers, or colleagues, we need to remember to make our expectations of each other clear and to use the reciprocal nature of relationships to help build interpersonal cooperation and trust.

It is also easier to communicate successfully with our bosses, employees, customers, and colleagues if we understand their frames of reference. One way to do this is to determine their style of communication. Do they tend to be more closed, blind, hidden, or open? And which is *our* preferred communication style? Are the styles compatible? We need to realize that there is no perfect style. Each style has its own strengths and weaknesses; each style is effective in some situations and less so in other situations. Each style varies in the amount of feedback obtained from others and disclosure volunteered to others. If you are interested in changing your style or becoming more flexible in style use, carefully monitor your feedback and disclosure and plan to make minor changes in how you use them as needed for specific situations. We aren't recommending that you make a drastic change in your communication style; it's better to know your style's best and worst sides and then build on your strengths and minimize your weaknesses.

CHECKPOINT

Before continuing to the next chapter, check your understanding of Chapter 3 by completing the following exercises:

1. Analyze the climate and attitudes of your organization or club. Is your organization or club one that encourages strong interpersonal relationships? Why or why not? How has your communication behavior been affected by your organization or club?
2. Ask willing members of your department (including management) to take the Survey of Communication Styles in Appendix A. Ask members to write their styles on slips of paper (anonymously if they wish). Discuss the results. Are the communication styles compatible? If not, discuss possible solutions.
3. If you wish to become more flexible in your use of styles, select either feedback or disclosure and list five specific ways you plan to change. For example, to become less hidden, you might list "I will share at least one personal feeling or thought with my group at each weekly meeting." Keep a record of your attempts to become more flexible.
4. Write about a problem that you or someone you know is experiencing at your workplace. Using the four communication styles, discuss how adapting communication styles could help solve the problem.[37]

NOTES

1. Eric M. Eisenberg and H. L. Goodall, Jr., *Organizational Communication: Balancing Creativity and Constraint* (New York: St. Martin's, 1993), p. 225.
2. Tom Peters and Nancy Austin, *A Passion for Excellence* (New York: Random House, 1985); Michael Hammer and James Champy, *Reengineering the Corporation* (New York: Harper-Business, 1993); Rosabeth Moss Kanter, *When Giants Learn to Dance* (Simon & Schuster, 1989); Kenneth Johnson, *Busting Bureaucracy* (New York: Irwin, 1992).
3. Charles Conrad, *Strategic Organizational Communication: Cultures, Situations, and Adaptation* (New York: Holt, Rinehart & Winston, 1985), p. 11.
4. Excerpt from p. 224 of Gerald M. Goldhaber, *Organizational Communication*, 6th ed. Copyright © 1993 by Brown & Benchmark. All rights reserved. Reprinted by permission of the publisher.
5. W. Charles Redding, "The Organizational Communicator," in *Business and Industrial Communication: A Source Book*, W. Charles Redding and George A. Sandborn, eds. (New York: Harper & Row, 1964), p. 29.
6. Excerpt from p. 209 of Charles Conrad, *Strategic Organizational Communication: Toward the Twenty-First Century*, 3rd ed. Copyright © 1994 by Harcourt Brace. Reprinted by permission of the publisher.
7. Robert L. Kahn, "Productive Behavior Through the Life Course: An Essay on the Quality of Life," *Human Resource Management* 23 (Spring 1984), p. 14.
8. Much of the material in this section is based on Chapter 8, "Interpersonal Communication and Organizing," by Gary L. Kreps, *Organizational Communication*, 2nd ed. (New York: Longman, 1990), pp. 149–155. See also S. W. Duck, *Understanding Relationships* (New York: Guilford, 1991).
9. Goldhaber, p. 69.
10. Kreps, p. 150.
11. Kreps, p. 150.
12. Kreps, p. 153.
13. Kreps, p. 153.
14. Kreps, p. 154.
15. David L. Bradford and Allan R. Cohen, *Managing for Excellence: The Guide to Developing High Performance in Contemporary Organizations* (New York: Wiley, 1984), p. 148.
16. Bradford and Cohen, p. 149.
17. Fritz Steele, *The Open Organization: The Impact of Secrecy and Disclosure on People and Organizations* (Reading, MA: Addison-Wesley, 1975), pp. 7–8.
18. Joseph Luft, *Of Human Interaction* (Palo Alto, CA: National Press Books, 1969).
19. Jay Hall, "Communication Revisited," *California Management Review* 15, 3 (1973), pp. 56–57. Reprinted in *Emerging Concepts in Management*, Max S. Worthman, Jr., ed., and Fred Luthans, 2nd ed. (New York: Macmillan, 1975), pp. 135–148.
20. Robert E. Lefton, V. R. Buzzotta, Manuel Sherberg, and Dean L. Karraker, *Effective Motivation Through Performance Appraisal: Dimensional Appraisal Strategies* (Cambridge, MA: Ballinger, 1980).
21. Rensis Likert, *The Human Organization: Its Management and Value* (New York: McGraw-Hill, 1967), Chs. 2 and 3, pp. 3–46.
22. Bradford and Cohen, pp. 43–98.
23. Dan Finkelman and Tony Goland, "The Case of the Complaining Customer," *Harvard Business Review* (May–June 1990), pp. 9–21.
24. Term used by Robert Blake and Jane S. Mouton, *The Managerial Grid III: The Key to Leadership Excellence* (Houston: Gulf, 1985), p. 12.
25. Steele, p. 38.
26. Lawrence B. Rosenfeld, "Self-Disclosure Avoidance: Why I Am Afraid to Tell You Who I Am," *Communication Monographs* 46 (1979), pp. 72–73.
27. Luft, pp. 132–133.
28. W. Worthy, A. Gary, and G. M. Kahn, "Self-Disclosure as an Exchange Process," *Journal of Personality and Social Psychology* 13 (1969), pp. 59–63.
29. Worthy, Gary, and Kahn, pp. 59–63.
30. P. Cozby, "Self-Disclosure: A Literature Review," *Psychological Bulletin* 79 (1973), pp. 73–91.
31. Lawrence R. Wheeless and Janis Grotz, "The Measurement of Trust and Its Relationship to Self-Disclosure," *Human Communication Research* 3 (1977), pp. 250–257.

32. H. A. McAllister, "Self-Disclosure and Liking: Effects for Senders and Receivers," *Journal of Personality* 48 (1980), pp. 409–418.
33. Steele, p. 37.
34. John P. Lombardo and Robert D. Wood, "Satisfaction with Interpersonal Relations as a Function of Level of Self-Disclosure," *Journal of Psychology* 102 (1979), pp. 21–26.
35. W. Barnett Pearce and Stewart M. Sharp, "Self-Disclosing Communication," *Journal of Communication* 23 (1973), pp. 409–425.
36. Shirley Gilbert, "Empirical and Theoretical Extension of Self-Disclosure," in *Explorations in Interpersonal Communication*, Gerald Miller, ed. (Newbury Park, CA: Sage, 1976), pp. 197–215.
37. Suggested by Shelley D. Lane, Collin County Community College, Plano, Texas.

4 Effective Listening[1]

L istening is not just a trick or a succession of techniques. It is an attitude, a way in which you relate to the world. To be a good listener you must make listening a part of the way you live.

LYMAN L. STEIL,
JOANNE SUMMERFIELD,
GEORGE DEMARE,
Listening—It Can Change Your Life [2]

Are you a good listener? Most of us assume that we are. We take for granted that listening just comes naturally, when in fact listening is as complicated and strenuous as the other forms of communication—reading, writing, and speaking. One of the interesting aspects of listening behavior is that very few overt motor skills are necessary to engage the listening process. With writing, reading, and especially with speaking, we must put forth physical effort to adequately perform the communication behavior. The effort involved in listening is primarily mental, and this may account for deceiving ourselves that listening is easy.

One reason listening is so important is that we do so much of it each day. According to research, listening occupies 80 percent of our waking hours.[3] That makes it our most frequently used communication skill. The business world is certainly aware of the importance of listening. Studies confirm that good listeners make good managers[4] and that good listeners advance more rapidly in their organizations.[5] Active listening was selected as the most crucial management skill by 282 members of the Academy of Certified Administrative Managers.[6] In another survey, 170 people in business organizations were asked to select the most important communication skills they were presently engaged in at work and the communication skills they wished they had studied in college. Listening was the number one response to both questions.[7] Still another study determined that 40 percent of the typical professional's salary is earned through listening, and that figure becomes higher as the person rises in the organization. For example, 80 percent of an executive's salary is earned through listening.[8]

It is no wonder that corporations such as Sperry-Rand have targeted listening as the communication skill they most want their employees to improve. Sperry has spent millions of dollars training its employees in more effective listening practices. The company recognizes that listening consumes a large portion of the time spent on the job and that most employees' listening skills are not as efficient as they could be.[9] Indeed, most working professionals recognize that listening is a skill that can and should be improved. Only through knowledge and application can we become more effective listeners. The information in this chapter will provide you with the knowledge to become a better listener on and off the job, but it will take effort on your part to apply it. To get an idea of how much effort will be needed, complete the Awareness Check.

AWARENESS CHECK: LISTENING SKILLS[10]

How are your listening skills? To check your skills, take the following quiz.

Directions: For each of these statements about your listening skills, select one of the following: (A) yes, (B) sometimes, or (C) no.

_____ 1. I feel comfortable when listening to others on the phone.

_____ 2. It is often difficult for me to concentrate on what others are saying.

_____ 3. I feel tense when listening to new ideas.

_____ 4. I have difficulty concentrating on instructions others give me.

_____ 5. I dislike being a listener as a member of an audience.

_____ 6. I seldom seek out the opportunity to listen to new ideas.

_____ 7. I find myself daydreaming when others seem to ramble on.

_____ 8. I often argue mentally or aloud with what someone is saying even before he or she finishes.

_____ 9. I find that others are always repeating things to me.

_____ 10. I seem to find out about important events too late.

Number of times you answered (A) "yes"_____
Number of times you answered (B) "sometimes"_____
Number of times you answered (C) "no"_____

ANSWERS

If you answered "yes" or "sometimes" on less than three questions, you perceive yourself to be a good listener. If you answered "yes" or "sometimes" on three to six questions, you are an average listener. If you answered "yes" or "sometimes" on seven or more questions, you need immediate improvement of your listening skills.

THE IMPORTANCE OF EFFECTIVE LISTENING IN ORGANIZATIONS

Most of us consider listening important when we know that the information we are receiving can benefit us in some way. At other times, we are likely to feel that careful listening is a waste of time. But there is no guarantee that what we ignore is unimportant. How will we know unless we listen? An attitude of "I already know what they're going to say" can land us in a situation in which we have incomplete information. In the working world, three different sources of information demand effective listening: customers, employees, and supervisors.[11]

Listening to Customers

Several popular business-related books, such as *In Search of Excellence*[12] and *Further Up the Organization*,[13] contend that the best-run companies in the United States actively listen to what their customers are saying. By listening to customers, the organization can learn objective information about its products or services. For example, customers can suggest desired product improvements that the research and development department may have overlooked.

Listening to customers can tell us a great deal about the competition. Most companies like to compare and contrast themselves with other companies' people, information, goods, and services. It is simply good business practice to do so. Customers will communicate their opinion of you, your company, and its competition if they are encouraged.

Listening to customers can also increase sales and customer satisfaction. Consider the following example from the training manager for Macy's department store in New York:

> One big difficulty with new, inexperienced sales clerks is that they don't listen. Here's what an inexperienced clerk often does: A customer steps to the counter and says, "I want that blouse on display there. I'd like size 14 with short sleeves." [The clerk] rushes away and brings back a blouse, size 14, but with long sleeves. The customer again explains, "Short sleeves." Back goes the clerk, and again the customer waits. In a store the size of ours, such incidents can run into money. There's useless work for the clerk, unnecessary handling of merchandise and, most important, possibly an irritated customer. That's why in our training we stress, "Listen before you act."[14]

As mentioned in Chapter 3, an irritated customer rarely keeps quiet about his or her unhappiness; word-of-mouth complaints can actually decrease a company's business by as much as 2 percent.[15]

Listening to Employees

In *The Change Masters*, Rosabeth Moss Kanter tells of a textile company that for years had a high frequency of yarn breakage. Management considered the breakage an unavoidable business expense until a new manager, who listened to his employees, discovered a worker with an idea about how to modify the machines to greatly reduce the breakage. The new manager "was shocked to learn that the man had wondered about the machine modification for *thirty-two years*. 'Why didn't you say something before?' the manager asked. The reply: 'My supervisor wasn't interested, and I had no one else to tell it to.'"[16]

Management can't afford not to listen to employees. Listening to employees is a way of showing support and acceptance, which make for a more open climate, and an open climate makes employee satisfaction and productivity more likely. To show that they are listening, managers' responses must communicate acceptance of the person. If you are a supervisor, check your usual responses against the list of nonacceptance responses in Table 4.1. If you are not a manager, see if you recognize your boss' typical responses. Do they make you feel like no one supports or listens to you?

Listening to Supervisors

Perhaps it is obvious that employees of an organization should listen to their bosses because their positions depend on pleasing higher authority. However, many employees do not recognize how important it is to appear to be listening. Of course, giving the appearance of listening without actually listening is unwise, but effectively listening to a supervisor involves not only good listening skills but also an indication that listening is taking place. Too often, managers who give instructions, orders, or suggestions must guess at the comprehension level of the employee receiving the information. Managers who suspect that the information was not correctly received (because the employee does not make an appropriate listening response) may repeat themselves, ask for feedback, or become frustrated. All of these alternatives are time-consuming and could hurt the career of the employee who appears not to be listening.

Effective listening can help you improve your relationship with your boss by making clear the boss' expectations and frame of reference. Allan Glatthorn and Herbert Adams offer the following suggestions for listening and responding to your boss:[17]

- *Listen to know your boss.* When does your boss prefer meetings? What nonverbal behaviors does your boss use? Their meanings? When is your boss the most receptive to bad news?
- *Use that knowledge of your boss to guide your general interactions with him or her.* Mention bad news in the manner that your boss finds most acceptable. If the boss prefers certain jargon terms such as *team player*, use these terms in your comments when appropriate.

Table 4.1 Responses That Can Communicate Nonacceptance

Listener's Response	Implied Message
Ordering, demanding: "You must try . . ." "You have to stop . . ."	Don't feel, act, think that way; do it my way.
Warning, threatening: "You'd better . . ." "If you don't, then . . ."	You'd better not have that feeling, act, or think that way.
Admonishing, moralizing: "You should . . ." "It's not proper to . . ."	You are bad if you have that feeling, act, or think that way.
Criticizing, blaming, disagreeing: "You aren't thinking about this properly . . ."	You are wrong if you have that feeling, act, or think that way.
Advising, giving answers: "Why don't you . . ." "Let me suggest . . ."	Here's a solution so you won't have that feeling, act, or think that way.
Praising, agreeing: "But you've done such a good job . . ." "I approve of . . ."	Your feelings, actions, and opinions are subject to my approval.
Reassuring, sympathizing: "Don't worry . . ." "You'll feel better . . ."	You don't need to have that feeling, act, or think that way.
Persuading, arguing: "Do you realize that . . ." "The facts are . . ."	Here are some facts so you won't have that feeling, act, or think that way.
Interpreting, diagnosing: "What you need is . . ." "Your problem is . . ."	Here's the reason you have that feeling, act, or think that way.
Probing, questioning: "Why . . . ?" "Who . . . ?" "When . . . ?" "What . . . ?"	Are you really justified in having that feeling, acting, or thinking that way?
Diverting, avoiding: "We can discuss it later . . ." "That reminds me of . . ."	Your feelings, actions, and opinions aren't worthy of discussion.
Kidding, using sarcasm: "That will be the day!" "Bring out the violins . . ."	You're silly if you persist in having that feeling, acting, or thinking that way.

Source: Norma Carr-Ruffino, *The Promotable Woman: Becoming a Successful Manager* (Belmont, CA: Wadsworth, 1985), p. 230. Used by permission.

- *Develop the expertise your boss values.* Without competing with your boss, build your knowledge and expertise in needed areas (preferably in areas in which your boss is weak). Make yourself valuable.
- *Be loath to give advice.* If you are right, the boss may resent it; if you are wrong, you may get blamed. Instead, serve as a sounding board for the boss. Ask questions and paraphrase in an attempt to help the boss think through the problem.
- *Use your boss' ideas to advance your own.* Don't make countersuggestions; instead, piggyback your ideas off the boss'. For example,

> Your boss says, "We could increase sales if we changed our advertising agency." You think the packaging is the problem. So you say,

Effective listening involves more than actual listening—the listener must also appear to be listening. (© *Superstock*)

"That sounds good. That would give us a shot in the arm, and if we did that, we could have them take a look at the way we package the product. There are probably some other ways they could help us as well. What do you think?"[18]

- *Know how to praise appropriately.* "Your praise is one of the few rewards you have for your boss." Avoid extravagant or insincere praise. Use tact; be subtle.
- *Don't criticize your superior.* Behind-the-back criticism has a way of traveling through the grapevine back to the boss. Direct criticism, even when sought, may not be appreciated. Be gentle and use tact.

SIGNS OF POOR LISTENING

Regardless of how you previously perceived yourself, after reading this far you may be wondering, "How good a listener am I?" Fortunately, there are certain hints or signs that can alert you to poor listening skills on the job.[19] And because most people will not tell you that you are a poor listener, you have to monitor your own habits. By watching for these signs, you may be able to detect whether poor listening is affecting your performance on the job.

As a manager, one of the surest signs of poor listening is that employees go around you to talk to others. This breaking of the chain of command—frustrating for both the manager and the employee—results when poor listening on the manager's part leaves the employee with no alternative. Employees feel that to effectively carry out their responsibilities they must have someone in authority who will listen to them. The following example illustrates this sign of poor listening:

> Jim was the shift supervisor and Bob's boss at a chemical plant. Jim and Bob had worked together for over a year when Jim began to notice that Bob had quit discussing safety problems with him. Jim was glad because he really felt that Bob was somewhat paranoid and cried wolf much too often. Recently, however, the operations vice president called Jim and demanded to know why Jim was unaware of or unconcerned with the safety problems in the plant. Obviously Bob had been discussing safety problems with the vice president. When confronted by Jim about his discussions, Bob replied, "Safety is too important not to have someone listen to the problems in this plant!"

If you find that others are going around you or over your head to talk about issues that are really your business, it may indicate (as it did to Jim) that you have demonstrated poor listening skills.

Another sign of poor listening involves learning about important events too late. In many organizations, oral messages are not always followed up by written memos or letters. Managers are expected to act on information without having it repeated. When important events occur without your knowledge or participation, poor listening may be the culprit. A manager in the corporate office of a restaurant chain related the following story:

> I arrived at work one day and was surprised to find that all of my colleagues were missing. I asked one of the secretaries where everyone was and was shocked by her reply: "All of the corporate managers are in a special meeting with our public relations firm. Aren't you supposed to be there?" When the special meeting was over, I asked one of my colleagues when the meeting was called, and he replied that it was announced in our weekly meeting with the president. I was at that meeting, but never heard (listened to) the announcement.

If you find that you must rely on others or on memos to ensure that you are on top of important events, or if these events pass you by, you can take this as a sign of poor listening.

One of the elements of good management practice is spotting problems before they reach the crisis stage. If you find that you are always putting out fires, or having to handle problems after they have reached crisis proportions, this too could be a sign of poor listening. Obviously, most comments by others directly indicating that problems are imminent are going to be listened to. Often, however, comments about problems are indirect. It is important to pick up on this type of information to head off problems before they get out of control. "I'm not sure I can handle this alone" or "We may want to consider replacing it soon" are indirect comments that could be warning of problems to come. Listening for these indirect comments takes special effort but is well worth it to prevent small problems from becoming large ones.

If you find that your supervisor or coworker has to constantly repeat information for you, it is probably a sign of poor listening. Repetition is costly for the manager, the employee, and the organization. Every time that information must be repeated, time is wasted. Just as important is the harm that repetition does to your professional reputation and chances for promotion. Supervisors may say, "I cannot recommend Tom for promotion because he doesn't seem to catch on very fast. I always have to repeat orders, instructions, or data for him!" The truth is not that people don't catch on very fast, but that they do not use listening skills to their advantage.

Supervisors may be communicating that they do not trust your listening skills when they avoid delegating complicated responsibilities to you. Tasks once trusted to you and now being given to others may be a sign of poor listening. Clearly, your career advancement is threatened: Promotions and raises often are based on one's ability to take on complex tasks.

Another sign of poor listening is that you are receiving an undue and unusual amount of written communication (memos, letters) when a more appropriate channel would be oral communication (face to face, telephone). Especially when information is lengthy or complicated, senders may feel that in writing you will not misunderstand it. Assuming that the receiver's listening skills are good, oral communication is often the better method because it is more rapid and allows for instant feedback. Written communication takes more time to produce and feedback is typically slower. Those who choose to write memos or letters to you, with the added effort involved, are aware that your listening skills are not what they should be.

CAUSES OF POOR LISTENING

People are not born with the ability to listen effectively; listening skills are learned. Unfortunately, many of us have developed poor listening habits. Poor listening can be attributed to several causes, many of them involving bad habits that can be broken. Before describing these habits, however, we will look at some other barriers to effective listening.[20]

Physical Barriers

Some barriers to effective listening are not directly under our control. For example, noisy office equipment, a loud conversation, or a nearby vacuum cleaner could prevent us from hearing an important message. Visual distractions also pose barriers to effective listening. For instance, during a conversation with your boss, you see someone make an obvious filing mistake; while a subordinate is delivering a report, you are watching birds land on the ledge outside your window; while listening to a technician's report, you can't help but be distracted by his inappropriate three-piece suit or (supposing the technician is a woman) by her heavy green eye shadow. (See the section on appropriate dress and grooming in Chapter 5.)

Because many physical barriers are difficult for us to control or eliminate, we have to control ourselves when these barriers are present. It may be difficult to devote our entire mental effort to the message we are supposed to be receiving, but it is necessary for effective listening.

Personal Barriers

We might assume that it is easier to control the numerous personal barriers to effective listening because we create them ourselves. This is not always true; in fact, some of them are long-standing or even subconscious aspects of our personalities. The first step is learning to recognize them.

Obviously, our physical well-being affects the listening process. Illness, fatigue, and discomfort make us unable to concentrate. Our main concern is relief of our aches and pains. When we go to work ill, we jeopardize the opportunity to listen well.

Psychological distractions are another type of personal barrier. Psychological distractions can arise from almost any source. Personal problems such as finances, buying a house or car, or the behavior of a spouse or children could all be psychologically distracting. Distractions can also originate in events or conditions at work. We may be worried, for example, that our ideas or projects will not be received favorably.

Attitudinal biases against the speaker are still another personal block to listening. Answer the following questions honestly:

- Do you have trouble listening to a colleague of the opposite sex?
- Do you have trouble listening to a coworker from an ethnic group other than your own?
- Do you have trouble listening to someone much older, or much younger, than you?
- Do you have trouble listening to coworkers with whom you feel competitive?

- Do you have trouble listening to someone whose manner or personal appearance displeases you?
- Do you have trouble listening to coworkers whom you judge to be less competent than you?[21]

You probably answered yes to at least one of these questions. Everyone has some biases. As the work force becomes more socially and culturally diverse (by the year 2000 over three-fourths of new workers will be women and minorities),[22] it will be even more important for communicators to acknowledge attitudinal biases and learn to manage them. Effective listeners acknowledge the bias and try to minimize its effect. For example, "I know I have a problem listening to that young know-it-all engineer—I'll watch it in tomorrow's meeting."

Personal barriers are a natural human tendency, but when they interfere with the ability to listen effectively, they can lead to problems. It is critical to eliminate or put aside physical, psychological, and attitudinal distractions and concentrate on the immediate events in a listening situation.

Semantic Barriers

The word *semantic* refers to the meaning of words. How often have you and someone else disagreed over the meaning of a message simply because the two of you had different frames of reference and interpreted the words differently? Many ideas, objects, and actions can be referred to by more than one word. Additionally, many words have several different definitions or meanings (referents) associated with them. Consider the following example:

> Boss to her new secretary: "Here, burn this!" Thinking to follow orders, the secretary destroys the only copy of an important document instead of making a copy as [the boss] intended. "Burn" and "copy" mean the same in some businesses.[23]

Even the sounds of words can be the same but have entirely different meanings (*red*, *read*). Semantic barriers can be frustrating because the problem stems from oddities in our communication system (language), not from the listeners' lack of effort.

Bad Listening Habits

One reason for studying listening is to know what to expect from an audience when you are speaking. In his research on listeners, Ralph Nichols has identified several bad habits that people develop in their listening behavior. When you speak, you can expect your audience to have many of these same listening problems. Understanding them will allow you to plan ways to minimize these problems. Also, when you are the listener, make sure that you are not guilty of any of these bad listening habits.[24]

The Ineffective Listener Criticizes the Speaker's Topic by Calling It Uninteresting or Boring ■ Many poor listeners justify their inattention by declaring the speaker's topic uninteresting. Of course, everything people need to know to perform their jobs effectively is not necessarily interesting. Nevertheless, good listeners try to find some fact or idea that they can use in the future. Only after listening to the entire presentation can they say that it contained nothing of value or interest.

The Ineffective Listener Criticizes the Speaker's Delivery ■ Poor listeners make a game of criticizing speakers. The moment that a speaker begins to talk (if not sooner), the poor listener condemns the speaker's walk, clothes, mannerisms, voice, grammar, or dialect. Thus, the poor listener feels justified in not listening and begins to think about something else. In contrast, the good listener notices the speaker's faults but concentrates on the message anyway. Listeners should remember that a speaker's message is much more important than the way it is presented.

The Ineffective Listener Interrupts to Challenge or Disagree with the Speaker or Mentally Builds Arguments Against the Speaker's Ideas ■ Poor listeners are easily provoked to disagree. Instead of listening, they are planning a rebuttal. Good listeners pay attention to the entire idea before deciding whether they agree or disagree with the speaker. A well-known psychologist, Carl Rogers, says that "the major barrier to mutual interpersonal communication is our very natural tendency to judge, to evaluate, to approve or disapprove the statement of the other person or the other group."[25] Until listeners are sure that their facts are complete, they should withhold evaluation.

The Ineffective Listener Listens Only for Facts ■ Isolated facts by themselves are difficult to remember and are often meaningless. Although facts are important, the best way to remember them is to relate them to a theme, principle, or concept. Also, the facts are often more meaningful when the feelings behind them are clear. Good listeners, therefore, make sure they understand not only the speaker's facts and feelings, but also any principles to which they relate.

The Ineffective Listener Makes Detailed Outlines While Listening ■ Although taking notes does improve people's memory of content,[26] trying to write down everything the speaker says has the opposite effect. Poor listeners become so involved in taking notes that they are not really listening, and they have to write so fast that their notes are almost impossible to understand later. The best notes are brief key words and phrases that will later refresh the listener's mind. They do not have to be in outline form; many speakers don't even follow an outline.

The Ineffective Listener Pretends to Listen to the Speaker ■ Poor listeners have a habit of pretending to listen (by staring at the speaker and appropriately nodding from time to time) while really thinking about something else. Faking attention is a bad habit that can lead to communication breakdown. Speakers expect listeners to know the facts that were presented. Remember the corporate manager who was late for the important meeting because he was thinking about something else when the meeting was announced.

The Ineffective Listener Tolerates or Creates Distractions While the Speaker Is Talking ■ We have all been in situations in which two or more people converse while a speaker is talking. Such behavior is very distracting to those sitting near the conversationalists and can be distracting to the speaker. Allowing these distractions to continue is just as bad as creating them. Either way we miss the speaker's message. Good listeners will either ask the conversationalists to be quiet or ask the speaker to talk louder.

The Ineffective Listener Avoids Listening to Difficult Material ■ When the speaker's topic is complicated or includes difficult or technical terms, many poor listeners immediately tune out. If listeners pay attention only to entertaining speakers, they will never improve their listening skills. Periodically, we all should attend complicated training sessions or watch challenging TV programs to practice our listening skills.

The Ineffective Listener Reacts Emotionally to Some Messages by Tuning Out the Speaker ■ Sometimes a speaker will use a particular word that causes listeners to react negatively or emotionally. Consider, for example, a male speaker who refers to his secretary as "my girl." The women in the audience might immediately consider the speaker a male chauvinist. While they are criticizing him mentally, they miss everything else he has to say. Good listeners may not care for certain words, but they do not let their reactions block what the speaker is saying.

The Ineffective Listener Tends to Daydream During Long Presentations ■ Compared to your thinking speed (400 to 800 words a minute), most speakers are slow to medium talkers (100 to 175 words a minute). This means that listeners can follow everything the speaker says and still have spare time. Poor listeners fill this time by thinking of other topics. Thinking of other topics is not such a bad habit as long as the listeners continue to monitor the speaker. However, poor listeners usually become so engrossed in their own thoughts that they forget to tune in the speaker again. Good listeners use this spare time to ponder the speaker's ideas, to evaluate the quality of evidence used, and to commit important ideas to memory.

Overcoming bad listening habits will make you a more important member of the organization. The process is not easy because habits are long-practiced. It will take a concerted effort on your part even to recognize that your listening skills are not optimal. At the same time, as a speaker you can expect to have several poor listeners in your audience. Knowing the typical bad listener habits allows you to prepare for them ahead of time. For example, you could avoid any words that might trigger an emotional response from your audience, and you could use visual aids to maintain audience attention and interest (see Chapter 12 for visual suggestions).

IMPROVING LISTENING SKILLS

In the previous section we made several suggestions for improving bad listening habits. This section will further explore strategies that can make you a more effective listener and a more effective speaker.

Understanding the Stages of Listening[27]

One way to improve your own listening skills is to understand what is involved when you listen. The basic stages of listening (as shown in Figure 4.1) are *sensing, interpreting, evaluating, responding,* and, if the other steps are completed correctly, *memory* of what we hear.[28]

Sensing Stage ■   In this stage listeners select or ignore one or more stimuli from the multitude of stimuli that bombard us continually. It's impossible to notice every sound, every sight, every smell, or to acknowledge every feeling that occurs around us. We have learned to become highly selective; we pay attention to things that are important to us or of interest to us; the other things we essentially tune out. Arthur K. Robertson, in his book *Listen for Success,* illustrates the sensing stage with this example:

> Eugene Raudsepp of Princeton Creative Research tells the story of a zoologist walking down a busy city street with a friend amid honking horns and screeching tires. He says to his friend, "Listen to that cricket!"

Figure 4.1 Stages of listening. *(Source: Lyman K. Steil, Larry L. Barker, and Kittie W. Watson,* Effective Listening: Key to Your Success *[Reading, MA: Addison-Wesley, 1983])*

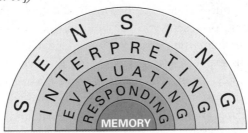

The friend looks at him with astonishment. "You hear a cricket in the middle of all this noise?" The zoologist takes out a coin and flips it into the air. As it clinks to the sidewalk a dozen heads turn in response. The zoologist says quietly, "We hear what we listen for."[29]

In addition to needs and interests, listeners' sensing abilities are also affected by gender, age, cultural background, bias, emotion, and environmental distractions, to name a few.

Interpreting Stage ■ In the interpreting stage, listeners assign meaning to the messages that they have seen, heard, and felt in the sensing stage. In other words, they attempt to decode what the speaker really means. The difficulty is that we often have different meanings for the same word. As a result, some of the most serious listening problems occur in the interpreting stage. Sometimes these problems occur because of semantic barriers (recall the boss we mentioned earlier who told an employee to "burn" a document). Sometimes they occur because listeners assume that they understand and don't bother with questions, or paraphrasing (summarizing the speaker's ideas in their own words). Sometimes they result from jumping to conclusions or from fatigue or information overload. However, many times interpreting problems arise because both speakers and listeners believe in the communication fallacy discussed in Chapter 1—that is, that 100 percent understanding is possible as long as the speaker is clear and the listener is paying attention.

Evaluating Stage ■ In this stage, listeners "think about the message, make more extensive inferences, evaluate and judge the speaker and the message."[30] In assigning a value judgment to what they have sensed and understood, listeners must decide whether the speaker is qualified, the information and evidence are accurate, and the comments are relevant and worth the time.

Listeners' evaluations are often affected by their attitude toward the speaker. Imagine yourself speaking before business colleagues who think you are too young, or resent you for your gender or ethnic group, or mistrust the department you represent. Listeners' evaluations are also affected by previous experiences, expectations, and even their beliefs and emotions. As a result, listeners sometimes make evaluations based on assumptions without waiting to make sure they have all the facts. A rescue squad member related this incident about a call for help the squad received from a patrolman:

> A 38-year-old man had pulled off the road and hit an obstruction. [After calling the rescue squad, the] patrolman had called back: "Cancel the call. The man is not really injured. He's just complaining of chest pains and probably bumped into the steering wheel." The squad went out anyway. When they arrived they could see immediately that the man was having a heart attack. "What happened," he told them between gasps, "was that I had this chest pain and went off the road." And with that he passed out. We got to work on him right away and got him to a hospital, but it was too late. Now he had told the patrolman the same thing he had told us— "I had this chest pain and went off the road." The patrolman heard him, perhaps understood him but despite his knowledge and experience did not evaluate what he heard and in this case not evaluating correctly was fatal. I never forgot that.[31]

When speaking to others, remember that the words you use (language code), the enthusiasm and pleasing quality of your speaking voice (paralanguage code), and your appearance, gestures, and visual aids (nonverbal code) are as important to your listeners as the ideas you present.

Responding Stage ■ When listeners have sensed, interpreted, and evaluated you and your ideas, they are ready to respond. This stage is very important because, without feedback, speakers can only assume that they have communicated. Listeners won't always agree, but their responses show whether they were listening and whether they understood. Listener response can take many forms, and it isn't always easy to interpret. Ideally, listeners will verbally indicate their understanding (agreement, disagreement, or confusion). If not, watch for nonverbal facial expressions (such as frowning or head nodding). Although accurately interpreting nonverbal responses is very difficult, Chapter 5 will discuss specific nonverbal cues that may be helpful. Also, don't forget that listeners often fake attention to speakers. Just because everyone's eyes are staring up at you while you speak

	REMEMBER: IN THE FIVE STAGES OF LISTENING, LISTENERS . . .	
1.	*Sense*	Hear what is important to them
2.	*Interpret*	Assign meaning to what is seen, heard, and felt
3.	*Evaluate*	Determine speaker credibility and message importance
4.	*Respond*	React to speech usually through nonverbal cues
5.	*Remember*	Retain parts of message in memory

doesn't mean that they are listening attentively. Speakers make a big mistake when they assume that attentive posture and intent eyes equal listening. People who are listening may move around, doodle on their papers, cough, glance at the clock, and look at the floor. Normally, *the only people who sit perfectly still are people who are mentally someplace else.*

Memory Stage ■   Memory storage is the end result of effective listening. Listeners (assuming that they completed the sensing, interpreting, evaluating, and responding stages) decide what parts, if any, of your message to retain and then attempt to store them in memory. Unfortunately, no matter how brilliant the speaker's ideas, or how intently people listen, most of us will remember only about 10–25 percent of a presentation the next day, week, or month.[32] Listeners are more likely to remember information that is organized, effectively delivered, repeated, related to their backgrounds and interests, and accompanied by professional-looking visual aids. The power of visual aids cannot be overstated. Audience retention and comprehension are definitely increased when visual and verbal communication are properly teamed. (Chapter 12 discusses the benefits and power of using visual aids.)

Listening More Each Day

As you recall from the beginning of the chapter, we spend a great deal of time listening each day. However, we probably could listen more than we do. A very successful businessman once said that the more listening he did, the less speaking he did, and the more successful he became. He discovered that by listening more, not only did he learn more about his job, his colleagues, and the product they were making, but he said the wrong thing less often, he appeared more industrious, and people talked to him more about pertinent issues. All of these factors contributed to his successful career.

As an experiment, figure out how much time you spend listening and speaking on a typical day. Don't include time spent reading, writing, reflecting (thinking), or watching TV. Just log the time you spend interacting with other people. Once you get a reasonably accurate idea of your average listening and speaking time, deliberately attempt to adjust those percentages, spending more time listening and less speaking each day. The mere act of consciously attempting to listen more will alert you to the process of listening and provide you with practice in being a good listener.

Using Your Listening Time Wisely

Instead of daydreaming or allowing yourself to get distracted, improve your listening by following these simple guidelines:

- *Identify the speaker's main points with a key word or phrase.* Key words and short phrases are easier to remember than complete sentences. Recalling a key word will trigger your mind to recall related facts as well.
- *Take brief notes while you listen.* Writing down phrases or key words will help reinforce your memory. However, studies show that those who take notes while listening but who never review those notes retain no more than the person who listens without taking notes.[33] It's best to review while listening and not wait until later.
- Therefore, *constantly summarize the speaker's previous points by repeating the key words in your mind.* Refer to your notes any time you are uncertain. With practice, you should be able to summarize a list of ten items and still not miss anything the speaker says. This type of rehearsal can increase the length of time ideas are held in short-term memory and may actually transfer them into long-term memory.[34]
- *Relate information to current policies and procedures.* When listening to information about the organization, good listeners associate what is said with current policies and procedures. Associated information is easier to understand and remember.
- *Avoid prejudice.* We all have prejudices, and we need to remember that they affect the information we process. Good listeners listen to information objectively first and then evaluate it according to their beliefs. Allowing prejudice to intrude during the listening process affects the meaning of the message.

Payoffs of Effective Listening

When we listen more effectively, we gain several advantages. The following list is not exhaustive, but it does suggest payoffs most people can obtain through more effective listening.[35] Your own personal payoffs will be even more numerous!

- *Effective listeners discover the values, needs, expectations, and goals of those with whom they work.* When listening is effective, we get a better understanding of what motivates our superiors, colleagues, and subordinates. We recognize that their values and expectations are either similar to or different from our own, and this information facilitates our own and the organization's goals. The following example from a business manager amplifies this payoff of effective listening:

  > For several years I became quite angry with several of my subordinates when they would gripe, "We are not appreciated around here." Their discontent was not reduced by several pay raises, which were quite generous. It was not until I really listened to their complaints that I found money was not the appreciation they desired. Verbal recognition was the answer. I now praise my employees each time they do a good job. They seem much happier and more motivated, and I am saving the company money, which would have been spent on excessive salaries.

  Another manager said that not until his plant and the labor union really started listening to one another did they determine that both parties in the labor dispute were trying to attain the same goal: job security for the workers. The values, goals, and needs of organizational members can be quite revealing and useful when we listen more effectively.

- *Better management–employee relations develop.* When employees know that their managers are really listening and responding appropriately to their messages, good relationships will develop (refer to Chapter 3 on interpersonal relationships). Managers are not always able to grant requests or comply with suggestions made by employees. But when employees know that they have been heard and receive responses that explain the manager's situation and position, they are much more likely to accept the decision and respect the manager. In making decisions, good managers take employee concerns into consideration. They can do this only by listening to and understanding those employee concerns.

- *We learn from others' experience.* Managers and employees who listen effectively realize that other members of the organization experience many of the same problems that they do. By listening carefully, we can learn from others' successes and avoid their mistakes. All of these advantages make us more valuable employees.

SUMMARY

Effective listening is not a passive communication activity. It takes a great deal of effort and motivation to become and remain an effective listener. However, good listening is a prerequisite for success in business and the professions. Effective listening is certainly not the answer to all business problems, but it is one of the first steps leading to solutions. The case cannot be made strongly enough that *organizational effectiveness is hampered by employees and managers who do not listen well.* Individual career advancement also can be hindered by poor listening. Unfortunately, poor listening is often more apparent to others than it is to the poor listener.

The suggestions made in this chapter should be used as a guide to help you to develop your listening skills. Some of these suggestions may be more beneficial than others. It is up to you to try them and monitor how they are working. Becoming an effective listener takes a great deal of work, but the payoffs are worth the effort. Very few people are effective listeners. Once you attain this skill, you will be in a very elite group indeed.

CHECKPOINT

Before continuing to the next chapter, check your understanding of Chapter 4 by completing the following exercises:

1. In your opinion, who appear to be better listeners—managers or employees? Why do you feel this way? What experiences have you had to believe this is the case?
2. If you are currently employed or are active in some organization, take a minute to assess your on-the-job listening strengths and weaknesses. Then verify your judgment by asking at least three colleagues and one supervisor to answer the following questions:

    a. How would you rate my overall listening skills?   Good   Fair   Poor

    b. Do I interrupt people when they are speaking?   Seldom   Sometimes   Often

    c. Do I show in a physical way that I am listening?   Seldom   Sometimes   Often

    d.   Do I listen better with some people than others? If so explain.

    e.   What one thing would you suggest I do to be a better listener?

3.   Assess your listening strengths and weaknesses with friends and family. Ask at least two friends or family members to answer the questions listed in the above exercise.

4.   As a customer, think of two service organizations you deal with regularly. Do they listen to customers? What specific things do they do to give you this impression? What, if anything, should they do instead?

NOTES

1.   This chapter was written for the second edition by Dan O'Hair of the University of Oklahoma, Norman, and Blaine Goss of New Mexico State University, Las Cruces, and revised by Hamilton and Parker for subsequent editions.

2.   Lyman K. Steil, Joanne Summerfield, and George deMare, *Listening—It Can Change Your Life: A Handbook for Scientists and Engineers* (New York: Wiley, 1983), p. 121.

3.   J. T. Powell, "Listen Attentively to Solve Employee Problems," *Personnel Journal* 62 (1983), pp. 580–582.

4.   L. E. Penley, E. R. Alexander, I. E. Jernigan, and C. I. Henwood, "Communication Abilities of Managers: The Relationship to Performance," *Journal of Management* 17 (1991), pp. 57–76.

5.   B. D. Seyper, R. N. Bostrom, and J. H. Seibert, "Listening, Communication Abilities, and Success at Work," *Journal of Business Communication* 26 (1989), pp. 293–303.

6.   S. L. Becker and L. R. V. Ekdom, "That Forgotten Basic Skill: Oral Communication," *Association for Communication Administration Bulletin* 33 (1980), pp. 12–25.

7.   V. DiSalvo, D. C. Larsen, and W. J. Seiler, "Communication Skills Needed by Persons in Business Organizations," *Communication Quarterly* 25 (1976), pp. 269–275.

8.   Ralph G. Nichols and Leonard A. Stevens, *Are You Listening?* (New York: McGraw-Hill, 1957), pp. 6–8; cited in V. Yates, *Listening and Note-Taking*, 2nd ed. (New York: McGraw-Hill, 1979), p. 2.

9.   M. Booth-Butterfield, "She Hears . . . He Hears: What They Hear and Why," *Personnel Journal* 63 (1984), pp. 36–42.

10. Adapted from L. Wheeless, "An Investigation of Receiver Apprehension and Social Context Dimensions of Communication Apprehension," *The Speech Teacher* 24 (1975), pp. 261–263.

11. T. R. Horton, "Using Your Managerial Ear," *Management Review* 72 (1983), pp. 2–3.

12. T. J. Peters and R. H. Waterman, *In Search of Excellence* (New York: Warner, 1982), p. 196.

13. R. Townsend, *Further Up the Organization*, 2nd ed. (New York: Knopf, 1984), pp. 168–170.

14. Ernest G. Bormann, William S. Howell, Ralph G. Nichols, and George L. Shapiro, *Interpersonal Communication in the Modern Organization* (Englewood Cliffs, NJ: Prentice-Hall, 1969), p. 175.

15. Dan Finkelman and Tony Goland, "The Case of the Complaining Customer," *Harvard Business Review* (May–June 1990), pp. 9–21.

16. Rosabeth Moss Kanter, *The Change Masters* (New York: Simon & Schuster, 1983), p. 70.

17. Allan A. Glatthorn and Herbert R. Adams, *Listening Your Way to Management Success* (Glenview, IL: Scott, Foresman, 1983), pp. 71–74. Copyright © 1983 by Allan A. Glatthorn and Herbert R. Adams. Reprinted by permission.

18. Glatthorn and Adams, pp. 72–73.

19. Horton, pp. 2–3.

20. W. G. Callarman and W. W. McCartney, "Identifying and Overcoming Listening Problems," *Supervisory Management* 30 (March 1985), pp. 38–42.

21. Glatthorn and Adams, p. 9.

22. W. B. Johnson and A. E. Packer, *Workforce 2000: Work and Workers for the Twenty-First Century* (Indianapolis: Hudson Institute, 1987); see also A. M. Simon, "Effective Listening:

Barriers to Listening in a Diverse Business Environment," *The Bulletin* 54 (September 1991), pp. 73–74.

23. From the film "Meanings Are in People," by David K. Berlo, produced by BNA Incorporated, 1965.

24. Adapted from R. G. Nichols, "Listening Is a Ten-Part Skill," *Nation's Business* 45 (1957), pp. 56–57; also Nichols and Stevens.

25. Carl R. Rogers, *On Becoming a Person* (Boston: Houghton Mifflin, 1961), p. 330.

26. Frances J. DiVesta and G. Susan Gray, "Listening and Note-Taking," *Journal of Educational Psychology* 63 (February 1972), pp. 8–14.

27. Adapted from Cheryl Hamilton, *Successful Public Speaking* (Belmont, CA: Wadsworth, 1996), pp. 72–77.

28. Based on the SIER Listening Model in Lyman K. Steil, Larry L. Barker, and Kittie W. Watson, *Effective Listening: Key to Your Success* (Reading, MA: Addison-Wesley, 1983), p. 21.

29. Arthur K. Robertson, *Listen for Success: A Guide to Effective Listening* (Burr Ridge, IL: Irwin, 1994), p. 45.

30. Blaine Goss, "Listening as Information Processing," *Communication Quarterly* 30 (1982), p. 306.

31. Steil, Summerfield, and deMare, pp. 27–28.

32. Nichols and Stevens.

33. K. A. Kiewra, N. F. DuBois, D. Christian, A. McShane, M. Meyerhoffer, and D. Roskelley, "Note-Taking Functions and Techniques," *Journal of Educational Psychology* 83 (June 1991), pp. 240–245; see also J. Hartley, "Notetaking Research: Resetting the Scoreboard," *Bulletin of the British Psychological Society* 36 (1983), pp. 13–14; K. A. Kiewra, "Investigating Note-taking and Review: A Depth of Processing Alternative," *Educational Psychologist* 20 (1985), pp. 23–32.

34. S. Hellyer, "Supplementary Report: Frequency of Stimulus Presentation and Short-Term Decrement in Recall," *Journal of Experimental Psychology* 64 (1962), p. 650.

35. B. Robinett, "The Value of a Good Ear," *Personnel Administrator* 27 (1982), p. 10.

5 Nonverbal Communication in the Organization

Warning: Knowledge of nonverbal communication can be an extremely important tool for the business and professional communicator. However, unless this knowledge is used carefully, serious misunderstandings may occur. We urge you to use caution in your interpretations of others' nonverbal behaviors.

M anagers and employees, regardless of their positions in the organization, constantly send messages to those around them. Some of these messages are sent intentionally, but many are sent without the sender even being aware of them. Managers at all levels send messages with their clothes; the size and location of their offices; the arrangement of their office furniture; where they sit during meetings; their facial expressions, gestures, and posture; their distance from others when standing; and even the time they arrive at meetings or social gatherings. Employees are sending just as many silent messages with their eye contact; their posture while standing and sitting; their facial expressions, gestures, and clothing; their distance from others; the time it takes them to complete their work; and even the way they decorate their desks.

The success of communication in an organization often depends on how well managers and employees can read these silent messages from others. Earlier, we learned that nonverbal code is responsible for more than half of the meaning of a sender's total message, and that when the language, paralanguage, and nonverbal codes send conflicting messages, people tend to pay even more attention to the nonverbal code. Successful use of nonverbal communication may also help us in establishing and maintaining needed interpersonal relationships. In Chapter 3, we discussed the reciprocal nature of relationships: What one partner does or discloses tends to obligate a similar action or disclosure from the other partner. Dean Barnlund claims that in nonverbal interaction there is also a reciprocal quality to relationships: "The habits of posture, gesture, and touch of one person tend to prompt similar acts from the other,"[1] thereby improving rapport and decreasing awkwardness. *The importance of nonverbal communication for your future success in business cannot be overemphasized.* This chapter, therefore, will concentrate on improving your knowledge and skills in understanding, detecting, and sending nonverbal messages.

NONVERBAL COMMUNICATION: DEFINITION AND PRINCIPLES

Although the term can be defined in several different ways, in this text we shall define **nonverbal communication** as all intentional and unintentional messages that are neither written, spoken, nor sounded. Although many texts include paralanguage as part of nonverbal communication, our definition omits it because we feel that the three codes (language, paralanguage, and nonverbal) are easier to understand when each is considered separately. (See Chapter 1 for a discussion of paralanguage.)

To accurately determine the meaning of a silent (nonverbal) message in the business or professional setting, you must know the sender's personal frame of reference, the specific situation, and the cultural back-

Figure 5.1 Cultural iceberg.

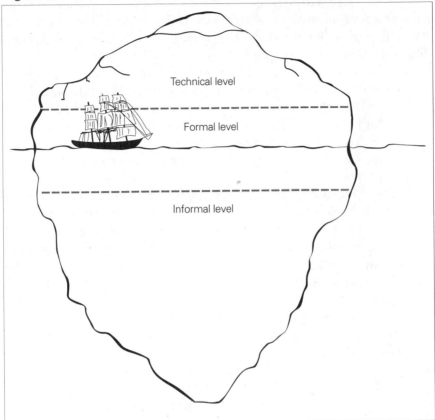

Technical level

Formal level

Informal level

ground of the sender. Although research supports the idea that some facial expressions such as laughing, smiling, frowning, and crying are fairly universal,[2] the meaning of most nonverbal messages depends on the culture in which they occur. For example, in the United States nodding your head usually means agreement; in Japan nodding the head means only that the message was received;[3] in Bulgaria, nodding the head shows disagreement.[4] Another example of cultural differences is illustrated by the gesture made by forming a circle with the thumb and forefinger: In the United States this gesture means "A-OK"; in France it means zero or worthless; in Australia, Brazil, and Germany it is considered an obscene gesture.[5]

In *The Silent Language*, anthropologist Edward Hall states that culture operates on three different levels: technical, formal, and informal.[6] To better understand the relationship between culture and nonverbal communication, we will compare the three levels of culture to an iceberg that extends far below the surface of the water (see Figure 5.1).[7] The cap of the iceberg, which everyone can see, represents the *technical level* of culture.

On this level, the rules for cultural and nonverbal behaviors are openly known and easily stated by most citizens of a particular culture. Parents and teachers deliberately impart the information at the technical level, and they give reasons for the rules. However, no one gets very upset when technical rules or behaviors are broken; the mistakes are simply corrected.

Technical information about various health and educational practices, the technical aspects of occupations or professions, and government, business, or military regulations are some examples of technical-level information that is deliberately taught. Other examples include how to introduce people appropriately, how to use language correctly, how to tell time, how to use various machines, and even how to participate properly in various ceremonies.

The second level of the cultural iceberg is the *formal level*, which lies just above and below sea level. On the formal level, the rules for behavior are known, but the reasons for them are not; they are simply accepted without question by most people. For example, tradition says the groom's family sits on one side of the church and the bride's family sits on the other. But how many people are aware of the reason for this tradition? The formal level includes rituals, traditions, and etiquette that are taught by "Do this" or "Don't do that" orders or warnings.

Compared with many other countries, the United States has few formal rules. Furthermore, many of these formal rules allow for a fairly wide range of variation before the rule is violated. However, when a violation does occur, it causes an emotional response. As a child, when you made an error at the formal level, you were warned in a tone of voice indicating that the error was unacceptable. Seldom were you encouraged to question the reason for the rule. If you persisted, you were probably told, "I don't know why. That's just the way things are!" Formal rules do change, but they change very slowly. These are examples of traditions that are changing: Young girls shouldn't call boys on the phone, only dark clothes should be worn to funerals, and people should dress up to go to church. Each cultural group has its own formal rules for such things as child-rearing practices, the value of work, the proper length of time between the death of a mate and subsequent dating, and so on. Some more generally accepted examples of the formal level in our country include the following: A week is made up of 7 days, a workweek is 40 hours, honesty is the best policy, punctuality is required for appointments, personal rewards are related to performance, bosses should be shown respect, and position in the organization is related to responsibility.

The *informal level* of the cultural iceberg is hidden far below sea level. The rules at this level are unconsciously learned by imitation (modeling ourselves after others). Once the behaviors of the informal level are learned, they usually become automatic and are taken for granted. We expect others to act in similar ways. We are unaware that these behaviors are dictated by rules. However, when someone breaks one of these unstated rules, we become anxious, then extremely uncomfortable, and finally we may withdraw from the situation or react angrily (for example, when someone stares at us longer than we feel is polite). Rules for gestures, eye contact, status, office size, the appointment arrival time, and the proper physical distance for conversations between strangers, friends, or intimates are a few examples of nonverbal behaviors at the informal level of culture.

There are many different cultures and subcultures in the United States, so it is dangerous to make assumptions about nonverbal meanings. However, the majority of our business-related nonverbal behaviors are at the informal level of culture. Because people are generally unaware of the rules governing behavior on the informal level, it is no wonder that so many people overlook the importance of nonverbal messages to successful communication.

TYPES OF NONVERBAL COMMUNICATION AND THEIR EFFECTS ON BUSINESS COMMUNICATION

Under our definition of communication, the types of nonverbal communication are almost limitless. However, in this chapter, we will cover only those types of nonverbal communication that are most applicable to business communications: facial expressions and eye contact, other body movements and gestures, clothing and personal appearance, distance and personal space, physical environment, and time.

Facial Expressions and Eye Contact

Researchers have estimated that the human face is capable of more than 250,000 different expressions[8] and that the face is responsible for most of the meaning in nonverbal messages. If you have ever felt uncomfortable around someone without knowing why, you were probably subconsciously picking up the person's facial expressions. When speakers are filmed and the films are played back in slow motion, they show that speakers often make rapid and dramatic changes in facial expression—for example, from a smile to a frown and back to a smile. Two researchers found that facial expressions lasting less than two-fifths of a second were not consciously noticed, although the observer may have "felt" that something was not quite "right."[9] These brief, unnoticed changes in facial expressions may be a more accurate indication of a person's real feelings than the perceived, more obvious facial expressions.

Although you may not be able to interpret or even perceive all facial expressions, raised or lowered eyebrows, nervous tics, unusual swallowing, clenched teeth, or tensed, pursed lips give clues to a person's feelings, thus enabling you to improve communication.

The eyes are the most expressive part of the face and have considerable effect on communication. In American culture, eye contact performs several functions.

Eye Contact Shows Interest and Attentiveness ■ In American culture, people in business or the professions expect those to whom they are speaking to look at them. Lack of eye contact on the part of the listener is interpreted as disinterest or even disrespect. At the same time, lack of eye contact on the part of the speaker may cause the listener to interpret the message less favorably.[10]

The informal rules do not call for constant or prolonged eye contact (except in cases of extreme anger or intimacy). In general, a person tends to look at others more while listening than while speaking. Speakers tend to look away at the beginning of an utterance (perhaps to plan what to say), look back occasionally to check the listener's response, and look again at the end to signal that feedback is expected.[11] Although women tend to look at others more often and with longer gazes than do men, generally two people conversing will maintain mutual eye contact only 31 percent of the time; the average length of a mutual gaze is only 1.18 seconds.[12] Even when the gaze is not mutual (for example, when the listener looks at the speaker, who has glanced away), it lasts an average of only 2.95 seconds.[13] Researchers have also found that a person will like you more if your gazes are longer and less frequent rather than shorter and more frequent.[14] Eyes that are constantly shifting or darting communicate discomfort or even dishonesty.

Eye Contact Signals the Wish to Participate or the Wish to Be Left Alone ■ For example, Tonya, a young nurse at a large hospital, complained that in the six months she had been working at the hospital, she had been appointed to four committees although she hadn't volunteered for any of them. Each time one of the head nurses asked for volunteers, Tonya sat quietly and said nothing. What the young nurse did not realize was that whenever the head nurse commented, "We need one more volunteer," Tonya looked directly at the head nurse, nonverbally signaling "I volunteer," thus the response, "Tonya, how about you?" Her nonverbal volunteering was just as loud as the verbal assents given by other nurses. Nurses who did not wish to volunteer most likely looked down and refused to meet the searching eyes of the head nurse. Avoiding eye contact can signal a desire to be left alone.

You have probably had a similar experience when your leader, boss, or teacher asked the group a question. The moment you made eye contact with the person, you knew that you were going to be called on—and you were, weren't you?

Eye Contact Controls the Flow of Communication ■ In American culture, eye contact signals others that it is okay to talk. Consider, for example, the project director who, after explaining the project, asked for individual responses from the group but looked directly at Joe. Even though Joe was looking down and missed the signal, no one else spoke—they had not received permission yet. Only when the director glanced across the group with slightly raised eyebrows did someone else speak. Because response to eye contact is at the informal level of the cultural iceberg, quite possibly neither the director nor the members were consciously aware of what had happened.

Lack of eye contact can also control the flow of communication by signaling that it is time for a conversation to end. Suppose, for example, that you are busy on an important task when a colleague stops by and asks if you have a minute to discuss a problem. You reply that you are busy but can spare 5 minutes or so. For 5 minutes, you give the visitor your complete attention. However, at the end of 5 (or maybe even 10) minutes, the visitor shows no signs of leaving. Either you can tell the person that you must get back to work or you can terminate the conversation nonverbally by turning back to your desk and breaking eye contact with the person. If you choose the latter course, in most cases the person will automatically end the conversation, thank you for your help, and leave without really being aware of the role that eye contact played.

Eye contact is such a powerful control that a seminar speaker who stands facing the left side of the audience with his or her back slightly toward the right side of the group will usually get comments only from those on the left. If, halfway through the seminar, the speaker turns and faces those on the right side of the room, those who have eye contact with the speaker will begin to respond, and the other side will become silent.

In the food service industry, eye contact is a valuable way to move customers rapidly while still giving them the feeling that they are receiving personal service. In line at a cafeteria one day, we observed a food server who would say, "May I help you with a meat dish?" but would look at the food while speaking. When no one replied, he would repeat the question several times and finally look up in exasperation. At that point, the person he made eye contact with would say, "Oh, I'll have the . . ." That server must have been exhausted by the end of the day! The salad server had much more success simply by making direct eye contact with each customer and raising her eyebrows slightly.

Because nonverbal expressions have different meanings in various cultures, be careful about assigning *your* culture's meanings for eye behavior to *all* people. In parts of the United States, the informal rules governing eye contact for African Americans and Hispanics differ somewhat from those for whites. The following example illustrates this point:

> A New York department store manager fired a young Hispanic clerk suspected of pilfering. "She wouldn't meet my eyes when I questioned her," he told a union representative. "I knew she was lying."
>
> The union representative, himself Hispanic, explained, "What you don't understand is that a well-bred Hispanic girl will not make eye contact with a man who is not a relative. It's just considered too bold. . . . She'll look away or drop her eyes."[15]

One researcher feels that different eye expectations may actually contribute to perceptions of racism, especially between whites and blacks. According to F. Erickson, many Caucasian listeners use a combination of three things to show attentiveness—fairly direct eye contact, vocal noises (like "uh huh"), and head nodding. However, many African Americans show attentiveness with only one of these (usually head nods).[16] Therefore, although Caucasians may view a single nonverbal behavior as insufficient to show attentiveness, African Americans may consider use of all three nonverbal behaviors as unnecessary and as a sign of hostility or superiority. This research was published in 1979. Do you think Erickson's observation is still true today?

What other cultural differences dealing with facial expressions and eye contact have you observed in your part of the country? As we learned in Chapter 1, assuming that you and another person have the same frame of reference usually leads to misunderstanding.

Other Body Movements and Gestures

Movements and gestures of other parts of the body are even more closely tied to culture than are facial expressions and eye contact. Therefore, it is extremely misleading to isolate a single body movement (such as crossing the legs) and give it a precise meaning as do many popular body language books. Keep in mind, however, that your body movements and gestures may be given specific meaning by others regardless of your intentions. For example, poor posture during an interview may be interpreted as disrespect, lack of enthusiasm, or indicative of poor work habits. Audiences may consider speakers' poor posture and nervous movements as proof that they are insincere or even inept. In one-to-one or small-group situations, posture can indicate liking: Leaning forward indicates a positive feeling

What nonverbal signals indicate that this meeting isn't going well? (© *Bill Bachman/Leo de Wys*)

toward others; leaning backward, a negative feeling.[17] The way a person stands may indicate self-confidence, status, friendliness, mood, and so on. Even weak or overly strong handshakes will be given some significance by many people. For example, Michael Houglum found that both men and women respond positively to firm handshakes from men; however, women feel negative toward women who give firm handshakes. Men respond the same to women whether the handshake is firm or weak.[18] Most Americans react negatively to the flaccid or "dead-fish" handshake.[19] Personnel managers from thirty companies were surveyed about the importance of handshakes during an interview. A firm handshake by the applicant was considered important by 90 percent of the managers.[20]

Gestures and body movements can be divided into four categories: emblems, illustrators, regulators, and adaptors.[21]

- **Emblems** are intentional body movements and gestures that carry an exact verbal meaning. For example, even if no words accompanied an obscene gesture (or the traffic patrol officer said nothing as she raised her hand with the palm facing you), the chances are good that you would understand the meaning of these gestures completely.
- **Illustrators** are intentional movements or gestures that add to or clarify verbal meaning. Examples of illustrators would be pointing in the correct direction while explaining how to get to the mall, or

making a left-to-right hand movement while telling a child to draw a parallel line.

- **Regulators** control the flow of a conversation. For example, the interviewer who breaks off eye contact with the interviewee may be signaling that it's time to wrap up the discussion; the listener who nods her head several times while saying, "Yeah. Yeah. Right." is probably signaling that it's time to switch speakers.

- **Adaptors** are habitual gestures and movements we use in times of stress. Flipping your hair behind your ear, scratching your nose or cheek, or rubbing the back of your neck are examples of adaptors.[22] Adaptors often contradict the message we wish to send. Suppose you are a customer trying to negotiate a price reduction on a certain item. Any nonverbal adaptors the salesperson displays indicate to you that the salesperson is weakening, and you renew your efforts to reduce the price. Or consider this example: A probation officer tells you that he cannot understand why the young parolees don't seem to trust him although he goes out of his way to help them. While he is speaking, the officer takes out a pocketknife and begins cleaning his nails in a slow, deliberate manner. This nonverbal action (although completely unconscious) clearly contradicts his verbal sincerity.

As a business or professional person, you can improve your communication techniques by monitoring your conscious and unconscious body movements and gestures. Ask colleagues and family for feedback, and review a videotape of yourself (taped during a meeting, interview, or oral presentation).

Clothing and Personal Appearance

Clothing and personal appearance also communicate nonverbal messages. In business or professional life, what *you* think of your clothes and appearance isn't nearly as important as what *others* think of them. Your appearance and clothing help others determine your status, credibility, and persuasiveness. Consider the following research findings:

- People who are perceived as more attractive are more persuasive.[23]
- Attractive people are more likely to get both emergency and non-emergency assistance when they requested it.[24]
- Attractive people are more likely to be found innocent when charges are brought against them in court; when found guilty, they are more likely to receive a lighter sentence.[25]
- Taller men get better jobs and larger salaries and are perceived as having more status.[26]

- Clothing also indicates your status.[27]
- People have more influence on others when wearing high-status clothing.[28]
- Clothing is more likely to affect the perceptions of strangers and less likely to affect the perceptions of friends.[29]
- Unattractive people improve their perceived attractiveness by wearing high-status clothing. Likewise, attractive people decrease their perceived attractiveness by wearing low-status clothing.[30]

Businesses and professions that have dress codes or that specify uniforms for their employees have learned from experience that the public's perception of their firms and their products or services depends, at least initially, on the appearance and dress of their personnel. For example, think of all the fast-food franchises that require uniforms. Many department stores, such as J. C. Penney and Sears, have employee dress codes. IBM has a strict dress code; representatives and executives of the company are known for their dark suits and white shirts.[31]

Hertz Corporation is one of many companies to have a very strict dress policy.[32] Hertz specifies that the following uniform items must be purchased through the company and gives both men and women strict guidelines on what combinations are allowed: shirts, pants, skirts, ties, scarves, sweaters, blazers, and jackets. In addition, men are advised on shoes, socks, jewelry, and hairstyles; women on shoes, hosiery, handbags, jewelry, hairstyles, and makeup. A few details:

- Other than the engagement/wedding ring, all jewelry must be gold.
- Watches should be gold with a black or gold band.
- Shoes and handbags must be black.
- Men must always wear a black or yellow tie.
- Men wear a black belt; women a brown belt.
- Skirt hems should be at midknee or slightly below.
- Earrings must be gold and no larger than 1 inch in diameter.
- Barrettes must be gold or tortoise.

Clothing is so important to an organization's image and sales that many companies have hired image consultants to help select the most appropriate clothing or uniform for their employees. The *Directory of Personal Image Consultants* profiles image consultants across the nation.[33] Image consultants are especially concerned with color and style of clothing. According to Nancy Golden, image consultant and author of *Dress Right for Business*, color shows status or rank in business offices just as clearly as uniforms show rank in the military. The darker the color, the higher the rank.[34] Another image consultant, John T. Molloy, the author of *New Dress for Success* and *The Woman's Dress for Success Book*, agrees.[35] In businesses where high-status clothing is important, Molloy has found that—for both men and women—the darker the suit, the more authority it communicates. Research seems to support this belief. Mary Damhorst and Julia Ann P. Reed found that male interviewers tended to rate applicants who were dressed in darker colors as more competent than applicants dressed in lighter colors.[36] Therefore, for the best effect, Molloy states that men should wear a shirt that is lighter than the suit, with a tie that is darker than the shirt. Although he found the skirted suit to be the best business "uniform" for women, dresses or skirts worn with solid navy or camel blazers, dresses with matching jackets, and conservative dresses can also be worn with success.

The most basic business colors are navy, gray, and neutrals such as tan or beige. How often you may wear other colors and which other colors are advisable depend on your profession, your rank, and your particular company. For example, Janet Wallach, author of *Looks That Work*, suggests that a woman's wardrobe and colors depend on which professional profile she fits into: corporate, communicator, or creative.[37] The *corporate* woman, who seeks to project efficiency and objectivity, could be a banker, accountant, attorney, or supervisor. The *communicator*, who wants to look friendly, sincere, and credible, could be a sales agent, reporter, media personality, fund raiser, politician, small business owner, or educator. The *creative* woman, who wants to emphasize her imagination and innovation, could be an artist, author, fashion designer, cosmetician, interior designer, photographer, or musician. Women in each profile would dress differently and emphasize different colors.

In addition to color, most image consultants also emphasize style. William Thourlby, author of *You Are What You Wear*, states,

> Although they don't say it, most managers when pressed agree that "You never get promoted to a position you don't look like you belong in." Understanding this can help you realize you dress for the position you want, not the one you're in.[38]

Style is especially important in the employment interview. For job interviews, Molloy recommends a dark blue suit with a white shirt for men and a navy suit with a pale blouse or a light gray suit with a dark blue blouse for women. Thourlby suggests two interview outfits for men: a medium-to-dark gray suit, white shirt, and regimental striped tie for the first interview with the personnel director, and a darker suit, white shirt, and dressier tie for the second interview with the line supervisor who will make the hiring decision.[39]

Golden claims that "jackets are the most important garments in any business wardrobe" and send "strong professional messages."[40] Vicki Keltner and Mike Holsey suggest that wearing a suit is important to the female manager because it allows her to look part of the team. People who don't look part of the team aren't considered team material.[41] Suit jackets are a great equalizer between men and women. During a long work session, men will often remove their jackets and drape them over the back of their chairs. Women in suits can do the same; women in dresses are at a disadvantage.

Although dressing for success is important, overdressing can lead to failure. For example, a three-piece suit is normally worn only by those in authority. Golden warns: "If you wear high-authority symbols on a low-authority job, managers may consider you foolish and your coworkers may feel threatened. You may lose the trust you've worked hard to gain."[42]

Don't overlook the importance of professional demeanor, which may be as important as or even more important than what you wear. Research by Myron Boor, Steven Wartman, and David Reuben revealed that physical appearance (especially grooming and neatness) had some effect on the hiring decisions of evaluators but that professional demeanor had "a marked influence" on hiring decisions.[43] Professional demeanor includes such things as direct eye contact and pleasant social interaction. (See Chapter 8 for a more thorough discussion of successful nonverbal behaviors in interviews.)

This advice obviously does not apply to all business and professional people. For example, in the fashion industry people are generally expected to dress in the latest fashions; in professions such as medicine, law enforcement, and pharmacy, authority is maintained with uniforms; and in professions requiring manual labor (such as bricklayers, carpenters, and truckers) still different dress is required. If your company has a more casual dress code, follow the style set by management. If you aren't sure, err on the side of conservatism. The following basic rules are suggested for both men and women in the typical "business" environment:[44]

- Dress conservatively.
- Simple, classic lines.
- Neutral colors (gray, navy, tan, beige, brown; black is also a good neutral color for women).
- Clothes as expensive as you can afford.
- Natural fabrics (wool, cotton, silk).
- Real leather shoes, briefcase, and so on.
- Simple hairstyles.
- Very little jewelry.

Figure 5.2 Distance categories in the United States.

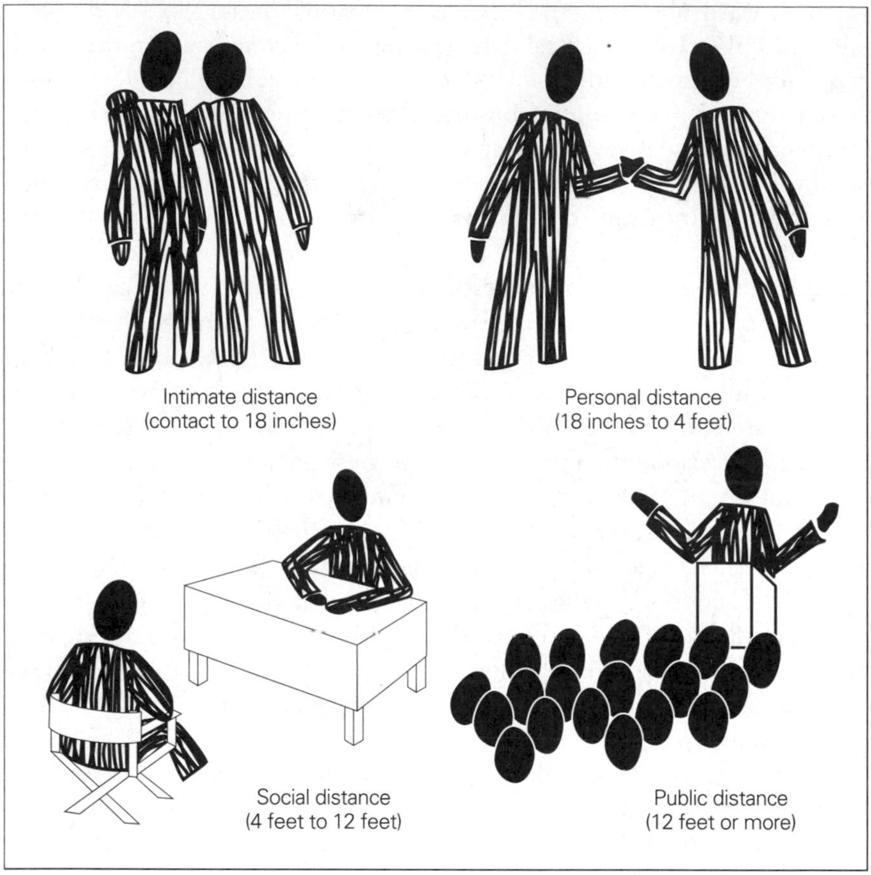

Intimate distance
(contact to 18 inches)

Personal distance
(18 inches to 4 feet)

Social distance
(4 feet to 12 feet)

Public distance
(12 feet or more)

Distance and Personal Space

The informal distance rules for conversing in various situations differ from culture to culture, family to family, and person to person. When you violate an individual's personal space requirements, that person becomes uncomfortable and will move to correct the distance. Many people are completely unaware of their personal distance requirements because, as we mentioned earlier, such requirements usually are at the informal level of culture.

Careful observation of business and professional people in the United States has led one anthropologist to divide personal reactions to distance into four categories (see Figure 5.2).[45] Except for comforting gestures (such as an arm around the shoulder) or greetings between very close friends, the *intimate distance* (from touching to 18 inches) is not used by Americans in public. Instead it is usually reserved for family and loved ones in private. *Personal distance* (from 18 inches to 4 feet) is used by close

Figure 5.3 Dispatcher's approach to truckers.

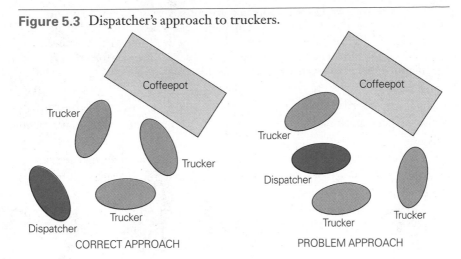

CORRECT APPROACH   PROBLEM APPROACH

friends or colleagues as they eat lunch together or stand around the coffee-pot during a break. How closely they sit or stand within the personal distance range depends on their own personal space requirements, the environment, and how much they like one another. Most business trans-actions are conducted within the *social distance* (from 4 to 12 feet). People attending a social function after work, or people who normally work to-gether or meet to solve problems, converse approximately 4 to 7 feet apart. Distances of 7 to 12 feet are reserved for formal business transactions with strangers. Finally, *public distance* (from 12 to 15 feet or farther) is main-tained between a speaker and a large group of listeners.

Knowledge of these distances is important to your business or profes-sional success. Although there may be times when you wish to deliberately ignore the unwritten rules of appropriate distances (for example, to dem-onstrate power or status), generally you will want to improve communi-cation by ensuring that everyone feels comfortable. People vary in their proximity preferences, and you should be aware of any nonverbal reactions that signal discomfort. This example, illustrated by Figure 5.3, demon-strates the problem:

> A dispatcher at a trucking company had a habit that routinely annoyed all the truckers. Several truckers would be standing at a personal distance, drinking coffee, and relaxing after making their deliveries. The minute the dispatcher received a delivery request from headquarters, he would, according to instructions, present the request to the appropriate trucker. The problem was that instead of calling to the trucker, or joining the group by also adopting a personal distance, he would walk between two truckers to present the message, thus violating the intimate space of both people.

When the truckers complained to the supervisor, they could not verbalize exactly what the dispatcher did that irritated them. All they could say was that he seemed rude and unfriendly. Although he had never noticed the dispatcher behaving rudely, the supervisor was forced to replace him after several truckers threatened to quit.

If the supervisor or any of the employees had been aware of the importance of personal distance requirements, the problem might have been solved.

Distance and personal space are also important in selecting the seating arrangements for various tasks. Some of the most helpful research findings are diagrammed in Figure 5.4.[46]

Why are these research findings on seating arrangements important to you? Regardless of who you are or what job you hold, an individual will usually be more comfortable talking with you if you are not separated completely by a desk. However, if the individual is positioned at any angle to you narrower than 45 degrees, he or she may become nervous. Also, if you are conducting a meeting, you can control the amount of discussion by the seating arrangement you select. To keep discussion to a minimum, arrange the chairs in straight rows; to encourage discussion, try circular seating. Even if you select circular seating, you should know who the participants are and whether you should designate individual seats (by place cards, for example) to control interaction. As one text suggests:

> Groups could conceivably change the patterns of interaction among their members by changing who sat across from whom. Putting two holders of conflicting points-of-view alongside instead of across from each other could silence the verbal expression of their conflict. The opponents might stew in silence but their verbal disagreements would be very difficult to express. In some cases, however, a group might welcome opposing viewpoints as a stimulus to discussion and might want opposites in opinions to be physically opposite in the meeting. The powerful fact here is that seating arrangements can influence the direction of talking and even the amount of talking.[47]

Physical Environment

Have you ever noticed how some rooms and offices seem friendly and inviting, while other rooms (or buildings) seem cold and unfriendly? Do you feel uncomfortable talking to your boss (or instructor) in his or her office? You may simply be reacting to the fact that the office is the boss' territory, which gives the boss the upper hand. However, your negative reaction may be caused by the room itself.

Physical environments reveal characteristics of the owner of the territory; they also affect how people communicate. One prominent psychol-

Figure 5.4 Seating arrangements.

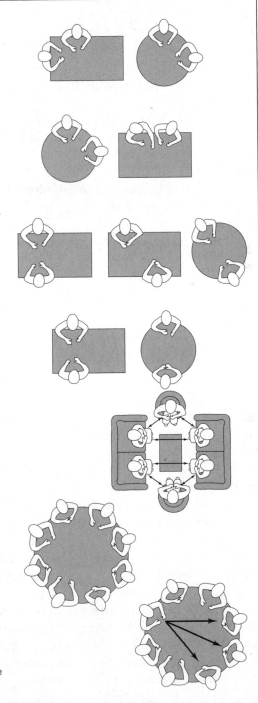

People (whether in a doctor's office, in the boss' office, or at home) are more comfortable conducting *conversation* when they are at right angles (90° or 45°) and no more than 4 feet apart.

When working closely together, *cooperating* on a task, people prefer corner seating or side-by-side seating.

When people are working on different tasks, *co-acting*, but need to be in close proximity to each other, they prefer more distant seating, facing opposite each other.

Competing people also prefer to sit opposite each other, with more distance between them.

People sitting side by side (on a sofa, for example) rarely converse with each other, preferring to converse with those across or at right angles to them.

Individuals in a group are more likely to participate if the group is seated in a circular pattern rather than in a rectangular pattern or in straight rows.

When a group sits in a circle, individuals are more likely to ask questions of or make comments to the persons directly across from them. Again, they are less likely to communicate with those sitting closest to them.

ogist states that for each person, the environment produces an emotional response, with "approach" (positive) or "avoidance" (negative) behaviors.[48] Various research studies have found that when participants perform tasks in "ugly" rooms, they experience "monotony, fatigue, headache, discontent, sleep, irritability, and hostility." However, when performing tasks in "attractive" rooms, participants experience "feelings of pleasure, comfort, enjoyment, energy, and desire to continue the activity"—even after an 8-hour period.[49]

Color also affects avoidance or approach behaviors and is a determining factor in whether an environment is judged as attractive or not. One researcher found that students in schoolrooms painted either yellow, rose, blue, or green showed more improvement than students in a room painted buff and white (the more common colors in schools).[50]

More businesses of all sizes are becoming aware of the impact of color on people. Manufacturers and sellers are aware of the emotional and even the physical effects of their products' colors:

> One detergent manufacturer sprinkled red granules throughout his white soap powder, and housewives subsequently complained that the detergent was too rough on their hands. He changed the color to yellow, and women said it was easier on their hands but that the clothes were not as clean. Finally, he changed the granules to a blue color, and the women said it was just right. Nothing had changed but the color of the granules.[51]

Police departments experimenting with color have found that solitary confinement and drunk holding cells painted a shade of pink cause less hostility and more compliance. Restaurant proprietors who want customers to eat and leave quickly may choose red and orange for their restaurant decor. Most companies use color in their headquarters to create a pleasant work environment.[52]

Another environmental factor that affects communication is *lighting*. White light can cause headaches, while light that is too blue can cause drowsiness.[53] A lighting design expert tells us that "most offices are generally overlit—with often twice as much light as they need . . . the result can be inefficiency, fatigue and perhaps a sense of dislocation."[54] For example, an Office of the Year winner, Purdue University's Administration Service Building, operated at a light level of approximately 150 footcandles. However, when the energy crunch necessitated lower electrical bills, the offices experimented with less light. On two floors, light was reduced from 150 to between 50 and 60 footcandles, and one floor dropped to the 30- to 40-footcandle range. Surprisingly,

Reaction was almost 100 percent in support of the change. Excessive light had apparently been a problem for many of the staff, but the problem had not surfaced in the initial reaction testing nor had it become concerted enough to merit attention in the period before the energy crunch.[55]

Room size can also alter communication. According to one management consultant:

> The amount of available space can also affect the success of a meeting. I always avoid a small classroom in my training sessions because the audience is much more argumentative and hard to control. The same holds true for a business meeting. . . . However, if you want to hold an efficient, spirited meeting, keep the space tight.[56]

Given the same number of people, an overly large room tends to inhibit relaxed discussions, while a smaller room seems to encourage discussion (and frank disagreement). The size of a room can also affect listener attitudes toward the event or the speaker. For example, an individual who walks into a small room with plenty of empty seats is likely to think, "I guess the speaker isn't any good. Look how few people showed up." The same person can walk into a crowded smaller room (with the same size audience) and think, "This speaker must be great. Look at all the people here."

Odor, too, communicates nonverbally, especially in a dental or medical office. Odors from disinfectant spray and dental chemicals can communicate uncomfortable associations, perhaps stir up unpleasant memories, and increase already existing anxiety. Of course, noise level, heat, ventilation, lack of windows, and furniture arrangements are other environmental factors that can nonverbally affect communication.

Closely related to physical environment is *ergonomics*, the science of mating machines to human requirements. Poor ergonomics can result in eyestrain, backache, headache, and fatigue. For people who spend a large portion of their day at the same workstation, using word processors or computer terminals, ergonomics can be extremely important to physical well-being and, therefore, to communication. Consider, for example, two current ergonomic problems and their solutions:

PROBLEM

Eyestrain and fatigue from glare and reflections from the CRT (cathode ray tube) screen.

SOLUTIONS[57]

1. Use an adjustable monitor or screen that you can tilt to avoid glare (and neck strain).
2. Place antiglare coating or a filter over the screen.
3. Position the terminal so that you are not facing a window (eyes must constantly adjust from bright to dim light).
4. Position the terminal so that it is not directly facing a window (causes reflections on screen).
5. Avoid highly reflective work surfaces.
6. Attach a glare hood to the terminal if glare is really bad.

PROBLEM

Back, neck, and arm strain from sitting before a CRT for a long period of time.

SOLUTION[58]

The home row of the keyboard [should] be approximately at elbow height. The forearm should be parallel to the floor with the wrist slightly bent. Feet should be flat on the floor with the seat at a height that provides some thigh clearance at the front. . . . The screen itself needs to be positioned so that the operator's line of sight is from 10 to 30 degrees below horizontal.

When we feel better, we communicate better. Perhaps your communication could be improved by ergonomic changes in your working environment.

Time

Time is another nonverbal communication factor in the business world. If you have a 1:00 appointment to discuss a production problem with an important manager or supervisor, is it permissible to arrive 15 or 20 minutes late? If you do, what message are you likely to be sending the manager? In contrast, suppose you arrive on time but are kept waiting for 15 or 20 minutes. What nonverbal messages would this behavior communicate to you?

Although your interpretation of time depends on your cultural and regional background, on the situation, and on the other people involved, you are most likely as fanatical about schedules and being on time as the majority of Americans. American reactions to time occur at all three levels of the cultural iceberg. Reading the correct time from a watch or clock is one of the technical aspects of time. Tradition determines the formal rules (a week consists of seven consecutive days, a workweek includes only five days, and so on). However, business life is generally regulated on the informal level. For example, whether it is acceptable to arrive late for an appointment often depends on whether you are meeting someone of equal rank, someone more important, or someone less important.[59] Also, anyone who is consistently late for appointments or in completing work assignments may be deemed inconsiderate or undependable. The amount of time an important person spends with us also has informal significance. For example, an employment interview that lasts longer than 30 minutes may mean that the interviewee's chances of getting the job are good.[60] The amount of time that a physician spends with a patient may tell the patient how much the physician cares.[61] Finally, the informal aspects of time in business are manifest in the use of *ASAP* (as soon as possible), *in a while*, and other similarly vague terms.

Although most Americans are schedule- and time-conscious and assign essentially the same nonverbal meanings to the types of time behaviors just discussed, reactions vary depending on where the individual was raised and the individual's cultural background. A woman born and reared in the North moved to the South and found it frustrating to adjust to what she called the southern concept of appointments. For example, the cable TV representative refused to give her an exact appointment time other than "sometime during the morning," and the plumber who promised to show up at 1:00 finally arrived at 6:00, just as she was leaving for the evening. In contrast, when a southern family moved to the North, they were just as frustrated by what they considered the hectic pace set by northerners. Expecting a repairman to arrive late, they went shopping only to return and find they had missed him and he would be unable to return for at least a week!

Although cultural and regional differences do add some confusion to the nonverbal aspect of time, when we deal with people from other nations, we all become American in our view of time. As a Japanese businessman told us, "If you keep Americans waiting long enough, they will agree to anything."

NONVERBAL STATUS SYMBOLS IN BUSINESS

Clothes are a nonverbal status symbol. Molloy tells us that "the tie is probably the single most important denominator of social status for a man in the United States today. Show me a man's ties and I will tell you who he is or who he is trying to be."[62] Several researchers have found that people are more likely to take orders from and follow the lead of people, even strangers, who are dressed in high-status clothing.[63]

Figure 5.5 Possible office arrangements.

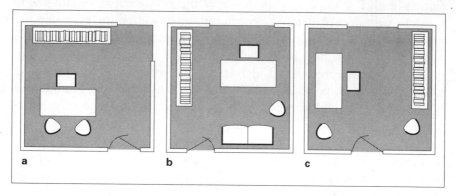

Other important status symbols are the location and size of a person's office. The following observations on office status are adapted from Michael Korda's popular book on power:[64]

- Because corner offices are usually larger and have more windows, corner offices carry more status; therefore, "offices in the middle of a row are less powerful than the ones at either end of it."
- Offices that are out of the traffic mainstream confer more power than do others. However, a secretary gains power by having a view of as many directions as possible.
- "In most cases, power diminishes with distance. Put someone's assistant next to his superior's office, and he benefits from being close to the source of power. Promote the assistant to a larger office that is farther away, and his power is likely to decrease. Only if he is given a title and a job that allows him to create his own power base can he benefit from moving."

Along with size and location, the interior arrangement of an office conveys the authority of its owner.[65] Which office arrangement shown in Figure 5.5 conveys the most authority?

Office *a* nonverbally assigns the most authority to its owner mainly because visitors are allotted only a small amount of space and because the desk separates visitors from the owner. Visitors would probably feel more comfortable and would communicate more freely in office *c* because they could sit at a right angle to the owner. Of the three, however, office *b* gives the owner the most flexibility; he or she can speak to the visitor from behind the desk when authority is necessary, or come from behind the desk to sit either in the chair or on the sofa for relaxed conversation with the visitor.

Other office amenities that lend a person status are solid-wood furniture, green plants (provided by the company), and quality artwork. And, of course, it doesn't hurt to have a personal secretary!

Time—that is, how it is handled—is another nonverbal indicator of status. For example, your boss may call a meeting at a specific time. The boss is allowed to arrive late, but you are not. A salesperson is kept cooling her heels in a doctor's waiting room, but a hospital board member is ushered in immediately (even if a patient has to wait). A job interview that lasts 45 minutes or longer usually conveys the prospective employer's interest, while a 10-minute interview may indicate disinterest. If you wish to talk with your supervisor, you are expected to make an appointment; however, your supervisor may stop by your office without giving you any prior notice.

A male executive can nonverbally indicate that he is more powerful than female executives or even other male executives by putting a comforting arm around them or always opening the door for them.[66] Of course, these gestures may have other meanings, but the recipients of such gestures need to be aware of their possible status implications. One way to counteract them as status symbols is simply to return them.

There are many ways to convey status. For instance, a person with status is more likely to have a preferred parking space, to demand (nonverbally or verbally) direct eye contact from others, to violate subordinates' personal space by touching or closeness, and to be allowed more space by lower-status people.

Others' perceptions play a large role in a person's success. For example, why aren't more women in management positions? Because many people who promote and hire do not *perceive* that women are as capable as men in power positions. Even hard work will not bring about a woman's promotion unless the promoter's perception changes. Korda notes:

> If a woman were elected President and chose a male Vice-President, we would doubtless see the Vice-Presidency transformed into a position of serious responsibility and power, while the Presidency was downgraded until the President and Vice-President could be treated as if they were a "team" of equals.[67]

Maybe women would be perceived as having more power if they used more nonverbal power indicators. Typically, women react nonverbally in a submissive or shrinking way while men react in a dominant, expanding way.[68] For example, women may smile too much. Mary Parlee found that women who smile less and use fewer facial expressions (than the average) are judged to have higher status.[69] Summarizing the research, Norma

Figure 5.6 (*a*) Powerful and (*b*) weak nonverbal behaviors.

a b

Carr-Ruffino lists the following strong and weak nonverbal behaviors for both men and women (see Figure 5.6):

SIGNS OF POWER

- Expansive movements.
- Tall, upright posture.
- Relaxed, affable, familiar behavior.
- Ability to turn one's back on another.
- Comfortable, relaxed seated positions: legs crossed, arms asymmetrically placed, body leaning sideways and reclining slightly.

SIGNS OF WEAKNESS

- Small, controlled movements.
- Any form of bowing or bowed posture.
- Tenseness, vigilance.
- Hesitantly standing or sitting forward attentively with feet together on the floor, with arms in lap or in another balanced position.[70]

Signs of power are more often used by bosses, while signs of weakness are more often displayed by subordinates. Even if we don't know the two people involved in a face-to-face discussion, their nonverbal body behaviors will usually clearly signal the status of each.[71]

To learn to use the more powerful postures:

- Picture yourself assuming specific power postures.
- Practice power postures in private, with feedback from a friend or a mirror.
- Adopt appropriate power postures.[72]

Some of you, especially those just beginning in a business or profession, may be thinking, "This is all ridiculous. I don't want to play these games. I can work well in extremely casual clothes, and where my desk or office is located makes no difference to my performance." And you may very well be right. Many companies have tried to downplay status differences. However, keep in mind that *the message that counts is the one received.* People are receiving nonverbal messages about you regardless of whether you intend to send them or not. Although you are capable of handling a particular job, you will not be assigned that job unless other people (especially your boss) think you are capable. Their perceptions of you are probably affected by their opinions of your dress, office, and many other things. Even if separate offices are eliminated, the people closest to the boss are perceived as having higher status; if personnel are required to wear the same uniforms, status will be determined by some other indicator. Look around you. What are the most successful managers wearing? Where are their offices located? You cannot go wrong by following the example of people in the positions you desire to achieve.

NONVERBAL MESSAGES AND INTERNATIONAL BUSINESS TRANSACTIONS

The nonverbal symbols and gestures discussed in this chapter apply to and are understood by most people in the United States. However, people of other countries and cultures have different nonverbal symbols and meanings for each level of the cultural iceberg. For example, people from different cultures use touch quite differently. In a study of how often adult couples in coffee shops touch, Sidney M. Jourard found that couples in San Juan, Puerto Rico, touched 180 times per hour; couples in Paris, France, touched 110 times per hour; couples in Gainesville, Florida, touched only twice per hour; and in London, England, couples touched once per hour.[73] It is just as difficult for the American businessperson, even one prepared for differences, to interpret accurately the nonverbal communication used in other countries as it is for businesspeople from other countries to interpret ours. Part of the difficulty is that many nonverbal meanings are hidden in the informal level of the cultural iceberg: People from all over the world are typically unaware of the informal rules governing their behavior! An informal rule in the United States may even be a formal or technical rule in another nation.

When a company sends representatives (sometimes with their families) abroad to conduct business or to manage or work in a plant comprised primarily of employees from the host country, two mistakes are often made. The first mistake is the company's. American representatives, for example, are usually given very little training in the language and customs of the country they will visit. Instead, the company assumes that the employee will cope. But without training, how would you know that the Japanese nod to acknowledge hearing, not agreement? (Wouldn't we assume the opposite?) What if, while visiting in Taiwan, you and several Taiwanese colleagues go to a restaurant. Without prior training, how would you know that the host, the person in charge who is paying the bill, always sits facing the door? If you were supposed to pay the bill but chose the wrong seat, or if you were not the host but sat facing the door, the group would likely become upset. Business relations would be strained.[74]

The second mistake is made by the visiting employees, who assume the people in the foreign country behave basically the same as Americans. When the natives do not react as expected, the visitors tend to develop *culture shock*.

People develop **culture shock** when they become confused because they cannot understand or be understood by the people of another culture. Many visitors become angry and suspicious, negatively stereotype the natives' behavior, and withdraw from personal contacts. An international student visiting the United States expresses the strain of culture shock:

> During those several months after my arrival in the U.S.A., every day I came back from school exhausted so that I had to take a rest for a while, stretching myself on the bed. For, all the time, I strained every nerve in order to understand what the people were saying and make myself understood in my broken English. When I don't understand what American people are talking about and why they are laughing, I sometimes have to pretend to understand by smiling, even though I feel alienated, uneasy and tense.[75]

To become culturally sensitive, Americans need to realize how people from other countries view us. Below are a list of actual comments made by foreigners while visiting the United States. Do you think these observations are accurate? If so, how would you explain them?

India "Americans seem to be in a perpetual hurry. Just watch the way they walk down the street. They never allow themselves the leisure to enjoy life; there are too many things to do."

Kenya   "Americans appear to us rather distant. . . . It's almost as if an American says, 'I won't let you get too close to me.' It's like building a wall."

Turkey   "Once we were out in a rural area in the middle of nowhere and saw an American come to a stop sign. Though he could see in both directions for miles and no traffic was coming, he still stopped!"

Colombia   "The tendency in the United States to think that life is only work hits you in the face. Work seems to be the one type of motivation."

Indonesia   "In the United States everything has to be talked about and analyzed. Even the littlest thing has to be 'Why, Why, Why?' I get a headache from such persistent questions."

Ethiopia   "The American is very explicit; he wants a 'yes' or 'no.' If someone tries to speak figuratively, the American is confused."

Iran   "The first time . . . my [American] professor told me, 'I don't know the answer; I will have to look it up,' I was shocked. I asked myself, 'Why is he teaching me?' In my country a professor would give the wrong answer rather than admit ignorance."[76]

Complete the following Awareness Check to see if you would experience culture shock in any of these situations.

AWARENESS CHECK: NONVERBAL SYMBOLS ACROSS CULTURES

Are you aware of the nonverbal symbols and meanings used by people from other countries in their everyday lives? Check your knowledge by selecting the best response to each of the following hypothetical situations.[77]

Situation 1   A German firm, an English firm, and a U.S. firm decide to work together in producing household appliances. The executives of each firm agree to house the top corporate executives in England. Almost immediately, unhappiness arises over the type of offices they will have. You are called in to mediate a settlement. Your first task is to determine just exactly what each country's executives want. Identify whether each of the following viewpoints belongs to the German, the English, or the American executives:

(continued)

_____ **a.** These executives insist on private offices with heavy doors, which should remain shut except when people are moving in and out.

_____ **b.** These executives insist on offices, but want all office doors to remain open unless a personal conference is in progress.

_____ **c.** These executives prefer working in open space and feel that offices are unnecessary. They consider the offices preferred by the other two countries' executives a waste of money.

Situation 2 You take a job working in an English manufacturing plant. You and your family are able to find a nice home to rent, and you are very happy to notice that the couple living next door are approximately your age. The afternoon you move in, you and your family go next door to meet your neighbors. Although they are polite, they do not seem very friendly. Several days later, while preparing dinner for an important associate, you run out of flour and rush next door to borrow a cup. Again you receive a polite but cool reception by your neighbors. What is the problem?

_____ **a.** The neighbors evidently do not like Americans, so you must approach them slowly.

_____ **b.** You appeared pushy by introducing yourselves the moment you arrived.

_____ **c.** Britons do not necessarily socialize with their neighbors so you should not feel insulted.

_____ **d.** English culture dictates that newcomers to a neighborhood must wait for an established neighbor to initiate the association.

Situation 3 You have worked long and hard on a business proposal to present to a Japanese business firm. With the help of an interpreter, you have even prepared your transparencies (visuals) in Japanese. When representatives from the Japanese firm arrive, you are surprised to see six people (all of important status) enter the room. Although you feel outnumbered, after the introductions you and the interpreter get right to business and outline what you know to be an excellent presentation. The Japanese are smiling so you feel fairly comfortable that the presentation is going well. At the end of two days of presentations and discussions, the Japanese representatives promise to look over the proposal and get back in touch with you. But they never do. Whenever you call, they politely give a reason for not meeting with you "at this time." What went wrong?

_____ **a.** You offended the Japanese by not socializing and getting to know them before beginning the negotiations.

_____ **b.** Your interpreter did a poor job of relaying your ideas to the Japanese.

_____ **c.** You conveyed to the Japanese representatives that your company has no status. Because position, rank, and status are extremely important in Japanese business deals, they did not wish to conduct business with an unimportant firm.

_____ **d.** The people in charge of the evening's entertainment apparently offended the Japanese in some way.

ANSWERS

Situation 1 Answer *a* is the viewpoint of the German executives. Germans have a greater desire for privacy than either the English or the Americans. To them doors should be heavy, soundproof, and snug fitting. One can violate a German's space simply by looking into his or her office. Therefore, open doors cause many Germans to feel exposed. Also, open doors are considered unbusinesslike and disorderly. Answer *b* is the American position. Americans want private offices but generally like to keep the doors open. Closed doors indicate to Americans that something illicit or secret is happening inside. Therefore, they would be suspicious of Germans who preferred closed doors. Answer *c* is the English position. In England, social class rather than amount of space determines status. The English have learned to communicate without private offices. Even members of Parliament function without private offices. Privacy comes from within.

Situation 2 Although some Britons may still hold the Revolutionary War against Americans, dislike is not the answer to this situation. Instead, answer *b* is probably the main reason. A cardinal rule of English society is not to be pushy. People like to get to know each other gradually and believe that friendship has to be worked for or it's not worth anything. By introducing yourselves the day you arrived, you appeared pushy. Generally, it takes a long time to become established in English neighborhoods. Answer *c* may also be true in some British neighborhoods. Social class is very important in England. Therefore, families do not socialize with their neighbors just because they happen to live next door but because they are of the same social status. In contrast, in the United States, where people live determines with whom they socialize and with whom their children play.

Situation 3 It is true that the Japanese do a great deal of socializing before getting down to business (and it would be wise for you to do likewise). However, it is doubtful that this oversight by a foreigner would cancel a business deal. Answer *c* is the best answer in this situation. Status is very important in Japanese culture. When conducting any type of business deal, Japanese businesspeople will bring along two or more important people to add to their own importance. In this situation, you had only one person with you—a relatively unimportant (in terms of business status) interpreter. Nonverbally, you indicated your lack of status or importance, which reflected negatively on your company.

How did you do with the Awareness Check situations? Try some additional hypothetical situations in the Checkpoint at the end of the chapter.

IMMEDIACY BEHAVIORS

When your nonverbal communication is combined with your vocal and verbal communication, you can promote a sense of closeness and personal interaction with business colleagues and customers; this interaction is referred to as **immediacy behavior.** Research has found that students learn significantly more and have an improved attitude toward the classroom experience when instructors use immediacy behaviors.[78] Although research on immediacy behavior has focused on teachers and students, there is much similarity between a classroom and an office. Immediacy behaviors include the following:

- *Verbal behaviors* (language). Using humor sensitively, citing personal experiences during conversations, referring to colleagues or employees as "we" and "our," praising individuals for their work, actions, or comments, referring to individuals by name, asking for opinions and questions, and conversing with others before and after meetings.
- *Vocal behaviors* (paralanguage). Being vocally expressive when speaking—that is, using good volume, pitch, emphasis, rate, and so on.
- *Visual behaviors* (nonverbal). Making eye contact, smiling appropriately at individuals as well as the whole group, keeping a relaxed posture, gesturing naturally, and moving around rather than staying behind a barrier such as a desk.

IMPROVING NONVERBAL SKILLS

If you are serious about improving your skills in sending and receiving nonverbal messages, begin with these steps:

1. Develop awareness of nonverbal differences.
2. Do not judge others using your own nonverbal meanings.
3. Do not assign nonverbal meanings out of context.
4. Observe yourself on videotape.

To communicate effectively, you need to be aware that differences in nonverbal symbols and meanings exist on the technical, formal, and informal levels. You have to be extremely observant to perceive even a few of these differences. According to Bernard Beegle of Sperry-Rand Corporation,

> It is in your own interest to observe how others communicate through their gestures and mannerisms. It is also in your interest to act on nonverbal messages as legitimate messages that deserve attention. When subordinates communicate with you nonverbally, they are signaling you to get involved. They are asking you to take initiative to talk to them, to find out if problems exist, and to take action to solve them quickly. Your responsiveness to nonverbal communications shows the extent of your awareness and interest in subordinates—and they will respond accordingly.[79]

Unobtrusively observe the nonverbal behaviors of your family, friends, coworkers, and even strangers. And, of course, be aware of your own nonverbal reactions in various situations and what those reactions are saying about you to others.

When you observe nonverbal behaviors, do not jump to conclusions or assume that you know what a particular behavior means. Judging others according to your own nonverbal system is a natural reaction, but it leads to errors and misunderstandings. You will make fewer errors in interpretation if, instead of analyzing only one nonverbal response at a time, you evaluate several responses as a whole. For example, suppose you are interviewing an employee about some missing machinery. If the employee fails to look you in the eye while responding, it might indicate that he or she is guilty. But it might also indicate embarrassment that you are questioning the employee's integrity, or it might be a gesture of respect for your authority, or it might indicate any number of other meanings. Suppose, however, that the employee squirms in her seat, begins to perspire, gives evasive answers to your questions, and makes nervous hand gestures in addition to avoiding eye contact. Now you have much stronger support for your assumption that the employee is guilty. However, guilty of what? You are still making an *assumption!* Perhaps the employee appears guilty because she knows who took the machinery but does not want to squeal on anyone. Be careful about jumping to conclusions.

We must not assign meanings to nonverbal behaviors out of context. We must consider the specific situation, environment, time factor, cultural background, and personal frame of reference. There is no nonverbal behavior that means exactly the same thing in all situations. If someone asks you the meaning of a certain word, you might reply, "Well, how was it used in the sentence?" In other words, you know that the context of the sentence determines the specific meaning of the word; for example, the word *run* has so many different meanings that it is almost meaningless out of context. Nonverbal behavior is no different; it, too, is meaningless out of context.

One suggestion for improving your nonverbal skills is to watch yourself on videotape and observe your nonverbal behaviors. Participate in a small-group discussion of job-related problems and record the session on videotape. Analysis of the videotape should indicate both positive and negative nonverbal behaviors. If videotaping is not possible, ask for specific feedback on your use of nonverbal communication from the other group members.

Another way to observe your nonverbal skills is to role play in hypothetical situations. For example, you might play the role of an employer who is interviewing an unfriendly or shy job applicant, played by a colleague. Again, videotapes of these sessions can be very revealing. Simulated pressure situations like this give participants insight into the effects of their own and others' nonverbal (and verbal) behavior. One businessman comments on the success of role playing:

> The observers will often be surprised at how quickly they can tell if one of the role players is falling under attack or is trying to mislead the others. Even though a role player thinks he is hiding his discomfort or impatience, observers read the hidden messages quite clearly.[80]

One more way to improve your nonverbal skills is by associating with as many different types of people as possible. If you aren't sure what certain nonverbal responses mean, ask. Of course, the others may not be able to help you if the response is from their informal level of culture, and they may even deny that any nonverbal message was sent. Don't argue with them; just observe and learn.

SUMMARY

We have looked at nonverbal communication at the technical, formal, and informal levels of culture. In the United States, most nonverbal behaviors are governed by the informal level, where the rules for behavior are unstated and even unknown to most people. When an informal rule is violated, people become extremely uncomfortable and even angry without knowing why.

In an attempt to make you more aware of these often unknown rules, we covered the types of nonverbal communication most applicable to business life: (1) facial expression and eye contact, (2) other body movements and gestures, (3) clothing and personal appearance, (4) distance and personal space, (5) physical environment, and (6) time. Nonverbal status symbols in business, such as clothing, office size, and the manipulation of time, strongly influence how others perceive us and thus are key factors in career advancement. For success in international business dealings, we must be aware of differences between our nonverbal messages and those of other countries.

Knowledge of nonverbal communication can be an important tool for the business and professional communicator if it is used correctly. After all, a large portion of the meaning of a person's message is carried by the nonverbal code. However, as with many things, a little bit of knowledge can be dangerous. *We urge you to be very careful in your interpretations of others' nonverbal behaviors.* Don't jump to conclusions, and don't read nonexistent meanings into simple gestures. Overreacting to nonverbal messages will cause just as many misunderstandings as ignoring them.

CHECKPOINT

Before continuing to the next chapter, check your understanding of Chapter 5 by completing the following exercises:

1. Walk the corridors of the place where you work, paying particular attention to various office arrangements. What nonverbal characteristics do you feel create a favorable impression, and what nonverbal characteristics account for any unfavorable impression?
2. Evaluate how successfully you use the six types of nonverbal communication covered in this chapter. Select two areas that need improvement and decide what you can do about them.
3. Check your awareness of cultural differences by responding to these additional hypothetical situations. Circle the answer that best explains the reason behind the behavior. Be sure to answer all questions before checking any responses with the answer key.

Situation 1   During a negotiation session with a Japanese corporation, you notice that every time the Japanese spokesman speaks to you, he avoids looking directly at you and usually looks sideways at the wall. It is important for you to know exactly how the Japanese are reacting to the proposal because you have an additional concession to offer only if it is necessary to close the deal. The best interpretation of the Japanese executive's behavior is:

a. This is probably his first negotiation session and he is just nervous.
b. He is trying to give you a nonverbal clue that his company is unhappy with your company's proposal.

c. He is simply showing good manners by not looking at you while he speaks.

d. He is probably misrepresenting the facts and is afraid to look you in the eye in case you see through him.

Situation 2   Your company hopes to arrange a very lucrative sale of machine parts to a French firm. A French representative, Mr. Deneuve, meets you at the Paris airport and greets you with a kiss on both cheeks. Although you are embarrassed, you step back, smile, and offer your hand. The airport is terribly crowded, and as you hold out your hand, a group of smiling travelers knocks against you and forces you closer to Deneuve. Even though he has room to move, he does not. You know he can smell on your breath the onions you ate at lunch, and you are feeling very embarrassed. You shift your suitcase so that it is between yourself and Deneuve. No deal is reached during this visit, so you return home, planning to try again next month. A few days later, you run into a mutual friend who tells you that Deneuve is unhappy with your company because he considers you too arrogant and too self-assured. What could be the cause of his reaction?

a. Mr. Deneuve has learned that one way to get more money out of a U.S. company is to pretend displeasure with the company's representatives. His reaction is only a negotiating ploy.

b. Your reactions to being crowded suggested to him that you thought you were too important to walk close to him.

c. His company is really not interested in buying your product, but in his culture it is impolite to say no directly. His comments to your friend are his way of getting the message to you.

Situation 3   You are excited that you have been selected to travel to England to help solve a technical problem at your company's English manufacturing plant. You have always wanted to visit London. The visit is very pleasant until you actually begin discussions with the English management. The managers continually stare at you and blink their eyes as though bored. This behavior on their part is very distracting. What nonverbal meaning, if any, can be drawn from their behavior?

a. The managers resent the fact that an American outsider, especially a mere technician, was sent to handle such a minor problem. They are nonverbally communicating to you their unhappiness.

b. The English smog is so bad that most British have eye irritations. Just ignore the behavior.

c. In England, eye blinking is a sign that people are listening. No disrespect is meant.

d. In England, eye blinking indicates confusion. Somehow, you are not getting through to them.

Situation 4 You have arrived 5 minutes early for an appointment with a Latin American businessman. You check with the secretary and are told that the manager cannot see you yet. You have flown in especially to see this person, and he knows you have only a short time before your plane leaves. Forty-five minutes later you are still waiting, while two other businesspeople have entered his office. By this time, you are getting rather angry. How should you interpret the treatment you are receiving?

a. The Latin American manager is obviously not interested in speaking with you. Your chances of arriving at a deal with him are slim.
b. Schedules are not terribly important to Latin Americans; they view time as relative.
c. The manager is trying to show you that you are not as important as he is. Latin Americans feel that when their status is greater than the other person's, they will get a better business deal.

Situation 5 You are giving a well-planned, second presentation to a group of Thai businesspeople who speak excellent English. You and your company's executives feel confident that the Thais are interested enough in your company's product to sign a contract. To show how relaxed you are with the group, you sit on the desk and cross your legs. For some reason, the group immediately freezes. The contract falls through. What caused their change in behavior?

a. When you crossed your legs, you directed the bottom of your foot toward several Thais, who interpreted this gesture as an insult.
b. Thais consider all business to be formal and were insulted when you showed how unimportant they were by the informal gesture of sitting on the desk.
c. You nonverbally showed how confident you were; this irritated them.

Situation 6 You volunteer for assignment at your company's plant in a West African country. You are aware of how difficult it is to step into a manager's position where the majority of the managers are not of your nationality. To get to know the other managers better, you host several informal cocktail parties in your home. None of your guests reciprocate by inviting you to a party at their homes, and several of them failed to attend your last party. What could be the reason for this behavior?[81]

a. Informal parties in West Africa are only for family; business parties are expected to be formal affairs.
b. Many of your African associates can only afford to entertain on a much smaller scale, and they are not sure you would be interested in their parties.
c. Your guests think you are cheap and probably feel insulted because you served no food at your parties.

d. Africans generally are not a social, party-loving people. No insult is intended.

ANSWERS

Situation 1   Based on American culture, *d* probably seems the most logical answer because lying or nervousness in the United States is usually indicated by avoidance of eye contact. However, Japanese usually try to cover up any feelings of nervousness or embarrassment by laughing or giggling, which was not done. The best answer in this situation is *c*. Looking directly into the eyes while talking is bad manners in Japan. Therefore, in this case, the spokesman is being polite and possibly showing you respect at the same time. He probably considers you both rude and arrogant for using direct eye contact while speaking.

Situation 2   Answer *b* is the best for this situation. A distance of 2 feet seems very close to Americans but is perceived as distant by the French. Therefore, your nonverbal reactions (obvious discomfort, stepping back, and using your suitcase to create more distance between the two of you) were misinterpreted as arrogance and self-importance.

Situation 3   Although the English managers may be upset that an outsider has been sent to solve one of their problems, eye blinking is not the way the English show unhappiness. Actually, the British use prolonged eye contact and eye blinking as a way to show that they are paying attention (answer *c*). Because private offices are rare in England, the grunting noises Americans make to show they are listening would intrude on nearby conversations almost as much as loud talking. Both are considered examples of extremely poor manners and low class! Actually, absence of eye contact and eye blinking might be one nonverbal sign that you were not getting through to the managers.

Situation 4   The best answer to this situation is *b*. Perception of time is much more relaxed in Latin American countries. A 45-minute wait to Latin Americans is approximately equal to a 5-minute wait in the United States. No insult is intended. Also, you may discover, when you are finally ushered into his office, that the other two guests are still there and that the businessman will try to talk to all of you at the same time. Again, this is not intended as an insult; it is simply the way business is conducted in Latin America.

Situation 5   In the Thai culture, feet are considered the most degraded part of the body and should never be directed toward anyone, touch anyone, or even be used to perform a task (such as pushing open a door when your hands are full). The bottoms of the feet are shown only when a serious insult is intended. When you crossed your legs and pointed one foot toward the audience, you insulted them. Therefore, *a* is the best answer. Sitting on the desk was also an insult but not of the sort described in answer *b*. The top of the desk is a place where people often rest their heads, and the head is considered sacred to the Thais. Therefore, the act of placing a lower, unclean part of the body on an area that the head might touch is also a cultural taboo.

Situation 6   Africans enjoy parties and usually are happy to reciprocate with parties that include both food and drink. Although your guests may have been surprised by your American-style (drinks only) party, it is doubtful that this was more than a slight influence in this situation. The best answer is probably *b*. When they get to know you better, you will probably be invited to their homes. Be patient.

NOTES

1.   Dean C. Barnlund, *Communicative Styles of Japanese and Americans: Images and Realities* (Belmont, CA: Wadsworth, 1989), p. 127.
2.   Paul Eckman and Wallace Friesen, "Constants Across Cultures in the Face and Emotion," *Journal of Personality and Social Psychology* 17 (April 1971), pp. 124–129.

3. David L. James, "The Art of the Deal (Japan-Style)," *Business Month* (November 1989), p. 93; see also Barnlund.
4. Roger E. Axtell, *Gestures: The Do's and Taboos of Body Language Around the World* (New York: Wiley, 1991), p. 47.
5. Mary Munter, "Cross-Cultural Communications," *Business Horizons* 36 (May–June 1993), p. 76.
6. Edward T. Hall, *The Silent Language* (Garden City, NY: Anchor, 1973), pp. 60–69.
7. Sharon Ruhly, "Orientations to Intercultural Communication," in *MODCOM: Modules in Speech Communication*, Ronald L. Applebaum and Roderick P. Hart, eds. (Chicago: Science Research Associates, 1976), pp. 8–11.
8. Ray Birdwhistell, *Kinesics and Context* (Philadelphia: University of Pennsylvania Press, 1970).
9. E. A. Haggard and K. S. Isaacs, "Micromomentary Facial Expressions as Indicators of Ego Mechanisms in Psychotherapy," in *Methods of Research in Psychotherapy*, L. A. Gottschalk and A. H. Averback, eds. (Englewood Cliffs, NJ: Prentice-Hall, 1966).
10. R. Exline and C. Eldridge, "Effects of Two Patterns of a Speaker's Visual Behavior upon the Perception of the Authenticity of His Verbal Message," a paper presented to the Eastern Psychological Association Convention, Boston, 1967.
11. Loretta A. Malandro, Larry Barker, and Deborah Ann Barker, *Communication*, 2nd ed. (New York: Random House, 1989); J. M. Wiemann and M. L. Knapp, "Turn-Taking in Conversations," *Journal of Communication* 25 (1975), pp. 75–92; A. Kendon, "Some Functions of Gaze-Direction in Social Interaction," *Acta Psychologica* 26 (1967), pp. 22–63.
12. R. G. Harper, A. N. Wiens, and J. D. Matarozzo, *Nonverbal Communication: The State of the Art* (New York: Wiley, 1978), pp. 77–118, 171–245; M. Argyle and R. Ingham, "Gaze, Mutual Gaze and Proximity," *Semiotica* 6 (1972), pp. 32–49, as reported by Mark L. Knapp, *Essentials of Nonverbal Communication* (New York: Holt, Rinehart, & Winston, 1980), p. 184.
13. Argyle and Ingham, pp. 32–49.
14. A. Kendon and M. Cook, "The Consistency of Gaze Patterns in Social Interaction," *British Journal of Psychology* 60 (1969), pp. 481–494.
15. Julius Fast, *Subtext: Making Body Language Work in the Work Place* (New York: Viking, 1991), p. 29.
16. F. Erickson, "Talking Down: Some Cultural Sources of Miscommunication in Interracial Interviews," in *Nonverbal Behavior: Applications and Cultural Implications*, A. Wolfgang, ed. (New York: Academic, 1979), pp. 99–126.
17. Albert Mehrabian, "Significance of Posture and Position in the Communication of Attitude and Status Relationships," *Psychological Bulletin* 71 (1969), pp. 359–372.
18. Michael Houglum, Steven Mandel, and Paul D. Krivonos, "Affective Response to Handshakes," unpublished manuscript, Department of Speech Communication, California State University, Northridge.
19. G. I. Nierenberg and H. H. Calero, *How to Read a Person Like a Book* (New York: Pocket, 1973).
20. Reported by Thomas E. Harris, *Applied Organizational Communication: Perspectives, Principles, and Pragmatics* (Hillsdale, NJ: Erlbaum, 1993), p. 147, from C. Forbes, "Firm Handshake More Important Than Buttering a Roll, Etiquette Expert Says," *Birmingham Post-Herald*, April 12, 1990, p. C10.
21. P. Ekman and W. Friesen, "The Repertoire of Nonverbal Behavior: Categories, Origins, Usage, and Coding," *Semiotica* 1 (1969), pp. 49–98.
22. Ken Cooper, *Body Business* (New York: AMACOM, 1987).
23. J. Mills and E. Aronson, "Opinions Change as a Function of the Communicator's Attractiveness and Desire to Influence," *Journal of Personality and Social Psychology* 1 (1965), pp. 73–77; H. Sigall, "Psychologist 'Proves' Good Looks Helpful," Associated Press Release, 1974; R. N. Widgery and B. Webster, "The Effects of Physical Attractiveness upon Perceived Initial Credibility," *Michigan Speech Journal* 4 (1969), pp. 9–15; Martin L. Hoffman, "Sex Differences in Empathy and Related Behaviors," *Psychological Bulletin* 84 (1977), pp. 712–722.
24. P. R. Mims, J. J. Hartnett, and W. R. Nay, "Interpersonal Attraction and Help Volunteering as a Function of Physical Attractiveness," *Journal of Psychology* 89 (1975), pp. 125–131; S. G. West and T. J. Brown, "Physical Attractiveness, the Severity of the Emergency and Helping: A Field Experiment and Interpersonal Simulation," *Journal of Experimental Social Psychology* 11 (1975), pp. 531–538; P. L. Benson, S. A. Korabenick, and R. M. Lerner, "Pretty Please,

the Effects of Physical Attractiveness, Race and Sex on Receiving Help," *Journal of Experimental Social Psychology* 18 (1976), pp. 409–415.

25. M. G. Efran, "The Effect of Physical Appearance on the Judgment of Guilt, Interpersonal Attraction, and Severity of Recommended Punishment in a Simulated Jury Task," *Journal of Research in Personality* 8 (1974), pp. 45–54.

26. E. E. Baker and W. C. Redding, "The Effects of Perceived Tallness in Persuasive Speaking: An Experiment," *Journal of Communication* 12 (1962), pp. 51–53; see also Knapp, p. 107.

27. R. Sybers and M. E. Roach, "Clothing and Human Behavior," *Journal of Home Economics* 54 (1962), pp. 184–187; L. Bickman, "Social Roles and Uniforms: Clothes Make the Person," *Psychology Today* 7 (1974), pp. 48–51.

28. M. Lefkowitz, R. Blake, and J. Mouton, "Status Factors in Pedestrian Violation of Traffic Signals," *Journal of Abnormal and Social Psychology* 51 (1955), pp. 704–706; Bickman, pp. 48–51.

29. R. Hoult, "Experimental Measurement of Clothing as a Factor in Some Social Ratings of Selected American Men," *American Sociological Review* 51 (1955), pp. 324–328.

30. Hoult, pp. 324–328; Bickman, pp. 48–51 (the Bickman study was conducted on men, but there is no reason to suspect that women would be any different).

31. D. Anderson, "Whatever Happened to the Corporate Dress Code?" *TWA Ambassador,* March 1977, pp. 43–45.

32. From a thirteen-page Hertz Corporation interoffice document, December 27, 1983 (to all employees from the zone training manager).

33. *Directory of Personal Image Consultants, 1988–1989,* edited by Jacqueline A. Tompson and Image Industry Publications (New York: Image Industry Publications, 1988–1989).

34. Nancy Golden, *Dress Right for Business* (New York: Gregg Division, McGraw-Hill, 1986), p. 39.

35. John T. Molloy, *New Dress for Success* (New York: Warner, 1988); John T. Molloy, *Dress for Success* (New York: Warner, 1976); John T. Molloy, *The Woman's Dress for Success Book* (New York: Warner, 1978).

36. Mary Damhorst and Julia Ann P. Reed, "Effects of Clothing Color on Assessment of Characteristics of Job Applicants," paper presented at the seventy-first annual meeting of the American Home Economics Association, 1980; see also *The Psychology of Fashion,* Michael R. Soloman, ed. (New York: D. C. Heath, 1985).

37. Janet Wallach, *Looks That Work* (New York: Viking Penguin, 1986), p. 16.

38. William Thourlby, *You Are What You Wear* (New York: Signet, 1978), pp. 36–38.

39. Thourlby, pp. 36–38.

40. Golden, p. 41.

41. Vicki Keltner and Mike Holsey, *The Success Image: A Guide for the Better Dressed Business Woman* (Houston: Gulf, 1982), p. 14.

42. Golden, p. 46.

43. Myron Boor, Steven A. Wartman, and David B. Reuben, "Relationship of Physical Appearances and Professional Demeanor to Interview Evaluations and Rankings of Medical Residency Applicants," *Journal of Psychology* 113 (1983), p. 64.

44. Norma Carr-Ruffino, *The Promotable Woman: Becoming a Successful Manager,* rev. ed. (Belmont, CA: Wadsworth, 1985), p. 87.

45. Edward T. Hall, *The Hidden Dimension* (Garden City, NY: Anchor, 1969), chap. 10.

46. Edward T. Hall, "Proxemics," in *Foundations of Nonverbal Communication: Readings, Exercises, and Commentary,* A. M. Katz and V. T. Katz, eds. (Carbondale: Southern Illinois University Press, 1983); Mark L. Hickson and Don W. Stacks, *NVC: Nonverbal Communication: Studies and Applications,* 2nd ed. (Dubuque, IA: Wm. C. Brown, 1989); Malandro, Barker, and Barker, p. 157; Albert Mehrabian, *Public Places and Private Spaces* (New York: Basic, 1980); Mark Cook, "Experiments on Orientation and Proxemics," *Human Relations* 23 (1970), pp. 61–76; Robert Sommer, *Personal Space: The Behavioral Basis of Design* (Englewood Cliffs, NJ: Prentice-Hall, 1967), pp. 61–64; N. Russo, "Connotation of Seating Arrangement," *Cornell Journal of Social Relations* 2 (1967), pp. 37–44; Robert Sommer, "Further Studies of Small Group Ecology," *Sociometry* 28 (1965), pp. 337–348; D. Byrne, "The Influence of Propinquity and Opportunities for Interaction on Classroom Relationships," *Human Relations* 14 (1961), pp. 63–70; Bernard Steinzor, "The Spatial Factor in Face-to-Face Discussion Groups," *Journal of Abnormal and Social Psychology* 45 (1950), pp. 552–555.

47. Mele Koneya and Alton Barbour, *Louder Than Words . . . Nonverbal Communication* (Columbus, OH: Merrill, 1976), pp. 69–70.

48. Mehrabian, *Public Places.*
49. N. L. Mintz, "Effects of Esthetic Surroundings: Prolonged and Repeated Experience in a 'Beautiful' and 'Ugly' Room," *Journal of Psychology* 41 (1956), pp. 459–466; see also A. H. Maslow and N. L. Mintz, "Effects of Esthetic Surroundings: I. Initial Effects of Three Esthetic Conditions upon Perceiving 'Energy' and 'Well-Being' in Faces," *Journal of Psychology* 41 (1956), pp. 247–254.
50. H. Ketcham, *Color Planning for Business and Industry* (New York: Harper & Brothers, 1968).
51. Malandro, Barker, and Barker, p. 157.
52. Walter A. Kleinschrod, "From Detail and Care, a Total Success," *Administrative Management* 42 (February 1981), pp. 24–28; see also B. Wayne Fishback and Carol Krewson, "Design Team Simplifies Interiors to Aid Patient Recuperation," *Hospitals* 55 (February 16, 1981), pp. 151–156; and Jeffrey S. Prince, "A Functional Interior from a 'Crystal' Design," *Administrative Management* 41 (May 1980), pp. 32–33, 60.
53. A. G. Abbott, *The Color of Life* (New York: McGraw-Hill, 1947).
54. William Kowinski, "Shedding New Light," *New Times* 4 (March 7, 1975), p. 46.
55. Robert S. Sorenson and J. Marshall Hemphill, "Purdue Revisited: The Soundness of the Open Plan," *Administrative Management* 42 (January 1981), pp. 28–31, 74.
56. Cooper, pp. 19–20.
57. James R. Clark, "How Does Ergonomics Affect the Secretary?" *Secretary* 42 (May 1982), p. 9.
58. Clark, pp. 9–10.
59. Virginia P. Richmond, James C. McCroskey, and Steven K. Payne, *Nonverbal Behavior in Interpersonal Relations* (Englewood Cliffs, NJ: Prentice-Hall, 1987), pp. 182–183.
60. Hall, *The Silent Language*, p. 150.
61. M. R. Dimatteo, L. M. Prince, and A. Taranta, "Patients' Perceptions of Physicians' Behavior: Determinants of Patient Commitment to the Therapeutic Relationship," *Journal of Community Health* 4 (1979), pp. 280–290.
62. Molloy, *Dress for Success*, p. 93.
63. Hoult, pp. 324–328; Bickman, pp. 48–51.
64. Michael Korda, *Power: How to Get It, How to Use It* (New York: Ballantine, 1975), pp. 75, 79–80.
65. R. L. Zweigenhaft, "Personal Space in the Faculty Office: Desk Placement and the Student–Faculty Interaction," *Journal of Applied Psychology* 61 (1976), pp. 529–532.
66. Korda, chap. 8.
67. Korda, p. 256.
68. N. M. Henley, *Body Politics* (Englewood Cliffs, NJ: Prentice-Hall, 1977), p. 136.
69. Mary B. Parlee, "Women Smile Less for Success," *Psychology Today* 12 (1979), p. 16.
70. Carr-Ruffino, 1st ed., p. 407, reprinted by permission of Wadsworth Publishing Co.; Mehrabian, 1980; M. LaFrance and C. Mayo, *Moving Bodies: Nonverbal Communication in Social Relationships* (Monterey: Brooks/Cole, 1978), pp. 155–170.
71. Martin Remland, "Developing Leadership Skills in Nonverbal Communication: A Situational Perspective," *Journal of Business Communication* 3 (1981), pp. 17–29.
72. Carr-Ruffino, 1st ed., p. 407. Reprinted by permission of Wadsworth Publishing Co.
73. Sidney M. Jourard, *Disclosing Man to Himself* (Princeton, NJ: Van Nostrand, 1968).
74. Told to us by a Taiwanese businesswoman attending a communication seminar.
75. La Ray M. Barna, "Intercultural Communication Stumbling Blocks," in *Intercultural Communication: A Reader*, 5th ed., Larry A. Samovar and Richard E. Porter, eds. (Belmont, CA: Wadsworth, 1988), p. 296.
76. From Nancy J. Adler, *International Dimensions of Organizational Behavior*, 2nd ed. (Boston: PWS-Kent, 1991), pp. 77–79.
77. The hypothetical situations in the Checkpoint section of Chapter 5 were written by the authors on the basis of friends' experiences or adapted from experiences reported by Edward T. Hall in *The Silent Language, The Hidden Dimension*, and *Beyond Culture* (New York: Anchor Press/Doubleday, 1976) and by Hall and W. F. Whyte in "Intercultural Communication: A Guide to Men of Action," *Human Organization* 19 (Spring 1960), pp. 5–12.
78. Judith A. Sanders and Richard L. Wiseman, "The Effects of Verbal and Nonverbal Teacher Immediacy on Perceived Cognitive, Affective, and Behavioral Learning in the Multicultural Classroom," *Communication Education* 30 (October 1990), pp. 431–453; Joan Gorham and Diane M. Christophel, "The Relationship of Teachers' Use of Humor in the Classroom to Immediacy and Student Learning," *Communication Education* 39 (January 1990), pp. 46–62;

and Joan Gorham, "The Relationship Between Verbal Teacher Immediacy Behaviors and Student Learning," *Communication Education* 37 (January 1988), pp. 40–53.

79. Bernard B. Beegle, "The Message That Is Sent Without Words," *Supervisory Management* (February 1971), pp. 12–14.

80. Michael B. McCaskey, "The Hidden Messages Managers Send," *Harvard Business Review* 57 (November–December 1979), p. 148.

81. Adapted from "Cross-Cultural Relations Quiz," *The Bridge: A Journal of Cross-Cultural Affairs* 1 (Winter 1976–1977), p. 9.

6 Obstacles to Organizational Communication

A barrier is a roadblock that brings communication to a halt. An obstacle is a temporary blockage to communication that can be removed with effort.

Regardless of your business or professional position, you have probably acquired a few poor habits that create obstacles to communication. These obstacles can be overcome with patience and practice, but first they must be identified. To help you identify your own communication obstacles, this chapter describes those that are most common in organizations. Anyone, employee or employer, can create such obstacles. As you read this chapter, determine how skilled you are at recognizing and avoiding each obstacle.

COMMUNICATOR ANXIETY

Whether you are expressing your ideas to a colleague, participating in a group discussion, interviewing or being interviewed, or giving a presentation, communicator anxiety can definitely be an obstacle to effective communication in the work environment. Research indicates that people who experience a high level of communication anxiety are at a disadvantage when compared with more talkative, outgoing employees. For example, people with high anxiety are perceived as less competent, are less likely to be offered an interview, make a poorer impression during interviews, typically hold lower status and lower paying positions, experience less job satisfaction, and are less likely to be promoted to supervisory positions.[1]

For many people, giving a presentation causes more anxiety than other forms of communication. In fact, a study by R. H. Bruskin Associates found that fear of public speaking was the number one fear of the American people—even greater than the fear of death![2] On the other hand, in 1987 *The Wall Street Journal* reported research by AT&T and Stanford University that found that the single best question to predict high earning was, "Do you enjoy giving speeches?"[3] Those who answered that they did enjoy it were making "big bucks"; those who said, "You've got to be kidding!" were making much less. Thus, overcoming your speaking anxiety could have an impact on your potential earnings. The remainder of our discussion will concentrate on speaker anxiety, although the suggestions will apply to all types of communicator anxiety.

Before you can manage your anxiety, you need to know what kind of anxiety you have. Anxiety is composed of two types: situational and trait. **Situational anxiety**[4] refers to anxiety caused by factors present in a specific situation, such as speaking for the first time before an audience, speaking in front of the boss or instructor, and being graded or critiqued while speaking. **Trait anxiety**[5] refers to the internal anxieties an individual brings to the speaking situation, such as feelings of inadequacy, or fear of looking like a fool in front of others. In other words, situational anxiety is caused by a new or different situation while trait anxiety is caused by the speaker's personal feelings that exist regardless of the situation. Your own anxiety may be situational, it may be trait, or it could be a combination of both.

Situational Anxiety

Feeling nervous prior to a new communication situation is perfectly normal. Firing a troublesome employee, being interviewed for a job, presenting a controversial idea to your boss, selling a product to a new client, or approaching a banker for a loan are all examples of situations that could cause a nervous, butterfly-in-the-stomach, anxious feeling in just about everyone. Anytime we become anxious, afraid, or excited, our body's nervous system prepares us for action with a big shot of adrenaline, which accelerates the heart rate, sends extra oxygen to the central nervous system, heart, and muscles, dilates the eyes, raises the blood sugar level, and causes perspiration.

Actually, we should be grateful for this boost from our nervous system. Can you imagine a runner at an Olympic competition with absolutely no anxiety? The runner's performance would no doubt fall far short of winning a medal. Speakers who view increased heart rate, dry mouth, and sweaty palms as normal excitement necessary for a dynamic job of communicating find that their anxiety becomes manageable and often disappears completely. Poor communicators, who tend to view physical reactions to situational anxiety with fear and as further proof that they are poor speakers, often find that their anxiety becomes worse as the presentation proceeds.

Even very experienced speakers—like Mike Wallace of "60 Minutes"—experience speaker anxiety. Accept the fact that almost every speaking situation will produce butterflies in your stomach. According to Edward R. Murrow, a great journalist of the past, "The only difference between the pros and the novices is that the pros have trained their butterflies to fly in formation."[6] The following advice will help you control your butterflies.

Prepare and Practice! ■ Nothing will make you more nervous than knowing you are not adequately prepared. After all, isn't your nervousness really fear that you will look foolish in the eyes of your colleagues, boss, or customers? Lack of preparation makes such a possibility much more likely. First of all, analyze your audience and plan your presentation and any visual aids for this particular group. Read Chapters 11 to 13 in this book for helpful suggestions on preparing presentations and visual aids.

Next, prepare easy-to-follow notes and practice your presentation three or more times from beginning to end, speaking aloud. Mentally thinking through your speech is *not* the same as practicing aloud. The environment you practice in should be as close as possible to the actual speaking environment. If you will be standing during your presentation, stand while practicing; if you will be using visual aids, practice presenting them. Time yourself to see if you need to shorten or lengthen the presentation. Finally, anticipate possible audience questions and prepare to answer them. Knowing that you are well prepared will help ease much of your anxiety.

Warm Up ■ Prior to giving your presentation, warm up your neck and arm muscles and your voice. Sing up and down the scale, as singers do before a concert; read aloud a memo or page from a book, varying your volume, pitch, emphasis, and rate; do several stretching exercises such as touching your toes and rolling your head from side to side; practice various gestures such as pointing, pounding your fist, or shrugging your shoulders. Speakers are no different from singers who warm up their voices, musicians who warm up their fingers, or athletes who warm up their muscles before a performance. Warm-up helps them relax and ensures that they are ready to perform their best.

Use Deep Breathing ■ One quick way to calm your butterflies is to take in a deep breath, hold it while you count to five, then slowly exhale. As you exhale, your stress and tension drain away. Do the same thing a second time if needed.

Use an Introduction That Will Relax You as Well as Your Listeners ■ Most speakers find that once they get a favorable audience reaction, they relax. This is one reason why so many speakers start with humor; it relaxes them as well as their listeners. If a humorous introduction is inappropriate or you are not comfortable with humor, perhaps relating a personal experience would work. Whatever your preference, make your introduction work to put *you* at ease.

Concentrate on Communicating Your Meaning ■ Instead of worrying about how you look or how you sound, center your energy on getting your *meaning* across to your listeners. Pay close attention to their nonverbal reactions. If they look confused, explain the idea again or add another example. A speaker who is really concentrating on the listeners soon forgets about being nervous.

Use Visual Aids ■ Some speakers do not know what to do with their hands. Using visual aids, such as transparencies or flip charts, not only adds eye-catching movement to your presentation but also keeps you so busy there is no time to worry about hand gestures. Chapter 12 gives specific advice on preparing and using visual aids.

Trait Anxiety

Whereas nearly everyone experiences situational anxiety, fewer people experience trait anxiety. Trait anxiety, or communication apprehension, is a personal, internal feeling about communication. People with high trait anxiety often feel that they are different from other speakers, have a history of negative speaking experiences, and consider themselves inferior to others.[7] So, if you feel like you are going to be more nervous than anyone else in your group, or if you have had several negative speaking experiences in the past, or if you are worried that your audience will know more about your topic than you and could do a better job of presenting it, there is a good chance that you have trait anxiety.

By the way, although some speakers do show outward signs of nervousness, most nervousness is internal and is rarely obvious to an audience. The best way to prove this to yourself is to videotape yourself. Most people are amazed that their inner turmoil is essentially invisible to others.

Although many procedures have been used to manage trait anxiety,[8] most of them require professional assistance. One successful way to manage trait anxiety that you can do by yourself is called **positive imagery** (or visualization).[9] Using positive imagery requires using your imagination. Instead of thinking of all the things you will do wrong and how nervous you will feel when you speak, create a detailed positive and vivid mental image of yourself confidently preparing for and giving a successful presentation. In other words, instead of imagining failure—as most speakers with trait anxiety do—imagine success.

Positive imagery has been used in athletic programs for years. One of the first studies investigated the effects of positive imagery on basketball players. Students were divided into three groups. All three groups were shown how to effectively shoot a basket. Group one was then told to practice shooting baskets for 20 minutes a day for three weeks. Group two was told not to touch a basketball for three weeks; instead they were to spend 20 minutes a day imagining themselves shooting baskets. If they imagined a miss, they were to correct it and continue practicing. Group three had no physical or mental practice of any kind. After three weeks, the students in all three groups were tested. Those who had practiced mentally had improved the same as the students who had practiced physically (about 24 percent); however, the students with no practice had not improved at all.[10]

Athletes such as golfer David Duval commonly use positive imagery to enhance performance. Here, Duval is checking the lay of the green for his putt and visualizing the path he wants the ball to take. (© *Al Behrman/AP Laserphoto*)

Sports psychologist Jim Loehr says that 80 to 85 percent of the top athletes use positive imagery in their training.[11] Tennis players Chris Evert and Martina Navratilova, figure skaters Kristi Yamaguchi and Brian Boitano, and gymnast Mary Lou Retton are just a few of the athletes who regularly use mental imagery. In an interview about her Olympic gold-medal-winning performance of 1984, Retton recalls: "Before I dropped off to sleep inside the Olympic Village, I did what I always do before a major competition—mind-scripted it completely. I mentally ran through each routine, every move, imagining everything done perfectly."[12]

Psychologists tell us that we act as the person we "see" ourselves to be. If we say to ourselves and others such things as, "I don't see myself as a person who speaks out in meetings" or "I couldn't possibly get up in front of 100 people," then we won't. *No amount of lecture, encouragement, or practice will make you into a confident professional speaker as long as deep down you believe yourself to be a nervous or ineffective speaker.*

Therefore, to change any negative pictures you have of your speaking ability into positive ones, look two or three months into your future and picture yourself as the speaker you would like to be. Write down the specific characteristics you desire to develop. Now close your eyes and mentally picture this ideal you on the day of your speech, feeling confident and giving a great presentation. For example, see yourself walking confidently up to the front of a group; see how professionally you are dressed; see yourself giving a clear, well-organized, and entertaining talk; feel yourself enjoying the talk; feel relaxed and warm; notice the direct eye contact you use and the way you retain your composure when a late arriver slams the door; hear yourself giving a great finish to the presentation and the audience applause as you walk proudly back to your seat. Say to yourself, "I am a good speaker," and say it like you mean it.

As you picture yourself being successful, don't forget to feel successful. Words + vivid mental pictures + feelings = confidence. You need to say it, see it, and feel it if you want to change a negative mental picture into a positive one. Positive imagery works because your subconscious does not know the difference between your real and your imagined experiences. Each time you vividly imagine yourself giving a successful presentation your confidence will grow just like it would if you had actually given a successful presentation. "Numerous studies have confirmed the fact that vividly experienced imagery, imagery that is both seen and felt, can substantially affect brain waves, blood flow, heart rate, skin temperature, gastric secretions, and immune response."[13] In other words, imagining yourself being attacked while walking to your car creates many of the same physiological responses as actually being attacked. In fact, neuroscientists using brain-imaging technology on athletes recently found that athletes who imagined a movement activated the same areas in the brain as athletes who actually performed the movement.[14]

The following Awareness Check is a positive imagery exercise written by a seminar participant in an attempt to overcome her speaking anxiety. You will want to write and practice your own imagery exercise to include the specific speaker qualities of interest to you. As you complete this exercise, imagine that you are the person being described.

AWARENESS CHECK: POSITIVE IMAGERY

Directions: For the best effect, have someone read this to you, or tape it and then listen to it.

It is important to get in the mood to visualize. Close your eyes and get as comfortable as you can. Remember to keep an open body posture with your feet flat on the floor and your arms resting comfortably but not touching. Now, slowly take a deep breath . . . hold it . . . and exhale slowly. As you exhale feel the tension draining away. Take another deep breath . . . hold it . . . and slowly exhale through your nose. Now one more time, breathe deeply . . . hold it . . . slowly exhale and begin normal breathing. Imagine yourself as the "I" in the following visualization:

(continued)

I am leaning toward the mirror in my bathroom so I can get a good look at my face. Suddenly, the mirror clouds over. When it clears, I am looking at myself sitting in my usual seat in speech class on the day of my first speech. It is my turn to speak.

As I rise from my seat, I direct the butterflies of excitement in my stomach into positive energy. I can do this because I have practiced carefully and know I am well prepared. As I turn to face my colleagues, I draw in a deep breath, stand up straight, and begin to speak. An aura of confidence radiates from within as I speak. My body shows no tension. My breathing is paced. My motions are fluid, and my gestures are graceful. My shoulders stay relaxed and down. My voice does not quiver or shake. It is pitched low and is well modulated and easy for everyone to hear. My eyes scan from student to student, drawing their complete attention. My mind is rested and calm, allowing my words to flow evenly and to be clear and concise.

As I speak, I have no trouble remembering each point of my speech. I can see the outline of my speech clearly in my mind and refer to my notes only briefly. I make use of dramatic pauses to stress important points within the speech. It is obvious that the audience is understanding what I am saying and that they are enjoying my speech. My words continue to flow smoothly and my transitions are especially good. Each idea is spoken clearly and confidently. There are no mistakes.

As the speech winds down, my words are chosen carefully and powerfully. The audience is paying complete attention. I end with a bang! I know from the enthusiastic applause and positive comments that my speech has been a total success! I feel so proud as I gather my visuals and walk to my seat. The mirror clouds over again, and I am back in my bathroom. I feel confident and happy. I am looking forward to giving my speech. I begin to dress for the day. . . . Now take a deep breath . . . hold it . . . and slowly let it out. Do this several more times and slowly return to the room.

How did you do? Could you see yourself? If you couldn't, don't be concerned. Visualizing is easier for some people than for others. If you are used to picturing your speaking abilities negatively, trying to see yourself in a positive light may feel not only phony but almost impossible. However, if we can't even imagine ourselves giving a confident presentation, how can we expect to actually give one? To become confident speakers, we must think of ourselves as confident. Two recent studies found that speakers who participated in a similar exercise only one time had less communication anxiety than speakers who did not use it or who used some other anxiety reduction method.[15] However, you may need to practice positive imagery for up to four weeks before you begin to feel comfortable with the new you.

We do not have to take a backseat to other more confident people. Taking control of nervousness and anxiety is much easier once we identify it. Almost everyone experiences situational anxiety in new situations. We can manage this type of anxiety with specific means: preparation and practice, warming up, deep breathing, relaxing introductions, concentrating on our message, and effective visual aids. Many people also find that positive imagery makes situational anxiety more manageable.

Trait anxieties are personal anxieties that we bring to a communication situation. Although more difficult to control than situational anxiety, trait anxiety can be effectively managed through positive imagery. As Gail Dusa, president of the National Council for Self-Esteem, says, "Visualization, in many ways, is nothing more complicated than involving your imagination in goal-setting. It's not hocus-pocus or magic. When you use your imagination to enhance goal-setting you get fired up, excited. This enthusiasm equips you with more mental energy to put into the task."[16] Don't forget also that positive imagery can be used to manage more than just speaker anxiety: It can help us control our anxiety in employment interviews, problem-solving discussions, meetings with angry customers, or any situation where our confidence needs a boost.

INADEQUATE PREPARATION

Inadequate preparation can make communicator anxiety even worse. Unfortunately, many of us view communication as a simple process requiring almost no special preparation.

> Cass Carlyle, the manager of a television station, found out the hard way the results of poor preparation. Several newscasters had complained about errors in a special newscast prepared by Al Mendez, the man Carlyle was grooming for the position of top newscaster. Although Carlyle thought Mendez's newscast was exceptionally good, he promised to speak to Mendez about the matter. He was discussing a problem sponsor with his secretary when Al walked by. Acting without thinking, Carlyle called Mendez into his office. Al noticed the uneasiness in Carlyle's voice and wondered what was wrong.
>
> "I've, uh, wanted to talk to you about your news special," Carlyle began. "We don't . . . we aren't always as careful of the basic infor-

mation ... the foundation of facts as it were ... not as careful as we should be."

"What do you mean?" Al asked, standing and putting his hands flat on Carlyle's desk.

"Well, it's just that some of the others feel you plunged ahead a little too fast without checking on certain basic background information."

"Are they questioning my competence as a news analyst?"

"No, no, it's nothing like that ... they just note, for example, that your treatment of the Middle East crisis was not historically accurate."

Mendez leaned over the desk and raised his voice, "They're saying I did a bad job of research, is that it?"

"Well, no, I wouldn't say that precisely." Carlyle wasn't sure what he wanted to say. Things weren't going as he had expected.

From this point on, with both men emotionally upset, the simple, friendly conference that Carlyle had intended turned into a shouting match and ended with Al's resignation. It had never occurred to Carlyle that the final result of the conference would be so disastrous. He had lost an extremely valuable employee, one he might not be able to replace.[17]

If Carlyle had planned what he wanted to say and the possible effect it would have on Mendez, and if he had selected a time when his own mind was free from other problems, the conversation could have ended very differently.

Good communicators are aware the communication is *irreversible* (once a particular idea has been expressed, its effect cannot be completely erased). As a result, they know that they must plan their messages carefully. How carefully do you prepare your comments, orders, and instructions before meeting with people?

VAGUE INSTRUCTIONS

Many of us give vague, easily misunderstood instructions due to lack of preparation. But in some cases, we give confusing instructions even when we prepare the instructions ahead of time.

Try the following exercise, which we will call Project F, before reading further in the chapter.[18] Project F will give you an idea of how difficult it is to communicate instructions to others. Chances are that your listeners will interpret your instructions differently from what you intend. Be careful about blaming your listeners if they don't follow your instructions correctly—you may be the problem.

AWARENESS CHECK: GIVING INSTRUCTIONS

SITUATION: PROJECT F

You are an engineer in an aerospace corporation and are working on a control panel for a top secret missile. A demonstration is planned for the Air Force this afternoon. The unit was sent to the demonstration site by Federal Express. To make sure no one tampered with the panel, you designed a secret access device, composed of parts that must be properly assembled into an F shape (F for fail-safe) and then scanned by a computer.

Solution

Five minutes before the demonstration is to begin, you receive an urgent message by telex from a technician asking for the secret instructions for assembling the access device—the two engineers who know the instructions and were to conduct the demonstration have not arrived. The Air Force is insistent that the demonstration must go on at the scheduled time. Knowing there is no time for him to ask questions, how would you instruct the technician to assemble the pieces? Try the following experiment:

Directions: Using the copy machine, enlarge and then cut out the pieces of the fail-safe device at the bottom of this paragraph. Carefully plan the easiest way to explain Project F, and then, giving each person a set of the cut-out parts (but not the solution), instruct various people (colleagues, employees, friends) on how to assemble the device. Stand far enough from them so that you cannot see what they are doing. Have them sit so that they can't see each other's work. Don't let them ask any questions. Remember, they must finish in 5 minutes!

Were you successful? If not, compare your instructions with the sample instructions included in Checkpoint item 2 at the end of this chapter. Then compare your instructions with the following eight rules for giving clear instructions.[19]

1. Begin with an overall picture.
2. Use a minimum number of words.
3. Use simple, easily understood words.
4. Be specific.
5. Use simple comparisons.
6. Use repetition.
7. Number or "signpost" objects, steps, or sets of instructions.
8. Use good delivery techniques.

Let's take a careful look at each step. Although you probably don't instruct people at work on how to draw geometric shapes, we are using such tasks to clarify certain steps. The principles in giving instructions are the same regardless of whether you are explaining how to boot a new computer, how to assemble a piece of machinery, or what work must be completed by your employees before noon.

Rule 1: Begin with an Overall Picture ■ The first step in giving instructions of any kind is to give a brief, but vivid, mental picture of the task. In other words, give a frame of reference from which the person can interpret your instructions. For example, the overall picture for geometric shape *a* in Figure 6.1 might include the following information:

> Before we begin with specifics, let me give you a brief overview. The drawing includes three squares that are 1 inch on each side. The squares are stacked on top of each other so that only one corner of each square touches the one below it; they do not overlap. They resemble a child's stack of building blocks that is beginning to topple to the left. I will begin my instructions with the top square and work downward. Okay . . . now draw a 1-inch square in the top left portion of your paper. . . .

This overall picture will give the listeners a mental image of the drawing that should make it easier for them to accurately follow your subsequent instructions.

To make accurate decisions, employees must be aware of all relevant information. Therefore, an *overview* could include the following information: the importance of the assignment, management's ideas about the task, the importance of accomplishing the task by a certain time or date, and why past attempts at completing the task failed.

Figure 6.1 Geometric shapes.

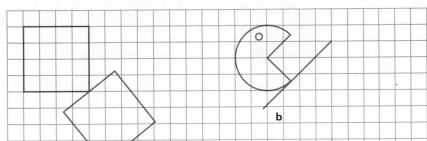

Rule 2: Use a Minimum Number of Words ■ The more words you use, the more likely you are to cause confusion. If you are prepared and know what you want to say, you should be able to convey your message in as few words as possible. For example, compare "Draw a 1-inch square in the center of your paper" with the following wordy instructions:

> In the center of your paper draw a 1-inch line that is parallel with the top of the paper. Now go to the right end of that line and draw a 1-inch line downward that is parallel to the right side of the paper. Next go to the left end of the original line and draw another 1-inch line downward. You should have three lines of a square. Complete the square by connecting the bottom points of the two vertical lines.

Although these instructions are fairly clear, they are unnecessary and a waste of time.

Rule 3: Use Simple, Easily Understood Words ■ In giving instructions, you should not be trying to impress people with your vocabulary. Do not assume that everyone knows certain words, especially jargon or technical terms.

> A plumber wrote to the U.S. Bureau of Standards about using hydro-chloric acid to clean drain pipes. . . .
> Several days later he received this reply, "The efficacy of hydro-chloric acid is indisputable but the corrosive residue is incompatible with metallic permanence."

Confused, he wrote again and asked if the acid is "okay to use or not."

A second letter advised him, "We cannot assume responsibility for the production of toxic and noxious residue and suggest that you use an alternative procedure."

Still baffled, he wrote, "Do you mean it's okay to use hydrochloric acid?"

A final letter resolved the question. "Don't use hydrochloric acid. It eats the hell out of pipes!"[20]

The skilled communicator uses terms that fit into everyone's frame of reference. For example, suppose you were explaining how to draw the second square in geometric shape *a* in Figure 6.1. You might tell your listeners:

Go to the bottom right corner of your first square and draw a 1/2-inch line at a 45-degree angle toward the northeast corner of your paper. Then go back to the same point and extend that line 1/2 inch downward toward the southwest corner of your paper.

Most adults should know what a 45-degree angle is and where the north, east, south, and west sides of the paper are located. They should also know the meanings of such words as *perpendicular, tangent, parallel, horizontal, vertical, diameter, circumference,* and so on. Unfortunately, however, many adults do *not* know such terms. Even when jargon or technical terms are used regularly in your business, you should briefly define their meaning. Those who are to follow your instructions might not be feeling well that day, or they might be preoccupied with personal problems. Using simple words increases the likelihood that your instructions will be accurately followed. It also reduces the risk that you will misuse a term (such as saying "horizontal" when you mean "vertical").

Rule 4: Be Specific ■   In addition to using few words and simple words, you must also be as specific as possible. For example, a specific yet simple explanation of how to position the second square in geometric shape *a* (Figure 6.1) is shown in Figure 6.2. For the right-hand triangle in geometric shape *c*, you might use instructions like those in Figure 6.3.

Rule 5: Use Simple Comparisons ■   People learn more easily when they can compare or contrast a new task with an old one. Mentioning that today's task is identical to yesterday's except for one additional step makes today's task much easier. To make sure that your comparisons fit into the frames of reference of those who are to follow your instructions, keep all compar-

Figure 6.2 Instructions for second square of shape *a* in Figure 6.1.

1. Draw a one-inch square in the upper left-hand portion of your paper.

2. Now in pencil, or in your mind, label the upper left-hand corner "a," the upper right-hand corner "b," the lower right-hand corner "c," and the lower left-hand corner "d."

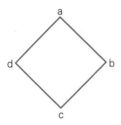

3. Picture the second square in your mind. The second square is identical to the first in size and has the same lettered corners, but will be rotated so that corner "a" points toward the top of the paper, corner "c" toward the bottom of the paper, corner "b" toward the right of the paper, and corner "d" toward the left.

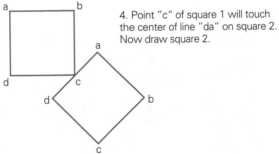

4. Point "c" of square 1 will touch the center of line "da" on square 2. Now draw square 2.

isons simple. For example, you might compare the geometric shapes in Figure 6.1 as follows:

- Shape *a* resembles a stack of building blocks toppling to the left.
- Shape *b* looks like a pie rolling down a hill with one-fourth of the pie missing; or it looks like Pac-Man.
- Shape *c* looks like a large ball wedged between two bookends.

Rule 6: Use Repetition ■ Most people need information repeated before they completely understand it. When giving instructions, repeat each set of instructions or steps. If the instructions are especially long or

Figure 6.3 Instructions for right-hand triangle shape *c* (Figure 6.1).

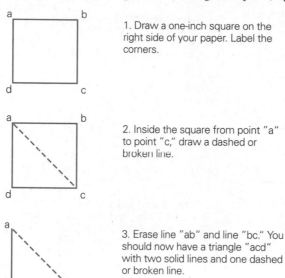

1. Draw a one-inch square on the right side of your paper. Label the corners.

2. Inside the square from point "a" to point "c," draw a dashed or broken line.

3. Erase line "ab" and line "bc." You should now have a triangle "acd" with two solid lines and one dashed or broken line.

complicated, give a brief summary after explaining several steps. And finally, after you've given all instructions, review the entire procedure. Some managers eliminate the final summary because they are rushed, but the final summary often clarifies a confusing item or points out an area of possible misunderstanding. The final summary also gives you a chance to ensure that all necessary instructions were given correctly.

Rule 7: Number or "Signpost" Objects, Steps, or Sets of Instructions ■ Instead of saying "And the next step . . . ," say "The third step . . . ." Instead of saying "When you finish that, I want you to . . . ," say "The third thing I want you to do before noon is . . . ." This makes it easier for everyone to keep track of the instructions. Also, when possible use mnemonic devices (memory formulas such as acronyms, rhymes, and acrostics) to simplify retention of your instructions.[21] For example, remembering the rhyme "Thirty days hath September . . ." to remember the days of the month, or the acronym NATO to remember North Atlantic Treaty Organization, or the acrostic "Every good boy does fine" to remember that the lines on the treble clef are EGBDF, are a few examples of mnemonic devices we use regularly. Make it as easy as possible for your listeners to understand and remember your key ideas.

Rule 8: Use Good Delivery Techniques ■ Glance directly at your listeners while speaking, and watch for nonverbal indicators of confusion (such as a frown or raised eyebrows). Look and sound confident. If you don't appear to have confidence in your instructions, why should others? And of course, make sure you speak loudly enough to be heard easily.

If you follow these eight rules, your instructions will be understood. However, don't assume that you have communicated what you meant. It is not uncommon for listeners to think they understand completely when they really do not. Therefore, when possible, ask them to rephrase your instructions in their own words, encourage them to ask for clarification of any confusing points, and supply a written copy of your instructions for further clarification.

JUMPING TO CONCLUSIONS

Jumping to conclusions (or inference–observation confusion) occurs when a person fails to distinguish between what was actually observed firsthand and what was only inferred (or assumed). The following incident shows an employee who made an inference and then acted on the inference as though it were fact:

> Arlene Johnson, 36, had worked for the Farwell Sheet and Tube Company as an inside salesperson for ten years. Her duties consisted of handling telephone orders from customers, processing orders placed by outside Farwell salespeople, and responding to letters of inquiry about company products.
>
> Outside sales positions paid substantially more and held more prestige than inside jobs. Johnson had requested a transfer to outside selling at the time of her annual performance review in December. Henry Browning, sales manager, had promised her the first opening in a sales territory. The most likely possibility was George Madison's territory, since Madison was to retire on his sixty-fifth birthday in March. It became general office knowledge that Johnson was to have Madison's post.
>
> Arlene had had two years of college but was forced to withdraw when her father became chronically ill. She had always hoped to complete her education. She had taken several night courses but somehow had never been able to accumulate enough credits to graduate.
>
> Arlene had not progressed as fast as she had anticipated and occasionally remarked to friends that she felt the lack of a college degree had held her back. However, she felt she had worked hard at Farwell. During the last two years she had developed several shortcuts in order-processing procedure. Browning had complimented her for initiative in introducing these innovations.
>
> In mid-January, Browning began interviewing applicants for sales positions in the firm. Johnson heard via the grapevine that the company was looking for a salesperson from the outside to take over Madison's territory. Johnson decided to check with Browning and was again assured that the next vacant territory would be hers.

Two weeks later, Johnson, whose desk faced Browning's inner office, saw a tall, well-groomed young man enter the sales manager's office at 9:30 Monday morning. Around 10:00 a.m., Browning, Madison, and the young man emerged. Johnson heard Browning tell Madison, "Although Mr. Calvin will not graduate officially until next week, he's finished his exams and is ready to start at once. I suggest you take him along with you, George, for the rest of the day and tomorrow as well, so he can get the feel of your territory."

Henry Browning shook hands with Calvin and said, "Good luck, Sam. We're glad to have you with us. I knew your father well."

At lunch, three other members of the office staff told Arlene the word around the office was that a new man was being hired to take over Madison's territory. Johnson blurted out, "Well, that's about all I can take!" She returned to her desk, collected her personal effects, and stomped out of the office.

The next morning, two events occurred that, to Browning, seemed unrelated. He received a bitter letter of resignation from Johnson, and he placed Sam Calvin on the payroll—as a trainee for the inside sales force.[22]

Obviously, Johnson jumped to a conclusion that had an unhappy consequence for her.

AWARENESS CHECK: FACTS VERSUS INFERENCES

To evaluate your skills at distinguishing facts from inferences, carefully read the following story and answer the statements by circling either T (definitely true), F (definitely false), or ? (not stated in the story).[23]

STORY A

John Phillips, the research director of a Midwestern food products firm, ordered a crash program of development on a new process. He gave three of his executives authority to spend up to $50,000 each without consulting him. He sent one of his best men, Harris, to the firm's West Coast plant with orders to work on the new process independently. Within one week Harris produced a highly promising new approach to the problem.

STATEMENTS ABOUT STORY A

1. Phillips sent one of his best men to the West
   Coast plant.   T   F   ?
2. Phillips overestimated Harris' competence.   T   F   ?
3. Harris failed to produce anything new.   T   F   ?

4. Harris lacked authority to spend money without consulting Phillips.　　　　　　　T　F　?

5. Only three of Phillips' executives had authority to spend money without consulting him.　　T　F　?

6. The research director sent one of his best men to the firm's West Coast plant.　　　　T　F　?

7. Three men were given authority to spend up to $50,000 each without consulting Phillips.　T　F　?

8. Phillips had a high opinion of Harris.　　　T　F　?

9. Only four people are referred to in the story.　T　F　?

10. Phillips was research director of a food production firm.　　　　　　　　　　　T　F　?

11. Although Phillips gave authority to three of his best men to spend up to $50,000 each, the story does not make clear whether Harris was one of these men.　　　　　　　　　　　T　F　?

The answers to Story A are given in the Checkpoint section at the end of this chapter.

It is quite possible that your job requires you to make a certain number of inferences or assumptions, and sometimes the nature of the job may also require that you act on those inferences. However, in such cases, you know that you are making an inference and you also know that there is a certain amount of risk involved. In other words, you are taking a calculated risk. As long as you recognize the risk and are willing to make changes upon receiving more evidence, there should be no problem. Problems arise when people are unaware that they have made any inferences and think, instead, that their inferences are facts. When these inferences include other workers, management, job assignments, possible promotion, and interests of clients or customers, communication breakdown is likely to occur. How often do you jump to conclusions in your communication with others?

BYPASSING

When a person assumes that words have definite meanings and that other people use the same meanings, **bypassing** (talking past one another) may occur. One source of bypassing is that people have *different meanings for* *the same word.* Consider the example of the secretary who ordered engraved stationery for his boss. He told the inexperienced salesperson that his boss was tired of the old stationery and wanted something different. Several possibilities were discussed and rejected. Finally the secretary said, "Let's keep it simple. Put the name in the center." When the 500 sheets of stationery arrived, the secretary was shocked to find his boss' name in the exact middle of each sheet instead of in the center at the top as he had intended.

To keep similar problems from arising, and to clarify the meanings of the term *urgent*, a printing company published the following definitions:

- "As soon as possible" = Complete in two or three days.
- "Rush" = Complete today.
- "Hot" = Don't drop what you're doing, but do it next.
- "Now" = Drop everything.

Managers and employees often have different meanings for the same words. When a boss tells an employee that a raise is "likely"—which to the boss means a 51 percent chance but to the employee means an 85 to 95 percent chance—misunderstanding and disappointment are sure to arise.

To further your understanding of bypassing, select four people with whom you regularly communicate and ask them each to take the test in the following Awareness Check without looking at the others' answers. See how closely all of you agree on meanings. Do you see any terms that could cause future misunderstandings among you?

AWARENESS CHECK: MEANINGS OF TERMS

Directions: Decide what percentage of certainty (from 0 to 100 percent) is implied when you use each of the following terms. For example, if you tell someone that your attendance at the staff party is "likely," do you mean there is an 85 percent chance of being there, a 30 percent chance, or what? Write the percentage that expresses your usual meaning next to each term. Ask three other people to do the same thing, and compare answers.

TERMS COMMONLY USED IN BUSINESS[24]

____ 1. Absolute

____ 2. Certain

———   **3.** A cinch

———   **4.** Indefinite

———   **5.** Open to question

———   **6.** Possible

———   **7.** Probable

———   **8.** Risky

———   **9.** Settled

———   **10.** A sure thing

———   **11.** A toss-up

———   **12.** Unlikely

Vague phrases such as "good job," "as soon as possible," "in a couple of minutes," and so on are sure to have different meanings for different people and will often cause misunderstandings if you are not careful.

Another way bypassing happens is when people have *different words for the same meaning.* For example, an American motorist made the following observations about the meaning of British road signs:

> If we saw a sign ROADUP, we came to learn that it meant "Road Taken Up" or "Road Repairs Ahead." Near Chepstow we were asked to detour (the British call it DIVERSION) because, said the man who directed us, there had been a BUMP down the road. We could see two cars locked together in a collision. Near London, you may find a warning DUAL CARRIAGE WAY, meaning "Divided Highway." Instead of "No Passing" the sign reads NO OVERTAKING. When the danger zone is passed, you come to END OF PROHIBITION! You are told not to "Stop" but HALT at highway intersections. If you try to park in a no-parking area, you find a sign NO WAITING.[25]

To prevent bypassing, both managers and employees should ask for feedback from one another to determine what each really means. Assuming that the listener's frame of reference is the same as yours can only lead to misunderstanding. Refer to Chapter 1 for additional examples of frame of reference differences that can cause bypassing.

GENDER DIFFERENCES

The work force in most U.S. organizations over the last twenty-five years has dramatically changed. The influx of women into occupations and positions traditionally held by men (the number of female managers has doubled since 1972[26]) and the movement of men into traditionally female occupations such as nursing and office jobs have increased the likelihood of gender-related obstacles to communication. As Judy Pearson states in her book *Gender and Communication:*

> Without a knowledge of the contrasting and similar communication styles of women and men, you are likely to encounter defeat in your interactions with others. It is less probable that you will have satisfying personal relationships, and your chances for success in your career are reduced.[27]

Complete the following Awareness Check to see if your perception of male–female communication differences agrees with current research findings.

AWARENESS CHECK: GENDER COMMUNICATION DIFFERENCES

Directions: For each statement, write "M" if you think it is more accurate of men; write "W" if you think it is more accurate of women. Then compare your responses with the answers and explanations drawn from the latest research.[28]

_____ 1. In office discussions, who usually talks more often?

_____ 2. Who is better at interpreting nonverbal cues?

_____ 3. When speaking to others, who tends to attach more tag questions (such as, "Don't you agree?") to statements?

_____ 4. Who is more likely to view talk in a competitive rather than cooperatitive manner?

_____ 5. In office discussions, who usually works harder to keep the conversation going?

_____ 6. During a conversation, who tends to interrupt more often?

_____ 7. Who is less likely to ask questions, especially if asking will reveal lack of knowledge?

_____ 8. When speaking, who tends to receive more attention from audience members?

_____ 9. Who do subordinates see as the more effective communicator?

_____ 10. When others are talking, who is more likely to make listening noises (to show interest and attention)?

1. *Men.* Despite the folklore that women talk more, research shows that in the classroom and the workplace, men talk more than women. In one experiment, male and female subjects were asked to orally describe pictures. The women's average description was approximately 3 minutes, while the average time for men was 13 minutes. Deborah Tannen reports a study of seven university faculty meetings that concluded that men "spoke more often and, without exception, spoke longer. . . . The longest contribution by a woman was still shorter than the shortest contribution by a man."[29]

2. *Women.* Women generally tend to be more proficient than men at nonverbal decoding. In a meta-analysis of sixty-one relevant studies, J. A. Hall found that women were more accurate decoders than men.[30] Anthropologist Edward Hall argues that greater nonverbal sensitivity is required of people who are in a subordinate position—as women traditionally have been.[31] Women's success at decoding may also be due to the high priority they tend to place on relationship development.

3. *Women.* Women use more tag questions such as "Isn't it?" They use more qualifiers such as "maybe" or "perhaps," exhibit excessive politeness, and use disclaimers such as, "This may sound silly, but . . ." Women are more likely to answer questions in a nonassertive, hedging style, rather than making a firm, declarative statement.[32] Even though, in the business world, this tentative style may be perceived as lacking power (something women should be aware of), it does leave "open the door for others to respond and express their opinions."[33]

4. *Men.* According to Julia Wood, communication rules taught during child play differ for men and women. Females are "encouraged to create and sustain interpersonal connections and respond to others" while males are "encouraged to emphasize independence and status."[34] As a result, women tend to use talk *cooperatively* ("It's important to invite others into conversations, wait your turn to speak, and respond to what others say."); men tend to use talk *competitively* ("Communication is an arena for proving yourself. Use talk to gain and hold attention, to wrest the talk stage from others; interrupt and reroute topics to keep you and your ideas spotlighted.").[35]

5. *Women.* Women work much harder than men to maintain a discussion. Sociologist Pam Fishman's research on married couples concludes that women initiate many more topics than do men. Men often "kill" topics by failing to respond or giving a minimal response, such as, "um" or "uh-huh."[36]

6. *Men.* D. Borisoff and L. Merrill found that men are more likely to interrupt others and are especially likely to interrupt women.[37] Judy Pearson and colleagues paired men and women and found that men interrupting women accounted for 96 percent of all interruptions.[38] On the other hand, after reviewing the current research on interrupting behavior, Deborah James and Sandra Clarke found the results inconclusive.[39]

7. *Men.* Although both genders certainly ask questions, Deborah Tannen notes that men tend to be more aware that asking a question is a public statement of lack of knowledge and that they may be judged less capable by those in power—reputation and even career may be affected. As a result, men are less likely to ask questions.[40] The problem is illustrated by an intern who received a low grade from her supervising physician: "It took her by surprise because she knew that she was one of the best interns in her group. She asked her supervisor for an explanation, and he replied that she didn't know as much as the others. She knew from her day-to-day dealings with her peers that she was one of the most knowledgeable, not the least. So she asked what evidence had led him to his conclusion. And he told her, 'You ask more questions.'"[41]

8. *Men.* Male trainers are seen as more authoritative and credible than are female trainers. Not only in training situations but also on professional newscasts, men are viewed as more credible anchors than women. One study demonstrated that audiences respond more favorably to messages from a man than from a woman. Thus, 92 percent of commercial voice-overs employ male voices.[42] A. Cann and W. D. Siegfried found that 82 percent of subjects preferred a male supervisor.[43]

9. *Women.* Despite the reluctance of many people to work for a female manager, women are seen as more supportive communicators. Female managers are viewed as more considerate, more open to new ideas, and more supportive of workers'

(continued)

efforts than are male managers. Both male and female subordinates report higher morale and job satisfaction when supervised by a woman.[44]

10. *Women.* According to Julia Wood, to show that they are attentive and interested in others, women are more likely than men to make listening noises (such as "um-hm," and "I know what you mean") while others are speaking. She attributes this to the differing cultural rules each is taught while young: Women are taught the importance of empathy and support; men generally are not.[45]

To summarize the Awareness Check answers, female communicators typically are better at decoding nonverbal cues in messages, view communication as a cooperative tool, make listening noises to show interest and attention, and work harder to maintain discussions. At the same time, they tend to be more tentative when making statements, often attaching tag questions (such as, "Isn't it?") to the ends of comments. Male communicators, on the other hand, talk more often and longer, view communication as a competitive tool, and are considered by others to be more credible and authoritative. At the same time, they tend to interrupt more often, may even stop conversations by responding with "Um" or "Uh-huh," and are less likely to ask questions.

Are differences in the way men and women communicate due to real, biological differences between the sexes or are they learned behaviors that correspond to social stereotypes? The general stereotype about men and women in business is that men are more assertive, rational, self-confident, and willing to lead, while women are more submissive, emotional, nurturing, and less willing to take responsibility.[46] In other words, men are seen as more task-oriented while women are seen as more supportive. However, the research is not conclusive on this point. For example, in studying gender and leadership style, two researchers concluded that the majority of studies do uphold the belief that men are more task-oriented while women are more supportive.[47] On the other hand, reviewing the statistical procedures used in gender research, three other researchers concluded that "very few expected sex differences have been firmly substantiated by empirical studies of isolated variables."[48]

It is important to point out that much of the research on gender was conducted in the laboratory setting using volunteer college students who had little organizational experience outside the classroom. This awareness led one researcher (reviewing studies on women in management) to report that research "conducted in the laboratory have yielded gender differences, while those conducted in the field [using real employees and managers] have not."[49]

Another problem with research on gender differences is that most laboratory studies use mixed male–female groups. Studies involving single-sex groups generally have found communication behavior (especially task-related acts) to be the same for both sexes. For example, Edwin Megargee found that when a high dominant woman was paired with a low dominant woman, the high dominant woman would assume leadership—the same as when high and low dominant males are paired. However, when a high dominant woman was paired with a low dominant man, the woman would "actively assign" the leadership to the man in 91 percent of the groups tested![50] If women behave differently in the presence of men, perhaps it is because they are reacting to social expectations, which lends support to the view that management style is more a function of sex-role socialization than of biological sex.

Even if men and women used the same communication techniques, would others perceive them in the same way? A study of training groups found that even when female trainees used more appropriate decision-making techniques than male trainees, they were evaluated less favorably by group members.[51]

Perhaps the business communicator of the future will be a more androgynous individual. The term *androgyny* comes from *andro*, meaning male, and *gyne*, meaning female, and denotes the integration of both masculine and feminine characteristics.[52] Sandra Bem believes that not all males are masculine and not all females are feminine; some androgynous individuals have both masculine and feminine personality characteristics.[53] Evaluating groups using Bem's Sex-Role Inventory,[54] the following was found:

1. The task-oriented leadership role was preferred by masculine individuals of both sexes.
2. The social-emotional leadership role was preferred by feminine individuals of both sexes.
3. Androgynous individuals of both sexes could use either role, and tended to adopt whatever role was not being used in the group.[55]

More research on communication and gender differences needs to be conducted before we can confidently answer whether gender differences are due to traits or to role expectations. Probably there are both biological and socialization differences between men and women. As more women move up in their organizations and women managers become commonplace, many of the gender-related obstacles to communication will likely disappear. In the meantime, the most effective communicators of both sexes will be those who understand the communication principles discussed throughout this text and who apply them in a considerate and flexible manner.

SEXUAL HARASSMENT

One of the surest obstacles to communication in the workplace is sexual harassment. The confirmation hearings for Supreme Court Justice Clarence Thomas refocused America's attention on this unpleasant topic. We would like to think that sexual harassment occurs rarely, but a survey of federal employees conducted in 1980 and again in 1988 by the U.S. Merit Systems Protection Board found that 42 percent of the women and 15 percent of the men reported having experienced sexual harassment.[56] And it's not only an American problem. One survey of several European countries reported that nearly 50 percent of those surveyed had experienced sexual harassment, and in a survey of Japanese women 70 percent reported some type of harassment.[57]

On July 3, 1991, the European Community adopted a sexual harassment code that defined sexual harassment as "unwanted conduct of a sexual nature, or other conduct based on sex affecting the dignity of women and men at work, including unwelcome physical, verbal or nonverbal conduct."[58]

Since the Civil Rights Act of 1964 it has been unlawful to discriminate in hiring on the basis of sex in the United States. However, it wasn't until 1980 that sexual harassment became a violation of Title VII of the Civil Rights Act.* Harassment is judged by its effects on the recipient, not by the intentions of the harasser. Because some people may regard any particular behavior as offensive and others not, the courts use what is called the *reasonable person rule* to determine whether a "reasonable person" would find the behavior in question offensive. There seems to be a gender problem in applying this rule to sexual harassment because "a reasonable woman and a reasonable man are likely to differ in their judgements of what is offensive."[60]

Although both women and men consider blatant behaviors, such as sexual bribery or sexual assault, to be harassment, they disagree in other areas. For example, women are more likely to consider gestures, stares,

---

* The 1980 "Guidelines of the U.S. Equal Employment Opportunity Commission" state: "Unwelcome sexual advances, requests for sexual favors, and other verbal or physical conduct of a sexual nature constitute sexual harassment when (1) submission to such conduct is made either implicitly or explicitly a term or condition of an individual's employment, (2) submission to or rejection of such conduct by an individual is used as the basis for employment decisions affecting such individual, or (3) such conduct has the purpose or effect of unreasonably interfering with an individual's work performance or creating an intimidating, hostile, or offensive working environment."[59]

and teasing harassment;[61] men do not typically consider these behaviors harassment.[62] Women tend to view sexual overtures from men at work to be insulting, whereas men often view similar overtures to be flattering.[63] Therefore, gender differences make the reasonable person rule difficult to apply.[64]

Effective communication requires trust and respect between communicators. By its very name sexual harassment creates an "intimidating, hostile, or offensive working environment" that interferes with communication and individual work performance. Therefore, it is not only a person's dignity that suffers but individual productivity as well. According to Susan Webb, turnover, absenteeism, and lost productivity caused by sexual harassment are costing large companies an average of $282.53 per employee each year.[65] Individuals and organizations need to become more sensitive to individual rights and differences. We will all benefit.

COMMUNICATION TECHNOLOGY

Although some people still view the recent advances in communication technology as "technobabble,"[66] the fact is that employees and managers who know when and how to harness the power of technology are the ones with an edge on the competition. Many of the most recent technological advances in telecommunications are listed in Table 6.1. The people who can keep these technological innovations from becoming obstacles to communication are those who are concerned with the cultural, social, and communication aspects of technology acquisition.[67] For example, what are the social and communication implications of call waiting? How does being put on hold in the middle of an important call affect a client or even a close friend, especially if it happens several times during the conversation? Does being put on hold send a message that we don't think the caller is as important as someone else? Businesses who are aware of the communication aspect of telephone technology have employees who know how to answer this question: When (if ever) does a call from a long-distance client take precedence over a call from a local client?

What are some possible effects of E-mail on the communication of a traditional organization? Suddenly, everyone can communicate instantly with everyone else in the company. Whereas Bill Gates claims much of Microsoft's success is due to their E-mail system, some companies have found it necessary to restrict E-mail use and have even eliminated electronic discussion groups completely.[68]

E-mail has both positive and negative aspects. The positive aspects include *task uses,* such as increased access to information as well as faster retrieval of information, and *social uses,* such as hobbies and recreational

Table 6.1 New Communication Technologies

- **On-line information services**   Personal access to services such as CompuServe or AOL as well as specialized databases such as Nexis and the Dow Jones News/Retrieval.

- **Electronic bulletin boards**   In the security of their homes, people discuss politics and environmental issues, get information about business opportunities and legal, tax, and accounting questions, play computer games together, and comment on hundreds of other possible topics.

- **Smart telephones**   Includes autodialing, call waiting, call forwarding, redialing, conference calling, and caller ID.

- **Modems and facsimile**   Fax and computer modems can transmit documents from one end of the country to the other in less than a minute.

- **Voice mail**   Directs phone calls, takes messages, and even distributes recorded messages to other phones.

- **Electronic mail (E-mail)**   Sends messages directly from your computer to any other computer.

- **Videoconferencing**   Electronic meetings that allow people at great distances to see and hear one another.

- **Workgroup computing**   Allows people to work together as teams by sharing information and coordinating activities.

- **Electronic data interchange (EDI)**   Documents, shipping orders, and so on are passed directly to another organization's computer over a telecommunications network, increasing transaction speed and reducing the need for paper storage.

Source: Adapted from Kenneth C. Laudon, Carol G. Traver, and Jane P. Laudon, *Information Technology and Society* (Belmont, CA: Wadsworth, 1994), pp. 204–215.

activities. A study conducted by Xerox Corporation supported their belief that their employees' social use of E-mail outweighed the costs. They found that social use of electronic mail had the following advantages:[69]

- Employees learned to use the system more rapidly.
- Social contacts often became valuable in later work tasks.
- Quality of work life improved for some employees.
- Creativity was enhanced.

On the other hand, there are some definite disadvantages to using E-mail. For example, messages sent by E-mail are not private and may live as long as "five years in someone's backup file or memory bank."[70] Also, because E-mail messages are usually brief and informal, senders often do not give them the same care they would give to a letter or memo. According to Charles Steinfield,

> In the absence of immediate feedback and the tempering effects of non-verbal cues and the physical presence of receivers, electronic messages can sometimes be perceived as overly critical or blunt, or can simply be misinterpreted. . . . In situations in which a response is meant to be critical, the absence of context can lead to its being interpreted as stronger criticism than intended.[71]

The following precautions should be followed:

- Don't send E-mail when you're angry.
- Don't write anything you wouldn't want published in the company newsletter.
- Realize an E-mail message is no more private than a phone message.
- Plan what you say. No message should be a flaming arrow.[72]

Kathleen Kelleher and Thomas Cross found that electronic meetings have many advantages over traditional meetings. For example, they are shorter, more task oriented, more organized and orderly, more equal in participation regardless of status, and more open in exchange of ideas than face-to-face meetings.[73] Other studies have found that participants consider the teleconference to be less threatening than face-to-face meetings, are less swayed by group norms, and reach decisions faster and are more innovative because more people are involved (meetings at one organization used to be attended by only six senior executives; now "more than 100 managers at 14 sites are able to participate in the monthly meetings").[74] Teleconferencing by computer exchange has the added advantages of allowing members to use the system when convenient for each of them rather than all at once and allowing time for research and careful thought before responses are given.[75]

Teleconferencing is not for everyone—especially not for people who don't know each other. In Chapter 2 we said that memos are best used to follow up a face-to-face meeting; this may be true of teleconferences as well. How and when to use teleconferences depends on the communication needs and capabilities of the participants and planners. Technological innovations can become obstacles to communication unless we consider them as just another resource to improve communication.

SUMMARY

Communication obstacles are some of the most common communication problems for managers and employees. Communicator anxiety (both situational and trait) can hinder communication success in one-to-one, group, interview, and public speaking situations. Positive imagery is one method of managing such anxiety. Inadequate preparation is another bothersome obstacle. The experiment with Project F demonstrated the problem of vague instructions. Jumping to conclusions occurs when we fail to distinguish between what was observed firsthand and what was only inferred. Bypassing is a problem due to the multiple meanings of words—we either have different meanings for the same word, or we use different words for the same meaning. The differences between the communication styles of men and women in the workplace (gender differences), whether real or perceived, cause many communication problems unless we are sensitive to them. Sexual harassment causes loss of human dignity and decreased productivity in the workplace. And finally, even technological advances in communication can cause obstacles to understanding if not used with care.

Successful communication is a result of constant effort. If you are willing to work at avoiding communication obstacles, your communication and even your business success should improve.

CHECKPOINT

Before continuing to the next chapter, check your understanding of Chapter 6 by completing the following exercises:

1. Check your answers about Story A (page 188):
    1. T   That's what the story says.
    2. ?   Story does not say whether he did or not.
    3. F   Story says he did produce something new.
    4. ?   Story does not say whether or not Harris had authority to spend.
    5. ?   Story does not say whether other than the three mentioned had such authority.
    6. T   That's what the story says.
    7. ?   Not all executives are necessarily men.
    8. ?   Story suggests this but does not specify it.
    9. ?   If Harris is one of the three given authority to spend $50,000, this would be true, but the story does not specify whether he is one of those three.
    10. T   That's what the story says.

11. ?   Story does not specify whether Phillips gave such authority to his best men.

2. If you have not attempted to explain Project F (see page 181) to at least one person, try it now. Then compare the instructions you used to the following instructions developed by Cindy Lewis, a communication workshop participant. Her instructions were given orally to five people (guests of the workshop participants); all five guests completed the puzzle within 5 minutes.

PROJECT F: ONE PERSON'S SUCCESSFUL INSTRUCTIONS

The five different shapes when assembled will be in the form of a capital letter *F*. Before you start putting the shapes together, let me briefly summarize.

By giving each shape a letter name *A* through *E*, then arranging them from the bottom of the *F* upward, you will form the capital letter *F* and complete the project. The top of your workspace will be considered north.

Start by laying each shape face up—you will see the black outline on the face of each piece. [Pause]

Locate the shape that best resembles an arrow, and name it Piece *D*. [Pause to give person time to find piece and name it]

Now, name the largest shape Piece *B*. [Pause]

Name the smallest of the shapes Piece *C*. [Pause]

Of the two remaining trianglelike shapes, name the one with the longest hypotenuse (longest side of a triangle) Piece *E*. [Pause]

Name the remaining shape Piece *A*. [Pause, then repeat *D* through *A*]

To arrange these shapes to form the capital letter *F* starting from the bottom, start with Piece *A*. The side with a 90-degree angle at each corner is the bottom of the figure. [Pause and repeat]

Piece *B* fits next, aligning the side with the same length as Piece *A* directly north of Piece *A*. Pieces *A* and *B* make the bottom half of the capital letter *F*. [Pause and repeat]

Next is Piece *C*. Piece *C* is similar in shape to Piece *A*, only smaller. Turn Piece *C* so the line with a 90-degree angle at each corner is at the bottom. You'll notice Piece *A* is also positioned this way. Place Piece *C* above Piece *B* so the lower-left corner of *C* meets the upper-left corner of *B*. [Pause and repeat]

Now position Piece *D* with the point of its arrow shape in a northwest direction, or pointing to the 11:00 position of a clock, above *C*. The same length sides will meet. [Pause and repeat]

Finally, position Piece *E* to complete the capital letter *F* shape by matching the same length side to Piece *D*. [Pause and repeat]

[If time remains, repeat all instructions briefly]

Congratulations on completing Project F!

3. In your experience, who are more often guilty of the obstacles covered in this chapter—managers or employees? Which obstacle causes you the most trouble? Plan ways to improve.

4. Select a situation in which anxiety seems to bother you (conversations, interviews, group discussions, or public speeches). Determine which type of anxiety bothers you the most, situational or trait. Plan some specific things you can do in the future to manage this anxiety. Discuss your plans with someone you trust.

5. Read the following communication situation involving Wolfson, John-
    son, and the buyers. Make a list of everything each person or group did
    that contributed to the breakdown. Refer to the information in Chapters
    1 to 6 in making your list. For example, was there a problem with the
    organization as a whole? Were any of the elements of communication
    involved in the breakdown—differences in frame of reference, poor
    channel choice, and so on? Did nonverbal messages contribute to the
    problem? Was anyone guilty of creating obstacles to communication?
    What type of managers or employees were they (hidden, blind, open,
    closed)? When you have finished, compare your answers with those
    given at the end of the story.

COMMUNICATION SITUATION: INPUT SYSTEMS, INC.[76]

Two months after Input Systems, Inc., moved to its new multimillion-dollar
home office after years of being housed in an old four-story building, a problem arose in the procurement section of the company over the placement of
the buyers' desks in a "bullpen" arrangement. Henry Wolfson, director of
the procurement (purchase) division, was in the midst of a crisis over delay in
delivery of an important installation when his secretary indicated he was
wanted on the phone. "Who is it now, Peggy?"

"Mr. Johnson, sir. He says it's urgent."

"Yeah, Bill. What is it?" Bill Johnson was the manager of the procurement
section and lately he had been a headache with his insistence that the buyers
were unhappy.

"It's the buyers, Henry. Five of our top employees are threatening to
resign unless . . . ."

"Can't you handle them, Bill?" Wolfson interrupted. "I've got enough
problems right now!"

"They insist on meeting with you."

"All right!" Wolfson growled. "Be here at 2:00 sharp!"

Johnson couldn't help smiling as he replaced the receiver. For the past
three weeks he had been trying to convince Wolfson that a serious problem
was brewing. Well, it certainly wasn't his fault that Wolfson had refused to
listen to him. He had tried!

At 2:00 a sullen group assembled in Wolfson's office. Just looking at all of
them angered Henry. They didn't have half the problems he had. Well, he
might as well get this mess over. "What's the trouble, this time?"

No one spoke. Tension mounted. Finally, Tom Rider, who had been the
ringleader behind the threatened resignations, stood up and blurted out, "All
right, I'll tell you what's wrong. Nobody tells anybody anything around here.
We did not know until the ground was already broken that our desks—I can't
say offices—were to be in a bullpen like that."

"Your facilities are certainly much better than they were in the old plant,"
Wolfson said, trying to reason with Tom.

"They are not. You can't do any work here. There's too much noise."

"Oh, come on now. The entire building is acoustically designed for low
noise level."

"Yeah, well, you haven't tried working out there. There's no privacy."

"We have conference rooms."

"They aren't available when you need them. Not only that, but you have
to sign up for them and then take the group into a room away from your
desk. The old way where we could meet in our office was much better."

Gradually the built-up resentment boiled over and the story was repeated. They were unable to work in the present conditions. It was bad enough trying to deal with the engineers without having to go through all the red tape of signing up for and scheduling a meeting room.

Kim Nelson finally said, "Let me give you an example. Just Monday I was supposed to have a meeting with the vice president of Norton's Tool and Die and their engineer and their salesman. When they got hung up over Chicago they came in an hour late and I couldn't find a meeting room available. Now there I am. Can I hold that meeting out in the bullpen?" Then fairly shouting with anger, Kim said, "You know what I finally did? Pete Wilson is the engineer who provides my specs. He invited us to his office over across the building. And we met in his office!"

"I bet you really had control of that meeting, didn't you," Jose said, "after demonstrating to that VP from Norton's that your own company treated you like a flunky."

Wolfson's face was red from anger. He knew things were out of hand, but had no idea what to do about it. Input Systems, Inc., did not treat their buyers like flunkies! Finally, in self-defense Wolfson jumped to his feet and roared, "I can see that the complaints I've been receiving about this department are true. No wonder research and development and engineering are complaining about the unnecessary delays in getting parts and materials! If you, and this includes you too, Bill, spent as much time working as you do complaining, we might get something done around here. And furthermore . . . ."

ANSWERS

Wolfson

1. *Frame of reference* completely different from that of the buyers. Wolfson was ignorant of buyers' real complaint—loss of prestige because they had no offices. He was only concerned with his crisis over a delayed delivery. Wolfson used his own frame of reference to decode the buyers' messages.

2. Operated in both *closed* and *blind* manager styles. Although it is possible that Wolfson was normally an open manager who just had a few bad weeks because of overwork, the evidence seems to indicate otherwise. He apparently failed to involve the buyers in the planning for the new building, never explained the rationale for the bullpen, and never listened to buyer feedback—typical of a closed manager. Wolfson seemed authoritarian in his dealings with Johnson on the phone and with the buyers during the meeting; he seemed to ignore feedback and concentrated on telling others how things must be; the buyers finally forced feedback on him—typical of a blind manager.

3. Poor use of *feedback*. He seldom asked for feedback, held no regular feedback sessions, used no paraphrasing or perception checking.

4. Selected a poor *environment* for the meeting. Although he felt more comfortable in his own territory, meeting in his private office only further angered the buyers who did not have offices. In the circumstances, it would have been better to meet in a neutral place or in the bullpen or a conference room.

5. *Inadequately prepared* for the meeting. Wolfson should have met with Johnson and one buyer before the general meeting to clarify the problem. He should have looked at the conference room scheduling records, checked with the building architect for problems and possible corrective measures, found out which buyers were coming to the meeting, carefully selected a meeting place and seating arrangement, and so on.

6. Poor use of *language code* to open the meeting. The buyers had been trying to talk with Wolfson for three weeks. Saying, "What's the trouble, this time?" in an accusing, let's-get-this-mess-over-with tone of voice was not a good way to instill confidence. Wolfson should have opened the meeting with an *overall picture* that would *stimulate, motivate,* and *create goodwill,* such as: "I understand we have a serious problem here. I've checked the scheduling sheet for the conference rooms, looked at. . . . I understand your concern and would have met with you sooner except for a crisis

in shipping. Such problems affect us all and must receive priority as you know. However, I see no reason why we can't work out a solution to this problem that is agreeable to us all. Let's begin by . . ."

7. His *paralanguage* (tone of voice) and the *nonverbal* frowning and sitting behind his desk did not indicate interest or concern for the buyers' problems.

8. Poor *listener.* He was especially guilty of bad listening habits (he got overstimulated and reacted emotionally to the word *flunky*).

Johnson

1. Seemed to have poor *attitude* and wanted to *blame* his problems on Wolfson (as shown by his response after speaking to Wolfson on the phone).

2. Chose a poor *channel* (telephone) for such an important message. Use of the telephone allowed for no nonverbal responses and made it impossible for Johnson to control the environment of the communication. (He was unaware that Wolfson was involved in a crisis.) A face-to-face meeting would have been much more productive, even if over lunch.

3. Seemed to operate partly as a *closed manager* because he *placed blame* for his problems on upper management and was fairly uncommunicative. The buyers had been unhappy for months, yet he had only recently communicated this to Wolfson. Johnson also operated as a *hidden manager.* He seemed to take pleasure in Wolfson's problem with the buyers, did not take an active role in the meeting even though he could have helped, and probably did not trust Wolfson.

4. Failed to give Wolfson a good *overall picture* of the problem. Although this was partly Wolfson's fault, Johnson did not make any real effort to communicate with Wolfson. He did not *encode* the message for Wolfson's *frame of reference.*

Buyers

1. Concerned only with their problems and completely ignored Wolfson's *frame of reference.*

2. Failed to *prepare* for the meeting. They did not have a list of complaints or any research to support them, had not selected a spokesperson, and worse yet, had no workable solutions to present as an alternative.

3. Poor *decoders* (viewed everything from their frame of reference) and worse *encoders* (didn't think how the word *flunky* might sound to Wolfson, and didn't organize their ideas).

4. Spent their time planning rebuttals instead of *listening* carefully.

5. Allowed their *nonverbal* facial expressions and tone of voice (*paralanguage*) to show unhappiness, which angered Wilson.

Summary

Wolfson, Johnson, and the buyers would have had a good chance of saving the situation if any one of them had employed good communication techniques. For example, even with angry buyers and a noncommunicative manager, Wolfson could have set the mood for cooperation by serving coffee, meeting in the bullpen or a conference room, and presenting the overall picture described above. Even with Wolfson upset and Johnson of no help, the buyers could have saved the situation by planning carefully and controlling their emotions. When Wolfson asked, "What's the trouble, this time?" one of the buyers should have thanked Wolfson for his time and then in detail (with visuals) presented the problem, supported with research, and suggested some workable solutions. Even Johnson could have saved the situation by meeting with Wolfson earlier, advising the buyers on how best to approach Wolfson, and helping to conduct the meeting in a friendly yet business-like manner.

NOTES

1. Virginia P. Richmond and James C. McCroskey, *Communication: Apprehension, Avoidance, and Effectiveness,* 4th ed. (Scottsdale, AZ: Gorsuch Scarisbrick, 1995), pp. 74–75.
2. "Fears," *Spectra* 9 (December 1973), p. 4.
3. Kurt Sandholtz, "Do You Have What It Takes?" *Managing Your Career,* published by *The Wall Street Journal,* Fall 1987, p. 10.

4. Situational anxiety is often referred to by researchers as state anxiety. See M. Motley, "Stage Fright Manipulation by (False) Heart Rate Feedback," *Central States Speech Journal* 27 (1976), pp. 186–191; and S. Booth-Butterfield, "Action Assembly Theory and Communication Apprehension," *Human Communication Research* 13 (1987), pp. 388–398.

5. Trait anxiety is often referred to by researchers as communication apprehension, or CA; see James A. Daly and Gustav W. Friedrich, "The Development of Communication Apprehension: A Retrospective Analysis of Contributory Correlates," *Communication Quarterly* 29 (1981), pp. 243–255.

6. Quote reported in Robert N. Bostrom, *Communicating in Public: Speaking and Listening* (Edina, MN: Burgess, 1988), p. 57.

7. Dissimilarity, prior experience, and subordinate status are discussed by Richmond and McCroskey, pp. 64–65; see also Michael J. Beatty, "Situational and Predispositional Correlates of Public Speaking Anxiety," *Communication Education* 37 (January 1988), pp. 28–39; and Michael J. Beatty, Gary L. Balfantz, and Alison Y. Kuwabara, "Trait-Like Qualities of Selected Variables Assumed to Be Transient Causes of Performance State Anxiety," *Communication Education* 38 (July 1989), pp. 277–289.

8. Systematic desensitization, cognitive restructuring, rational emotive therapy, and skills training are discussed in Richmond and McCroskey, pp. 93–109; see also Melanie Booth-Butterfield and Steve Booth-Butterfield, *Communication Apprehension and Avoidance in the Classroom* (Edina, MN: Burgess, 1992), pp. 110–120.

9. Research has found positive imagery (visualization) to be especially effective for trait anxiety, to have a long-term effect, and to be easy to administer. See Joe Ayres and Theodore S. Hopf, "The Long-Term Effect of Visualization in the Classroom: A Brief Research Report," *Communication Education* 39 (January 1990), pp. 75–78; Joe Ayres and Theodore S. Hopf, "Visualization: Is It More Than Extra-Attention?" *Communication Education* 38 (January 1989), pp. 1–5; Joe Ayres and Theodore S. Hopf, "Visualization: A Means of Reducing Speech Anxiety," *Communication Education* 34 (1985), pp. 318–323; see also Joe Ayres, "Coping with Speech Anxiety: The Power of Positive Thinking," *Communication Education* 37 (October 1988), pp. 289–295, and John Bourhis and Mike Allen, "Meta-Analysis of the Relationship Between Communication Apprehension and Cognitive Performance," *Communication Education* 41 (January 1992), pp. 68–76.

10. Alan Richardson, *Mental Imagery* (New York: Springer, 1952), p. 56.

11. Jim Loehr, "Seeing Is Believing," *World Tennis* 36 (March 1989), pp. 16ff.

12. Robert McGarvey, "Rehearsing for Success: Tap the Power of the Mind Through Visualization," *Executive Female* (January–February 1990), p. 35.

13. Jean Houston, *The Possible Human* (Los Angeles: J. P. Tarcher, 1982), p. 11.

14. K. M. Stephan, G. R. Fink, R. E. Passingham, D. Silbersweig, A. O. Ceballos-Baumann, C. D. Frith, and R. S. J. Frackowiak, "Functional Anatomy of the Mental Representation of Upper Extremity Movements in Healthy Subjects," *Journal of Neurophysiology* 73 (January 1995), pp. 373–385.

15. Ayres and Hopf, 1989, 1985.

16. McGarvey, p. 35.

17. Adapted from William S. Howell and Ernest G. Bormann, "The Case of the Hasty Resignation," in *Presentational Speaking for Business and Professions* (New York: Harper & Row, 1971). Copyright © 1971 by William S. Howell and Ernest G. Bormann. Reprinted by permission of Harper & Row, Publishers, Inc.

18. The instructions were developed by Cheryl Hamilton and Cordell Parker. The puzzle pieces are from "How to Assemble a Framus," by Marshall Sashkin and William C. Morris, *Organizational Behavior: Concepts and Experiences* (Englewood Cliffs, NJ: Prentice-Hall, 1984), pp. 127, 137. Copyright © 1984. Reprinted by permission of Prentice-Hall, Englewood Cliffs, NJ.

19. Adapted in part from John Stewart, "Clear Interpersonal Communication," in *Bridges Not Walls: A Book About Interpersonal Communication*, John Stewart, ed. (New York: Random House, 1973). Copyright © 1973 by Newbery Award Records, Inc. Reprinted by permission of Random House.

20. John Dunworth, "Six Barriers to Basics: Education Depends on You," *Vital Speeches* 46 (January 1, 1980), p. 190.

21. Harry Lorayne, *Memory Makes Money* (Boston: Little, Brown, 1988); John A. Glover, Vicky Timme, Dave Deyloff, Margie Rogers, and Dale Dinell, "Oral Directions: Remembering What to Do When," *The Journal of Educational Research* 81 (September–October 1987), pp. 33–40; F. S. Bellezza, "Updating Memory Using Mnemonic Devices," *Cognitive Psychology* 14 (1982), pp. 301–327.

22. Garrett L. Bergen and William V. Haney, *Organizational Relations and Management Action: Cases and Issues* (New York: McGraw-Hill, 1966), pp. 107–108. Reprinted by permission.

23. Modified version of "Test Your Judgment," *Nation's Business*, January 1962, pp. 66–69, 81. The text portion of this article was prepared for *Nation's Business* by William V. Haney. Reprinted with permission from *Nation's Business*.

24. Adapted from Arnold E. Schneider, William C. Donaghy, and Pamela Jane Newman, *Organizational Communication* (New York: McGraw-Hill, 1975), pp. 22–23.

25. Clyde S. Kilby, "Signs in Great Britain," in *Word Study* (Springfield, MA: G. & C. Merriam, 1944); quoted in William V. Haney, *Communication and Organizational Behavior: Text and Cases*, 3rd ed. (Homewood, IL: Irwin, 1973), pp. 259–260.

26. O. C. Brenner, J. Tomkiewicz, and V. E. Schein, "The Relationship Between Sex Role Stereotypes and Requisite Management Characteristics Revisited," *Academy of Management Journal* 32 (1989), pp. 662–669.

27. Judy C. Pearson, *Gender and Communication* (Dubuque, IA: Wm. C. Brown, 1985), pp. 8–9.

28. Several of the questions and answers were adapted from Hazel J. Rozema and John W. Gray, "How Wide Is Your Communication Gender Gap?" *Personnel Journal* 66 (July 1989), pp. 98–105.

29. Deborah Tannen, *Talking from 9 to 5: How Women's and Men's Conversational Styles Affect Who Gets Heard, Who Gets Credit, and What Gets Done at Work* (New York: Morrow, 1994), pp. 279–280; see also Deborah Tannen, *You Just Don't Understand: Women and Men in Conversation* (New York: Morrow, 1990).

30. J. A. Hall, "Gender, Gender Roles, and Nonverbal Communication Skills," in R. Rosenthal, ed., *Skill in Nonverbal Communication: Individual Differences* (Cambridge, MA: Oelgeschlager, Gunn & Hain, 1979), pp. 32–67; see also J. A. Hall, *Nonverbal Sex Differences: Communication Accuracy and Expressive Style* (Baltimore: Johns Hopkins University Press, 1984).

31. Discussed in Rozema and Gray, pp. 98–105.

32. R. Lakoff, *Language and Women's Place* (New York: Harper & Row, 1975); see also B. Bate, *Communication Between the Sexes* (New York: Harper & Row, 1988).

33. Julia T. Wood and L. F. Lenze, "Gender and the Development of Self: Inclusive Pedagogy in Interpersonal Communication," *Women's Studies in Communication* 14 (1991), pp. 1–23.

34. Julia T. Wood, *Gendered Lives: Communication, Gender, and Culture* (Belmont, CA: Wadsworth, 1994), p. 275.

35. Julia T. Wood, *Everyday Encounters: An Introduction to Interpersonal Communication* (Belmont, CA: Wadsworth, 1996), p. 110.

36. Pam M. Fishman, "Interaction: The Work Women Do," *Social Problems* 25 (1978), pp. 15–21.

37. D. Borisoff and L. Merrill, *The Power to Communicate: Gender Differences as Barriers*, 2nd ed. (Prospect Heights, IL: Waveland, 1992).

38. Judy Pearson, L. H. Turner, and W. Todd-Mancillas, *Gender and Communication*, 2nd ed. (Dubuque, IA: Wm. C. Brown, 1991).

39. Deborah James and Sandra Clarke, "Women, Men, and Interruptions: A Critical Review," in Deborah Tannen, *Gender and Conversational Interaction* (Oxford: Oxford University Press, 1993), pp. 231–280.

40. Tannen, *Talking from 9 to 5*, pp. 26–29.

41. Tannen, *Talking from 9 to 5*, p. 26.

42. Rozema and Gray, pp. 98–105.

43. A. Cann and W. D. Siegfried, "Sex Stereotypes and the Leadership Role," *Sex Roles* 17 (1987), pp. 401–408.

44. Rozema and Gray, pp. 98–105.

45. Wood, *Everyday Encounters*, p. 111; see also Julia T. Wood, *Gendered Relationships* (Mountain View, CA: Mayfield, 1996).

46. Linda Putnam and S. Heinen, "Women in Management: The Fallacy of the Trait Approach," *MSU Business Topics* (Summer 1976), pp. 47–53.

47. A. H. Eagly and B. T. Johnson, "Gender and Leadership Style: A Meta-Analysis," *Psychological Bulletin* 108 (1990), pp. 233–256.

48. Barrie Thorne, Cheris Kramarae, and Nancy Henley, eds., *Language, Gender and Society* (Cambridge, MA: Newbury House, 1983), p. 13.

49. Ellen A. Fagenson, "At the Heart of Women in Management Research: Theoretical and Methodological Approaches and Their Biases," *Journal of Business Ethics* 9 (1990), pp. 267–274.

50. Edwin E. Megargee, "Influence of Sex Roles on the Manifestation of Leadership," *Journal of Applied Psychology* 53 (1969), pp. 377–382.

51. Arthur G. Jago and Victor H. Vroom, "Sex Differences in the Incident and Evaluation of Participative Leader Behavior," *Journal of Applied Psychology* 67 (1982), pp. 776–783.

52. Robert L. Quackenbush, "Sex Roles and Social Perception," *Human Relations* 40 (1987), pp. 659–670.

53. Sandra L. Bem, "Gender Schema Theory: A Cognitive Account of Sex Typing," *Psychological Review* 88 (1981), pp. 354–364.

54. Sandra L. Bem, *Bem Sex-Role Inventory: Professional Manual* (Palo Alto, CA: Consulting Psychologists Press, 1981).

55. Karen Korabik, "Androgyny and Leadership: An Integration," paper presented at the meeting of the Association for Women and Psychology, Boston, 1981; see also Karen Korabik, "Androgyny and Leadership Style," *Journal of Business Ethics* 9 (1990), pp. 283–292.

56. U.S. Merit Systems Protection Board, *Sexual Harassment in the Federal Workplace: Is It a Problem?* (Washington, DC: U.S. Government Printing Office, 1981); U.S. Merit Systems Protection Board, *Sexual Harassment in the Federal Government: An Update* (Washington, DC: U.S. Government Printing Office, 1988).

57. Susan Webb, *Step Forward: Sexual Harassment in the Workplace* (New York: MasterMedia, 1991), pp. xiv, xvii.

58. "Sexual Harassment Abroad," *Parade Magazine*, January 12, 1992, p. 14.

59. *Federal Register* 45 (November 10, 1980), pp. 74675–74677.

60. Stephanie Riger, "Gender Dilemmas in Sexual Harassment Policies and Procedures," *American Psychologist* 46 (May 1991), p. 498.

61. A. Deutschman, "Dealing with Sexual Harassment," *Fortune*, November 4, 1991, pp. 145–148; J. W. Adams, J. L. Kottke, and J. S. Padgitt, "Sexual Harassment of University Students," *Journal of College Student Personnel* 23 (1983), pp. 484–490; D. Kirk, "Gender Differences in the Perception of Sexual Harassment," paper presented at the Academy of Management National Meeting, Anaheim, CA, August 1988; U.S. Merit Systems Protection Board, *Sexual Harassment in the Federal Workplace.*

62. A. M. Konrad and B. A. Gutek, "Impact of Work Experiences on Attitudes Toward Sexual Harassment," *Administrative Science Quarterly* 31 (1986), pp. 422–438; D. Lester, B. Bants, J. Barton, L. Mackiewicz, and J. Winkelried, "Judgments About Sexual Harassment: Effects of the Power of the Harasser," *Perceptual and Motor Skills* 63 (1986), p. 990; G. N. Powell, "Effects of Sex Role Identity and Sex on Definitions of Sexual Harassment," *Sex Roles* 14 (1986), pp. 9–19.

63. B. A. Gutek, *Sex and the Workplace* (San Francisco: Jossey-Bass, 1985).

64. Riger, p. 499.

65. Webb, p. 49; see also Diane Filipowski, "Texaco's Penalty for Sex Discrimination," *Personnel Journal* 70 (December 1991), pp. 72–78.

66. Peter G. W. Keen, *Competing in Time: Using Telecommunications for Competitive Advantage*, updated and expanded (Cambridge, MA: Ballinger, 1988), p. 2.

67. Urs E. Gattiker, *Technology Management in Organizations* (Newbury Park, CA: Sage, 1990), pp. 284–285.

68. L. Sproull and S. Keisler, "Computers, Networks, and Work," *Scientific American* 265 (September 1991), pp. 116–123.

69. Charles W. Steinfield, "Computer-Mediated Communications in the Organization: Using Electronic Mail at Xerox," in *Case Studies in Organizational Communication*, Beverly D. Sypher, ed. (New York: Guilford, 1990), pp. 289–291.

70. Sharon M. Haddock, "Beware! Your E-Mail Could Haunt You Later," in *Communication Skills for Business and Professions*, Paul R. Timm and James A. Stead, eds. (Upper Saddle River, NJ: Prentice-Hall, 1996), pp. 148–149.

71. Steinfield, p. 292.

72. Timm and Stead, p. 149.

73. Kathleen Kelleher and Thomas Cross, *Teleconferencing* (Englewood Cliffs, NJ: Prentice-Hall, 1985), p. 52.

74. Jay Misra and Byron Belitsos, "Teleconferencing," in *Business Telecommunications: Concept, Technologies, & Cases in Telematics* (Homewood, IL: Irwin, 1987), pp. 363–365; and Ronald E. Rice and George A. Barnett, "Group Communication Networking in an Information Environment: Applying Metric Multidimensional Scaling," in Margaret L. McLaughlin, ed., *Communication Yearbook 9* (Beverly Hills: Sage, 1986), pp. 316–317.

75. Misra and Belitsos, pp. 374–375.

76. Adapted from "The Case of Information Systems, Inc.," in Ernest G. Bormann, William S. Howell, Ralph G. Nichols, and George L. Shapiro, *Interpersonal Communication in the Modern Organization* (Englewood Cliffs, NJ: Prentice-Hall, 1969), pp. 19–24. Copyright © 1969. Reprinted by permission of Prentice-Hall, Inc., Englewood Cliffs, NJ.

7

Basic Information for All Types of Interviews

I n few communication formats [public speaking, conferences, or interviewing] is greater involvement expected of a participant than in an interview. . . . It is only in the interview that approximately equal participation is expected of both parties.[1]

JAMES M. LAHIFF,
"Interviewing for Results"

Whether you are a production worker, supervisor, teacher, assistant manager, police officer, executive, or self-employed, you will spend much of your business time conducting some type of interview. The interviewing process often begins when a person is seeking a job, but the overall concept of interviewing is much more comprehensive. By the term *interview*, we are referring to all types of planned, face-to-face encounters in which at least one of the participants has a specific objective in mind. Interviewing, according to this definition, includes gathering information and research, appraising employee performance, settling grievances, and many other interactions. Although most interviews are one-to-one interactions, some employment interviews involve either a panel of interviewees, a panel of interviewers, or both. Don't forget that interviewing is a form of communication. Therefore, all the communication theories, skills, and obstacles discussed in earlier chapters are equally important for interviewing success. Also remember that interviewing is a reciprocal process: Interviewees should actively question, paraphrase, add information, and so on.

TYPES OF INTERVIEWS

There are far too many types of interview situations to completely list here. However, the basic approach to each type is similar. An understanding of the following types of interviews can easily be transferred to other interview situations.[2]

Counseling Interview

The intent of the counseling interview is to help the interviewee uncover and solve "career-related personal or interpersonal problems."[3] Counseling interviews may deal with such things as job stress, problems with a job change or transfer, relationship problems with a boss or coworkers, and personal problems such as alcoholism, smoking, drug abuse, or family discord. The communication skills covered in the first six chapters of this text are especially important in a counseling interview in which the interviewee may be emotional, defensive, suspicious, or has all but given up. Empathetic listening, use of nonevaluative feedback, careful paraphrasing, and sympathetic nonverbal responses will help to establish the needed climate of trust. In some cases, a directive approach in which the interviewer takes complete control works best; in other situations, a nondirective approach in which the interviewer is merely a facilitator is needed; at other times, a combined approach may be best.[4] Although the traditional/

classical organization discussed in Chapter 2 may not see the need for counseling interviews, the "best" companies try to meet all the needs of their employees.[5]

Employment Interview

As it is typically used, the employment interview involves one prospective employee and one prospective employer. However, you should be aware that some companies use various group approaches:

1. Two or more interviewers and one interviewee.
2. One interviewer interviewing two to ten interviewees at the same time.
3. Several interviewers questioning several interviewees at a time.

Although the prospective employer usually takes the lead during the interview, the person seeking employment is at the same time interviewing the prospective employer. This type of interview is one of the most important because in it some of the most critical organizational and personal decisions are made. The ultimate productivity of an organization depends on the ability of its management to recruit and select the best personnel. However, "30 years of research indicate that the interview as conducted in American business, when compared to other selection procedures, has little or no value in predicting employee success."[6] Poorly trained interviewers and poorly prepared interviewees contribute to this problem. Chapter 8 offers information and advice to both interviewers and interviewees who wish to improve the employment interview.

Exit Interview

Whether an employee was laid off, fired, or simply quit, it could be to the organization's benefit to discover the perceptions of this employee who has "nothing to lose." Potential company problems can be identified and corrected while they are still small. The exit interview is also a good way to create goodwill for the organization. Exit interviews require careful listening and reading between the lines because many people will only hint at their real reason for leaving—never saying, for example, that the boss is impossible to work with. In some companies, such as Corning Glass and Firestone, exit interviews include outplacement counseling to help employees find and qualify for new jobs.[7]

Grievance Interview

The grievance interview is any type of one-to-one encounter involving conflict and its resolution. Examples of situations leading to grievance interviews include employer–employee disputes over working hours or wages, customer–salesperson conflicts, and teacher–student conflicts. The grievance interview is unique in that emotions often run at a much higher level than in other types of interviews. However, the basic structure of a grievance interview includes many of the same factors that operate in other interview situations. The interviewer in a grievance interview must be both a good listener and a problem solver. The basic problem-solving procedure discussed in Chapter 9 is an effective way to organize the interview.

Interrogation Interview

The interrogation interview differs from all others in that there is usually some type of offense involved. An interrogation can occur, for example, between firm representative and customer in a case of shoplifting, between employer and employee in a case of missing company funds, or between police and suspect.

Performance Review

One of the keys to the successful operation of any firm or organization is the accurate and consistent evaluation of the performance of employees, regardless of their levels. The performance review, planned and executed under the proper conditions, is an excellent way to

- Recognize and reward employee contributions
- Give employees feedback on their standing in the eyes of the company
- Help discover and solve communication problems between employees or between employer and employee
- Motivate employees by setting future performance objectives

Keep in mind that the content of the performance review "must be relevant to the job," must include "observable" aspects of the job only, and must avoid vague factors such as "desire to succeed."[8] The performance review will be more productive if the employee is actively involved in assessing his or her performance. The performance review should include a written as well as an oral appraisal; the written form is normally kept in the employee's file. The written appraisal protects the employee from unfair dismissal and, at the same time, gives the company concrete support for dismissing a person with a consistently poor job record.

Persuasive Interview

Many employee–customer situations are really persuasive (or sales) interviews. Although it influences the choices a customer makes, persuasion is not coercion or trickery. A successful persuasive interviewer must appeal to the values and needs of the interviewee very much like a persuasive speaker. The facts and evidence the salesperson or persuader must use also depend on the interests and opinions of the interviewee. Selling is not the only place we find persuasive interviews. Convincing your boss you deserve a raise and persuading your colleagues to go along with your suggested office rearrangements are also examples of persuasive interviews. According to Charles Stewart and William Cash, persuasive interviews are more likely to succeed if you can convince the interviewee that your proposal:[9]

- Will satisfy one or more unmet needs
- Is consistent with important beliefs, attitudes, and values
- Is feasible, workable, practical, and affordable
- Has benefits that outweigh any objections
- Is the best course of action available

Group Interview[10]

Although interviews having one interviewer and one interviewee are the most common, group interviews are gaining in popularity. When there are more interviewees than interviewers, the term *panel interview* is used. Product researchers use panel interviews as a way to get more customers' opinions and suggestions on a product in a shorter time and as a way to cut costs. Psychologists also use the panel interview as a counseling and diagnostic tool. For example, in an attempt to help a child who has been stealing items from school, a family counselor might interview the entire family at the same time. As a result, it is easier to observe family interaction styles and relationships; at the same time, having the whole family present indicates that the child's problem is also the family's problem. Employment personnel in both profit and nonprofit organizations use panel interviews as a way to save time and to determine employee leadership and communication skills. For example, airlines use panel interviews extensively for reservation clerks and flight attendants. Many health care professionals also use panel interviews.

When there are more interviewers than interviewees, the term *board interview* is used. Board interviews are used by nonprofit, public, educational, and business organizations. The Oliver North hearing conducted by the U.S. Senate was a board interview. Other examples include parole board hearings, graduate student oral examinations, and selection interviews (such as those used by educational institutions, government agencies, and even museums). Board interviews allow interviewers to share responsibility and expertise and to check interviewee answers under stress.

Because group interviews can catch you off guard, the following are a few suggestions to keep in mind if you are the interviewee:[11]

GENERAL SUGGESTIONS FOR GROUP INTERVIEWS

- *Be prepared for confusion and noise.* The more people in a room, the greater the confusion has to be. Don't let the noise make you rush your answers or feel pressured.
- *If possible, determine names of panelists ahead of time.* Find out as much about them as you can (for example, who is in charge, who has the most clout, and so on).
- *If possible, determine why group interviews are being used.* Maybe it's for everyone's convenience, maybe it's to create stress, maybe it's merely to save the interviewer time and money. This information may indicate how to focus your answers.
- *Appear confident and in control.* Try to keep a relaxed posture, including open body with chin down, direct eye contact, appropriate dress, natural gestures, and a positive, relaxed attitude.
- *Make your answers direct, brief, honest, and sincere.*

SPECIFIC SUGGESTIONS FOR THE PANEL INTERVIEW

- *Try to speak to everyone, not just the interviewer.* The interviewer is probably interested in how you interact with a group, so think of the other applicants as your friends. The interviewer may ask the interviewees to direct their answers to the group; if so, consider the interviewer as part of the group and speak to everyone.
- *Take an active role but don't always speak first.* In other words, use good communication skills. If the group is asked to solve a problem, listen carefully, draw in nontalkers, help structure the process, and use other good leadership skills.

SPECIFIC SUGGESTIONS FOR THE BOARD INTERVIEW

- *Try not to be one of the first applicants interviewed.* During the first interview, there may be confusion about who is responsible for a particular area of questioning, who will take the lead, and so on. It may take several interviews before board members become organized and feel comfortable with one another.

- If possible, sit where you won't have to constantly move your head back and forth to see all the interviewers.

- *Make eye contact with all interviewers* and not just the person who asks a question. You want to establish rapport with everyone. Also be aware that some interviewees tend to speak to those on their right while ignoring those people on their left, or vice versa.

- *Stick by your answers.* If challenged, "defend your view or just acknowledge that there are several ways to look at it and you subscribe to one particular view."[12]

Informational Interview

An *information-giving* interview often occurs in a professional setting and is characterized by a need or desire on the part of at least one of the participants to impart important information. Examples would be a dental hygienist advising a client on how to brush teeth, a nurse explaining a medical procedure to a patient, an automobile salesperson describing the correct operation of the cruise control to a customer, or a supervisor informing an employee about a new company policy.

In an *information-seeking* interview, the interviewer is getting information from the other person. A police officer or lawyer interviewing crime victims or witnesses, a physician interviewing a patient about his medical history, a journalist conducting a public opinion poll, or a student interviewing a business professional about a specific type of job to help in career planning—these are all examples of information-seeking interviews.

Because information-seeking interviews can be used to find out all types of information, they are one of the most often used. They are especially useful for people planning a career, anticipating a career change, or planning for future promotion. For example, just about any job hunting guide recommends that readers conduct several information-seeking interviews before actually going on a job interview.[13] These interviews, which should take no longer than 15 minutes, provide a wealth of information to help you decide what career you really want or to make sure you are prepared to get the job or promotion you already know you want. Some of the questions you might ask include:

Exactly what does your job entail?

What are the educational requirements for the position?

What experience is required or recommended?

What do you like most about the position? Like least?

If you could do things over again, would you choose the same career? Why or why not?

What problems could I expect to encounter in a position of this type?

What future changes do you see in this field (or position)?

Describe the ideal person for this career (position).

What is the average salary for a person just starting out in this career (position, job)?

What questions could I expect if I were interviewing for a job of this type?

What are the professional organizations (journals, newsletters) that you recommend?

Could you give me the name of another person that you would suggest I interview?

Find people to interview through personal contacts provided by friends, coworkers, professors, and even parents and bosses. You may also want to call the human relations (personnel) department of a particular company and ask for the name of a person to interview. When conducting an information-seeking interview, be sure to follow the opening, question–response, and closing phases suggested later in this chapter. In the opening phase, thank the interviewee for his or her time, say how valuable the information will be in helping you plan your career (future job, and so on), and assure the person that everything will be kept in the strictest confidence. During the questioning phase, take only minimal notes, use verbal and nonverbal probes, ask follow-up questions, and listen carefully. Appearing to be more interested in which question to ask than in what the person is saying is sure to lower the interviewee's motivation to help. During the closing phase, summarize the basic areas covered, ask if the interviewer can think of any additional information you should know, and end with a handshake. Follow up with a thank-you note. Later, if an interview suggested to you by the previous interviewee uncovers a helpful bit of information, why not call and share it. This way you are not only developing friendships, but future references as well.

BASIC INTERVIEW ORGANIZATION

The basic organization is generally the same for all interviews. Most interviews consist of three phases: the opening phase, the question–response phase, and the closing phase.[14]

> ## BASIC INTERVIEW OUTLINE
>
> I. Opening Phase
>   A. Rapport
>   B. Orientation
>   C. Motivation
> II. Question–Response Phase
> III. Closing Phase

Opening Phase

To omit the opening phase of an interview is just as serious a mistake as forgetting to introduce the topic in an oral presentation. To leave out the opening phase of an interview is to make assumptions that may not be true. We know one manager who completed an entire interview before he discovered that the woman he was talking to was not the person he was scheduled to see. Interviews for the position she wanted were being held in another department two doors down the hall. Because the manager had omitted the opening phase, neither person was aware of the error.

The opening phase of an interview includes three basic steps: rapport, orientation, and motivation. Normally, these steps are followed in the order listed. However, their order is not as important as making sure that all of them are included. Feel free to order the steps in the way that best fits the type of interview, your preference, and the specific occasion.

Rapport ■ Usually, the first thing an interviewer should do in the opening of the interview is establish rapport. Rapport is a comfortable, I-respect-you-as-an-individual, relaxed feeling that makes both participants receptive to the interview and willing to talk. The initial 1 to 4 minutes may be the most important of the entire interview—their impact on its ultimate outcome cannot be overstated.[15] First impressions are difficult to erase. If both parties establish a good relationship—rapport—during the opening minutes, the purpose of the interview is more likely to be achieved. In an employment interview, the applicant who makes a good first impression has a better chance of being hired (see Chapter 8 for more on the relationship between first impressions and hiring). In a grievance interview, rapport is likely to make the conflict easier to resolve. In a performance review, rapport will typically make the employee more likely to accept the review. In a persuasive interview, rapport between the salesperson and the customer usually makes it easier to sell the product. And in an informational interview, rapport makes the information easier to obtain.

It is very difficult to tell a person how to establish rapport or how to make a good first impression. The interviewer can aid the process by supplying a relaxed but businesslike environment, selecting a spot relatively free from distractions, and coming from behind the desk to sit near the interviewee. (An exception might be an interrogation interview in which the interviewer wishes to maintain a psychological distance.) When the interviewee arrives, the interviewer should stand up, shake hands, and make the person feel welcome. To start a relaxed conversation, the interviewer might refer to a mutual acquaintance or interest, a local or national event, or even the weather if it is unusual. In some types of interviews, such as the grievance interview, the interviewer might create rapport by sharing some personal feelings or opinions to give the interviewee a feeling that someone understands and cares. However, some interviewees can be put at ease by an immediate reference to the subject of the interview. In such cases, the interviewer can ask the interviewee to verify facts or to summarize the purpose of the interview. Once interviewees start talking, they are likely to forget to be nervous.

The interviewee can create a good first impression by being on time, dressing appropriately, being well prepared, and appearing confident and relaxed. The interviewee can also help establish rapport by referring to a mutual acquaintance or some topic of mutual interest.

Orientation ■ In addition to establishing rapport in the opening of an interview, the interviewer should give the interviewee a clear orientation, or overall view, of the interview. In this phase, the purposes of the interview are clearly established and understood by both parties. The orientation should include at least the following information:

- *Verification of the interviewee's name* (if not included earlier).
- *The interviewer's name and why he or she is conducting the interview* rather than someone else. Why a particular person is conducting the interview could be especially important in an exit interview, a grievance interview, and a performance review.
- *The purpose or desired outcome of the interview.* In some interviews, such as a grievance interview, the interviewer may be unaware of the exact purpose. In other interviews, such as a performance review, the interviewee may be unsure of the purpose. But even when it is fairly obvious, such as in an employment interview, the purpose should be summarized—never assumed!

- *What information is needed, if any, and how it will be used.* Interviewees in grievance interviews and performance reviews will probably be more willing to talk openly if they know how their comments will be used. The interviewer may wish to assure the interviewee of the confidentiality of his or her responses. On the other hand, a police officer is required by the Miranda decision of the U.S. Supreme Court to tell arrested suspects that "anything you say can and will be used against you." In an employment interview, applicants are interested in how the information they disclose will be used in determining whether they will be hired. In counseling, exit, or survey interviews, interviewees are hesitant to talk until they know how their responses will be used.
- *Approximate length of the interview.* It is only common courtesy to give the interviewee a general idea of how much time will be needed to complete the interview.

Motivation ■   The third step the interviewer should take in the opening phase of an interview is to motivate the interviewee to give straightforward, complete answers. The fact that the interviewee shows up for the interview does not mean that the interviewer will get factual answers that reflect careful thought. The type of motivation to use depends on the person and the circumstances. Listed here are some sample motivational approaches for three types of interviews:

EMPLOYMENT INTERVIEW

This interview is an important part of the application process with our company, Mr. Riley—not just a formality. I feel sure that you are as interested as we are in finding you a position in which you will be most successful. To place you appropriately, we need accurate, detailed information from you, okay?

EXIT INTERVIEW

Management is interested in your perceptions of our company. Anything you tell me will be kept in strict confidence. After your comments are added—anonymously, of course—to our exit interview suggestion pool, this form will be destroyed. No mention of this interview will be added to your permanent file. So I hope you will feel free to be candid. Your comments may make our company a better place to work for the friends you are leaving!

INFORMATION INTERVIEW

Ms. Smith, so far you are the only witness to the robbery. Our ability to apprehend the thieves depends on you and how much information you can give us about them. Thieves tend to come back to the same neighborhood, so I'm sure you want them apprehended just as much as we do.

Question–Response Phase

The question–response phase is truly the heart of the interview encounter, for in this phase both interviewer and interviewee have the opportunity to ask questions, respond to statements, and provide feedback. It is during the question–response phase that the primary objective of the interview is explored and treated.

Regardless of the type of interview, both participants should carefully prepare for the question–response phase. Very few interviewers can compose effective questions on the spur of the moment, and even fewer interviewees can give good answers to questions that take them completely by surprise. Realizing the importance of careful preparation by both participants, the authors of a book on performance appraisal urge that employees be given, ahead of time, the list of questions that will be discussed during the appraisal interview.[16] Knowing the questions in advance allows the employee to give answers based on a more complete and honest self-appraisal.

To plan for the question–response phase of an interview, the interviewer should decide what information needs to be sought, verified, or given and then plan the necessary questions. The interviewer should also anticipate possible interviewee responses and be prepared to change the type and the organization of the questions if necessary. The advantages and disadvantages of various types of questions and how best to organize questions are discussed later in this chapter.

Likewise, the interviewee should carefully outline the information he or she wishes to communicate to the interviewer. For example, in a grievance interview, the interviewee should be prepared to give a clear picture of the grievance with documentation if available. In a performance review, the interviewee should come prepared with a list of strengths, weaknesses, accomplishments for the year, and future performance objectives, all with documentation if possible. Similarly, for an employment interview, the applicant should come prepared with a list of strengths, areas of knowledge, and past accomplishments (usually in resume form). And the interviewee in a planned informational interview should make sure that all necessary information to answer the interviewer's questions is readily available.

In preparing for the question–response phase of an interview, the interviewee should also anticipate possible questions and carefully think through honest answers to each one. When appropriate, the interviewee should get a list of possible questions from the interviewer or talk to someone who has been through a similar interview. Suggestions on answering various types of questions are covered later in this chapter.

Closing Phase

The closing phase of any type of interview should begin with a summary of the major points covered in the interview and of any conclusions reached. Summaries allow both parties to make sure that all important topics have been discussed and that no informational errors have been made. When appropriate, the closing phase should also include agreement on what steps should be taken in the future and an arrangement for the next meeting if one is needed. For example, a person applying for a job needs to know if there is a chance of being hired, and, if so, when the prospective employer is going to make a decision and how candidates will be notified of their acceptance or rejection. Interviewees in grievance interviews or performance reviews are especially concerned with what steps will be taken in the future and how these steps may affect their standing in the organization. Also, witnesses to crimes in informational interviews are anxious to know if they will be interviewed again and if they will be called to appear in court.

Giving the interviewee a chance to ask questions is another item to include in the closing phase of an interview. Finally, the interview should always end with each participant thanking the other for the time given and the cooperation shown.

USING QUESTIONS EFFECTIVELY IN THE INTERVIEW

In order to effectively use questions in an interview—whether you are the interviewer or the interviewee—you must understand the different types of questions that can be used.

Determine the Types of Questions to Ask

Different types of questions elicit different types of responses. An effective interviewer knows what types of questions to ask to get particular responses. An ineffective interviewer has no real idea why interviewees respond as they do. Consider the interviewer who could not understand why an employee in a grievance interview would not talk much. After all, the employee was the one with the grievance! The interviewer did not realize it, but she was asking only direct and closed questions, which are designed to get short, brief answers. To encourage the employee to talk, she should have asked open-ended or hypothetical open questions. To improve your interviewing skill, carefully study the following types of questions that can be used in any interview.

Open-Ended Questions ■   These are broad, general questions that allow the respondent maximum freedom in deciding how much and what type of information to give. The following are examples of open-ended questions:

> "In your own words, evaluate your accomplishments this year."
>
> "Tell me about your complaint."
>
> "Tell me what you know about our company."
>
> "Why are you leaving our company?"
>
> "Describe for me the ideal boss."

Open-ended questions can be effective because they relax some interviewees, who discover the questions easy to answer and nonthreatening. Also, these types of questions reveal what the interviewee thinks is important and may uncover information or attitudes previously unknown to the interviewer. A person who is trying to hide information may let it slip out while answering open-ended questions. Such questions also give the interviewer an opportunity to discover areas that may need further probing. Most interviews should begin with open-ended questions.

However, open-ended questions can sometimes be ineffective. The responses to these questions are time-consuming, may cover information of little interest to the interviewer, and could cause the interviewer to lose control of the interview. Also, open-ended questions make some interviewees nervous because they do not know where to begin their answers.

Hypothetical Open Questions ■   These questions allow the respondent maximum freedom in deciding how to respond to an invented, but possible, situation. Hypothetical open questions have the same basic advantages and disadvantages that open-ended questions have. In addition, they allow the interviewers great flexibility in designing a question to fit any situation, and the responses give the interviewer an idea of how the respondent would react in a specific circumstance. The following are examples of hypothetical open questions:

> "On your first day of work, you arrive an hour late. How would you explain this and to whom?"
>
> "Suppose you were on regular patrol duty and observed an elderly woman run a red light. You signal her to stop, and she pulls into a busy parking lot. What would you do if she refused to roll down the window and accept the traffic citation?"
>
> "Suppose you were supervisor of this department and someone came to you with a complaint similar to yours. How would you handle it?"

Direct (or Specific) Questions ■ These are short questions requiring at least a short answer and may include a "yes" or "no" answer. Examples of direct questions are:

"Is the accusation against you accurate?"

"Did you accomplish your top priority this year?"

"Who recommended you to us?"

"What word-processing software can you use?"

"How long have you been in this field of work?"

"Do you think you should receive a promotion?"

Direct questions are generally valuable in that they control and limit responses, save time, and may be more relaxing for some interviewees than open-ended questions. However, researcher E. Duff Wrobbel has found that after giving a short answer or a "yes" or "no" answer, many interviewees will also add a reason or explanation to their response.[17] Therefore, an interviewer who really wants short answers without explanations should make this clear during the orientation step of the opening phase. Also keep in mind that direct questions give only limited information, especially if the interviewer does not know enough about the interviewee to determine which direct questions to ask. In most types of interviews, specific questions that must be answered "yes" or "no" should be kept to a minimum.

Closed Questions ■ These questions completely limit the respondent's choice of answers by requiring the respondent to select one of the answers supplied in the question. The following illustrate the closed question:

"Do you prefer to work with Doris, Carol, or Bob on this assignment?"

"Which would best help you meet your performance objectives— more guidance from me or more assistance from the other supervisors?"

"What size company do you prefer? Large, medium, or small?"

"How would you rate the president's handling of Third World countries?"

a. Superior   d. Poor
b. Good   e. Undecided
c. Fair

The advantage of closed questions is that they give the interviewer maximum control over the questions and answers. Moreover, the answers are easy to interpret, and more questions can be asked in less time. However, closed questions neither allow for detailed explanations nor allow the respondent to impart real feelings when the options given do not include his or her preferred choice. If you with to encourage an emotional or frustrated interviewee to talk freely, it is best to avoid closed questions.

Loaded Questions ■ These are questions that have no correct answers, but are designed to get an emotional response. Loaded questions are seldom used, even by expert interviewers; unless care is taken, they can backfire on the questioner. Loaded questions are valuable, however, when used to determine how well a person handles pressure (for jobs involving an unusual amount of stress) or to stimulate a reticent or hostile respondent. Examples of loaded questions are:

"Have you stopped drinking yet?"

"Are you still difficult to get along with?"

Leading Questions ■ A leading question implies the correct answer in the question itself. Leading questions can be helpful in determining the extent of the respondent's willingness to agree with the interviewer and in determining the consistency of current responses with earlier responses. The following are leading questions:

"You want the kind of car that gets good gas mileage, don't you?"

"We are looking for creative people here. What do you have to offer?"

"I don't think you have been working up to your potential. What do you think?"

"People who can solve their own problems are admired here. Do you have any solution in mind?"

Some interviewers think they are asking direct questions when actually they are asking leading questions. In such cases, all the interviewer is learning is that the respondent is smart enough to give the "correct" answer.

Third-Person Questions ■ Embarrassing or personal questions may be phrased in a less threatening way by involving a third person. For example, instead of asking, "What do you think about the latest merger proposal?" the interviewer can ask, "What does your group think about the latest merger proposal?" Instead of, "Do you think the new raise is fair?" the question may be phrased, "Do the employees in your department think the new raise is fair?" The answer will usually be the personal opinion of the respondent, which is generally what the interviewer really wants to know.

Verbal and Nonverbal Probes ■   Probes are used to urge the respondent to add more information to a previous response. Verbal probes are usually single words or phrases requesting more information or a judgment. "In probing for information," suggests one author, "useful questions begin with the words: *what, when, where,* and *who.* When seeking judgments, ask questions that begin with the words *why* and *how.*"[18] Repeating, in your own words, the response just given is also an excellent probe. The following are examples of probes:

"Tell me more."	"I see."
"Really?"	"Uh-huh."
"That's interesting."	"How do you mean?"
"Why?"	"Why do you feel that way?"
"Anything else?"	"What happened next?"

A nonverbal probe often can produce the same result as a verbal probe. Silence, raising the eyebrows, frowning, and nodding the head are all examples of nonverbal probes. Probes elicit additional information from the respondent, making long, involved questions unnecessary.

Knowing the different types of interview questions, their strengths and weaknesses, and the control each gives to the interviewer and interviewee leads to better interviews. Complete the following Awareness Check to see how many types of questions you can identify.

A W A R E N E S S   C H E C K :   T Y P E S   O F   Q U E S T I O N S

To check your knowledge of the various types of questions, take the following quiz.

Directions: Identify each question below. Is it (A) open-ended, (B) hypothetical open, (C) direct/specific, (D) closed, (E) loaded, (F) leading, (G) third-person, or (H) a verbal probe?

_____   **1.** What can our company do to make employees feel more a part of the organization?

_____   **2.** Do you still arrive late to most meetings?

_____ 3. About how long does it take you to drive to work?
Less than 15 minutes
16–20 minutes
21–30 minutes
31–40 minutes
Over 40 minutes
Don't know
Refused/NA

_____ 4. Tell me about your work experience.

_____ 5. Oh?

_____ 6. The communication teams in manufacturing are very excited about this procedural change. What do you think about it?

_____ 7. Could you give me an example?

_____ 8. Suppose you had an employee who was consistently late to work. Every time you talked to him about his lateness, he apologized and promised to do better, but he never improved for more than one day. How would you handle the problem?

_____ 9. If I could lower the price another $300, would you buy today?

_____ 10. Where did you work immediately after you graduated from college?

_____ 11. How did the majority of officers in A Company view the chief?

_____ 12. Which do you enjoy the most—working on your own or working under close supervision?

ANSWERS

1. A (open)
2. E (loaded)
3. D (closed)
4. A (open)
5. H (verbal probe)
6. F (leading)
7. H (verbal probe)
8. B (hypothetical open)
9. C (direct/specific)
10. C (direct/specific)
11. G (third-person)
12. D (closed)

If you had any problems in identifying the various types of questions, go back and reread those sections. Effective interviewees should not ask questions that they cannot identify, and interviewees will do a better job answering questions if they know what to expect.

Decide How to Best Organize Questions

Using questions effectively in an interview involves more than just knowing what type of questions to ask. Interviewers also must organize the questions carefully. Normally, questions should be organized into general areas. In an employment interview, these areas might include past work experience, leadership abilities, and educational background. All questions relating to past work experience would be asked first; then, questions about leadership abilities; and, finally, educational background. In a performance review, questions might be organized into (1) general performance over the past year, (2) ability to get along with other employees, (3) specific areas of achievement, and (4) possible areas needing improvement. Interviewers who jump from one general area to the next and then back again find it very difficult to remember what was discussed and what answers were given.

The questions asked within any general area are usually organized in either the funnel sequence or the inverted funnel sequence.

Funnel Sequence ■ Questions following the funnel sequence move from the general (open-ended questions) to the specific (closed questions). The following is a series of questions arranged in the funnel pattern:

1. "Tell me what overall problems you see occurring in the Harrison project." (open-ended)
2. "Why do you feel Shelton is an ineffective communicator?" (open-ended)
3. "Are you willing to accept Shelton and Jackson as coworkers on this assignment?" (direct)
4. "What makes you say that?" (verbal probe)
5. "Whom do you recommend for director of the Harrison project— Jackson, Shelton, or yourself?" (closed)

The funnel sequence is probably the most often used method of organizing an interview. Beginning with open-ended questions usually relaxes the interviewee and often eliminates the need to ask many of the planned questions because the information is volunteered. In many interviews, the interviewer does not know enough about the interviewee to begin with direct, specific questions. The funnel sequence gives the interviewer a chance to listen and learn more about the interviewee.

When you are conducting an interview, think of yourself as a detective. You are trying to gather enough facts to make a decision of some sort. In an employment interview, the decision would be whether to hire the applicant. You don't want to wait until the end of the interview to evaluate all the facts; instead, you want to rate the person on each general area as you cover it. For example, if you are using the funnel sequence to question a candidate on her educational background, at the conclusion of your questions you want to be able to say, no, she doesn't meet our educational requirements, or, yes, she does. Some interviewers assign a rating of 1 to 5 for each general area covered.

Inverted Funnel Sequence ■ Questions following the inverted funnel sequence move from specific to general. A series of questions in this order might be as follows:

1. "Whom do you recommend for director of the Harrison project—Jackson, Shelton, or yourself?" (closed)
2. "What makes you say that?" (verbal probe)
3. "Are you willing to accept Shelton and Jackson as coworkers on this assignment?" (direct)
4. "Why do you feel Shelton is an ineffective communicator?" (open-ended)
5. "Tell me what overall problems you see occurring in the Harrison project." (open-ended)

The inverted funnel sequence is typically used with reluctant, shy, or unmotivated respondents. Short, closed, or direct questions may prompt them to talk, while open-ended questions would cause only frustrated silence.

Remember that the effective interviewer is flexible and can switch from funnel to inverted funnel as needed. You may organize one general area of questions in the funnel sequence, and the next two areas in the inverted funnel sequence. Some topics seem more appropriately organized in one sequence than the other. Don't be afraid to use variety. Also, remember to place any private, threatening, or embarrassing questions in the middle of the interview. This gives you time to reestablish rapport with the individual before the interview is concluded. As the interviewer, don't hesitate to maintain control of the interview. A good interview covers as much as possible in as short a time as possible. Rambling interviews are frustrating to both participants. To keep the answers on track, interrupt when necessary with comments such as:

"I understand what you're saying, but let me ask you this . . . ."

"Let's go back to . . . for a minute."

"I am more interested in . . . . Could you expand on that particular topic for me?"

Although the funnel and inverted funnel are the most frequently used sequences for organizing your questions, there are two other sequences that you may want to use occasionally: the hourglass and the diamond sequences. These two sequences are used as followup when answers are unexpected or unclear.

Hourglass Sequence ■ When you have organized your questions into the funnel sequence and the interviewee's answer to the last question isn't at all what you expected, you will want to reopen the questioning to clarify the missing information. Each question would then become more and more general until you end with a final summary (open) question. A diagram of your questions would resemble an hourglass shape.

Diamond Sequence ■ The diamond sequence is used when the final question you ask in an inverted funnel results in an unexpected or unclear answer. To clarify the interviewee's opinion or information on the confusing answer, you need to reverse the order of your questions so that each question becomes more and more specific until you end with a closed (or specific) question. A diagram of these questions would resemble a diamond shape.

Be Prepared to Answer Questions

Just as effective interviewers need to know what type of questions to ask to get particular responses, effective interviewees need to come prepared to answer those questions. The following suggestions can help interviewees in any type of interview:

■ *Try to relax and be yourself.* A psychologist's suggestion to a friend who was testifying in court for the first time is good advice for all interviewees: Imagine how you feel when you are sitting in your own living room in a favorite chair, entertaining a guest (the interviewer). You are comfortable, relaxed, warm, and friendly.
■ *If a question catches you off guard, don't rush unprepared into an answer.* Think about your answer first. If you feel you are taking too much time, say something like, "I'd like to make sure I completely understand your question. You're asking . . ." (then paraphrase the question

Regardless of the type of interview (exit, counseling, informational, or job), the most successful interviewees are those who are prepared to answer a variety of questions. (© *Pickerell/The Image Works*)

as you understand it). Repeating the question aloud often helps stimulate thinking.

- *If you don't know or can't remember certain information, say so.* Never lie. Lies are too difficult to remember. On the other hand, there are things you probably should avoid mentioning. There is a fine line between disclosing too much and saying too little. Without falsifying facts, you should present as positive a picture of yourself as possible.
- *Don't be pressured into saying more than you want to say* by such interviewer techniques as silence, leading questions, or nonverbal probes.
- *Open-ended questions give you the floor.* Take this opportunity to present the information you want the interviewer to know. "Tell me about yourself" is one question that all interviewees should be prepared to answer. In an employment interview, you can tell your age, marital status, spouse's occupation, and number of children (all unlawful for the interviewer to ask about); or you can speak of your past career achievements, past employment, why you feel you are especially qualified for this job, and so on. Interviewers sometimes ask ambiguous open questions such as "Tell me a story" to see how you think on your feet and handle the unknown. Which story or experience you talk about is not important (although we suggest you stick to job-related stories) as long as you sound confident and fairly well organized.

- *Listen carefully to hypothetical open questions* to make sure you understand the situation. In some cases, the interviewer is using the hypothetical open as a follow-up question to check the consistency of your answers and even your commitment to an ideal. For example, you have just expressed your opinion that the best supervisor communicates in an open style. Later the interviewer asks how you would handle a very difficult situation with an employee to see if you would still select the open communicator style. Other interviewers ask hypothetical open questions to check your knowledge or to determine whether you rush to make decisions or carefully look at all angles of a problem.

- *Because direct (or specific) questions require only brief answers or "yes" or "no" answers, most interviewers use them to verify known information.* For these interviewers, keep your answers short. However, some interviewers are not very skilled at asking questions and really want you to give detailed answers. If they seem frustrated by your brief answers, try to answer their specific questions in an open manner. For example:

  Q: How long have you been in this field of work?

  A: Two years. (Most interviewers expect this.)

  A: I've been a certified financial planner for two years. After my training and apprenticeship with the Smith Company, I began working for Black's Financial Planners in . . . (Untrained interviewers might expect this.)

- *Closed questions, normally used in surveys, give the interviewer the most control of any type of question.* Always answer the question as given, but if your preferred answer is not one of the choices in the question, make sure to express it also. For example:

  Q: Which of the following college courses best prepared you for this position: psychology, technical writing, Pascal, or management theory?

  A: Of those four choices, I would select management theory. However, if I could pick any course, I would say my business communication course best prepared me to handle people as individuals.

- *Loaded questions are designed to put you under stress for some reason known to the interviewer.* Avoid answering "yes" or "no" to a loaded question. For example:

  Q: Are you still difficult to get along with?

A: Yes. (This doesn't sound good.)

A: No. (This sounds better but implies that you have had problems in the past.)

A: I have never been difficult to get along with. As a matter of fact, three months ago I was voted employee of the month by my colleagues. My leaving this company has nothing to do with my communication ability. (Best.)

- *Beware of leading questions.* They are normally trick questions designed to determine how much of a "yes person" you are or to get you to agree to purchasing a product. Don't let the interviewer put words in your mouth. Listen to the question carefully. If it is confusing, ask for an explanation. For example:

  Q: This product does meet the majority of your needs, doesn't it?

  A: Yes, but I still want to comparison shop.

- *Third-person questions are face savers that allow us to give our opinion without having to say that it is our opinion.* As such, they are good. However, be aware that these questions are often aimed at getting you to say more than you planned to say.

SUMMARY

Although there are many types of interviews, the same basic approach can be used in all interviews. Therefore, you will find that the information covered in this chapter can be applied to almost any situation, from counseling and grievance interviews to employment and performance reviews. All effective interviews are organized into the same three steps: opening phase (including rapport, orientation, and motivation), question–response phase (the body of the interview), and closing phase.

Interviews also include a variety of types of questions. The most common are open-ended, hypothetical open, direct, third-person, leading, loaded, and closed questions. They all have advantages and disadvantages, and the interviewer should use them with a specific purpose in mind. By grouping questions in general subject areas, the interviewer can evaluate information in coherent chunks as the interview progresses. The funnel sequence and the inverted funnel sequence are two common methods of organizing questions within general subject areas.

Interviewees, too, should be aware of the purposes of various types of questions and the types of responses expected. Effective interviewees know that open-ended questions give them the floor, but that direct and closed questions indicate a brief response is desired. They also know to answer leading and loaded questions with extreme care.

As with all skills, effective interviewing involves both knowledge and practice. The next chapter will look in greater detail at the employment interview.

CHECKPOINT

Before continuing to the next chapter, check your understanding of Chapter 7 by completing the following exercises:

1. If you are a supervisor, poll your employees to see how they currently evaluate your company's performance reviews. Otherwise, construct a set of questions that might be useful in a performance review. Use as many types of questions as you can in order to get the feel of asking all types of questions. Show your questions to two or three friends. Get their suggestions on which ones would be most effective in an actual interview.

2. Conduct a 15-minute information-seeking interview with someone who currently holds approximately the same job and title that you would like to have sometime in the future, say between six months and five years from now. You act as interviewer, and have the person be the interviewee. Ask him or her questions that will either help you decide whether you want this particular career (or position) or help you prepare effectively for the position. Keep in mind that it is better to conduct at least three information-seeking interviews so you can compare your results and feel confident in the advice you've obtained.

3. As an interviewee, what first impressions do you make? Get feedback from your boss and a few trusted friends to help you in your self-analysis.

4. Identify each of the following questions and decide whether the questions are organized in a funnel or inverted funnel sequence.

   a. "Tell me about your last position."
   b. "What were your main accomplishments?"
   c. "Did you save the company money?"
   d. "How much?"
   e. "Which was your greatest accomplishment—saving the company money or improving employee satisfaction through new management techniques?"

NOTES

1. James M. Lahiff, "Interviewing for Results," in *Business Communication: Strategy and Skills*, 3rd rev. ed., Richard C. Huseman and James M. Lahiff, eds. (Hinsdale, IL: Dryden, 1988).
2. Charles J. Stewart and William B. Cash, Jr., *Interviewing: Principles and Practices*, 6th ed. (Dubuque, IA: Wm. C. Brown, 1991); Phyllis Hodgson, *Practical Guide to Successful Interviewing* (New York: McGraw-Hill, 1987); Arthur H. Bell, *The Complete Manager's Guide to Interviewing: How to Hire the Best* (Homewood, IL: Dow Jones–Irwin, 1989).
3. Bell, p. 169.
4. Eric W. Skopec, *Situational Interviewing* (New York: Harper & Row, 1986), p. 101.
5. Peter C. Cairo, "Counseling in Industry: A Selected Review of the Literature," *Personnel Psychology* 36 (1983), pp. 1–18; Robert Levering, *A Great Place to Work: What Makes Some Employers So Good (and Most So Bad)* (New York: Random House, 1988); Tom Peters and Nancy Austin, *A Passion for Excellence: The Leadership Difference* (New York: Random House, 1985).
6. Bell, p. 6. Original source Wayne F. Cascio, *Applied Psychology in Personnel Management*, 2nd ed. (New York: Reston, 1982).
7. Deborah A. Randolph, "Concerns Offer Counseling to Executives, Lower Level Workers Who Are Laid Off," *The Wall Street Journal*, May 22, 1980, p. 40.
8. Paul M. Muchinsky, *Psychology Applied to Work*, 3rd ed. (Pacific Grove, CA: Brooks/Cole, 1990), p. 233.
9. Stewart and Cash, p. 219.
10. For a very detailed discussion of group interviewing, see William C. Donaghy, *The Interview: Skills and Applications* (Glenview, IL: Scott, Foresman, 1984), pp. 390–400.
11. Donaghy, chap. 18, "The Group Interview," pp. 390–400; Janet Bamford, "Surviving the Group Interview," *Forbes* 137 (March 24, 1986), pp. 190–191.
12. Bamford, p. 191.
13. For example, see Richard N. Bolles, *What Color Is Your Parachute?* (Berkeley: Ten Speed Press, 1996) and Kathryn Petras and Ross Petras, *The Only Job Hunting Guide You'll Ever Need: The Most Comprehensive Guide for Job Hunters and Career Switchers*, updated and revised (New York: Simon & Schuster, 1995).
14. From an unpublished manuscript by Meredith Moore, Washburn University, Topeka, Kansas, January 1976.
15. Leonard Zunin and Natalie Zunin, *Contact: The First Four Minutes* (New York: Ballantine, 1975).
16. Robert E. Lefton, V. R. Buzzotta, Manuel Sherberg, and Dean L. Karraker, *Effective Motivation Through Performance Appraisal: Dimensional Appraisal Strategies* (Cambridge, MA: Ballinger, 1980).
17. E. Duff Wrobbel, "A Conversation Analytic Look at the Yes/No Question," a paper presented at the annual meeting of the Speech Communication Association, Atlanta, November 1991.
18. Joseph P. Zima, *Interviewing: Key to Effective Management* (Chicago: SRA, 1983), p. 70.

8

The Employment Interview

nterviews are one of the least efficient forms of professional communication available. . . . However, most professionals are willing to rely on such an admittedly inefficient form of communication because it is potentially one of the most efficient forms available.[1]

ERIC WILLIAM SKOPEC,
Situational Interviewing

Ⅰf you follow the current norm, you will be searching for a job several times during your lifetime. Arranging for employment interviews through telephone contacts, letters of application, computer searches, and a good resume (conventional and electronic), and then communicating effectively in the actual interview are important skills you need to practice. And, on the job, you may be interviewing others seeking employment. Knowing how to conduct an effective interview that accurately assesses the qualifications of applicants without restricting their individual rights (as specified by law) also requires up-to-date skills and information.

Chapter 7 covered the basic organization of an interview (the opening, question–response, and closing phases), the types of questions normally asked in interviews along with their advantages and disadvantages, and how to effectively organize the questions during the interview. This chapter will apply this basic information to the employment interview and add specific, current information that will help you become an effective employment interviewee and a skilled employment interviewer.

RESPONSIBILITIES OF THE INTERVIEWEE

If you are the interviewee, you cannot take a passive role in the employment interview process. You must become actively involved if you hope to find a job that specifically fits your abilities and interests. The following sections discuss some of the things you can do to increase the effectiveness of the employment interview.

Investigate the Employment Market

According to Richard Bolles in *What Color Is Your Parachute?* and George Shinn in *Leadership Development*, various conventional job-hunting methods show the following rates of success:[2]

- Networking (through informational interviews)—86 percent.
- Direct approach (cold-call on employer)—47 percent.
- Asking friends for job leads—34 percent.
- Asking relatives for job leads—27 percent.
- Using placement office at college attended—21 percent.
- Job agencies—10 percent.
- Newspaper ads—5 percent.

And we can now add a new job-hunting method:

- Electronic job banks—success rate unknown.[3]

Before applying for a job or making a career change, conduct between ten and forty information-seeking interviews. (© *Jeffrey Dunn/The Picture Cube*)

Although some methods obviously have a higher success rate than others, an aggressive job-hunting approach uses all methods. At any rate, you will certainly want to use the networking approach that is based on the information-seeking interview discussed in Chapter 7. A **network** is an intricate web of contacts and relationships designed to benefit the participants—including identifying leads and giving referrals. To begin networking (before any job interviews are held), conduct from ten to forty information-seeking interviews; interview people who do what you would like to do (and do it well), successful people (especially from your chosen field), people who have access to information you need, and people who have access to other people you may want to contact.[4]

It's not as difficult as you think to find qualified people to interview. For example, ask your friends, schoolmates, family members, family friends, acquaintances from organizations and clubs (including religious and volunteer organizations), business colleagues, or professors. In fact, one researcher claims each of us have approximately 40,000 people we could ask.[5] Warren Rosaluk says you start with 200 people you know— friends to mere acquaintances. Each of those 200 people also knows 200 people—thus, 40,000 people. Out of 40,000 people, how difficult can it be to come up with at least 60 names?

According to a survey of Goodrich & Sherwood Company, a human resources management consulting firm, serious networking reduces your job search. If you see 2 people a week, you may expect the search to last up to a year; if you meet 10 people a week, your search will usually be cut about six months. But if you see 20 people a week, you're likely to conquer a new job in 90 days or less.[6]

If all goes well, these information-seeking interviews will provide you with the following information:

- Information about the career, job, or specific company in which you are interested (including jargon terms, key words, future trends, potential problems, expected salary range, organizations to join, leading journals and magazines to read, and so on).
- Evaluation of your career goals, resume, interviewing skills, appearance, and so on.
- Names of other people (referrals) you can contact for further information.

Information interviews are best when conducted in person, but phone interviews can be made. Once you have all the information you need about a specific job area, you are ready to prepare a conventional and perhaps an electronic resume.

Prepare a Conventional Resume

In addition to the letter of application, the resume is a way of communicating with a prospective employer. If properly done, it can give you an advantage over others applying for the same position. Resumes vary greatly in length, style, and content, depending on the type of job, the work experience of the applicant, and the preference of the particular company or firm. There are many excellent resume books available.[7] The information you gathered during your information-seeking interviews will help you decide whether to use a short, one-page resume or a longer, more detailed, two-page resume. Sample resumes are shown in Figures 8.1, 8.2, and 8.3.

Regardless of the length, resumes usually follow either the chronological or functional style. The **chronological resume** (the most often used) "emphasizes what you did, when you did it, and for whom you did it."[8] Work experience (including responsibilities and achievements for each position) is highlighted and presented in reverse chronological order; dates are prominent. On the other hand, the **functional resume** emphasizes skills rather than work experience—"areas of achievement are highlighted in categories" with dates playing a less prominent role.[9] The functional resume is normally for very experienced job seekers who have a variety of experiences and wish to highlight specific skills. Because

Figure 8.1 Sample one-page employment resume.

Susan Feagin
1355 Edna Street, Napa, CA 94558
Home phone: (415) 555-5760
Office: (415) 555-5745

OBJECTIVE	Sales, Leading to Sales Supervision

AREAS OF KNOWLEDGE

Personal selling	Display arranging	Correspondence
Customer relations	Fluent in Spanish	Files and records
Stock handling	Word processing	Shorthand, 90 wpm
Complaint handling	Office procedures	Typing, 55 wpm

WORK EXPERIENCE

July 1992 to present

Salesperson, Fabric Imports, Napa, California
Responsible for sales and customer relations.
Achievements include being top salesperson for last three years and adding ten new accounts.

Jan. 1988 to July 1992

Secretary to Dean of Instruction, Richland College, Dallas, Texas
Responsibilities included full secretarial service, handling student complaints, handling all confidential faculty records, composing letters and memos on word processor, and taking dictation.

Feb. 1987 to Dec. 1987

Fountain Clerk (part-time), Jack-in-the-Box, Dallas, Texas

EDUCATION

Associate of Arts Degree, 1988, Richland College, Dallas, Texas. Major in business with emphasis in sales and secretarial science

High School Diploma, 1986, Willard High School, Dallas, Texas

EXTRACURRICULAR ACTIVITIES

Student Government Representative
Young Salespeople of America

REFERENCES

Available upon request

employers generally prefer them, the sample resumes in this chapter follow the chronological style.

Experts recommend that both chronological and functional resumes include the following basic information:

■ Name, address, home and work telephone numbers.

Figure 8.2 Sample two-page employment resume (continued on next page).

RESUME

Susan Feagin
1355 Edna Street
Napa, CA 94558
Home phone: (415) 555-5760
Office: (415) 555-5745

OBJECTIVE	Sales, Leading to Sales Supervision	
AREAS OF KNOWLEDGE	Personal selling	Word processing
	Customer relations	Office procedures
	Stock handling	Correspondence
	Complaint handling	Files and records
	Display arranging	Shorthand, 90 wpm
	Fluent in Spanish	Typing, 55 wpm

EXPERIENCE

July 1992 to present

Fabric Imports, Napa, California
POSITION: Salesperson
RESPONSIBILITIES:
• Personally sell to customers, including key accounts
• In charge of all Spanish-speaking customer accounts
• Handle customer complaints and adjust satisfactorily
• Assist in ordering stock and in promoting warehouse sales
• Arrange fabric displays
ACHIEVEMENTS:
• Top salesperson for the company for last three years
• Added ten new key accounts last year

Jan. 1988 to July 1992

Richland College, Dallas, Texas
POSITION: Secretary
RESPONSIBILITIES:
• Provided full secretarial service to dean of instruction and one assistant
• Maintained daily calendar for dean
• Handled student relations and complaints
• Composed any necessary letters and memos; took dictation

- Objective or position desired.
- Education and (for recent graduates) educational highlights; educational highlights include a brief list of some of the job-related courses you completed. If you have a college degree or a special certification or license, there is normally no need to list any high schools attended.
- Areas of knowledge or professional highlights.

Figure 8.2 (continued)

Susan Feagin
Resume, page 2

Feb. 1987 to Dec. 1987	Jack-in-the-Box, Dallas, Texas **POSITION:** Fountain Clerk (part-time) **RESPONSIBILITIES:** • Took orders from drive-through window • Prepared fountain items such as carbonated drinks and ice-cream orders • Cleaned counters and tables
EDUCATIONAL HIGHLIGHTS	**BUSINESS** Salesmanship Advertising Principles Retailing Principles Motivation Seminar **SECRETARIAL SCIENCES** Word-Processing Skills Shorthand Speed Building Office Machines Secretarial Procedures Business Correspondence in Spanish **ADDITIONAL COURSES** Business and Professional Speech Business Communication Human Relations Spanish I–IV
EDUCATION	Richland College, Dallas, Texas **Associate of Arts Degree** in 1988 in business with emphasis in sales and secretarial science
LANGUAGES	Speak and write fluent Spanish and am familiar with the Spanish dialects used in southern California and Texas
REFERENCES	Available upon request

■ Job experience, including job accomplishments and responsibilities.
Usually, your past jobs should be listed in reverse chronological order
beginning with the most recent job held. If you have very little or no
job experience, list your volunteer experience. The interpersonal and
supervisory skills that the volunteer develops are as valuable as those
developed in a paid position. "Many federal agencies will accept volunteer experience in lieu of paid experience."[10]

Figure 8.3 Another sample one-page employment resume.

JENNIFER MAXWELL STRAUSS

Present Address
P.O. Box 23383, Emory University
Atlanta, GA 30322
(404) 555-8550

Permanent Address
274 Alpha Road
West Chester, PA 19150
(215) 555-5939

OBJECTIVE An internship in advertising

EDUCATION **Emory University, School of Business Administration**
Atlanta, GA
Candidate for BBA degree, May 1996
Major: Marketing

ACTIVITIES **Panhellenic Representative, 1993–1994**
Delta Phi Epsilon Sorority
Participated in weekly meetings that were held to allocate funds to sponsor
various all-university events. Liaison between the Delta Phi Epsilon
Sorority and the Panhellenic Board.

EXPERIENCE **Administrative Assistant**
December 1993–January 1994
Summer 1994
The Craft Fashion Institute, Philadelphia, PA
Coordinated information to produce course syllabi. Proofread and oversaw
printing of course catalog. Installed a card catalog system in the library.
Organized and maintained the director of education's office.

Sales Clerk
Summer 1993
Kamikaze Kids, Philadelphia, PA
Promoted unique, upscale children's clothing. Responsibilities included
opening and closing of the store and making cash deposits. Cash register
experience.

Public Relations Intern
March 1992–June 1992
Elkman Advertising, Philadelphia, PA
Worked closely with the account executive for the McDonald's
Corporation. Responsibilities included following-up press releases and
television spots, calling various media offices, and arranging interviews
with local celebrities to promote McDonald's public relations interests.

ADDITIONAL Working knowledge of BASIC computer language.
DATA Extensive travel in the United States, Europe, and Mexico.
Hobbies include theatre, reading, and music.

REFERENCES Available upon request

■ Items of interest, if appropriate:

Military status.
Professional organizations.
Publications or patents.
Job-related hobbies, activities, or interests.
Accreditations or licenses.

REMEMBER, WHEN WRITING A CONVENTIONAL RESUME . . .

- *Put the most important information first.* The reader may only read the top half of the page. Don't start with education unless it is outstanding. If both education and experience are weak, begin with areas of knowledge or accomplishments.
- *Make it neat.* No misspelled words or erasures.
- *Make it easy to read.* Leave wide margins to make the resume appealing to the eye, and avoid complete sentences when possible. The reader should be able to glance quickly down the page to get basic information.
- *Keep it brief.* Usually one to two pages.
- *Type or print it on heavy bond paper.* If you use a printer, make sure the print is letter quality and do not use paper with perforated edges.
- *Include the basic information* listed on pages 238–242.
- *Make sure all information is job related.*

Scholarships, awards, or honors.

Language ability (including knowledge of computer languages and programs).

- References: Available upon request (some experts believe this statement, often included, is not necessary). Normally, family members should not be used as references. Select persons who know you well and can comment on your communication and people skills, your work abilities and experiences, or both. Usually, the more impressive your references, the better. Be sure to take your list of references with you to the interview.

To protect you from possible discrimination and to keep all items in your resume strictly job related, we suggest that you *not* include the following information in your resume:*

---

*Federal and state legislation make it unlawful to discriminate in employment hiring on the basis of race, color, religion, sex, national origin, and in most cases, age and physical disabilities. Even so, some companies prefer that personal data be included in the resume. It is not unlawful for you to include such data if you wish or if you feel it would be to your advantage. However, if you include personal data and other non-job-related items, there is no guarantee that this information will not be used against you in some way. For similar reasons, it is also advisable to omit specific salary preferences (even if requested). If desired salary is requested on an application form, you can write, "negotiable." Unless the information is pertinent in some way to the job, you are advised to omit personal data, salary, and non-job-related activities from your resume.

- Hobbies, activities, or interests that do not relate to the job. (However, hobbies, activities, and interests that reveal your creativity, leadership, and character usually should be included.)
- Past, present, or desired salary.
- Personal data, such as race, sex, age, date of birth, city and state of birth, marital status, spouse's name, health, height, weight, number and ages of children.

Prepare an Electronic Resume[11]

An **electronic resume** is a conventional resume that has been altered into a "computer friendly" form that can be scanned, read, stored, updated, and extracted accurately by computer. There are two reasons why electronic resumes are becoming important today: First, to cut down on the time and number of employees needed to handle the volume of resumes received, companies are turning to computers for storage, speed, and accuracy of evaluation. When a person with specific qualifications is sought, the computer analyzes the resumes on hand and extracts a list of those candidates that meet the necessary requirements; it does this by searching for key words used to describe the position.

The second reason for the increasing importance of electronic resumes is the growing number of electronic database companies (called *job banks*), which, for a small fee, collect resumes from people seeking jobs and make them available to employers wishing "to supplement their traditional recruiting strategies," says Peter Weddle, president of Job Bank USA. Because resumes are scanned into the database, they must meet certain readability guidelines not required on conventional resumes (for example, no color paper—it smudges when copied; no point size smaller than 12 point—scanners have problems reading small print). To save storage space, resumes are compacted and reduced to a format that looks something like the following (compare this compressed version with the electronic resume in Figure 8.4):

> - ®®Susan Feagin 1355 Edna Street Napa, CA 94558 (415) 555 5760 (Res) (415) 555 5745 (Bus) ®®**KEY WORD PREFACE** Sales and sales supervision. Four years in fabric import sales. Customer relations. Customer complaints. Stock ordering. Files & records. Correspondence. Word processing. Shorthand, 90wpm. Typing, 55wpm. Fluent in Spanish. Cultural sensitivity. A.A., Business—1988. ®®**EXPERIENCE Fabric Imports** Napa, California Salesperson 7/92–Present ®®Awarded top salesperson for the last three years. ®®Strengthened customer relations with Spanish speaking accounts. ®®Generated 10 new key accounts during last year. ■

Figure 8.4 Electronic resume.

Susan Feagin
1355 Edna Street
Napa, CA 94558

(415) 555-5760 (Res)   (415) 555-5745 (Bus)

KEY WORD PREFACE

Sales and sales supervision. Four years in fabric import sales. Customer relations. Customer complaints. Stock ordering. Files & records. Correspondence. Word processing. Shorthand, 90wpm. Typing, 55wpm. Fluent in Spanish. Cultural sensitivity. A.A., Business--1988.

EXPERIENCE

Fabric Imports   Napa, California
Salesperson   7/92–Present

- Awarded top salesperson for the last three years.
- Strengthened customer relations with Spanish speaking accounts.
- Generated 10 new key accounts during last year.
- Ordered stock, promoted warehouse sales, and designed showroom fabric displays.

Richland College   Dallas, Texas
Secretary   1/88–7/92

- Personal secretary to Dean of Instruction.
- Supervised office and office assistant.
- Maintained daily calendar for the Dean.
- Developed less complicated procedure for handling student complaints.
- Composed letters and memos; took dictation.

Jack-in-the-Box   Dallas, Texas
Fountain Clerk (part-time)   2/87–12/87

- Took orders from drive-through window.
- Prepared fountain items such as carbonated drinks and ice-cream orders.
- Cleaned counters and tables.

EDUCATION

Richland College   Dallas, Texas
Associate of Arts Degree in Business   May 1988

PROFESSIONAL AFFILIATIONS

Napa Sales Club. Chamber of Commerce. Phi Beta Kappa.

Once your resume has been read and identified for a job vacancy, it is extracted and returned to the form in which it was originally received (providing the computer read it accurately); then it is sent to the requesting company to enter into their conventional evaluation process. Therefore, an electronic resume must appeal both to the computer and to the human reader as well.

WHEN WRITING AN ELECTRONIC RESUME . . .

- *Use boldface* (for titles and subtitles) *but avoid using boxes, lines, italics, underlining, shading, or graphics*—they don't copy well. Bullets must be dark and filled in.
- *Use white paper* (20–60 lb.) *and black ink.* Send only original copies from a laser printer (or print shop).
- *Use simple fonts,* like Helvetica or Times in 12 to 14 point. 14 point is easier for a scanner to read but a one-page resume will become two pages.
- *Print on only one side of the paper.* If you use two pages, do not staple them. Use a paper clip instead. Be sure to put your name and page number at the top left side of the second page.
- *Write your information from left to right* so it will still be readable when compressed. Dates are normally easier to read when on the right side of the resume. Avoid columns; the scanner will read each column as a different page.
- *Include dates as May 1996 or 5/96.*
- *Send resume in a large envelope.* Do not fold it (folds make print impossible to read).

When writing an electronic resume, think in key words. **Key words** are used by employers to describe a specific job. If your resume does not include these key words (or their synonyms), it will not be selected. Peter Weddle suggests that the electronic resume begin with a Key Word Preface, which lists ten to twenty key words or phrases.[12] Or, if you prefer to use longer phrases to highlight your abilities, knowledge, and skills, begin your resume with a Summary of Qualifications. Don't forget, however, to include key words. In both sections, each word/phrase should begin with a capital and end with a period.

Electronic resumes generally include four headings: *Key Word Preface, Experience, Education,* and *Professional Affiliations and Awards.* References and Objective aren't needed—the first is already obvious; the second was replaced by the Key Word Preface. Although the chronological pattern is also effective for electronic resumes, Weddle advises that simply telling what you can do with the skills (listed as key words) isn't enough. You need to show "some benefit or improvement achieved by those actions."[13] For example, assuming "customer complaints" is a key word, you might state that you "handled customer complaints." However, saying that you "developed a faster procedure for handling customer complaints" not only shows *what* you can do, it indicates *how well* you can do it.

Figure 8.5 Sample letter of application.

1355 Edna Street
Napa, CA 94558
September 20, 1996

Mr. John F. Schmitz, Owner
Schmitz Furniture & Carpet
705 North Locust Street
Dulsura, CA 94661

Dear Mr. Schmitz:

Four years' sales experience at Fabric Imports, where I ranked as top salesperson for the last three years, prepared me for your position as carpet salesperson advertised in today's *Los Angeles Times*. I would like to interview for the position.

Last year at Fabric Imports, I added ten new accounts because of my ability to sell to walk-in customers. At the same time, I enjoyed the close working relationship with key accounts. In addition, my knowledge of Spanish and personal computers should allow me to make a positive contribution to your company.

I would like to personally meet with you to discuss more thoroughly my qualifications for this position. Although mornings work best for me, another time can be arranged at your convenience. My resume includes my home and work numbers, or you can leave a message at (415) 555-4332.

Thank you for your consideration. I look forward to hearing from you soon.

Sincerely,

Susan Feagin

Susan Feagin

Enc: Resume

Once you have completed your resume, you are ready to prepare a letter of application to send with your conventional resume.

Prepare a Letter of Application[14]

Keep in mind that the purpose of the letter of application is to give enough information about you and your capabilities to interest the employer in

WHEN WRITING A LETTER . . .

- *Type neatly and use correct grammar.* Ask someone to proofread the letter for errors.
- *Address it to a specific person* by name at a specific firm. Include the job title in the inside address. If you address your letter to the "Personnel Manager," "Manager," or a similarly vague title without a name, the letter may never reach the right person, or if it does, the letter may not be answered. Always address the letter to a specific person so that someone has the responsibility to answer it. Also, that person may be impressed that you cared enough to find out his or her name.
- *State the following:*

    Your purpose in sending the letter.

    How you heard about the opening.

    Your basic qualifications for the position and any accomplishments or career highlights that might interest the employer enough to contact you.

    Phone number(s) where you can be reached, and when you would normally be available for an interview.

    Any other information you feel is pertinent to the specific job for which you are applying, without repeating the same information found in your resume unless necessary to establish your basic qualifications.

- *Include a final paragraph that requests action,* with such sentences as "I am looking forward to hearing from you soon" or "I will call you during the week of _____ to arrange an appointment with you."
- *Include your return address, the date, an inside address, greeting, body, closing, and your signature.* Sign the letter in dark blue or black ink.

talking with you personally. Each letter should relate specifically to the company and person to whom you are writing (see Figure 8.5). Therefore, if you haven't already done so, find out as much as you can about the firm(s) and individual(s) you plan to ask for an interview. Try to talk with someone who has been working with the firm, ask for literature such as the annual report that explains the firm and its policies, or read about the organization in *The Wall Street Journal, Dun & Bradstreet Middle Market Directory* or *Dun & Bradstreet Million Dollar Directory, Moody's Industrial Manual, Thomas Register of American Manufacturers,* and other reference

books in your library. The only way to get information about small organizations is to call them and ask. A call to the company receptionist or the
sales, marketing, or public relations departments should give you the information you need. Don't be afraid to call the personnel office (often
called Human Resources) for information. Once you have discovered as
much about the company as possible, you are ready to complete your letter
of application.

Once you have completed a conventional and/or an electronic resume
and prepared your letter of application, you are ready to consider ways to
improve your effectiveness during the actual interview.

Have a Positive Attitude

Once your communication with the potential employer has produced a
date for a personal interview, the next step is to prepare for the interview
by adjusting your mental attitude as necessary. Regardless of the type of
interview involved, attitude is immensely important. You must feel that
you are a person of worth and integrity with a genuine right to be considered for the job. Do not be frightened about the unknown; rather, be
confident in your ability to respond openly and honestly with favorable
effect. You are just as important as the person who is interviewing you.
After all, you are also using the interview to decide whether *you* want the
job. Approach the interview with a positive attitude. Think success!

On the other hand, adjusting your attitude does not mean that you
should alter your personality or style just for the interview: Be yourself.
You will make a better impression if you avoid role playing and pretense.

Dress and Communicate for the Occasion

Dress has a lot to do with the first impressions an interviewer has of
you—and first impressions count. One study found that when a negative impression was created during the first 5 minutes of the interview,
applicants were not hired 90 percent of the time; however, when a positive impression was created in the first 5 minutes, applicants were hired
75 percent of the time.[15] The Research Institute of America surveyed
executives in hiring positions to learn which items of dress and appearance
gave them a bad first impression of salesmen and potential male employees
(see Table 8.1). Another study found that interviewers tend to hire people
who dress in the interviewers' images.[16] If you are poorly groomed, there
is a good chance that the prospective employer will view you as a person
with a low self-concept—a person unable to function effectively in the

Table 8.1 Male Dress Items Making a Bad First Impression
on Executive Interviewers

Item	Percentage of Executives That Noticed the Item
Needed a haircut	100%
Soiled shirt cuffs and collar	97
Frayed cuffs and collar	88
Needed a shave	83
Tie badly knotted	79
Scuffed shoes	79
Shirt collar badly fitted	76
Slacks needed pressing	76
Poor-fitting suits	59
Wrong suit style or color	46
Slacks too short	41

Source: Adapted from "Round Up," *Personnel* 56 (July–August 1979), p. 45, by Leslie B. Lawrence and David D. Steinbrecher. © 1979 American Management Association, New York. All rights reserved. Used by permission of the publisher.

position being discussed. (See Chapter 5 for suggestions on how to dress for acceptance in the business world.)

Interviewers' decisions are more heavily influenced by unfavorable impressions and behaviors than they are by favorable impressions and behaviors.[17] This is especially important now that videotaped interviews are becoming more common. Dress is not the only way interviewees create unfavorable first impressions; other nonverbal behaviors clearly affect professional interviewers' evaluations of applicants. In one study, twenty-six people interviewed candidates with good nonverbal behaviors and candidates with poor nonverbal behaviors. Good nonverbal behaviors included such things as direct eye contact, high energy level, smiles, and smooth delivery; poor nonverbal behaviors included very little eye contact, low energy level, nonfluent delivery, and few smiles. When asked if they would invite the candidates back for another interview, none of the twenty-six would invite the candidates with poor nonverbal behaviors back for another interview; however, twenty-three of the interviewers would invite back the candidates with good nonverbal behaviors.[18] Another study compared successful and unsuccessful interviewees. The successful interviewees were more likely to[19]

- Speak rapidly and forcefully.
- Gesture and smile often.
- Look directly at the interviewer.
- Nod their head in a positive manner.
- Lean forward while maintaining natural, comfortable postures.

And finally, Kittie Watson and Larry Smeltzer report that there are three things that interviewers remember most after the interviewee is gone: *eye contact, appearance,* and *facial expressions.*[20]

Be Prepared for Any Type of Interviewer

You cannot always predict which type of interviewer you will see. Normally, you can expect one or a combination of the following three types.[21]

The Nonstructured Interviewer ■   This interviewer usually expects you to take most of the initiative during the interview. Expect the nonstructured interviewer to ask open-ended questions such as, "Tell me about yourself." or "Will you please tell me why you feel qualified for this position?" This interviewer wants detailed, fairly long responses. In order to respond effectively, you must anticipate possible questions and carefully think through your responses in advance. Think of what you want to say; jot down the major points if you wish. Expand on them if you have an opportunity. This type of interview gives you a chance to demonstrate your intelligence, creativity, and ability to adapt to a difficult situation.

The Structured Interviewer ■   This interviewer is just the opposite of the nonstructured interviewer. The structured interviewer plans everything in advance and gives you little if any opportunity to be creative in your responses. The structured interviewer usually asks direct and closed questions and wants specific, to-the-point answers. This type of interviewer succeeds in learning a great deal of information in a short time.

   The best way to respond to the structured interviewer is to provide the most direct, forthright answers you can. Keep explanations brief while still including all necessary information. However, be aware that the interviewer may suddenly become silent. Some structured interviewers use this tactic to test how you handle the unexpected. Use this silence as an opportunity to expand on important areas.

The Hostile Interviewer[22] ■   On rare occasions, you may find an interviewer who seems to delight in constantly evaluating the interviewee, often with belittling and embarrassing comments or questions and subtle nonverbal signals. Usually, the hostile interviewer has low self-esteem or sees the interviewee as threatening.

A polite question or remark, such as "Why do you ask?" or "Thank you, but I do not wish to respond to that statement," is the best way to respond to this type of person. Such responses will usually be sufficient to end the hostile comments and encourage the interviewer to probe areas that are more critical to the job.

Be Prepared for a Group Interview

Group interviews are becoming more common in both profit and non-profit organizations and at all levels. *Panel interviews* usually comprise one interviewer and several interviewees; *board interviews* comprise two or more interviewers and usually only one interviewee. There are even some interviews that have two or more interviewers and two or more interviewees.[23] (See Chapter 7 for a more detailed explanation of panel and board interviews.)

Unless you know for sure that your interview will not be a group interview, be prepared just in case. In addition to being prepared for a possible group interview, you must be prepared for all probable questions.

Carefully Plan Answers to Probable Questions

Research suggests that, when answering questions, successful job applicants[24]

- Refer to technical jargon that is in common use in their field.
- Use active, positive, and concrete language.
- Support answers with specific examples, comparisons, illustrations, and statistics taken from personal experience, coworkers, company publications, supervisors, and so on. (See Chapter 12 for an explanation of supporting materials.)
- Use humor when appropriate. If the interviewer uses humor, then you can; if not, don't.
- Describe job weaknesses or physical disabilities in a positive manner.

Anticipate interviewer questions, plan your answers (don't forget to include the above research suggestions), and practice those answers aloud. Detailed lists of typically asked questions are located at the end of this book in Appendixes B and C. A few of the most typically asked "tough" questions are listed here:[25]

What do you know about our company?

Why do you want to leave your current job?

What do you think of your present job?

What salary are you expecting?

What do you want to be five years from now?

Describe yourself in three adjectives.

What is the best idea you've had in the last three years?

What is the hardest thing you've done in the last three years?

How would your coworkers describe you? Supervisor describe you?

Why should we hire you?

Your answers should always be truthful, should come from you, and should never sound memorized. However, getting an idea of some good answers to some tough questions may help you present the real you to the interviewer and may help calm your nerves. If the following responses don't fit you, at least they should stimulate your thinking:[26]

Q: Why do you want to leave your current job?

A: They went out of business.
I want to earn more money.
Because I'm looking for a job in which I can grow as well as contribute; I need more challenge.

Q: What are your weaknesses? [Or a newer version:] What do friends criticize about your personality?
[Try to give truthful "positive weaknesses." One or two weaknesses is enough; be prepared to give a positive illustration of each weakness.]

A: Impatience—I get impatient with people when they don't get their jobs done on time and impatient with myself for not growing fast enough.
Overdrive—I drive myself, and often others, too hard.
I'm very stubborn when I believe I'm right.

Q: What are your strengths? [Or a newer version:] How do your customers (or boss, subordinates, coworkers) describe you?
[Try to relate your strengths to qualities you know are needed on this job. Give examples to support your answer.]

A: My common sense in establishing work priorities.
I am able to handle not only business problems but also people problems.
My job knowledge and extensive training.

Q: Do you mind taking a personality test prior to joining our company?
[Such tests are often for research purposes and are not used to de-

cide between candidates. In any case, to be hired you will have to take the test.]

A: No, not at all.

Q: What are you currently making?
[If you are currently underpaid, state your current salary without hesitation, then add something like the following.]

A: That's precisely the reason I am here today.
[If you currently have benefits beyond the base salary, state your current salary, then add the following statement.]
The total value of my current financial package is $_____. This is made up of _____, _____, and _____.

Q: What do you want to make on your next job?
[If asked on the first or second interview, it's usually better to say something such as the following.]

A: I'm pretty flexible on that score. I'd rather talk about finances after we've decided together whether I'm the right person for this job.
[If asked on later interviews, give a positive, unapologetic answer. Be sure you've done your research and know the salary range. Most employers expect you to ask for at least a 20 percent raise.]

Q: What do you think of your present boss?
[Be positive even if it hurts. You may wish to refer to the positive characteristics of your boss's communication style as discussed in Chapter 3.]

A: My boss is very knowledgeable in sales and as a result I've learned some valuable sales techniques.

Q: What would you consider an ideal job?
[An answer similar to the following is probably better than listing some overworked buzzwords.]

A: I don't think there is an ideal job—meaningful jobs are what employees make them.

Q: What actions would you take if you came on board?
[It's best not to describe the changes you would make.]

A: The chances are I would not make any changes at all for a while, at least until I have a chance to really evaluate the situation from the inside.

It is impossible to predict exactly what is going to happen during an interview, but if you take time to consider probable questions and think through your answers, your confidence and chances of success will be greatly improved.

Exercise Your Responsibility During the Interview

First impressions, based mainly on nonverbal factors, are certainly important in an interview. However, it is possible to make a good first impression and then ruin it by your answers and behaviors. As an interviewee, you are responsible for the impressions you create. You also have the responsibility of making sure you discuss areas of interest to you and of introducing topics that the interviewer may have forgotten to explore. In addition, you are partly responsible for creating rapport in the interview and for achieving a friendly and cordial conclusion to the interview.

During the interview, avoid annoying mannerisms such as chewing gum, fiddling with things on the interviewer's desk, and other inappropriate behaviors.

Be Prepared with Questions to Ask the Interviewer

Most interviewers will invite you to ask questions. You should be prepared to ask a few—first, because you want to get enough information to decide if you really want this particular job (you want a company with an open climate), and second, because your questions show your interest. If the interviewer does not give you the opportunity to ask questions, simply say, "Excuse me, but I have a few questions I would like to ask about. . . ." Here are some of the questions you might want to ask:[27]

How creative am I allowed to be on this job?

Would the company support me if I went back to school?

What is the typical career path of an individual entering the organization at this level?

Would this position require travel?

Describe your ideal employee.

What type of training program would I receive?

What could I do or read while you are considering my application that might help me on the job if I'm hired?

May I see a copy of the job description?

Remember, your questions reflect your training and education, your ambitions, and your level of commitment.

Be Prepared to Follow Up the Interview If Necessary

Most interviews end with some plan for future action on the part of one or both of the participants. When the decision will be reached and how it will be communicated are usually specified by the interviewer. Make certain that you carry out whatever responsibility you have been assigned during the interview. Always send a thank-you card immediately after the interview; it could be a factor in whether you are called back for a second interview. If you do not hear from the company within a reasonable amount of time (usually five to seven days), write or call reconfirming your interest in the position and again thank the interviewer for his or her time.

RESPONSIBILITIES OF THE INTERVIEWER

If you are the interviewer, you usually have more responsibility for the manner in which the employment interview is conducted than does the interviewee. Keep in mind that interviewees prefer interviewers who

1. Show high levels of nonverbal immediacy (discussed in Chapter 5) such as eye contact and an open body posture.
2. Listen to interviewee answers and limit the number of interruptions.
3. Ask open questions and allow sufficient time to answer them.[28]

Interviewer responsibilities occur before, during, and after the interview.

Communicate with the Interviewee Before the Interview

Make certain you have informed the interviewee where and when the interview is to take place. In some instances, a phone call may be an appropriate reminder. Inform the interviewee if there are materials he or she should bring to the interview.

Plan the Environment

The nature of the interview usually determines the type of environment you will want to establish. In almost all instances, privacy is essential. Select an area that will be free from phone calls and distractions. The seating should be planned so that participants feel equal. An interviewee who must pass the guard posts of two secretaries only to find you sitting behind the desk is likely to be frightened and nervous. Come from behind the desk, and sit across from the interviewee, free from psychological and physical barriers.

Organize the Interview Carefully

Interviewers who conduct poorly planned, unorganized employment interviews learn very little useful information about the candidate during the interview. Consequently, their decisions will be based solely on gut reactions, often resulting in ineffective hiring. Such mistakes cost the company money. Interviewers cannot afford to make wrong decisions. Therefore, they must plan and organize each phase of the interview carefully. Some suggestions for organizing each phase are summarized here (see Chapter 7 for more detailed explanations).

Plan the Opening Phase ■ Establishing *rapport* (a relaxed feeling between individuals) is the first responsibility of the interviewer during the interview. The best way to establish rapport depends on the interviewee; each person should be handled individually. Look carefully at the resume and the letter of application for clues as to what subject would be of most interest to the person. If you plan to establish rapport by discussing general interest items, be careful not to overdo it. Some interviewees prefer to discuss only topics related to the purpose of the interview and become suspicious and nervous when idle talk continues for very long. Instead of discussing general subjects, you may want to ask the applicant to verify information listed on the resume or application form or to discuss his or her reasons for wanting the particular position.

Regardless of the topic discussed, remember that your purpose is to get the applicant talking, relaxed, and ready for the interview. Also, try not to be overly dependent on your first impressions of the applicant; they could be inaccurate.

As you establish rapport, give the interviewee a brief *orientation* to the interview. Don't assume! Verify the interviewee's name and the position sought. State your name and the reason you are the one conducting the interview. Give a clear overview of the job and any responsibilities connected with it. Once the specific job has been clarified, the interviewee may no longer be interested; if so, you have saved yourself valuable time. If the applicant is still interested, clarify the type of information you are specifically interested in and the types of responses you prefer—detailed or brief answers. Give the applicant a general idea of the length of the interview and ask whether that is agreeable.

Don't conclude the opening phase of the interview before *motivating the applicant* to give you candid, carefully thought-out answers. Most applicants are already motivated simply because they want the job. However, they may feel a need to impress you by pretending qualities or characteristics they don't have. Tell applicants that you are sure they are as interested as you in finding a position in which they will be most successful, and that to help you place them accurately you want them to answer all questions honestly and put aside false modesty. This will motivate most applicants. Explaining to them the importance of the interview to the overall application process is another way to motivate job applicants.

Plan the Question–Response Phase ■   Asking whatever question comes to mind is an extremely ineffective way to learn and remember information about the applicant. The skilled interviewer decides what general areas (such as past work experience, leadership abilities, personality characteristics, and so on) should be covered in the interview and then plans specific questions for each area. For example, one psychologist has found that the ideal employee has personality characteristics including sociability, stability, leadership, maturity, and industriousness.[29] If these were the personality traits desired by your company, you would need to plan a series of questions designed to help you rate the applicant on each one. For example, to determine the industriousness of a sales candidate you might ask:

> At what age did you commence work?
>
> How many jobs have you held since you left school?
>
> How many accounts did you work in your last position?
>
> How often did you see these accounts?
>
> What were your sales for the past year? Preceding year?[30]

To remember data and comply with EEOC (Equal Employment Opportunity Commission) regulations, interviewers must keep an accurate record of each interviewee. A rating of 1–5 or "well above average" to "well below average" should be given for each characteristic or topic area, on a form such as the one in Figure 8.6.

One expert suggests that the following general areas be investigated when candidates are applying for supervisory or management positions:[31]

> Has the applicant performed in a similar capacity?
>
> How does the applicant feel about his or her present job?
>
> Why does the applicant desire a change in jobs at this time?
>
> Do you find the applicant likable?
>
> What are the applicant's career objectives?
>
> Will the applicant maintain good relations with other managers?
>
> What is the applicant's level of self-esteem?

(See Appendix B for specific questions often asked of applicants seeking nonsupervisory positions, and Appendix C for additional questions asked of applicants seeking supervisory positions.)

Most employment interviewers organize their questions for each general area into the funnel sequence, which begins with open-ended questions and ends with direct or closed questions. Open-ended questions at the beginning of the interview usually relax the applicant, uncover a great

Figure 8.6 Form for rating job applicants. *(Source: Robert L. Brady,* Law for Personnel Managers: How to Hire the People You Need Without Discrimination, *p. 25. Used by permission of Robert L. Brady, J.D., Bureau of Law and Business, 64 Wall Street, Madison, CT 06643.)*

FORM FOR RATING JOB APPLICANTS

Candidate _____ Job Classification _____

Interviewer _____ Date _____

RATING

Skills/Aptitudes*	Well Above Average	Above Average	Average	Below Average	Well Below Average	Comments
Alertness						
Education						
Experience						
Job Knowledge/Skills						
Organizational Ability						
Communications Ability						
Personal Assessment*						
Attitude						
Maturity						
Stability						
Motivation/Ambition						
Assertiveness						
Initiative						
Confidence						
Leadership Ability						
Ability to Work with Other Employees						

* Evaluate only those characteristics which are appropriate for the position involved.

RATING SUMMARY

Strongest Points _____

_____

_____

Weakest Points _____

_____

_____

Recommended for Hiring? Yes _____ No _____

_____

Advancement Potential? Very Good _____ Good _____ Average _____

Below Average _____

deal of information (which means the interviewer will not have to ask so many questions), and reveal areas that need to be investigated in more detail. Organized questions will allow you, the interviewer, to make a more valid assessment of the applicant. Notes of important information taken discreetly during the interview will further help you in your assessment.

Plan the Closing Phase ■ The closing of the interview is as important as the opening, for you will want to make sure the interviewee leaves with a positive feeling and an accurate understanding of what will happen next. Let the applicant know that the interview is ending by summarizing its content and outlining the times and nature of any future contact. Give the interviewee a chance to ask questions, and thank the interviewee for his or her time and cooperation.

Ask Only Lawful Questions

In accordance with federal and state laws (see note 32 for a list of federal laws), there are certain questions that interviewers cannot ask of applicants during preemployment interviews. These laws are based on the belief that all persons—regardless of race, sex, national origin, religion, age, or marital status—should be able to compete for jobs and advance in the job market based on their "bona fide occupational qualifications": experience, education, and specific skills. An employer does not have to hire anyone who is not qualified, but race, sex, national origin, religion, age (in most cases), disabilities, or marital status cannot be used to determine whether a person is qualified (except in rare instances in which an employer can prove that one of these traits is job-related). Thus, skills, experience, and education are the only factors that should be used to determine whether a person is qualified for a particular job.

There are two basic guidelines to follow in deciding the legality of an interview question (whether it's asked during the interview or included on the application form):

1. *All questions must be job-related.* The interviewer must be prepared to prove that the questions are related to the specific job.
2. *The same basic questions must be asked of all applicants for the position.* In other words, an interviewer cannot have one set of questions for minorities, another for women, and still another for white males.

Using these two guidelines, determine whether the questions in the following Awareness Check (questions often asked in interviews and found on application forms) would be considered lawful if used by the average organization. Then compare your answers with the key. Be sure to read the discussion provided with each answer; additional questions are covered there as well.

AWARENESS CHECK: LAWFUL AND UNLAWFUL QUESTIONS

LAWFUL AND UNLAWFUL QUESTIONS FOR THE PREEMPLOYMENT INTERVIEW AND APPLICATION FORM

Directions: For each of the questions and statements below, select an "L" for those you feel are lawful, a "U" for those that seem unlawful, and a "Q" for those that seem questionable (could be either lawful or unlawful depending on the situation).

_____ 1. What is your wife's maiden name?

_____ 2. Are you a citizen of the United States?

_____ 3. Have you ever been arrested?

_____ 4. Do you play golf?

_____ 5. How old are you?

_____ 6. Would you be willing to submit a copy of your birth certificate or baptismal record to prove your date of birth?

_____ 7. How many words per minute do you type?

_____ 8. Do you have any physical disabilities?

_____ 9. Have you ever been fired from a previous job?

_____ 10. What work experiences have you had that you feel have prepared you for this job?

_____ 11. Tell me about your educational background and your grade point average.

_____ 12. Are you married, divorced, or single?

_____ 13. Do you have any children? Are you planning on having any children?

_____ 14. What foreign language(s) do you speak, read, or write fluently?

_____ 15. What personal qualities do you have that you think would be helpful in working with the people within our organization?

_____ 16. What type discharge did you get from the service?

_____ 17. What are the names and addresses of your parents, grandparents, an aunt, and an uncle?

_____ 18. Please include a photograph with your application form.

_____ 19. What religious holidays do you observe?

_____ 20. What office machines can you operate?

_____ 21. Of what clubs or organizations are you a member?

_____ 22. Do you own your own home?

_____ 23. What is your weight, height, and color of eyes, hair, and complexion?

_____ 24. You sound Oriental. Are you from Taiwan?

_____ 25. Can you get along with persons of different races?

ANSWERS[33]

1. *Unlawful.* Unless absolutely necessary to obtain information for a preemployment investigation, this question is unlawful. How can the maiden name of a man's wife in any way relate to his job qualifications?
2. *Lawful.* This information is necessary to ensure that the applicant has a legal work permit that allows permanent stay in the United States. It is unlawful, however, to ask if a person is a naturalized citizen of the United States or to ask when the person acquired citizenship.
3. *Unlawful.* Arrest does not necessarily mean conviction. An applicant could have been arrested simply because he or she happened to be driving the same type of car as a reported robbery getaway car. Should this be on the applicant's record? Unfortunately, some employers might feel that the applicant is suspect, regardless of the reason for the arrest, and refuse employment. It is lawful to ask if the applicant has been convicted of a felony, but this can be used for employment rejection only depending on the number of convictions, the nature and time of the convictions, and if the conviction is job-related. (For example, does the position require the employee to be bonded?)
4. *Questionable.* There is probably nothing wrong with asking this question, but if challenged the burden of proof would be on the employer to show that the question was job-related.
5. *Unlawful.* The Age Discrimination in Employment Act prohibits discrimination against persons between the ages of 40 and 60, and in most cases, to 70 years of age. Because of child protection laws in most states, it is legal (even required) to ask if the applicant is 21 or older. The exact age, however, should not be asked.
6. *Unlawful.* Both documents contain information that is unlawful to obtain. Even if the employer owned a liquor store and could not legally hire anyone under the age of 21, the employer could not ask for proof of age in the preemployment interview. Once the applicant has been hired, it is legal to obtain proof of age.
7. *Lawful.* This information would be job-related if the job requires the applicant to type. The employer may ask the applicant to take a standardized typing test if all applicants are given the same test.
8. *Unlawful.* This question is unlawful unless the job requires certain physical skills for successful performance of duties. It would be better to ask, "Do you have any physical or health problems that may affect your job performance?"
9. *Questionable.* Employer must be able to prove that the question is job-related.
10. *Lawful.* The response would tell of the applicant's skill and abilities.
11. *Lawful.* This is necessary to determine an applicant's qualifications. Employer should request applicant to sign a release form so that the schools in question may legally release this information.
12. *Unlawful.* Even men could be discriminated against by this question. Some employers consider a young man who is married to be more stable and therefore a better employee than a young man who is single.

(continued)

13. *Unlawful.* Questions referring to pregnancy, marital status, number or names of children, care of children when sick, and other similar questions are illegal because they are mainly used to discriminate against women and are not job-related. An employer who is worried that a woman may take off too much time to tend sick children merely needs to ask for the woman's attendance record for the past year.

14. *Lawful.* As long as the information is job-related, it is lawful. However, to ask how the applicant acquired the ability to speak, read, or write a foreign language is unlawful. If a definite competency level is required, all applicants can be given a language test.

15. *Lawful.* The response would tell of the applicant's job-related skills and knowledge.

16. *Unlawful.* Type of discharge is not job-related; neither is the branch of the military in which the applicant served. It is lawful to ask, "Are you a veteran?"

17. *Unlawful.* This could reveal information used to discriminate against the applicant.

18. *Unlawful.* A photograph could easily be used to discriminate against the applicant on the basis of race, sex, age, or national origin. Sometimes, a job applicant will send a photograph even when not requested. Normally it is advisable not to send a photograph because employers aware of federal regulations will separate it from the application and destroy it anyway. Once an applicant has been hired, the company can request a photograph or have the employee photographed.

19. *Unlawful.* This question could be used to discriminate against an applicant because of his or her religion. However, if the applicant has voluntarily stated religious preferences requiring special scheduling that the company will be unable to provide, the interviewer may ask, "Do you expect to have your religious holidays off?"

20. *Lawful.* This question is job-related if the job requires the operation of business machines.

21. *Questionable.* Asking for names of clubs, lodges, or organizations that relate to sex, race, or religion is unlawful. It is also unlawful to ask if the applicant is or was a member of a fraternity or sorority. However, it is lawful to inquire about any unions or trade or professional organizations that are job-related.

22. *Unlawful.* This is not job-related and tends to discriminate against the poor, young, and minority groups. For the same reasons, it is also unlawful to ask if an applicant owns a car (unless it's a job requirement) or has an established credit record.

23. *Unlawful.* Such personal data as asked for in this question are used to discriminate against applicants for the same reasons listed in answer 18. Personal data have rarely proven to be job-related. Applicants are not advised to include such data in their resumes or personal data sheets.

24. *Unlawful.* The Immigration Reform and Control Act (IRCA) prohibits discrimination based on national origin. Areas given special consideration by EEOC and IRCA include discrimination against a person who is foreign-looking, who speaks with an accent, who fails to meet company height and weight requirements, and who speaks a language other than English in personal conversations and on breaks.

25. *Questionable.* Although not actually unlawful, it would be hard for the employer to prove that the applicant's answer was not used in a discriminatory manner. The safest policy in this case would be to omit questions such as this one, or ask, "What types of people do you least like working with?"

You may have discovered while checking your answers that what seemed fair or reasonable to you may not be considered fair or reasonable in the eyes of the law. As an interviewer, you must depend on court rulings and not on personal opinions. Court rulings are constantly changing the interpretations of various laws, so stay up to date. Check with the *Federal Register* or an Equal Employment Opportunity official regularly. Some of the answers we have given here may have already changed. Ask your placement director or personnel supervisor about possible changes.

If you find job applicants are answering any of your questions in the ways listed here, you need to review your questions for possible discriminatory content:[34]

LESS EFFECTIVE ANSWERS TO UNLAWFUL QUESTIONS

- Silence.
- "That's illegal; you can't ask me that."
- "I prefer not to answer that question at this time."
- Ignoring the legality of the question and giving a candid answer. (Although employers may prefer this answer, why should applicants give information that may be used against them? Also, if applicants continue to answer unlawful questions, interviewers will continue to ask them.)

MORE EFFECTIVE ANSWERS TO UNLAWFUL QUESTIONS

- "I'm not clear on how that relates to my ability to handle this job. Could you clarify it for me?"
- With sincerity the applicant asks the same question of the interviewer. For example, if the interviewer asks if the applicant has children: "Yes, I have two lovely children. They are such a joy, aren't they? Do you have children?"
- Laughter, then, "Is having children a requirement for this job?"
- Answering the fear behind the question, not the question itself. For example:

  Q: Do you have plans for a family?

  A: If what you are concerned with is my ability to manage or my commitment to my job, I can assure you that I am quite aware of the job's responsibilities and take them seriously.

  A: If you are concerned about my regular attendance, let me assure you that I have only missed one day of work in the last three years and on that day I had the flu.

  Q: Do you have any physical disabilities?

  A: Any disabilities I may possess would not interfere with my ability to perform all aspects of this position.

As well as being careful to ask only lawful questions, you must be careful to listen to the person you are interviewing.

Listen Carefully to the Interviewee

It is fairly easy for an employment interviewer to become so preoccupied with the tasks of the interview that he or she forgets to listen carefully to what the applicant is saying. As an interviewer, you need to be aware of the mistakes that poor listeners tend to make. Some of the more common ones are listed here.

- Being distracted by something in the environment (for example, a stack of letters that must be read before quitting time).
- Listening only for the factual parts of the applicant's responses (ignoring the applicant's feelings toward these facts and the reasons behind the facts).
- Becoming so overstimulated by something the applicant says (such as a belief that all students should work while attending college) that you miss his or her following comments.
- Getting upset when the applicant uses emotional words.
- Making snap judgments about the applicant's worth based on only one or two comments.
- Failing to follow up on important information.

Additional listening errors were covered in Chapter 4. We suggest that you reread that chapter very carefully.

Remember, you can't listen while you're talking! Allow the interviewee to do most of the talking—while *you* listen. Researchers have discovered that interviewees are given the opportunity to talk for only 10 minutes in the typical 30-minute interview.[35]

Clarify and Verify Responses; Avoid False Inferences

Even interviewers who listen carefully can make mistakes when they assume they understand exactly what the interviewee means. In Chapter 1, we stated that everyone receives messages through a unique frame of reference. Because the interviewee and the interviewer have different frames of reference, it is easy for each to misinterpret the other's meanings.

When a statement is unclear, the interviewer should *clarify* the interviewee's response by asking questions. Ask a question when you don't understand exactly what the applicant is talking about. For example, you might say, "I'm not sure I understand. Would you explain . . . ?" Sometimes you may understand what the applicant is saying but fail to understand the reason behind it. Therefore, you should also ask a question when you are not sure why the applicant made a certain statement. You might clarify by saying, "I understand what you are saying, but I don't think I quite understand why you feel this is important. Why do you feel it's so important?'

Even when the applicant's statement seems clear, the interviewer should *verify* the response by paraphrasing—repeating the statement in your own words to see if you understood correctly. You might say, "Then what you are saying is . . . . Is that correct?" or "Are you saying . . . ?"

After clarifying and verifying applicant answers, interviewers may confuse inference with facts (see "Jumping to Conclusions" in Chapter 6) and reach a costly false assumption. A school superintendent gives some examples of invalid inferences drawn during employment interviews:[36]

FACT	INFERENCE
Knows subject matter	Can teach subject
Attended small, private school and is from rural community	Can't teach in an urban setting
Of same cultural and socioeconomic background as pupils	Will command respect of pupils
Big, strong, star athlete	Can handle "tough kids"

To avoid making costly hiring decisions because of false inferences, be careful to base your decisions on real facts and not on inferred or assumed information. Ask for clarification and verification of interviewee comments.

SUMMARY

Both the job-seeking interviewee and the employment interviewer have definite responsibilities if meaningful communication is to occur. Interviewees are responsible for investigating the employment market, preparing conventional and/or electronic resumes, preparing letters of reference, planning answers to possible questions, communicating effectively during interviews, and following up interviews when necessary. Neurobiologist Patricia Wade, in discussing tips for landing a job, sums up the interviewee's role when she says:

> The critical question really is do you want the job once you land it? Since you'll probably be spending as much as one-third of your total time at it, it's worth spending a good deal of time figuring out beforehand what is optimal for you. Someone who knows what he or she wants, has thought realistically and practically about the steps required to get it, and has a plan for implementing those steps is an extremely attractive job seeker. It's neither desirable nor necessary to do anything deliberately flashy or exotic to get a job. Being straightforward is so exotic in itself that amidst a sea of would-be wheelers, dealers, and the undecided, it's nearly irresistible.[37]

Interviewers are responsible for carefully planning and organizing the interview ahead of time, asking necessary but lawful questions, listening carefully to the interviewees, and clarifying and verifying responses as well as avoiding false inferences. The interviewer perhaps has the greatest responsibility for the success of the interview. Interviews that are poorly planned, poorly organized, and poorly executed result in neither participant learning anything valuable about the other. Often the wrong person is hired for the job—a costly mistake for everyone involved.

The advice offered in this chapter should help you make your next interview a more productive one.

CHECKPOINT

Before continuing to the next chapter, check your understanding of Chapter 8 by completing the following exercises:

1. Locate a newspaper advertisement or job description that you are willing to apply for. Carefully write a letter of application, a resume, your answers to probable questions, and questions you could ask the interviewer. If possible, arrange an actual interview for the job you have located.
2. Write or phone for applications from prominent firms in your community. And take a careful look at the application form used in your organization. Analyze each form carefully, and evaluate the appropriateness and effectiveness of each. Are any unlawful questions included?
3. Select five of the most difficult questions listed in Appendix B and Appendix C and carefully think through your answer to each question. If you are not sure about the quality of your answers, check with a personnel director, your boss, or someone you know who conducts regular interviews.
4. Exchange a letter of application and resume with a friend so that you can prepare to role play an interview with each other. Each of you will get valuable practice assuming the role of both the interviewer and the interviewee. If possible, videotape the interviews so you can analyze both your verbal and nonverbal behaviors. You may even want to ask a professional to watch the interviews and give you suggestions for improvement.

NOTES

1. Eric W. Skopec, *Situational Interviewing* (New York: Harper & Row, 1986), p. 5.
2. Richard N. Bolles, *The 1996 What Color Is Your Parachute?* (Berkeley: Ten Speed Press, 1996), pp. 57–63; George Shinn, *Leadership Development*, 2nd ed. (New York: Gregg Division/McGraw-Hill, 1986), p. 234.

3. For a list of the U.S. job banks, see Joyce Lain Kennedy and Thomas J. Morrow, *Electronic Job Search Revolution* (New York: Wiley, 1994).
4. This section on information-seeking interviews and networking adapted from Bolles, pp. 269–300; Kathryn Petras and Ross Petras, *The Only Job Hunting Guide You'll Ever Need: The Most Comprehensive Guide for Job Hunters and Career Switchers* (New York: Simon & Schuster, 1995), pp. 16–19; Bob Weinstein, *Resumes Don't Get Jobs: The Realities and Myths of Job Hunting* (New York: McGraw-Hill, 1993), pp. 57–68.
5. Warren J. Rosaluk, *Throw Away Your Resume and Get That Job!* (Englewood Cliffs, NJ: Prentice-Hall, 1983). Discussed by Weinstein, p. 65.
6. Weinstein, p. 65.
7. More detailed explanations of letters of application and resumes can be found in the following books: Jeffrey G. Allen, *The Resume Make Over* (New York: Wiley, 1995); Myra Fournier and Jeffrey Spin, *Encyclopedia of Job-Winning Resumes*, 2nd ed. (Ridgefield, CT: RoundLake, 1993); Richard H. Beatty, *175 High-Impact Cover Letters* (New York: Wiley, 1992); Ronald L. Krannich and Caryl Rae Krannich, *Dynamite Cover Letters* (Manassas Park, VA: Impact Publications, 1992); Martin J. Yate, *Resumes That Knock 'Em Dead* (Holbrook, MA: Adams, 1993); Samuel N. Ray, *Resumes for the Over-50 Job Hunter* (New York: Wiley, 1993); Burdette E. Bostwick, *Resume Writing: A Comprehensive How-to-Do-It Guide*, 4th ed. (New York: Wiley, 1990); Tom Washington, *Resume Power: Selling Yourself on Paper*, revised (Bellevue, WA: Mount Vernon, 1990).
8. Pat Brett, *Writing for Results: A Resume Workbook* (Belmont, CA: Wadsworth, 1990), pp. 25–26.
9. Brett, p. 26.
10. M. Zippo and H. Z. Levine, "Volunteer Experience: A Plus on Any Resume," *Personnel* (September–October 1984), pp. 40–42.
11. The information in this section comes from Peter D. Weddle, *Electronic Resumes for the New Job Market* (Manassas Park, VA: Impact Publications, 1995). Weddle is president of Job Bank USA, one the nation's largest electronic database companies.
12. Weddle, pp. 55–59.
13. Weddle, p. 63.
14. Rosaluk. See note 5.
15. Mary Bakeman et al., *Job Seeking Skills Reference Manual*, 3rd ed. (Minneapolis: Minnesota Rehabilitation Center, 1971), p. 57.
16. Kittie W. Watson and Larry R. Smeltzer, "Perceptions of Nonverbal Communication During the Selection Interview," *ABCA Bulletin* (June 1982), pp. 30–34.
17. Watson and Smeltzer, pp. 30–34; D. M. Young, E. G. Beier, and S. Beier, "Beyond Words: Influences of Nonverbal Behavior of Female Job Applicants in the Job Interview," *Personnel and Guidance Journal* 57 (1979), pp. 346–350.
18. Thomas McGovern and Harvey Ideus, "The Impact of Nonverbal Behavior on the Employment Interview," *Journal of College Placement* 38 (Spring 1978), pp. 51–53.
19. Lois J. Einhorn, "An Inner View of the Job Interview: An Investigation of Successful Communication Behaviors," *Communication Education* 80 (July 1981), pp. 216–228.
20. Watson and Smeltzer, pp. 30–34.
21. Many other types of interviewers are discussed by David Noer in *How to Beat the Employment Game: Secrets of the Personnel Recruiters* (Radnor, PA: Chilton Book Company, 1975).
22. Petras and Petras, pp. 233–234.
23. Researcher Katherine F. Shepard, in "Use of Small Group Interviews for Selection into Allied Health Educational Programs," *Journal of Allied Health* 9 (May 1980), p. 93, concluded: "Small group selection interviews consisting of two or more applicants and two or more interviewers appear superior to one-on-one interviews for use in allied health educational programs."
24. Einhorn, pp. 216–228; Auren Uris, *Action Guide for Executive Job Seekers and Employers* (New York: Arco, 1971), pp. 186–187.
25. Martin J. Yate, "Great Answers to Tough Interview Questions," *Knock 'Em Dead: The Ultimate Job-Seekers Handbook*, 9th ed. (Holbrook, MA: Adams, 1996), pp. 135–199; Ron Fry, *101 Great Answers to the Toughest Interview Questions*, 3rd ed. (Franklin Lakes, NJ: Career Press, 1993); Bob Weinstein, "'Tell Me About Yourself' and 16 Other Killer Questions," *Resumes Don't Get Jobs: The Realities and Myths of Job Hunting* (New York: McGraw-Hill, 1993), pp. 150–156; Petras and Petras, pp. 238–252; John T. Hopkins, "The Top Twelve Questions for Employment Agency Interviewers," *Personnel Journal* (May 1980), pp. 379–380, 404; Richard Payne, "Good Answers for Good Questions," *Data Processing Management Association Career Development Guide* (Fountain Valley, CA: Career Research Systems, 1983),

pp. 30–34; Jeremiah J. Sullivan, "Six Hundred Interviews Later," *ABCA Bulletin* (March 1980), pp. 2–5.

26. Adapted from Payne, pp. 30–34; Hopkins, pp. 379–380, 404; Weinstein, pp. 150–156; and Petras and Petras, pp. 238–252.

27. Taken in part from Charles J. Stewart and William B. Cash, Jr., *Interviewing: Principles and Practices*, 6th ed. (Dubuque, IA: Wm. C. Brown, 1991), p. 157.

28. Fredric M. Jablin, Linda L. Putnam, Karlene H. Roberts, and Lyman W. Porter, eds. *Handbook of Organizational Communication: An Interdisciplinary Perspective* (Newbury Park, CA: Sage, 1987), p. 691.

29. Robert N. McMurray reported by Ovid Riso, editor of *The Dartnell Sales Manager's Handbook*, 12th ed. (Chicago: The Dartnell Corp., 1977), p. 563. Reprinted by permission.

30. McMurray, p. 560.

31. D. Trevor Michaels, "Seven Questions That Will Improve Your Managerial Hiring Decisions," *Personnel Journal* 59 (March 1980), pp. 199–200, 224; see also Martin J. Yate, *Hiring the Best: A Manager's Guide to Effective Interviewing*, new expanded edition (Boston: Bob Adams, 1988), which includes more than 400 questions to ask applicants; A. Uris, *88 Mistakes Interviewers Make* (New York: AMACOM, 1988); Jack Gratus, *Successful Interviewing: How to Find and Keep the Best People* (New York: Penguin, 1988).

32. Federal legislation and guidelines include Title VII of the Civil Rights Act of 1964, amended 1972; the Age Discrimination in Employment Act of 1967, amended 1978; the Equal Pay Act of 1963, amended 1972; the Equal Employment Opportunity Act of 1972; OFCC (Office of Federal Compliance Commission) Affirmative Action Guidelines of 1972; the Rehabilitation Act of 1973; the Vietnam Era Veterans Readjustment Act of 1974, amended 1980; the Immigration Reform and Control Act of 1986 (IRCA); the EEOC 1987 policy statement regarding national origin discrimination and IRCA; and the newest law, the Americans with Disabilities Act of 1990 (ADA). Many states have employment laws stricter than the federal laws. Check the Federal Register to keep up to date on current federal rulings.

33. Answers adapted from Robert L. Minter, "Human Rights Laws and Pre-Employment Inquiries," *Personnel Journal* (June 1972), pp. 431–433; *How to Conduct a Lawful Employment Interview* (Des Moines: Batten, Batten, Hudson and Swab, 1978); Stewart and Cash, chap. 7; *Fair Employment Practices Manual* (Washington, DC: Bureau of National Affairs, 1982); James G. Frierson, "National Origin Discrimination: The Next Wave of Lawsuits," *Personnel Journal* 66 (December 1987), pp. 97–108; Nancy L. Perkins, "What You Need to Know About the Americans with Disabilities Act," *Supervisory Management* (March 1991), pp. 4–5; and *Americans with Disabilities Act* (New York: Wiley, 1992).

34. Adapted from Fredric M. Jablin and Craig D. Tengler, "Facing Discrimination in On-Campus Interviews," *Journal of College Placement* (Winter 1982), pp. 57–61; Bolles, pp. 353–356, also suggests answering the fear behind the question; see also Gerald L. Wilson, "Preparing Students for Responding to Illegal Selection Interview Questions," *The Bulletin of the Association for Business Communication* (September 1991), pp. 47–48.

35. Jablin, Putnam, Roberts, and Porter, p. 690.

36. Vincent Loretto, "Effective Interviewing Is Based on More Than Intuition," *Personnel Journal* 65 (December 1986), p. 102.

37. Prepared especially for this book by Patricia Wade, neurobiologist at Rockefeller University, New York.

9

Small-Group Communication and Problem Solving

When you accept poor meetings as a fact of life, you are in collusion with many others doing the same thing. In effect, you are aiding and abetting them in clogging the system and in eroding the quality of working life.[1]

RICHARD J. DUNSING

Have you ever been a member or leader of a committee, conference, or similar group and found it to be a very unsatisfying experience? You may have left the group convinced that "if you want it done right, you have to do it yourself!" If so, you may be one of many business and professional people who seldom use groups because they feel that while groups may sound good in theory, in reality they fail to work effectively.

Of course, there are times when an individual is more effective than a group. For example, an individual can make decisions more quickly, which can be crucial when time is short. And many individuals in managerial positions certainly have enough expertise and experience to make the right decision for others. It would be ridiculous to appoint a committee to make the minor, daily decisions necessary to run an office.

However, there are many times when groups can be more effective than individuals. Consider some of these advantages of group decisions:[2]

- Resistance to change is reduced, and decisions that are arrived at jointly are usually better received because members are committed to the solution and therefore are more willing to support it.
- Decisions may be superior and more accurate because people with different viewpoints gave input.
- Because decisions are better, they may be more readily accepted by those outside the group.
- Personal satisfaction and job morale are greater.
- Hostility and aggression are significantly reduced.
- Productivity is increased.
- Responsibility for the decision is diffused and therefore there is less risk for any individual. This is especially important when the solution is unpopular or unpleasant.

When a group is ineffective, the problem is not in the group process but in the way the group is organized and handled by the person or persons in charge. Handling groups effectively can be very difficult and complex; it requires that the leader and the members understand *group process*. Unfortunately, many group leaders as well as group participants know very little about working in groups.

To prepare you for managing and participating in groups in the business and professional environment, this chapter emphasizes problem-solving techniques. Chapter 10 will discuss how to be an effective group leader and participant.

DEFINITION OF A SMALL GROUP

Three distinct features differentiate a small group from a large group of people. **Small-group communication** involves a small number of people, usually engaged in face-to-face interaction, actively working together toward a common goal.

- *A small number of people (the optimum size is five).* Although some people consider two people to be a group (an interview would therefore be a group), a group of fewer than three people usually has difficulty supplying enough information for efficient decisions. A group of more than eight makes it difficult for everyone to participate as much as they would like. Five is considered the most productive size for a small group because it is large enough to supply needed information and to share the work load, yet small enough to give each member a chance for maximum participation. (In business, however, groups of fifteen or twenty are common—perhaps explaining why groups often seem to function poorly.) Having an uneven number of people in a group is also a good idea because it can prevent votes from ending in ties.
- *Face-to-face interaction.* Face-to-face group interaction is simply interaction that occurs in the presence of all the group members. The importance of this characteristic should not be overlooked. A successful group meeting conducted by mail or by phone would be much less likely because of the lack of instant feedback and the absence of nonverbal cues to meaning.*
- *Actively working together toward a common goal.* Just having the same goal is not enough. To be classified as a group, members must be working together specifically to achieve the common goal.

According to this definition, four people discussing politics while waiting for a bus to take them downtown would not constitute a small group. They may be engaged in face-to-face interaction and have the same goal, but they are not working together toward that goal. However, if the bus

---

*Teleconferences are appropriate when costs or circumstances prohibit face-to-face meetings. They must be carefully planned, and, in advance of the conference, the participants should receive a copy of the agenda, the conference objectives, and photos of participants they don't know. For more information, see Thomas M. Jenkins, "What It Takes to Teleconference Successfully," *Administrative Management* 43 (October 1982), pp. 28–44.

failed to arrive, and the people discussed how they were all going to get downtown—walk or pool their money for a taxi—they then would be considered a small group.

USE AND VALUE OF SMALL GROUPS IN THE EFFECTIVE ORGANIZATION

A brief look at business surveys indicates that the small group (the conference, committee, task force, quality circle, or performance team) may be one of the most often used communication methods within organizations. Consider the following survey information:

- A 1994 survey of Fortune 1000 companies found that 68 percent of them use "self-managing or high-performance teams."[3]
- Researchers estimate that the average supervisor spends as much as 40 percent of the workweek in meetings and conferences.[4]
- A survey conducted by a management consulting firm found that "the average executive spends almost 700 hours a year in meetings."[5] In other words, many executives spend two complete days of each five-day week in meetings!
- Pitney Bowes Corporation has all 18,000 employees stop work for 1 hour each month and meet in groups of approximately 12 along with their section supervisor.[6]
- Xerox has over 75 percent of its employees actively working in "quality-improvement or problem-solving projects."[7]
- In 5 years, 7,000 American organizations implemented quality circles.[8]
- Lockheed attributed $2,844,000 in documented savings to QCs over a period of two years, and Honeywell's QC reduced the costs of an assembly shop by 40 percent.[9]
- Northrop Corporation of Los Angeles documented a net savings of $106,000 from six quality circles.[10]
- Florida Power & Light Company used teams to build a nuclear power plant in an unbelievably fast six years. For example, because of the work of teams, "a slipforming technique was developed for pouring concrete around the clock, allowing the three-foot-thick, 190–foot-tall concrete shell to be finished in just seventeen days, compared with a year for other power companies."[11]

Because group communication is one of the most often used methods of communication within the organization, let's take a look at the types of groups generally used. Three general categories are found in business and professional organizations: (1) learning groups, (2) self-maintenance groups, and (3) problem-solving groups.

- *Learning groups* are involved in seeking or sharing information—for example, a department conference including the supervisor and the department employees, a management training seminar, or an orientation group for new employees.
- *Self-maintenance groups* seek to inspire desirable attitudes, understanding, and communication patterns rather than merely to inform. Companies that project a corporate culture use self-maintenance groups to train employees to interact, feel, and communicate as team members.
- *Problem-solving groups* make a series of decisions in an attempt to solve a particular problem.

> Decision making refers to the act of choosing between two or more alternatives. It focuses on evaluating alternatives that already exist so the group can choose the best. Problem solving is a . . . multi-stage procedure through which an individual or group develops a plan to move from some unsatisfactory present state to a desired goal state. Problem solving usually requires a group to make a multitude of decisions, but it also involves creating alternatives as well as deciding among them.[12]

Problem-solving groups are often referred to as committees, task forces, or quality circles (see Chapter 2 for a discussion of quality circles). Some examples of problem-solving groups are a group of purchasing representatives discussing how to expedite critically needed materials from a subcontracting firm behind in deliveries, a quality circle suggesting ways to improve the general work environment, a group of supervisors trying to figure out how to increase production in their departments without sacrificing quality.

Because problem solving is the most complicated yet the most often used type of group process, this chapter will concentrate on various problem-solving procedures.

CHARACTERISTICS OF EFFECTIVE PROBLEM-SOLVING GROUPS

Successful problem-solving groups have six basic characteristics in common: They are well organized, they receive periodic training, they

Many problem-solving meetings are ineffective because they fail to follow an organized procedure. (© *Comstock*)

carefully examine the assumptions and opinions of members, they thoroughly evaluate possible solutions, they try to avoid "groupthink," and they manage cultural diversity. Let's look at each of these characteristics in more detail.

Effective Groups Are Well Organized

Many problem-solving meetings are ineffective because they fail to follow an organized procedure. Any of the following could result:[13]

- Lack of group cohesiveness
- Uncertain leadership
- Less motivation to complete the task
- Less participation and coordination in decision-making activities
- Member uncertainty about expected role performance
- More anxiety among group members toward one another
- More task anxiety among group members
- Greater cost to the organization
- Greater opportunity for unproductive conflict

Although researchers generally agree that groups following an organized procedure are more productive, they are not certain which procedure is best.[14] If the members are trained and the task is complex, the "basic problem-solving procedure" works well.[15] However, when the members are untrained and the task is simple, other organizational methods are suggested: the "buzz group" procedure, the "single-question" procedure, or the "ideal-solution" procedure.[16] All four of these procedures will be discussed later in this chapter.

Not all groups follow exactly the same procedure, and they do not always move smoothly from step to step. Researchers have found that although effective groups tend to move toward a solution in a "linear" fashion, the actual process appears to be accomplished in a "spiraling" manner.[17] "Forward movement toward a solution is sometimes accompanied by backward steps to anchor ideas in prior discussion and lateral moves to consolidate the thinking of all members."[18] In other words, effective groups follow an organized procedure, but they aren't overly rigid; some overlapping and backtracking can be expected.

Effective Groups Receive Periodic Training

One way to ensure the failure of a problem-solving group is to not train the leader and participants in problem solving. Suppose a company, wanting to improve employee morale, job satisfaction, and productivity, decided to implement a program in which employees would be involved in group problem solving. To test the success of such a program, several experimental test groups were set up. Assume further that one influential person was opposed to such programs and wanted to ensure that the test groups were unsuccessful. What could the person do? Simply convince management that no training in group process was needed. The program would almost certainly be doomed to failure. Research shows that group productivity can be improved when training is improved.[19] One of the lessons learned from the three-year Tennessee Valley Authority (TVA) experiment involving employees in problem-solving groups was the importance of participant training.[20] The Federal Aviation Administration began a quality circle program after the 1981 air traffic controllers strike and is sold on the importance of training. Facilitators receive several days of training; QC leaders and members receive 8 hours of training and practice in problem solving; all receive yearly training updates.[21]

In discussing needed resources for self-managing teams, two professors of organizational behavior state,

> The first, and perhaps the most important [resource], is training. Team members need to be trained in basic problem-solving and group-dynamic skills. Over time, the employees' skill base should be broadened to include statistical quality control, conflict resolution and other useful problem-solving tools. Training in the philosophy of participation,

responsibility, and management–worker cooperation is also essential. . . . Keep in mind that it is necessary to continue providing training as new workers and managers enter the system; to periodically "retrain"; and, especially, to reinforce the training over time.[22]

Training can dispel a variety of myths and prejudices people have about groups. People who have had poor experiences with groups or who view groups as time-wasting talk expect all new group experiences to be negative. Employees may view problem-solving participation as a trick by management to shift blame for problems. Midmanagers may fear losing their authority, fear employees will use the procedure for their own bene-fit, or view group participation as a waste of time. One researcher devel-oped a scale to measure "grouphate" (how much or how little people enjoy working in groups). She found that those with a higher level of hostility toward groups had had no training in group communication skills.[23]

Effective Groups Examine Assumptions and Opinions

Researchers have recently found that ineffective groups tend to accept opinions and assumptions without adequately evaluating them and may even view such inferences as though they were facts; effective groups, on the other hand, challenge and question the opinions and assumptions ex-pressed by group members.[24] Here is an example of how an ineffective group handled assumptions in deciding how to punish a student caught plagiarizing:

A: Well, let's see, we could recommend anything from letting him off to kicking him out of school. . . .

B: Kicking him out is unreasonable, don't you think?

C: Yeah, no way that would be justified . . . this is his first offense . . . right?

B: Uh . . .

C: Has to be, I mean, he's a journalism student, right? They must write a lot of papers, and since the student has never been caught plagia-rizing before, this had to be the first time he did it. . . .

A: O.K. . . . So kicking him out of school is out . . . also failing him in the course would be out, too? Huh?

B: Has to be . . . if it's his first offense and all. . . .[25]

Effective Groups Evaluate Possible Solutions

The best way to evaluate a possible solution is to compare it to predeter-mined criteria—guidelines or rules that the group earlier agreed to use to reach a solution (how to establish criteria is discussed later in this chapter). For example, in selecting the employee of the month, a group of employees might agree on the following criteria:

- Employee's supervisor should have received at least one letter of recommendation from a satisfied customer.
- Employee should have at least a 20 percent increase in sales over the previous month.
- Employee should be liked by fellow workers.

Although researchers have found that both effective and ineffective groups weigh possible alternatives against preestablished criteria, effective groups are more thorough in considering the consequences of each alternative. In one study, however, ineffective groups

> appeared to test each alternative against the four pre-established criteria in almost a perfunctory manner—that is to say, they appeared to "go through the motions" . . . in most instances, members of the "ineffective" groups would simply ask each other whether the recommendations met each of the four criteria and would simply respond to each question with a simple "yes" or "no" response.[26]

Ineffective groups rarely brought up facts to support their "yes" or "no" responses and ignored the consequences of the possible solutions.

Effective Groups Avoid Groupthink

Groupthink, a term developed by Irving Janis, refers to an uncritical way of thinking, often characteristic of groups, in which the desire to avoid conflict and reach agreement is more important than careful consideration of alternatives.[27] Groups are often guilty of the following symptoms of groupthink:[28]

- *The illusion of invulnerability.* Like the military advisors who decided to concentrate on training and supplies rather than defense because they felt Pearl Harbor was impregnable, groups may make risky decisions, feeling that their decisions cannot possibly be wrong.
- *Shared stereotypes.* Ideas that conflict with the majority opinion are often presented stereotypically—for example, "Well, you know how those guys in engineering are! Always ready to push the panic button." Such stereotypes are easier for a group to discount as unimportant.

- *Rationalization.* Justifying or making excuses for a particular course of action hampers a group's critical thinking.
- *Illusion of group morality.* The unquestioned belief that the group's decisions will be moral and good keeps group members from considering the possible negative consequences of their decisions.
- *Self-censorship.* When members believe that they are the only one with doubts or are afraid any expression of doubt or disagreement will destroy the group's harmony, they remain silent.
- *Illusion of unanimity.* Self-censorship leads to the belief that everyone is in agreement when actually some members have doubts.
- *Direct pressure.* If a member does voice a doubt and is persistent in that objection, direct pressure is applied by the leader or other members to reestablish a feeling of harmony. Usually a simple comment, "Let's stay in agreement on this! I'm sure John didn't mean to upset the applecart," is enough to silence the doubter. If not, members may withdraw eye contact, reposition their chairs, and even refuse to listen by talking as though the deviant were not speaking.
- *Mind guarding.* Members protect each other from mental harm (information that might cause the group to question its decisions or opinions) just as a bodyguard protects a person from physical harm.

To groups guilty of groupthink, maintaining group harmony is more important than reaching good solutions. Groupthink is more likely to occur in groups with a hidden leader or hidden members. As you recall from Chapter 3, hidden communicators have a strong desire for social acceptance. As a result, they are unlikely to express openly any concerns or disagreements or even to introduce any ideas that might cause conflict. They smooth over any conflicts that do occur in an effort to reach a consensus and preserve the harmony of the group. In contrast, effective groups view conflict as a healthy way to ensure that all ideas are considered—conflicts are resolved, not smoothed over.

To avoid groupthink, Janis suggests the following:[29]

- Bring in outside experts with opinions that differ from those expressed by the group.
- Ask all members to be "critical evaluators" who look at all sides of the problem regardless of personal opinions.
- To keep from unduly influencing the group, the leader should

  Keep personal opinions to self until others have expressed their opinions.
  Occasionally miss a meeting and allow someone else to lead.
  Impress on the group the importance of looking at many options.

■ Once a tentative solution has been reached, give members a "second chance" to rethink their choice and to openly express any doubts before agreeing to the final solution.

Effective Groups Manage Cultural Diversity[30]

Increasingly, we will be participating in decision making with persons from other parts of the world. Not all cultures view or solve problems in the same way. For example, managers in the United States expect problems to occur and are quick to identify them when they do. However, managers in countries such as Thailand, Malaysia, and Indonesia are more likely to accept situations for what they are and take longer to identify problems. Also, in the United States a single individual usually assumes the final responsibility for decisions—thus our saying, "the buck stops here." However, in Japan, for instance, it is the group that makes and assumes responsibility for decisions. Americans put great value on speed and decisiveness. Other countries, such as Egypt, consider a fast decision to show how little importance was placed on the problem or business deal. Japan and China want to discuss all alternatives before making any decisions while Canada and the United States prefer to make decisions as the discussion proceeds.

Even though countries view problem solving differently, research discussed by Nancy Adler shows that multicultural groups have definite advantages: Because of their different backgrounds, they are less susceptible to groupthink and more likely to produce a creative range of alternatives. These advantages are especially important when problems are complex. However, Adler points out that successful groups do not ignore their diversity; they manage it. To manage diversity, Adler recommends that multicultural groups[31]

■ *Recognize actual differences.* Begin by describing the range of cultures present.
■ *Elect members for their task-related abilities.* Members should be "homogeneous in ability levels and heterogeneous in attitudes."
■ *Find a purpose or goal "that transcends individual differences."*
■ *Avoid cultural dominance.* Encourage equal participation.
■ *Develop mutual respect for each other.*
■ *Seek a high level of feedback from each other and the leader.*

THE BASIC PROBLEM-SOLVING PROCEDURE

To ensure productive meetings, both the leader and the group members should be trained in using the basic problem-solving procedure. If training is impossible—say, for example, a new group is formed to handle an emergency situation—then another method described later in this chapter would probably be more successful. The basic problem-solving procedure includes the following steps:[32]

1. Define the problem.
2. Research and analyze the problem.
3. Establish a checklist of criteria.
4. List possible alternatives.
5. Evaluate each alternative.
6. Select the best alternative as your solution and discuss how to implement it.

Each of these steps must be addressed for the basic problem-solving procedure to be successful.

Step 1: Define the Problem

Groups often skip steps 1 through 3 and begin with step 4, listing possible alternatives. Step 1 is usually omitted because the group members assume that everyone already knows exactly what the group's problem is. This is especially true when the group's task has been decided by management or someone outside the group. But eliminating step 1 can waste valuable time. Groups often are unaware that everyone's basic understanding of the problem is different until they are unable to agree upon a solution. Even when the problem seems obvious, the group should summarize the problem by stating it precisely in question form. If the group cannot agree on the specific wording, then the problem has not been defined clearly enough.

Defining the problem may be the only purpose of some meetings. If the problem is vague, or too broad, or even unknown, then a discussion of *observed symptoms* and *perceived size of the problem* may help the group to determine the specific problem. A supervisor, for example, who has noticed that production has dropped and that morale seems quite low knows the symptoms but not the problem.

Identifying the exact problem may also help to determine the *impact* or *effect of the problem*. One consultant found that average managers focus their evaluation on the problem itself, whereas "super executives," who solve problems with apparent ease, view "the problem as merely a stepping stone to the *problem impact*—the effect of the problem."[33] While the average person is considering the cause of the problem, the super executive is determining the cause of the problem impact and what to do about it. This is important because the initial focal (or takeoff) point generally determines the train of thought that follows . . . starting with the problem instead of the problem impact invariably results in a narrower evaluation of the total situation and final decisions are less prone to be fully responsive to overall needs.[34]

When the problem finally seems clear to everyone, test that understanding by writing down the problem in *question form*. Discuss the written question until all members are satisfied with the wording. Keep the following rules in mind when wording your question.[35] All questions should be

- *Written in a manner that allows for the widest range of answers.* "Yes" or "no" answers should be avoided. For example, a problem stated, "Should Tooling Incorporated adopt the metric system?" asks for only a "yes" or "no" answer. If the question is rewritten to read, "What position should Tooling Incorporated take toward adoption of the metric system?" the group would have a range of possible responses.
- *Specific rather than general.* For example, in the question, "Should we encourage employees to give to the United Way?" the words *we* and *encourage* are fairly vague. Who are "we" and what is meant by "encourage"? The question might be reworded to read, "What position should the management of Park's Furniture take toward employees giving to the United Way?"
- *Specific with regard to who should act.* In the question, "What can be done to clean up the debris around Johnson Lake?" the person or group who is to act has not been named. Should the question be directed toward the police, the Boy Scouts, the City Council, or the business community? A better question might read as follows: "What suggestions for cleaning up the debris around Johnson Lake should the local Parents League make to the City Council at the council meeting on Friday?"
- *Written in an unbiased manner.* Sometimes, questions are worded in such a way that the group's biases are obvious. "What can management do about the ridiculous hiring practices required by the Equal Employment Opportunity Commission?" is obviously not an objectively worded question. How can a group be objective in its answers when the stated question is biased?

Thus, an effectively worded problem avoids "yes" or "no" answers, is specific, states who is to act, and avoids biased phrasing. Can you see what is wrong with the following question: "Should the speed limit be raised to a decent speed?" This question violates all four rules! It can be answered "yes" or "no." It is too general. (What speed limit—national? state? or business property? What is meant by "decent speed"?) It fails to state who is to act (perhaps the U.S. Senate or the state legislature or the company policy board). And it includes biased phrasing ("decent speed" implies that the present speed is not decent).

You may also find it helpful to think of problem-solving questions as questions of either fact, value, or policy. In **questions of fact,** the group tries to determine whether something is a fact, is true, or to what degree something is a fact or is true. In **questions of value,** the group tries to assess the worth or desirability of some object, idea, or person. In **questions of policy,** the group tries to arrive at a specific course of action, usually a change from the present system. Questions of fact require the group to base the solution on detailed research. Questions of value require the group to base the solution on value judgments. Groups discussing a question of policy will consider both researched facts and value judgments (opinions) in order to reach the solution.

The last part of step 1 is to define any unusual or easily misinterpreted terms in the problem question. Defining terms further clarifies meaning and prevents misunderstandings. Of course, if your question has been carefully worded, few terms will need clarification.

Step 2: Research and Analyze the Problem

Groups that omit step 2 usually arrive at unsound solutions because they do not know enough about the situation to make an effective decision. If you are not aware of the qualities needed in a good secretary, how can you select the best candidate from a list of applicants? Even groups that do analyze the problem often reach ineffective solutions because their discussion is disorganized and continually jumps from topic to topic. To prevent these difficulties, there are three simple guidelines to follow.

List All the Topics or Ideas That Must Be Researched and Discussed ■ This will inform your group of the information needed on the problem to reach an intelligent solution. To answer the question, "What position should our county take toward the federal government's proposal to build a nuclear power plant in Glen Rose?" you would need to research current laws, public opinion, accident records of present nuclear power plants, safety features, and so on. Also, most problem-solving discussions should include research on causes of the problem and past efforts to solve the problem: What are the real causes of this problem? Has the problem come up before? How was it handled then? Was the solution successful? If so, why does the problem exist today? Make sure all members get a chance to comment. Combine and narrow the list if possible.

When the cause of a problem is unclear or totally unknown (such as when a piece of machinery suddenly begins to turn out inferior work), your group may find it helpful to answer the following four pairs of questions.[36] Write the answers on a chalkboard or flipchart so everyone can see.

1. What is involved? What is not involved?
2. Where is it found? Where is it not found?
3. When does it occur? When does it not occur?
4. To what extent (how much/how often) does it occur? To what extent does it not occur?

Look very carefully at the answers and ask these two additional questions for each pair: (1) What is the main difference, if any, between the answer to the first question of the pair and the answer to the second, and (2) what change, if any, caused the difference? When as many answers as possible have been found, summarize your information by stating the most likely cause. If this possible cause does not account for the facts obtained by answering the four pairs of questions, reject it and look for some other cause. Look carefully for differences and changes that might have been overlooked earlier.

Gather All Needed Information ■ At this point, the leader may wish to postpone the discussion to give members time to gather information on areas needing research. Information may be obtained from company records and data, from personal opinion surveys conducted by the group, or from the company or community library. Even when no outside research is needed, the discussion will take less time if members are given a chance to organize their thoughts or at least to do some careful thinking prior to the next discussion.

Discuss the Facts and Opinions for Each of the Listed Topics in an Organized Manner ■ One researcher found that most groups changed topics or themes on an average of every 58 seconds and that "though the same themes frequently reappeared several times, groups were often unable to complete discussion of these topics."[37] To improve the quality of your group's discussion, try using the following organizational pattern:

1. State the topic to be discussed.
2. Give all members a chance to cite their research and opinions on the topic.
3. Ask if anyone has anything further to say on the topic.
4. Summarize the group's findings on the topic.

5. State the next topic to be discussed and repeat the above process until all topics have been discussed.

Gathering, analyzing, and discussing information relevant to the problem are necessary components of the group's problem-resolution process.

Step 3: Establish a Checklist of Criteria

Establishing criteria is one of the most important steps of all. Without criteria, the procedure we have been discussing would not be "the basic problem-solving procedure." To clarify the importance of criteria, we will examine them from four angles: *what* are criteria, *types* of criteria, *when* in the procedure to use criteria, and *how* to use criteria in reaching quality solutions.

What Are Criteria? ■ **Criteria** are guidelines, boundaries, standards, or rules that a group agrees to follow in reaching a solution to their problem. For example, your group might agree that any solution selected should

- Receive unanimous support from all group members.
- Fall within current state and national laws.
- Treat all persons equally.
- Not result in any increase in taxes.
- Receive the backing of both the union leaders and management.

You can also view criteria as a checklist of items that must be met in order to be selected by your group. For example, a possible checklist of criteria to use in the selection of a chief executive officer of a corporation might be as follows:

- Should meet all requirements listed in the bylaws.
- Should have at least ten years' experience in policy-making positions.
- Should be a good public speaker and present self well on camera.
- Should have prestige with major companies in the United States and abroad.

Types of Criteria ■ First, criteria can be either task or operational. **Task criteria** relate to the actual problem or task being discussed. **Operational criteria** relate to group procedural matters. Task criteria might be stated as

- Should be an employee of the company for at least five years.
- Should have received merit pay at least once in the last five years.
- Should be a current member of a work team.

- Should have presented a suggestion to the company that saved $5,000 or more.

Operational criteria might be stated as

- Selection of employee of the year must be completed in two weeks.
- Selection should be unanimously supported by group members.
- Selection should be agreeable to the division manager.
- Selection costs (duplication of papers, and so on) should not exceed $50.

Second, criteria can be divided into musts and wants. **Must criteria** are required items, and **want criteria** are desired items. Must and want criteria can consist of either task criteria, operational criteria, or both. If an alternative fails to meet even one of the must criteria, it will be rejected by the group. *There is no need to rank must criteria. Want criteria, however, must be ranked to be effective.* For example, imagine that there are two solutions and that each meets all of your group's must criteria and three of the four want criteria. If solution A meets criteria 2, 3, and 4, but solution B meets criteria 1, 2, and 3, solution B will be the best solution because it meets the most important want criteria.

Once the want criteria have been ordered from most desirable to least desirable, your group might wish to assign a numerical weight to each criterion. For example, if there were five want criteria, the group might assign the most important criterion a numerical weight of 5, the next most important a weight of 4, and so on. Another method is to assign each criterion in the want category a weight of 1, 2, or 3 regardless of the number of items being considered:

1 = important
2 = very important
3 = extremely important (almost a must)

In deciding what personal computer to buy, you could arrive at the following criteria (used to evaluate solutions in step 5):

MUSTS

- Must not cost more than $1,500 (that is all the money in your savings account).
- Must use Easyword (a word-processing software program with which you are already familiar).
- Must have two disk drives.
- Must be portable.

WANTS	ASSIGNED WEIGHT
■ Bundled software included in cost of computer.	3
■ Cost of computer low enough to allow for the purchase of a printer.	3
■ Keyboard comfortable to use.	1
■ Screen easy to read—prefer green or amber.	2
■ XYZ compatible.	2
■ Runs games as well as business software.	1

Deciding when to establish criteria is just as important as deciding what your criteria will be.

When (in the Procedure) to Use Criteria ■ The point at which the group establishes criteria in the problem-solving procedure is very important. Other than limitations specified by management and given to the group at its first meeting, criteria should *not* be established before step 2 because the group will not know enough about the problem. For example, in the hypothetical list of criteria for selecting a chief executive officer, how did the group know that past experience in policy making was an important quality in a CEO? Because in step 2, one of the group members researched the experience of past corporate CEOs. In discussion of this topic, the group discovered that all past CEOs who were judged by their corporate structures to be effective had at least ten years' prior experience in policy-making positions. Therefore, experience would seem to be a necessary qualification or criterion for a successful CEO. If the group had found that experience seemed to make very little difference in the performance of past CEOs, then experience would not be listed as a criterion.

Whether criteria should be established before or after listing alternatives is more difficult to say with certainty. Research has produced conflicting answers. On the one hand, once solutions are listed, it is very difficult for group members to remain unbiased and objective. It is only natural that you will favor criteria that support your preferred alternative. For example, suppose CEO candidate A has only six years of policy-making experience and candidate B has twelve years of experience. You prefer candidate A. If your group discusses criteria *after* selecting these two candidates, you might become emotionally attached to candidate A and insist that experience should not be used as a criterion.

On the other hand, establishing criteria before solutions makes it more difficult to think of novel ideas. Once criteria are set, tunnel vision occurs. Therefore, if your group's main purpose is to produce a great number of ideas for group consideration, perhaps you should reverse steps 3 and 4.[38]

OUTLINE OF THE BASIC PROBLEM-SOLVING PROCEDURE

I. **Define the Problem.**
   A. Discuss symptoms (especially if problem is unknown).
   B. Discuss size (or seriousness) and impact (effect) of problem.
   C. Determine the exact wording of the problem in question form.
   D. Define terms in the question.

II. **Research and Analyze the Problem.**
   A. List topics that need to be researched or discussed, including causes and past efforts to solve the problem.
   B. Research the problem if needed.
   C. Discuss the research in an organized manner.
      1. State the first topic to be discussed.
      2. Give all members a chance to cite research or opinion on the topic.
      3. Ask if anyone has anything further to say on the topic.
      4. Summarize the group's findings on the topic.
      5. State the next topic to be discussed and repeat the procedure until all topics have been discussed.

III. **Establish a Checklist of Criteria.**
   A. List all possible criteria (give everyone a chance to respond).
   B. Discuss each criterion.
   C. Reduce the list to a workable length by combining criteria where possible.
   D. Rank remaining criteria from most to least important.

IV. **List Possible Alternatives.**

V. **Evaluate Each Alternative.**
   A. Read through the list of alternatives, eliminating those the group feels obviously do not meet the criteria agreed on in the third step.
   B. Reduce the list further by combining any similar alternatives.
   C. Discuss each remaining alternative's strengths and weaknesses (referring to research presented in the second step when necessary).
   D. Determine how well each alternative meets the criteria—number of criteria met and importance of criteria met.
   E. Continue reducing the list until the best alternative (or alternatives) is reached.

VI. **Select the Best Alternative(s) as Your Solution and Discuss How to Implement It (or Them).**

However, we suggest (as do many experts[39]) that you *establish criteria before listing alternatives* in the following situations:

- If the problem-solving task is complex.
- If the topic is emotional or involves value judgments.
- If the group members have little or no problem-solving experience and are likely to allow preferred solutions to dictate the criteria.

Once a group has decided *when* to establish criteria, they must focus on producing quality criteria.

How to Use Criteria Effectively ■ Criteria are easy to confuse with solutions. Criteria are guidelines for reaching solutions, but are not solutions. For example, in discussing whether city police officers should be allowed to strike, "The strike should not last longer than 48 hours" is a solution while "Citizen safety should be considered" is a criterion. To keep your group from confusing criteria with possible solutions, precede each criterion with this phrase: "Any decision we reach should (or should not) . . ." For example, "Any decision we reach should be agreeable to all sides," or "Any decision we reach should not result in any increase in taxes."

The following procedure is an effective way to organize your group's discussion of criteria:

1. List all possible criteria (make sure everyone gets a chance to respond).
2. Evaluate each criterion to determine its importance or unimportance, thereby

   a. Reducing the list of criteria to a workable length by combining or eliminating.
   b. Dividing the remaining criteria into two categories: "musts" (required) and "wants" (desired).[40]
   c. Ranking or assigning a numerical weight to criteria in the "wants" category.

Establishing criteria is the key to the basic problem-solving procedure. Once a group agrees on the criteria to be used in evaluating the solutions, the most difficult part of the process is over.

Step 4: List Possible Alternatives

List as many alternatives as are feasible within your group's time and budget limits. Most groups have trouble listing possible alternatives without evaluating them at the same time. However, to use step 4 effectively, all evaluations must be postponed until step 5. Evaluating alternatives as soon as they are mentioned tends to hamper creative thinking. Remember to *list first, then evaluate.*

Brainstorming ■ One way to obtain creative, detailed lists of alternatives in business and professional decision making is **brainstorming,** the spontaneous contribution of ideas by all members of the group. Neither a debate nor an evaluation session, it is merely a procedure used to generate lists of items. For effective brainstorming, follow these guidelines:[41]

- *Avoid negative feedback* (both verbal and nonverbal). The only comments allowed should be words of praise and encouragement or requests for clarification of an idea. When negative comments occur in a group, they usually put an end to creative thinking.
- *Strive for the longest list possible* rather than for a high-quality list. Discussions of the quality of the ideas should be postponed until step 5. The leader or a recorder should make a list of all ideas.
- *Strive for creative, unusual ideas.* It is often the crazy-sounding idea that proves to be the best when combined with other ideas. Even if it would not be acceptable to the group, a bizarre or extraordinary suggestion often stimulates someone to think of a valuable idea that may have been overlooked otherwise.
- *Try to build from previously mentioned ideas.* If the group is really thinking, there should be no long pauses. Effective brainstorming moves quite rapidly as one idea stimulates another.

Brainstorming can also be used effectively in step 1 to define the problem, in step 2 to generate the list of topic areas needing research, and in step 3 to generate the list of possible criteria.

The principal advantage of brainstorming is that the group members stimulate and build onto one another's ideas. However, it is possible that one or two members may monopolize the time, not giving others a chance to participate, or that some group members may be afraid to talk because of real or perceived group pressures. They may withhold an excellent idea simply because they are afraid someone will think poorly of them. Also, researchers have shown that individuals usually "produce more ideas per person when working alone."[42]

Nominal Group Technique ■ Because of the potential problems with brainstorming, many people in business and the professions prefer a procedure known as the **nominal group technique.**[43] NGT can be used both for generating lists of ideas and as a method of decision making.

When the nominal group technique is used as a method for generating ideas, these two steps are followed:

1. Ideas are silently generated by each individual. Each person writes down ideas or solutions privately. There is no discussion at this point.
2. Ideas are recorded on a chalkboard or flipchart. All ideas are recorded in a round-robin procedure: The leader accepts one idea at a time from each person until all ideas are listed, including any additional ideas that members have thought of while others were speaking. There is no discussion of ideas in this step. (We suggest the use of flipcharts because they can be rolled up and taken with you; chalkboards often get erased.)

NGT gives all group members a chance to participate and minimizes group pressures. There are two stages in the basic problem-solving procedure in which the nominal group technique may be used: to generate the list of possible alternatives needed in step 4 and to generate the list of topics needing research in step 2. The Federal Aviation Administration often uses NGT during regional meetings to help identify problems.[44]

The nominal group technique can also be used in steps 1 and 3 of the basic problem-solving procedure or as a separate method of decision making. For these purposes follow this four-step procedure:

1. Ideas are silently generated by each individual.
2. Ideas are recorded on a chalkboard or flipchart.
3. Each idea is discussed for clarification only. Debate, criticism, or persuasive appeals are not allowed; suggestions for combining or rewording ideas and for clarifying meaning are allowed.
4. Each member privately selects the top five (or more) items and ranks them according to importance. An individual, asked to select five items, would assign the most important a rank of 5, the next most important a 4, and so on. When all votes are recorded, one page of a flipchart for the problem "How can our department become more productive?" might look like the page shown in Figure 9.1.

For using NGT as a problem-solving procedure, the third and fourth steps may have to be repeated until a definite solution is clearly present—that is, until one idea wins the highest score.

The advantage of NGT—individual privacy—can also be its weakness. Researchers have found that the quality of both individual and group decisions is improved when open exchanges of information, ideas, and criticism are allowed.[45] NGT allows an exchange of information, but

Figure 9.1 NGT flipchart.

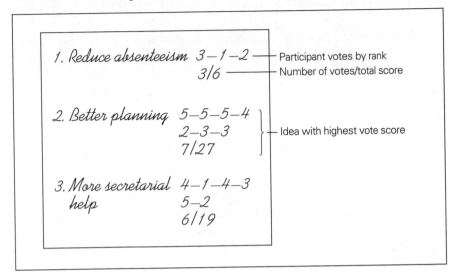

no criticism. Critical evaluation appears to be necessary for superior decisions.

Combination Methods ■ A combination of brainstorming (oral) and NGT (written) methods may also be effective. One popular combination method begins with the two-step nominal group technique and concludes with a brief brainstorming session. The new ideas derived from the brainstorming session are added to the flipchart. Another combination method calls for each member to suggest an idea. All ideas are recorded (even if they are the same or similar to previous ideas). Each member is asked explicitly to contribute.[46] This method follows the brainstorming procedure but takes the pressure of speed off the participants.

Another combination method called "brainwriting" was developed at the Battelle Institute in Frankfurt.[47] Brainwriting instructions are as follows:

- Write down four ideas on a sheet of paper, place the sheet in the center of the table, and exchange it for another sheet. No discussion is permitted.
- Use the ideas of the other group members for stimulation and list as many additional ideas as possible. These new ideas may be combinations and improvements of the listed ideas or entirely new ideas. [Keep exchanging sheets and adding your ideas until time is called.]

- There will be a 30-minute time limit. At the end of this time, all papers will be collected so that the ideas can be evaluated.[48]

Brainstorming and nominal group technique are effective ways to generate lists of items. Try them both to see which works the best for you and your organization.

Step 5: Evaluate Each Alternative

If the group has done a good job of determining criteria, step 5 in the basic problem-solving procedure becomes amazingly simple. The following guidelines will enable your group to evaluate the possible alternatives:

1. Read through the list of alternatives, eliminating those that the group feels obviously do not meet the criteria agreed on in step 3.
2. Further reduce the list to a workable number by combining any similar alternatives.
3. Discuss each remaining alternative's strengths and weaknesses (referring back to research presented in step 2 when necessary).
4. Determine how well each alternative meets the criteria—consider the number and the importance of criteria met.
5. Continue reducing the list until the best alternative (or alternatives) is reached.

One drawback to group problem solving is that so much time is required. Groups that use criteria correctly can substantially cut the time needed to reach a solution because criteria limit the solutions that must be considered. In our previous example of deciding what personal computer to buy, four must criteria were listed. Suppose that only three of the personal computers currently on the market meet our must criteria. At this point, we may wish to do additional research or personally test each of the three computers. Next we determine how well each of the top computers meet the want criteria (see Figure 9.2).

Step 6: Select the Best Alternative

The best solution is simply the solution (or solutions) that best fulfills the group's criteria. Sometimes, however, even after using criteria to eliminate poor solutions, the group is left with several alternatives—a decision must still be made.

A decision can be reached by one of several methods: consensus, compromise, or vote.[49] The best decision is the consensus. In a **consensus** decision, all members agree to accept a particular solution even though it

Figure 9.2 Using criteria to narrow down possible solutions.

Want Criteria	Assigned Weight		Computer A*		Computer B*		Computer C*	
—Bundled software	3	×	5 =	15	1. =	3	5 =	15
—Cost allowed for printer	3	×	1 =	3	3 =	9	4 =	12
—Keyboard comfort	1	×	5 =	5	3 =	3	5 =	5
—Green or amber screen	2	×	4 =	8	1 =	2	4 =	8
—XYZ compatible	2	×	5 =	10	5 =	10	5 =	10
—Runs games	1	×	3 =	3	1 =	1	5 =	1
				total = 44		total = 28		total = 51

* Each computer ranking (on a scale of 1–5) of how well it meets each criterion.

may not have been their original choice. Commitment to the solution is greater in groups that can reach consensus. However, the group needs to be aware of the phenomenon called groupthink, discussed earlier in this chapter.

If a consensus cannot be reached, the next best decision is a **compromise.** Of course, no one completely wins in a compromise—all parties must forfeit some of their requirements. But at least no one completely loses either.

If a consensus or a compromise is not possible, the group may have to **vote** for the best solution, which would be the alternative that receives more than 50 percent of the vote. Voting should be used only as a last resort because it often causes resentment and unhappiness by creating winners and losers. Most group members would rather agree to a compromise than find that their solutions had been voted out of consideration.

Discuss How to Implement the Best Alternative ■ Once the best alternative has been selected, the group must discuss how to implement it. In other words, the group must decide what can or should be done to ensure that the solution to the problem becomes a reality. During this discussion, the group may decide that although the solution sounds great in theory, it is too costly, or that management would never agree, or that in some other way the solution will not work. In this case, go back to step 5, select the second-best alternative, and discuss implementing it.

The group has then completed the decision-making process and is ready to report all recommendations to the appropriate person(s) or, if the group has the power, to initiate the implementation. (See Chapter 13 for suggestions on making presentations.) If the group is to remain a group even after the solution has been reached, it is important to follow up on the implementation and to keep a record of both successes and failures for future use.

OTHER PROBLEM-SOLVING TECHNIQUES

Although the basic problem-solving procedure can be modified to fit specific needs, it tends to work best when both the leader and members are trained in the process, the group is relatively small, and the members have had ample time to prepare. There are times in the business world, however, when problems need to be solved even though one or more of these conditions are missing. In such situations, the *single-question procedure*, the *ideal-solution procedure*, or a *buzz group procedure* might be more successful.

Single-Question Procedure

The single-question form of problem analysis is especially appropriate when one or more of the following is true:

- The group is fairly small.
- The task is simple.
- A one-time meeting is desired.
- The group has a pressing deadline.
- A temporary decision is needed (a more detailed problem-solving discussion will be held later).
- The group is untrained in problem solving.

C. E. Larson suggests the following five steps for the single-question procedure:

1. What is the single question, the answer to which is all that the group needs to know to accomplish its purpose?
2. What subquestions must be answered before we can answer the single question we have formulated?
3. Do we have sufficient information to answer confidently the subquestions? If no, continue below.
4. What are the most reasonable answers to the subquestions?

5. Assuming that our answers to the subquestions are correct, what is the best solution to the problem?[50]

When the group has more time and flexibility for problem solving, the ideal-solution procedure may be more appropriate.

Ideal-Solution Procedure

The ideal-solution form of analysis can be used successfully in the same situations listed for the single-question form. In addition, the ideal-solution procedure is useful when the group's task is to select the best of several alternatives or when members' feelings are likely to run high.

The ideal-solution procedure involves answering these four questions:

1. Are we all agreed on the nature of the problem?
2. What would be the ideal solution from the point of view of all parties involved in the problem?
3. What conditions within the problem could be changed so that the ideal solution might be achieved?
4. Of the solutions available to us, which one best approximates the ideal solution?[51]

When neither the single-question procedure nor the ideal-solution procedure seems viable, the group may turn to buzz group procedures.

Buzz Group Procedures

Buzz group procedures, named after a group technique called "Buzz," created by J. D. Phillips in the 1940s, are probably more effective than the basic problem-solving procedure when

1. The members are not especially well informed about the problem.
2. The leader is not familiar with the basic problem-solving procedure.
3. The size of the group is too large for a successful discussion.

The buzz group procedure[52] involves dividing a group into smaller groups (buzz groups) of five to eight people and instructing each group to discuss the problem, arrive at suggestions, and report back to the large group as a whole. Normally, all the buzz groups are located in the same room or auditorium and thus can benefit from the conclusions and thinking of the other groups.

The quality of information and suggestions reached by the individual buzz group depends on the participants' knowledge of the problem. If the person in charge of the large group believes the participants know little about the particular problem or if the amount of their knowledge is unknown, the person in charge might wish to brief the participants by arranging for a group of experts to discuss the problem in front of the entire gathering. After the experts' discussion, those present can be organized into buzz groups.

Many variations of buzz group procedures are possible; the following is an example:

1. Divide the gathering into small groups.
2. Have each group appoint a timekeeper.
3. Have each group appoint a secretary or leader to record ideas.
4. Have each group state the specific topic to be discussed.
5. Have each group member take 1 minute to express opinions (more time may be given if desired).
6. Have each group take 5 minutes (or more) to discuss its list and to select (by consensus) the best one or two ideas or suggestions.
7. Have each secretary then report the group's conclusions to the entire gathering.
8. Follow up with a general discussion by all those present.

When time is not as limited, a less rigid procedure can be used. Another variation, useful when the effects of group pressure need to be minimized, is to hand out a prepared list of ideas or solutions and have buzz group members select from or rank these items.

SELECTING THE GROUP FORMAT

We conclude this chapter on small-group communication and decision making by taking a brief look at various group discussion formats. The most often used format, generally referred to as the *roundtable*, is a small-group discussion conducted in private by means of the basic problem-solving procedure.

The **panel** discussion involves a small group of well-informed individuals discussing a problem or topic of interest in front of a larger group. All panel members contribute freely and equally and are usually guided through the basic problem-solving procedure or a similar one by a leader or chairperson.

The **symposium** is composed of a small group of experts, also in front of a larger group. Instead of the free exchange of ideas heard in the panel discussion, each member of the symposium presents a formal, 5- to 10-minute presentation on an area of the problem relating to the member's expertise. The chairperson introduces each presentation. When all presentations are finished, several procedures can be followed. For example, the symposium speakers may choose to discuss (agree or disagree with) the formal ideas presented by each speaker or to continue the discussion using the basic problem-solving process. However, if the symposium was intended to educate or stimulate the audience, the leader may invite everyone to enter the discussion.

When those present are allowed to participate following a panel or symposium discussion, the discussion is called a **forum.** Thus, both a panel-forum and a symposium-forum are possible. A forum may involve a simple question-and-answer period, a general discussion, or organized buzz groups. Most problem-solving groups select the roundtable format and conduct their discussions privately. However, if your group is asked to discuss a problem in front of a larger group, you will need to select either the panel or symposium format for your discussion. The basic problem-solving procedure can be used with both of these formats with only minor modification.

The basic problem-solving procedure works best with groups of from three to eight members. However, if your group is too large to use this procedure successfully or if your group is assigned a task but not given time to do research or prepare for the discussion, you may wish to use the single-question procedure, the ideal-solution procedure, or a buzz group procedure. Buzz group procedures can be used successfully with large groups (we have seen it used with as many as 300 people). A panel or symposium discussion can be used to educate or stimulate people before they are divided into smaller buzz groups.

SUMMARY

Group decision making is not the answer to all business or professional problems, but when used correctly, it can be very effective. Now that you have read this chapter, you should feel more confident about participating in and even leading committees, conferences, or similar groups. Most typically, you will be asked to work in small groups to solve problems. Unfortunately, problem solving can be one of the most difficult group tasks. Groups can be effective problem solvers if they are well organized, receive training in problem solving, carefully examine members' assumptions and opinions, evaluate all possible solutions, avoid groupthink, and manage cultural diversity. If the group follows the basic problem-solving procedure outlined in this chapter, decision making can be less frustrating and more productive. This six-step procedure can be altered to fit most group or individual problems. It would be a good idea, however, to master the steps as explained before trying to modify them. To practice the procedure, why not use it to solve family problems at home? Because your family group will not be familiar with the process, you will not have to use the terminology discussed here. A skilled leader, regardless of the setting, can guide a group through the six steps without the group even being aware of the process.

Now that we have covered the basic procedures of group discussion, the next chapter will discuss how individuals can become more proficient in small-group participation and leadership.

CHECKPOINT

Before continuing to the next chapter, check your understanding of Chapter 9 by completing the following exercises:

1. Evaluate the following discussion topics. Rewrite each of the discussion questions to conform to the guidelines in this chapter.

   a. Should General Motors produce electric cars?
   b. Should something be done to alter the ridiculous prices charged by phone companies for long-distance calls?
   c. What can be done to help eliminate waste in the federal government?

2. Assume that someone in your organization must be transferred to a branch store, and that the decision as to who will be transferred has been left to the employees themselves. The branch store is 18 miles from the location where you are presently working, and all jobs in this organization are considered functionally equivalent. Establish criteria to determine who should be transferred. Show your list to a fellow worker or friend and get some feedback.

3. Recall a recent decision-making meeting you attended. Was it an effective meeting? Why or why not? In what ways was the group more effective than an individual might have been?

4. Read the following example.[53] Do you think similar decision-making groups should be used more often in government? Why or why not?

   Susan Hagar, an engineer with the Environmental Protection Agency, tells how her agency used group decision making to determine how to divide three-quarters of a million dollars in federal grants among seventeen state and regional agencies:

   Congress had not given our agency any more than a vague prescription of what should be accomplished with the funds. However, half of the seventeen agencies had very definite, albeit very different, ideas on how to use the money, and the other half had no ideas at all. But all were uniformly clear on one point; that whatever method was used to allocate funding, it should maximize their agency's share.

Progress was finally made when agreement was reached to select a group of people who would represent the interests of all seventeen agencies and to abide by their recommendation. A very animated group of eight was chosen and the decision-making process began. After only one meeting, priorities had been set and several viable proposals were discussed; at the second meeting, consensus was reached on an allocation plan which withstood review by all others affected.

Although asking agency representatives to take responsibility for allocating their own funding is somewhat risky, putting these individuals face-to-face supplies the essential interpersonal contact needed to promote an understanding of the other's perspective. Writing a memorandum establishing a rationale for maximizing your agency's share of funding (and coincidentally minimizing everyone else's) is simple; defending it to a small group of people who have many of the same justifications you do, is a whole different ballgame.

ℓ NOTES

1. Richard J. Dunsing, "You and I Have Simply Got to Stop Meeting This Way" (Part 1), *Supervisory Management* (September 1976), p. 9.
2. William Bowen, "How to Regain Our Competitive Edge," *Fortune* 103 (March 9, 1981), pp. 74–90; Rensis Likert, *The Human Organization: Its Management and Value* (New York: McGraw-Hill, 1976), p. 76; Keith Davis, *Human Behavior at Work* (New York: McGraw-Hill, 1972); Frederick C. Hatfield, "Effect of Prior Experience, Access to Information and Level of Performance on Individual and Group Performance Ratings," *Perceptual and Motor Skills* 35 (August–December 1972), pp. 19–26.
3. B. Dumaine, "The Trouble with Teams," *Fortune* (September 5, 1994), pp. 65–70.
4. Thomas R. Tortoriello, Stephen J. Blatt, and Sue DeWine, *Communication in the Organization: An Applied Approach* (New York: McGraw-Hill, 1978), p. 81.
5. Stewart L. Tubbs, *A Systems Approach to Small Group Communication* (Reading, MA: Addison-Wesley, 1978), p. 5.
6. Gerald M. Goldhaber, *Organizational Communication*, 6th ed. (Dubuque, IA: Brown & Benchmark, 1993), p. 268.
7. J. G. Bowles, "The Human Side of Quality," *Fortune* (September 24, 1990), p. 24.
8. *Quality Circle Journal* 6 (December 1983), p. 25.
9. Joel E. Ross and William C. Ross, *Japanese Quality Circles and Productivity* (Reston, VA: Reston, 1982), p. 16; Phillip C. Thompson, *Quality Circles: How to Make Them Work in America* (New York: AMACOM, 1982), pp. 11–12.
10. D. Scott Sink, *Productivity Management: Planning, Measurement and Evaluation, Control and Improvement* (New York: Wiley, 1985), p. 396.
11. Discussed by Richard L. Daft, *Organization Theory & Design*, 5th ed. (St. Paul: West, 1995), pp. 199–200. Original source Ron Winslow, "Utility Cuts Red Tape, Builds Nuclear Plant Almost on Schedule," *The Wall Street Journal*, February 22, 1984, pp. 1, 18.
12. John K. Brilhart, *Effective Group Discussion*, 6th ed. (Dubuque, IA: Wm. C. Brown, 1989), p. 260.
13. Adapted from H. Lloyd Goodall, Jr., *Small Group Communication in Organizations* (Dubuque, IA: Wm. C. Brown, 1985), p. 230.
14. Brilhart; Goodall, pp. 229–230; Brant R. Burleson, Barbara J. Levine, and Wendy Samter, "Decision-Making Procedure and Decision Quality," *Human Communication Research* 10 (Summer 1984), p. 570; Randy Y. Hirokawa, "Consensus Group Decision-Making, Quality

of Decision, and Group Satisfaction: An Attempt to Sort 'Fact' from 'Fiction,'" *Central States Speech Journal* 33 (Summer 1982), p. 411; Marshall S. Poole, "Decision Development in Small Groups I: A Comparison of Two Models," *Communication Monographs* 48 (1981), p. 20; C. H. Kepner and B. B. Tregoe, *The New Rational Manager: A Systematic Approach to Problem Solving and Decision Making* (New York: McGraw-Hill, 1981); Larry J. Barker, Kathy J. Wahlers, Donald J. Cegala, and Robert J. Kibler, *An Introduction to Small Group Communication: Groups in Process*, 3rd ed. (Englewood Cliffs, NJ: Prentice-Hall, 1987), p. 146; A. Paul Hare, *Handbook of Small Group Research*, 2nd ed. (New York: Free Press, 1976), p. 330.

15. John K. Brilhart and Lurene M. Jochem, "Effects of Different Patterns on Outcomes of Problem-Solving Discussion," *Journal of Applied Psychology* 48 (1964), pp. 175–179; Marshall Scott Poole, "Decision Development in Small Group I: A Comparison of Two Models," *Communication Monographs* 48 (1981), pp. 1–24.

16. C. E. Larson, "Forms of Analysis and Small Group Problem-Solving," *Speech Monographs* 36 (1969), pp. 452–455.

17. Thomas M. Schiedel and Laura Crowell, "Idea Development in Small Groups," *Quarterly Journal of Speech* 50 (1964), pp. 140–145.

18. Brilhart, *Effective Group Discussion*, 3rd ed., p. 127. (Brilhart's new 6th ed. does not include this statement.)

19. Dale G. Leathers, "Quality of Group Communication as a Determinant of Group Product," *Speech Monographs* 39 (August 3, 1972), pp. 166–173; Willard E. Gutzner and William Fawcett Hill, "Evaluation of the Effectiveness of the Learning thru Discussion Method," *Small Group Behavior* 4 (February 1983), pp. 5–34.

20. Aaron J. Nurick, "The Paradox of Participation: Lessons from the Tennessee Valley Authority," *Human Resource Management* 24 (Fall 1985), pp. 353–354.

21. From a personal conversation with Hal Weller, FAA regional quality circle trainer.

22. Henry P. Sims and James W. Dean, Jr., "Beyond Quality Circles: Self-Managing Teams," *Personnel* (January 1985), p. 31.

23. S. Sorenson, "Grouphate," paper presented to the International Communication Association Annual Convention, Minneapolis, May 1981.

24. Randy Y. Hirokawa and Roger Pace, "A Descriptive Investigation of the Possible Communication-Based Reasons for Effective and Ineffective Group Decision Making," *Communication Monographs* 50 (December 1983), pp. 269–370. Used by permission of the Speech Communication Association.

25. Hirokawa and Pace, p. 370.

26. Hirokawa and Pace, pp. 370–372.

27. Irving L. Janis, *Crucial Decisions: Leadership in Policymaking & Crisis Management* (New York: Free Press, 1988); Irving L. Janis, *Groupthink: A Psychological Study of Foreign-Policy Decisions and Fiascoes*, 2nd ed. (Boston: Houghton Mifflin, 1982); Irving L. Janis, "Groupthink Among Policy Makers," in *Sanctions for Evil*, Nevitt Sanford, Craig Comstock, and associates, eds. (San Francisco: Jossey-Bass, 1971); Irving L. Janis, "Groupthink," *Psychology Today* 5 (November 1971), pp. 43–46, 74–76.

28. Janis, *Groupthink*, pp. 174–175; Janis, *Crucial Decisions*.

29. Janis, *Psychology Today*, p. 76.

30. The information in this section comes from Nancy J. Adler, *International Dimensions of Organizational Behavior*, 2nd ed. (Boston: PWS-Kent, 1991), pp. 132–137, 165–167, as well as Harry C. Triandis and Rosita D. Albert, "Cross Cultural Perspectives," in *Handbook of Organizational Communication*, Frederick M. Jablin, Linda L. Putnam, Karlene H. Roberts, and Lyman W. Porter, eds. (Newbury Park, CA: Sage, 1987), pp. 280–281.

31. Adler, pp. 139–141.

32. Based on John Dewey, *How We Think* (Boston: Heath, 1910), and Kepner and Tregoe, 1981.

33. Charles H. Ford, *Think Smart, Move Fast: Decision Making/Problem Solving for Super Executives* (New York: AMACOM, 1982), p. 6.

34. Ford, pp. 10–11.

35. Gerald M. Phillips, Douglas J. Pedersen, and Julia T. Wood, *Group Discussion: A Practical Guide to Participation and Leadership* (Boston: Houghton Mifflin, 1979), pp. 150–155.

36. C. H. Kepner and B. B. Tregoe, *The Rational Manager: A Systematic Approach to Problem Solving and Decision Making* (New York: McGraw-Hill, 1965).

37. David M. Berg, "A Descriptive Analysis of the Distribution and Duration of Themes Described by Task-Oriented Small Groups," *Speech Monographs* 34 (1967), pp. 172–175.

38. Brilhart and Jochem, pp. 175–179.

39. Ichak Adizes and Efraim Turban, "An Innovative Approach to Group Decision Making," *Personnel* (April 1955), pp. 45–49; Hirokawa and Pace, pp. 361–379.

40. Kepner and Tregoe, 1981.

41. A. F. Osborn, *Applied Imagination*, 3rd ed. (New York: Scribner's, 1963).

42. Charles H. Clark, *Brainstorming* (Garden City, NY: Doubleday, 1958); Thomas J. Bouchard, Jr., and Melana Hare, "Size, Performance and Potential in Brainstorming Groups," *Journal of Applied Psychology* 54 (1, Part 1), pp. 51–55; Warren R. Street, "Brainstorming by Individuals, Enacting and Interacting Groups," *Journal of Applied Psychology* 59 (4), pp. 433–436; for other sources see Hare, p. 319.

43. Andre L. Delbecq, Andrew H. Van de Ven, and David H. Gustafson, *Group Techniques for Program Planning: A Guide to Nominal Group and Delphi Process* (Westport, CT: Green Briar Press, 1986).

44. Weller.

45. Brant R. Burleson, Barbara J. Levine, and Wendy Samter, "Decision-Making Procedure and Decision Quality" *Human Communication Research* 10 (Summer 1984), pp. 557–574; J. H. Davis, *Group Performance* (New York: Addison-Wesley, 1969); Marshall Scott Poole, Robert D. McPhee, and David R. Seibold, "A Comparison of Normative and Interactional Explanations of Group Decision-Making: Social Decision Schemes Versus Valence Distributions," *Communication Monographs* 29 (March 1982), pp. 1–19.

46. Marshall Sashkin and William C. Morris, *Organizational Behavior: Concepts and Experiences* (Reston, VA: Reston, 1984), p. 195.

47. Arthur B. Van Gundy, *Managing Group Creativity: A Modular Approach to Problem Solving* (New York: American Management Association, 1987) and *108 Ways to Get a Bright Idea* (Englewood Cliffs, NJ: Prentice-Hall, 1983).

48. Arthur B. Van Gundy, "Brainstorming: Variations on a Theme," *Quality Circles Journal* 7 (June 1984), pp. 14–17.

49. J. T. Wood, "Consensus and Its Alternatives: A Comparative Analysis of Voting, Negotiation and Compromise as Methods of Group Decision-Making," in *Emergent Issues in Human Decision-Making*, G. M. Phillips and J. T. Wood, eds. (Carbondale: Southern Illinois University Press, 1984).

50. Larson, p. 453.

51. Larson, p. 453.

52. J. D. Phillips, "Report on Discussion 66," *Adult Education Journal* (1948), pp. 181–182.

53. Written especially for this book by Susan Hagar, engineer with the Environmental Protection Agency.

10

Participation and Leadership in Small Groups

A t least two things can be said about meetings. First, they are a necessary evil, and second, they cost organizations a great deal of money. Therefore, it is in the best interest of the organization to ensure that meetings are productive. . . . Unfortunately . . . organizations have failed to impress upon their supervisors that conducting a successful meeting is actually a supervisory skill to be as highly prized as any other supervisory function.[1]

LARRY G. MCDOUGLE,
School of Technical Careers, Southern Illinois University

T he basic problem-solving procedure and other procedures presented in the previous chapter are useful ways for a small group to organize its decision-making process. However, for a small group or task force to operate effectively, it must be more than well organized. Consider the following example:

> The owner of a small manufacturing company decided to create a task force to help him develop and implement revisions in his company's reward policy. He selected three second- and third-level managers from the company to serve on the task force. At the opening meeting the owner clarified the specific task for the managers—they were to make specific recommendations for changing the company's outstanding employees' benefit package so that it would create more initiative in personnel. The managers were instructed to consult with their employees so that the final recommendations would be welcomed by everyone connected with the company. The owner served as chairperson of the group meeting and guided the group through the basic problem-solving procedure. Everything should have gone well. But it didn't. The managers had few opportunities to give their opinions even though they had met previously with their employees and were prepared with valuable suggestions. In the end the owner made the final decisions because he couldn't get the quality of participation he felt he needed from the managers.

Why did the group process fail in this situation? First, the group failed because the managers knew very little about how to participate effectively in group decision making. They waited for the owner to initiate each step and then were angry when he did. They felt that they had played no real part in the decision-making process. Second, the group failed because the owner was confused about his role as leader of the group: He wanted to let the managers make the decisions, but felt that a leader must hold firm control if a group is to accomplish anything.

To help you avoid such problems in your groups, this chapter will discuss effective group participation and effective group leadership.

EFFECTIVE GROUP PARTICIPATION

Effective group participation requires members who are committed to the group's goals, who display the communication skills of active listening and open-mindedness, and who are aware of their responsibilities.

Committed Members

As seen in the example just discussed, a small group must be more than well organized to operate effectively. To begin, group members must be committed. A committed member is one who is willing to

1. Devote time and energy to the group by faithful attendance and by careful preparation for each meeting
2. Support the final decision of the group
3. Perform needed task and maintenance roles

Obviously, meetings run more smoothly when members are prepared. Probably the best way to prepare for a problem-solving discussion is to work through the six basic problem-solving steps (see Chapter 9) before the meeting. Come prepared with facts, possible criteria, possible solutions, and so on. Research and discuss all pertinent viewpoints and alternatives, thereby avoiding groupthink. When the facts and figures presented during a discussion point to a solution that is agreeable to most of the group but not supported by a few members, the majority opinion must stand until new evidence is presented. In the business world, members who are not willing to support their group's final decisions are not committed members. This does not mean, however, that the members should avoid disagreement or productive conflict during the discussion; however, once a solution is reached, it should be supported by the group's members.

Committed members should also be willing to perform any needed *task* or *maintenance functions* and be willing to handle any *nonfunctional behaviors* that may appear in the group. These functions and behaviors are explained next.

Task and Maintenance Functions ■ People perform numerous functions in their lives—many of them at the same time. For example, a person may be a spouse, a student, a member of the church board, a manager, and a friend—all at the same time. The same is true of task and maintenance functions in the small group; participants may perform many functions in the life of a group. **Task functions** are roles that must be performed if the group is to accomplish its task or solve its problem. **Maintenance functions** are roles that must be performed if the interpersonal relationships and harmony of the group are to be maintained. The number of task and maintenance functions that need to be performed in a particular group depends on such situational factors as the personalities of the group members, the task or goal of the group, and even the leadership style of the leader. Task functions are stressed more by the traditional/classical manager, while maintenance functions are stressed more by the human relations manager (see Chapter 2). The following lists give examples of various task and maintenance functions.[2]

Group Task Functions

- *Initiate.* Propose new ideas, procedures, goals, and solutions to get the discussion started.

- *Give information.* Supply evidence and experiences relevant to the task.
- *Seek information.* Request and clarify information from other members.
- *Give opinion.* State beliefs, attitudes, and judgments.
- *Seek opinion.* Solicit and clarify opinions and feelings of others.
- *Elaborate.* Clarify and expand the ideas of others through examples, illustrations, and explanations.
- *Energize.* Stimulate the group to be energetic and active.
- *Review.* Summarize the discussion throughout.
- *Record.* Record group suggestions and decisions.

GROUP MAINTENANCE FUNCTIONS

- *Encourage.* Provide a warm, supportive interpersonal climate by praising and agreeing with others (especially important during conflict).
- *Harmonize.* While recognizing the value of conflict to a group, members reconcile differences in a productive manner. Compromise and mediation may be used when necessary.
- *Relieve tension.* When necessary, relax the atmosphere through such things as informality or humor.
- *Gatekeep.* Control the flow of communication: Draw the nontalkers into the discussion and tactfully cut off the monopolizers and other nonfunctional members in an attempt to give all members an equal chance to communicate.

The positive behaviors of task and maintenance functions are necessary in groups, but *nonfunctional* or *negative behaviors* often occur also.

Nonfunctional Behaviors ■ Some behaviors are nonfunctional because they serve individual needs and inhibit organizational and group needs. Although these behaviors cause problems, they can also stimulate healthy conflict and jar a group out of its groupthink pattern. Some of the major nonfunctional behaviors are listed here.[3]

NONFUNCTIONAL BEHAVIORS

- *Blocking.* Constantly putting down the ideas and suggestions of others.
- *Aggression.* Insulting and criticizing other members, perhaps out of jealousy or dislike.
- *Storytelling.* Luring the group off track with irrelevant stories, often very interesting.

- *Recognition seeking.* Calling attention to personal achievements and successes.
- *Dominating.* Monopolizing group interaction; often, domination is the result of excellent preparation and involvement in the discussion.
- *Confessing.* Using the group as a sounding board for personal problems and feelings.
- *Special-interest pleading.* Representing the interest of another group, regardless of whether it fits the topic being discussed.
- *Distracting.* Distracting the group with antics, jokes, and comments at inappropriate moments.
- *Withdrawing.* Participating very little or not at all, possibly from lack of preparation, nervousness, or the climate of the group.

When it is obvious that these behaviors are causing unproductive conflict, handle them with care and tact. The key to handling these behaviors lies in the reason for them. Careful observation of both the verbal and the nonverbal behaviors of these group members should give the gatekeeper or leader valuable clues to their motives. Here are some suggestions to minimize the effect of negative behaviors:

- *Plan your opening remarks carefully.* When you are the leader, open the meeting with a reference to the short time allotted for the meeting and request that all remarks be brief and specific. Mention the fact that you will be interrupting conversations when necessary to keep the discussion on track. Giving a specific, overall picture of expected topics or listing the criteria for performance is surprisingly effective in directing group behavior. Most members are willing to conform to necessary limitations as long as they know what the limitations are and the reasons for them.
- If you know ahead of time that a person with potentially negative behavior will be present, *seat the person immediately next to the leader.* It is easier to bypass a person in this position. If the leader is sitting on one side of a rectangular table, make sure the person with nonfunctional behavior is not at one of the ends of the table (the traditional power seats) or across from the leader, where direct eye contact is impossible to avoid.
- *Avoid direct eye contact* with anyone performing nonfunctional behaviors. Eye contact in American society is a nonverbal signal that encourages talking. Therefore, when asking a question of the group, look only at those to whom you wish to speak.
- *Assign nonfunctional members specific tasks* to keep them occupied. For example, before the meeting you could ask a person who tends to be

distracting to help you relieve tension during the sure-to-come tense moments in the meeting. By concentrating on when tensions should be relieved, this nonfunctional person will likely become a productive group member. Recording is another important task that can be assigned to a nonfunctional member.

- *Ask members to speak in a specific order,* making sure that everyone gets a chance to participate. Such regimentation will make the group more formal and should be used only when necessary.
- When a person displaying a nonfunctional behavior pauses for breath, *break in*—briefly summarize the previous comments or quickly ask someone else for an opinion. Don't make the mistake of asking the nonfunctional speaker if your summary is correct; he or she will simply begin speaking again.
- *Place an extremely talkative member between two extremely quiet members.* Such seating may stimulate the quiet members and restrain the talkative member.
- *Encourage nontalkers* by giving only positive feedback to their comments or asking them direct questions about which you know they have information or opinions.
- *Give praise and encouragement* when possible to those who seem to need it, including the distracters, the blockers, and the withdrawn.

As you can see, these suggestions require some planning prior to the meeting, as well as attention during the meeting.

Communication Skills for Members

For successful communication to occur, group members must be both active listeners and open-minded participants.

Active Listening ■ Many times when we are discussing a problem with others, we listen selfishly. In other words, we listen to gather ammunition for our rebuttals and to determine when we can insert our viewpoints into the conversation. Active listening, however, requires us to listen from the speaker's viewpoint. The active listener

1. Receives the speaker's total message—verbal and nonverbal.
2. Interprets the speaker's meaning as closely as possible.
3. Checks the interpreted meaning for accuracy by rephrasing it for the speaker.
4. Repeats steps 1–3 until the speaker is satisfied with the interpretation.

For effective group participation to occur, group members must be active listeners and open-minded participants. *(© Zigy Kaluzny/Tony Stone Images)*

After you are sure that you understand the speaker's argument, you may agree or disagree and present your views. This type of active listening is necessary for effective group participation.

Open-Mindedness ■   While preparing for a group discussion, participants sometimes become convinced that a certain solution is best. They come to the discussion prepared to convince the other members to agree with *their* choice. If all participants were equally close-minded, the discussion would become a debate. Feelings would be hurt, productivity would decrease, and the meeting would drag on.

Productive group discussion requires that members listen with an open mind to all views and even respect those views. But open-mindedness does not mean that there can be no disagreement. Conflict over opinions can stimulate the group's thinking. If no one disagreed, the group could fall into a groupthink pattern and arrive at a risky or unsuccessful decision.

Open-minded participants try to reach a decision that benefits the group or company as a whole. They work together as a team, not as unyielding individuals.

EFFECTIVE GROUP LEADERSHIP

In addition to an organized procedure and committed participants, an effective group must have good leadership. There are many theories of leadership (see Table 10.1). Research does not completely validate any of

> REMEMBER, AS A GROUP MEMBER,
> YOUR RESPONSIBILITIES ARE TO . . .
>
> - Attend meetings faithfully.
> - Prepare carefully and completely for each meeting.
> - Be willing to support the decisions of the group.
> - Perform task and maintenance roles.
> - Avoid nonfunctional behaviors.
> - Use the communication skills of active listening and open-mindedness.

these theories, and they are not all equally helpful to those who want advice on how to become a good leader. Therefore, we summarize here those theories that are the most important for you to know.

Trait Theory of Leadership

When asked to serve as the leader of a small group or committee, do you generally say "yes" or do you say, "Oh, no, I'm not qualified to be a leader. I'm not leadership material"? If your answer resembles the second response, you probably agree with those who say that a leader must be intelligent, forceful, willing to lead, popular, and so on. In other words, the reason you are not a good leader is because you do not have the traits or characteristics necessary for a leader. You may also believe that leaders are born with the ability to lead.

Such a belief is based on the **trait theory** of leadership, which claims that there are certain traits or qualities that a person must have to become a leader. However, although it may be helpful and even desirable for the leader to be intelligent or forceful or persuasive, research on leadership does not completely support the trait theory. Keith Davis reports:

> Research has produced such a variegated list of traits presumably to describe leadership that for all practical purposes it describes nothing. Fifty years of study have failed to produce one personality trait or set of qualities that can be used to discriminate between leaders and nonleaders.[4]

In a search for leader traits, Ralph M. Stogdill reviewed more than 25,000 books and research articles on leadership and management and failed to find any "magic" traits that fit all leaders in all situations.[5]

In a more recent review of trait research, S. A. Kirkpatrick and E. A. Locke report that successful leaders do seem to be different from less successful leaders: Successful leaders are more likely to be ambitious, trust-

Table 10.1 Leadership Theories[6]

Behavior Theories

Trait	Leaders are born with certain leader characteristics.
Two-dimension	Leaders have either task orientation or people orientation. (Stogdill)
Function	Leadership determined by set of functions—task functions and maintenance functions. Anyone can perform these functions, thereby sharing leadership responsibility. (Benne and Sheats)
Three-dimension	Leader behavior thought of in terms of three basic styles: autocratic, democratic, or laissez-faire. (Lippitt and White)

Situational Theories

Situational contingency	Leader style determined by: (1) leader–member relations, (2) how clearly task is structured, (3) leader's power position (strong or weak). Different leader styles successful in different sets of circumstances. Leaders normally don't change styles. (Fiedler)
Situational leadership	Leaders can change styles to fit situation. Which of four styles to use—delegating, participating, selling, or telling—depends on ability and willingness of subordinates to carry out task. (Hersey and Blanchard)
Path–goal	Leader effectiveness depends on leader's abilities and group's needs. Leader is responsible for assisting followers in attaining their goals while providing needed direction—making the path to those goals clear. (House)

Recent Theories

Normative decision	Provides a step-by-step guide for selecting one of five basic decision-making strategies. (Vroom and Yetton; revised by Vroom and Jago)
Transformational	A charismatic leadership style that inspires employees to exceptional performance, enthusiasm, and loyalty. (Bass)

worthy, motivated to lead, self-confident, able to integrate and interpret large amounts of information, knowledgeable of their industry and of technical matters, creative, and able to adapt to people and situations.[7]

Even so, most experts believe that *good leaders are not born, they are trained.* Practically anyone willing to spend the time for training can become a small-group leader. People we know who seem to be natural leaders have actually had experience in leadership. Perhaps as children they observed their parents in leadership positions and automatically picked up the necessary skills and confidence for leadership. Perhaps they participated in Boy Scouts, Girl Scouts, or other clubs and organizations that provide leadership experience. Perhaps they had a mentor when they began in business—someone who guided, nurtured, and taught them how to become effective leaders.[8]

Function Theory of Leadership

Suppose that you have just been promoted to supervisor and the first day with your new employees will be in one week, or suppose that your boss has asked you to lead a problem-solving team that will meet in two weeks. Is it possible to train yourself to be a leader in one or two weeks? Not if you believe in the trait theory. You could have a nervous breakdown trying to mirror Kirkpatrick and Locke's list of "successful leadership characteristics": ambitious, trustworthy, motivated, self-confident, intelligent, knowledgeable, creative, and flexible. How long would it take to train yourself to be ambitious, self-confident, and creative? Thinking of leadership as a list of personality traits is counterproductive. We suggest instead that you think of leadership as an activity composed of various acts or functions.[9]

The **function theory** claims that there are certain roles or functions that must be performed if a group is to be successful. Any time you perform one of these functions, you are the leader for that period of time.

Leadership may be defined as the use of power to promote the goal accomplishment and maintenance of the group.[10] In other words, the leader is the person (or persons) who performs the task and maintenance functions discussed earlier in this chapter. In many groups, the appointed leader performs most of the task and maintenance functions. However, in democratic groups in which the members are committed and involved, the leadership functions are shared. Because it is difficult for one person, the designated leader, to guide a group through the basic problem-solving procedure and, at the same time, to be aware of all the functions that need to be performed, another member can handle some leadership functions. For example, you may be sitting next to someone who has been trying to participate in the conversation for several minutes, but the leader and the other members are so involved in what's being said that they haven't noticed. When you say, "Carol has a point she wishes to make," you are performing gatekeeping, an important leadership function. Furthermore, in some situations, the appointed leader is inept, and the only way the group will succeed is for one or more members to emerge as the real leaders. If you wish to develop leadership skills, we suggest you begin by simply learning to perform the task and maintenance functions discussed earlier.

Three-Dimension Theory of Leadership

To become a skilled leader, you should also be aware of your leadership style (the way you handle yourself and others in a group). The **three-dimension theory** of leadership (sometimes referred to as the stylistic approach) concentrates on three different leadership styles: autocratic, democratic, and laissez-faire. J. Kevin Barge summarizes the three main leadership styles as follows:

- *Autocratic leadership style.* Leaders are central authority figures who retain a high degree of control and power over their followers. Leaders make the decisions, whereas followers' participation in decision making is minimal. Leaders use one-way communication.
- *Democratic leadership style.* Leaders and followers make decisions together and jointly determine courses of action. They are viewed more as equals because two-way communication exists between leaders and followers.
- *Laissez-faire leadership style.* This style of leadership is best characterized by leaders who are not involved with the group's decision making. . . . Group members make work assignments and evaluate task completion among themselves.[11]

Autocratic Style ■ The *autocratic* or *authoritarian leadership* style is similar to Theory X and the blind communication style discussed in earlier chapters. Under an authoritarian leader, the group reaches a solution quickly, often makes few errors, and gets more work accomplished than groups that get bogged down in discussion. Even though members in authoritarian-led groups are happy that they reach solutions quickly, they tend to display more hostility and are discontented with their low level of participation. In addition, members develop a dependence on the leader rather than a trust in their own abilities and initiative. However, with large groups authoritarian leaders are more effective than democratic leaders—the larger the group, the more autocratic the leader must be to maintain control.

Democratic Style ■ The *democratic leadership* style is similar to both Theory Y and the open communication style discussed in earlier chapters. Although it takes more time under a democratic leader to accomplish a task, motivation, initiative, and creativity are at higher levels than in authoritarian-led groups. Also, under democratic leadership, group members experience a high level of personal enjoyment and are more committed to the group and its final decision.

In the business world, group commitment to decisions can be very important—especially because most people tend to resist change of any kind. Obviously, businesses *must* change to remain productive. Two businessmen see resistance to change as a real problem when they write:

> Reorganization is usually feared, because it means disturbance of the status quo, a threat to people's vested interests in their jobs, and an upset to established ways of doing things. For these reasons, needed reorganization is often deferred, with a resulting loss in effectiveness and an increase in costs.[12]

One way to reduce resistance to change is to allow company personnel to share their ideas in small groups and to take part in deciding how the change is to take place.[13] People who have been involved in a decision are much more likely to abide by it (even if they aren't completely happy with it) than people who have not. The democratic style of leadership, therefore, can be very effective when member satisfaction and personal commitment are crucial. Keep in mind, however, that the democratic style of leadership is more difficult to perform effectively than either autocratic or laissez-faire leadership, and it is time-consuming. It takes much skill and patience to become a good democratic leader.

Laissez-Faire Style ■ The style of leadership definitely affects the behavior of the group. For example, *laissez-faire leadership* tends to result in a low level of group productivity and poor member satisfaction. Most groups seem to need more guidance than the laissez-faire leader gives. Only one type of group may excel in a nonleadership environment: a group of highly trained, highly motivated experts (such as a group of vice presidents), who perform needed leadership roles themselves.

Situational Contingency Theory of Leadership

Another approach to leadership considers the situation and the contingencies involved. In choosing your leadership style, you would weigh several factors including the style with which you are most comfortable, the needs and expectations of the group, the situation, and the goals of the group. For example, if group members expect a good leader to be autocratic, they may not perceive you as a good leader if you use the democratic style.

Because of the normal pressures of the business world, the *situation* may be the primary factor that dictates the most effective leadership style.

Figure 10.1 The decision time line. *(Source: Marshall Sashkin and William C. Morris,* Organizational Behavior: Concepts and Experiences *[Reston, VA: Reston Publishing, 1984], p. 190. Reprinted by permission of Prentice-Hall, Inc., Englewood Cliffs, NJ.)*

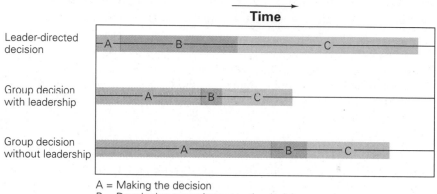

A = Making the decision
B = Developing commitment to the decision
C = Implementing the decision

Fred Fiedler is the best-known exponent of *situational contingency theory* (see Chapter 2, p. 63 for a more detailed explanation). In summary, Fiedler found that leadership in any given situation depends on the power of the leader, the nature of the task, and the relationship between the leader and the group members. He found that authoritarian leadership is effective when the leader is powerful, the task is well defined, and group–leader relations are good. Authoritarian leadership is also effective at the other extreme: The leader has little power, the task is poorly structured, and the leader is disliked by the group. Democratic leadership is more effective when the three conditions are somewhere between the other two extremes.

Another situational variable is the time factor. In selecting an appropriate leadership style, you need to consider the time needed to reach a decision, the time needed to get group commitment, and the time needed to implement the decision. The chart in Figure 10.1 compares the total time for the three leadership styles. Although we have traditionally considered the autocratic approach to be fastest, the chart shows that it is actually slowest if time required to implement a decision is included. The autocratic style is fast at reaching a solution but very slow at implementation, possibly because group members are not fully committed. The democratic style takes longer to reach a decision but is faster to implement, probably because the group has been actively involved in the decision.

Generally, the autocratic leadership style works best when

Group agreement is not required for implementation.

The group is very large.

Time for a decision is short.

Tasks are fairly simple.

Democratic leadership is suggested when

Greater employee satisfaction is needed.

Group commitment is needed for implementation.

Tasks are complicated and require lengthy discussion.

Increased productivity is needed.[14]

Reduced resistance to change is sought.

Selecting the wrong leadership style can result in an unnecessary waste of time, unacceptable solutions, unhappy or hostile employees, and resistance instead of commitment to an idea.

Remember the case of the company owner who appointed a task force to revise the company's reward policy? One of his main reasons for deciding to use a group was that he wanted a plan that would be accepted by all company personnel. He was hoping to please everyone and overcome possible resistance to change. In this situation, which leadership style should the owner have used? The laissez-faire leadership style probably would not have been successful because the managers in the group came from different departments, had different areas of expertise, and were not trained in group decision making. The autocratic leadership style selected by the owner produced a solution quickly but caused feelings of hostility and discontent among the group members—a result exactly opposite the owner's intent. Because the democratic leadership style allows more creativity, promotes member satisfaction, and helps reduce resistance to change through group commitment, the owner would have been most successful using the democratic style for this decision-making group.

Situational Leadership Theory

Believing that a good leader is flexible and can change styles when needed, P. Hersey and K. H. Blanchard describe the following four leadership styles (selection to depend on ability and willingness of subordinates to carry out a particular task):[15]

■ *Delegating.* Followers make and implement decisions on their own. This style works best when followers are both willing and able to do the job.

- *Participating.* Followers and leader share in decision making. This style works best when followers have the ability but require encouragement.
- *Telling.* Followers receive detailed instructions with close supervision. This style works best when followers are able but lack the knowledge needed to do the job.
- *Selling or coaching.* Followers receive structured but supportive instructions. This style is needed when followers have neither the ability nor the willingness to do the job.

Although research has yet to prove the validity of this theory, companies such as Xerox, Caterpillar, and Mobil Oil have found it a successful tool in their leadership training.[16]

Transformational Leadership

Franklin D. Roosevelt, Martin Luther King, Jr., Mary Kay Ash (of Mary Kay Cosmetics), and Lee Iacocca are examples of *transformational leaders*— charismatic leaders who inspired followers to exceptional performance, enthusiasm, and loyalty. You recall that it was Lee Iacocca who took over Chrysler Corporation when it was several billion dollars in the red and was able to convince Congress to approve a $1.5 billion loan guarantee. He was also able to convince Chrysler workers, who had sustained huge wage cuts, and Chrysler dealers, who were being wooed by Japanese franchises, to pull together to get the company back on its feet. And finally, by making personal appearances in advertisements, he also convinced the American public to buy Chrysler. As a result, Chrysler was able to pay back the federal loan seven years before it was due.[17]

As in Iacocca's case, transformational leadership (the theory developed by Bernard Bass[18]) refers to

> leaders who rely on their rhetorical skills to create a compelling vision of the future, which prompts shifts in follower beliefs, needs, and values. Transformational leaders do not depend on their ability to manipulate formal rewards and punishments; rather, they set an example for followers and use rhetorical skills to establish a common vision.[19]

According to Jerald Greenberg and Robert Baron, transformational leaders do more than "articulate a vision"; they "provide a plan for attaining their vision" that makes sense to their followers.[20] They are also careful to "mobilize commitment" from management and employees,[21] who feel a special kind of relationship with the transformational leader. As J. A. Conger notes, because of this relationship, the transformational leader can "make ordinary people do extraordinary things in the face of adversity."[22]

METHODS OF RESOLVING CONFLICT

In addition to being flexible in choice of leadership style, a good leader is effective at resolving conflicts among group members. Any group that meets for any length of time will have conflict of some kind. Gary Kreps points out that "interpersonal conflict provides organization members with important feedback about potentially problematic situations."[23] The success of the group often depends on how the conflict is handled. In developing your conflict resolution skills, you should determine

1. The strategy you feel most comfortable using
2. The strategy the group members prefer
3. When each strategy is the most productive

There seem to be five main strategies for coping with conflict. Kenneth Thomas calls them avoidance, accommodation, competition, compromise, and collaboration.[24] Robert Blake and Jane Mouton call them withdrawal, smoothing, forcing, compromising, and problem solving, as illustrated in Figure 10.2, the conflict grid.[25] (See also Figure 2.4 in Chapter 2, another version of the conflict grid.)

As the grid illustrates, the way you deal with conflict depends on where you place the most concern—people or production of results. Which of the following methods of handling conflict best describes the way you typically resolve conflict? The ways your boss or employees resolve conflict?

- *Withdrawal/avoidance.* This person

    Maintains neutrality at all costs; views conflict as a worthless and punishing experience.

    Removes self either physically or mentally from groups experiencing any type of conflict; stays away from any situation that might possibly produce conflict.

    Feels little concern for people or production of results but great desire for noninvolvement.

    Tends to lead in a closed management style (see Chapter 3 for a discussion of management styles).

- *Smoothing/accommodation.* This person

    Feels a high concern for people regardless of the production of results and, therefore, tries to smooth over or ignore conflicts in an attempt to keep everyone happy.

Figure 10.2 Conflict grid. *(Source: Adapted by special permission from* The Journal of Applied Behavioral Science, *"The Fifth Achievement," by Robert R. Blake and Jane Syrgley Mouton, Vol. 6, No. 4, p. 418, copyright 1970, NTL Institute.)*

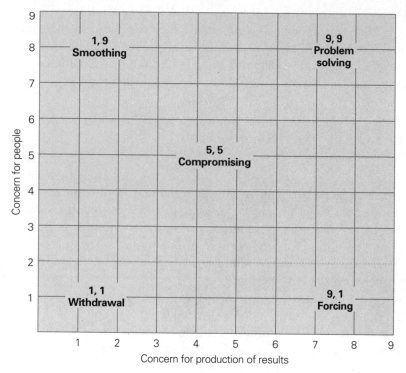

Believes that surface harmony is important to maintain good re-lationships and receive personal acceptance; has motto "If you can't say anything nice, don't say anything at all."

Views open conflict as destructive; gives in to the will of others if necessary.

Tends to lead in a hidden management style.

■ *Forcing/competition.* This person

Views production of results (usually his or her own personal goals) as much more important than people and therefore sees nothing wrong with using force when necessary.

Views conflict as a win-lose situation or as a contest-of-power situation: One person must fail so the other can succeed; no pos-sible compromise.

Has great respect for power and will submit to arbitration only because the arbitrator's power is greater.

Tends to lead in the blind management style.

■ *Compromising.* This person

Believes that everyone should have an equal chance to express opinions.

Tries to find a solution that everyone can live with.

Uses voting or other methods of compromise as a way to avoid direct confrontation; believes that a high-quality solution is not as important as a workable or agreeable solution.

Tends to lead in the open management style.

■ *Problem solving/collaboration.* This person

Gives equal consideration to people and production of results.

Views conflict as beneficial if handled openly; lays all cards on the table.

Guides group through the basic problem-solving procedure (see Chapter 9).

Attempts to reach a consensus agreement; willing to spend a great deal of time and effort to achieve it.

Tends to lead in an open management style.

This range of strategies allows you to combine the strategy with which you feel most comfortable with the strategy group members prefer.

Conflict Strategies: When to Use Them

There are certain times when the five conflict strategies are productive and other times when they are best avoided.[26]

Withdrawal (avoidance) may be the best response to conflict when[27]

■ The issue is trivial.
■ Parties lack the communication skills necessary to prevent destructive escalations.
■ Potential losses from an open conflict outweigh potential gains.
■ There is insufficient time to work through the issue adequately.

The drawback to handling conflict by avoidance is that the confrontation is usually only delayed or transferred to another issue.

Smoothing (accommodation) may be the best response to conflict when

- The issue is minor.
- The damage to the relationship would harm both parties.
- A temporary reduction in conflict is needed to give time for additional research or information.
- Tempers are too hot for productive discussion.

The drawback to handling conflict by accommodation is that it only temporarily solves the problem; it is like putting a Band-Aid on a serious cut.

Forcing (competition) may be the best response to conflict when

- A decision or action must be immediate.
- The parties in the conflict expect and appreciate the force and power necessary in a win-lose situation.
- The combatants recognize the power relationship between themselves.

The drawbacks to handling conflict by force are that the real cause of the conflict is usually not resolved, and because of the unmanaged emotions of the losers, the solution may be only temporary; when the losers gain more power, they may reinstate the conflict.

Compromise may be the best response to conflict when

- Both parties stand to gain.
- An "ideal" or "quality" solution is not required.
- Time is short.
- A temporary solution is needed for a complex problem (a problem-solving discussion will be held later to determine the best solution).
- The parties in the conflict are equals.

The drawbacks to handling conflict by compromise are that everyone loses something and the best solution is probably not reached.

Problem solving (collaboration) may be the best response to conflict when

- Members are trained in problem solving.
- The parties have common goals that require everyone's cooperation to be achieved.
- The conflict arises from misunderstandings or communication breakdown.

The drawback to handling conflict by collaboration is that it may not be successful when the parties have different values or goals. For example, a person who feels that conflict should be resolved in a competitive manner has goals and values completely opposed to the "everyone wins" view of the collaborator. Another important drawback to the problem-solving strategy is that it usually requires a long time.

The success of the five conflict strategies can be analyzed by dividing them into three categories:[28]

- *Win-lose.* Only one party achieves objective. Forcing and voting are win-lose strategies.
- *Lose-lose.* Neither party achieves objective, or both get only a small part of what was wanted. Compromise, arbitration, smoothing, and avoidance are examples of lose-lose strategies.
- *Win-win.* All parties receive acceptable gains. Problem solving and consensus are examples of the win-win strategy.

Although all of these methods can be used to handle conflict, the most productive and satisfying method over the long run is that used by the democratic problem solver. When conflict is handled correctly, it can be very productive.[29]

Imagine that you are the leader of a task force and that you are striving to use the problem-solving method of handling conflict. Under your guidance, all facts and opinions are openly discussed. But after a long and tedious discussion, the group cannot reach an agreement. Half of the group prefers solution A, while the remaining members insist on solution B. How will you handle the problem?

You might urge the group to compromise. If this also failed, you would then probably turn in anger to the forcing method. The group would be unhappy with their wasted time and your decision, as well as probably losing trust in you as their leader, who so easily switched from the democratic to the authoritarian style.

Of course, sometimes it is impossible to reach a consensus agreement, and compromise or even force is necessary to reach a solution. However, keep in mind that settling for just any solution could be worse than no solution. Group members who are told that they can make the decision and then find that the decision is taken away from them may feel that they are being punished. If you find yourself leading a group that seems to have reached a stalemate—that is, the problem-solving method is impossible—try the following procedure before yielding to compromise:

1. Clarify the situation to the group. Include such comments as, "The group seems to have reached an impasse. Further discussion along the same lines would be a waste of time. Obviously, a new approach is needed."

2. Urge the group to set the two conflicting solutions aside temporarily and to pretend they do not exist.

3. Guide the group to seek new solutions through brainstorming or the two-step nominal group technique (review the rules for each of these procedures in Chapter 9). Once a new list has been created, have the group evaluate these solutions and select the best one.

4. Guide the group in comparing the original two solutions with the new solution to see which of the three is now the best. Usually, the new solution is more creative and effective than either of the original conflicting solutions and is selected by the surprised group members as the best solution.

This four-step procedure is not a compromise, because no concessions are required to reach a consensus agreement. The group members believe that the new solution is better than the original solutions and usually wonder why they did not think of it sooner. However, if a consensus is still not possible, the conflict will have to be resolved by compromise, mediation, or even force.

LEADER RESPONSIBILITIES

If you are the designated leader of a small group, you should be ready to assume certain responsibilities, including the following:

- *Inform everyone involved when and where all meetings are to take place.* Distribute an agenda whenever possible.
- *Select a place for the meeting that will be conducive to effective discussion.* Pay attention to the surroundings—make them as pleasant as possible. Comfortable chairs that can be arranged in a circle are desirable. Serve refreshments if possible.
- *Check the facilities a few minutes before the meeting to see that everything needed is in place.* It can be disconcerting to discover that the media equipment is missing, that there are too few chairs, or that the room has another meeting scheduled at the same time as yours.
- *Welcome people as they come in.* You can set the tone of the meeting that follows. Handshakes, smiles, and friendly greetings go a long way toward creating a favorable climate.
- *Start on time.* People have busy schedules and are inconvenienced when meetings do not begin and end on time.
- *Preview the agenda.* It is always helpful to outline the plan for the meeting at the beginning of the meeting. Even if the participants already have access to this information, your time will be well spent if

> ### HELPFUL RESEARCH FINDINGS FOR
> ### LEADERS AND PARTICIPANTS IN BRIEF . . .
>
> - Well-acquainted groups make better decisions than ad hoc groups.[30]
> - As the size of a group increases, members contribute less.[31]
> - "Persons who believe that their skills are inferior to those of others in the group are less likely to use the skills they have."[32]
> - "Members of groups prefer positive feedback and are more willing to believe it."[33]
> - Feedback received by viewing a taped discussion is as effective in training as human evaluation.[34]
> - Instructions to problem-solving groups are better if specific rather than general.[35]
> - Persons who occupy the more central and clearly identified positions (for example, at the head of the table) will tend to become leaders.[36]
> - Group members seem to enjoy the process more and to agree more when the leader takes an active role in the discussion.[37]
> - In business, groups expect the chairperson or designated leader to be the sole leader. Leadership sharing by members may cause a decrease in group satisfaction and cohesiveness.[38]

you take a few moments to remind them of the content of the discussion. Assuming that they know the agenda or the specific topic or problem to be discussed is asking for trouble.

- *Stick to the agenda.* Rambling is a waste of time. Stay with what you have planned, and keep the discussion on track.
- *Encourage discussion.* It is your responsibility to encourage the more reticent members of the group to give their points of view and to tactfully block those who try to monopolize the discussion. You are in a favorable position to do both in your role as designated leader, and you can often do it more tactfully than someone else.
- *Ask questions skillfully.* Know the various types of questions and the kind of responses each question encourages. Such questions as open-ended, hypothetical open, direct, third-person, and closed can help ensure an intelligent, productive discussion (see Chapter 7 for types of questions).
- *Summarize.* You should summarize the main points as the discussion progresses and provide an overall summary at the conclusion.

- *Perform other necessary task and maintenance functions.* In many cases, these functions will be performed by members of the group. However, it is the responsibility of the leader to make sure that the group accomplishes its task in relative harmony.
- *Thank the participants and the audience* (if any). It takes very little time for you to express appreciation to the participants and the audience; it is one of your final responsibilities as leader to take a few moments to do this.
- *Make sure that everyone in the organization who needs results of the meeting is properly informed.* Do not just assume that the word will be passed around. If people are affected by the results of your meeting, inform them as soon as possible.

By following these suggestions, you can greatly improve your group's chances of success. You may want to add other items to the list depending on the specific meeting for which you are responsible.

Summary

An organized procedure such as the basic problem-solving procedure is not enough to enable a small group or task force to operate effectively. Effective group process requires other ingredients. First, it requires committed members, who are willing to devote time and energy to the group, support the decision of the group, and perform needed task and maintenance roles, as well as avoid nonfunctional behaviors. As participants in a group, you and the other members have a definite effect on its productivity. When members are active listeners and open-minded, are well prepared, view conflict as productive, and are willing to support the leader in any way necessary, the group has a very good chance of producing good decisions and ideas. If, however, the members fail to actively listen to one another, are set on their own opinions, fail to prepare or research their ideas prior to the meeting, view conflict as a win-lose situation, and expect the leader to make all the decisions, the group is certain to be nonproductive. Even an excellent, skilled leader would be unable to motivate such members to become a productive group.

Second, effective group process requires leaders who can perform necessary task and maintenance functions, who are adept and flexible at using the democratic, autocratic, and laissez-faire styles of leadership, and who can handle conflicts productively. As the leader of a group, you will directly affect the productivity of the group. According to Bernard Bass,

> The real test of leadership lies not in the personality or behavior of the leaders, but in the performance of the groups they lead. Groups, when

free to do so, appear to select as leaders members who create the expectation that they will be able to maintain goal direction, facilitate task achievement, and ensure group cohesiveness. . . . Some leaders are extremely effective in furthering task achievement. Others are exceptionally skilled in the art of building member satisfaction and intermember loyalty, which strengthen group cohesiveness. The most valued leaders are able to do both.[39]

In your future, you will most likely serve as a group member in some situations and as the group leader in others. This chapter has given you the necessary guidelines to help you perform both roles successfully and productively. Remember, the more you practice these skills, the more effectively you will be able to use them.

CHECKPOINT

Before continuing to the next chapter, check your understanding of Chapter 10 by completing the following exercises:

1. Recall specific personalities who have acted in nonfunctional ways in some of the groups in which you have participated. Could their behavior have been successfully handled in any of the ways suggested in this chapter?
2. Consider the last supervisor for whom you worked. What kind of leadership style was used—autocratic, democratic, or laissez-faire? What do you like and dislike about each of these leadership styles? If you are a supervisor, what leadership style do you normally use? Is it effective? Do your employees like it?
3. Think of four recent conflict situations in which you were involved. Did you react to the conflict by withdrawing, smoothing, forcing, compromising, or problem solving? Do you agree that the problem-solving approach to conflict is the most productive in the long run? Why or why not?

NOTES

1. Larry G. McDougle, "Conducting a Successful Meeting," *Personnel Journal* 60 (January 1981), p. 49.
2. Adapted in part from K. D. Benne and P. Sheats, "Functional Roles and Group Members," *Journal of Social Issues* 4 (1948), pp. 41–49. Used by permission.
3. Benne and Sheats, pp. 41–49.
4. Keith Davis, *Human Behavior at Work* (New York: McGraw-Hill, 1972), p. 3.
5. Bernard M. Bass, *Bass and Stogdill's Handbook of Leadership*, 3rd ed. (New York: Free Press, 1990), pp. 407–418.

6. Bass, *Bass and Stogdill's Handbook of Leadership*; John G. Geier, "A Trait Approach to the Study of Leadership in Small Groups," *Journal of Communication* 17 (1967), pp. 316–323; S. A. Kirkpatrick and E. A. Locke, "Leadership: Do Traits Matter?" *Academy of Management Executive* 5 (1991), pp. 48–60; K. D. Benne and P. Sheats, pp. 41–49; Ralph White and Ronald Lippitt, "Leader Behavior and Member Reaction in Three 'Social Climates,'" in *Group Dynamics: Research and Theory*, 3rd ed., Dorwin Cartwright and Alvin Zandor, eds. (New York: Harper & Row, 1968), pp. 318–335; Frederick E. Fiedler, *A Theory of Leadership Effectiveness* (New York: McGraw-Hill, 1967); F. E. Fiedler and L. Mahar, "The Effectiveness of Contingency Model Training: A Review of the Validation of Leader Match," *Personnel Psychology* 32 (1979), pp. 45–62; P. Hersey and K. H. Blanchard, *Management of Organizational Behavior*, 6th ed. (Englewood Cliffs, NJ: Prentice-Hall, 1988); R. J. House, "A Path–Goal Theory of Leader Effectiveness," *Administrative Science Quarterly* 16 (1971), pp. 321–339; Victor Vroom and Philip Yetton, *Leadership and Decision Making* (Pittsburgh: University of Pittsburgh Press, 1973); Victor Vroom and Arthur G. Jago, *The New Leadership: Managing Participation in Organizations* (Englewood Cliffs, NJ: Prentice-Hall, 1988); J. M. Howell and B. J. Avolio, "Transformational Leadership, Transactional Leadership, Locus of Control, and Support for Innovation: Key Predictors of Consolidated-Business-Unit Performance," *Journal of Applied Psychology* 78 (1993), pp. 891–902.
7. Kirkpatrick and Locke.
8. A. Zaleznik, "Managers and Leaders: Are They Different?" *Harvard Business Review* 55 (May–June 1977), pp. 67–78.
9. Benne and Sheats, pp. 41–49.
10. David W. Johnson and Frank P. Johnson, *Joining Together: Group Theory and Group Skills* (Englewood Cliffs, NJ: Prentice-Hall, 1972), pp. 203–204.
11. J. Kevin Barge, *Leadership: Communication Skills for Organizations and Groups* (New York: St. Martin's, 1994), p. 38; Ralph White and Ronald Lippitt originally described the three leadership styles in *Autocracy and Democracy: An Experimental Inquiry* (New York: Harper & Row, 1960), pp. 26–27.
12. Marvin Bower and C. Lee Walton, Jr., "Gearing a Business to the Future," in *Challenge to Leadership* (New York: The Conference Board, 1973), p. 126.
13. Lester Coch and John R. P. French, Jr., "Overcoming Resistance to Change," *Human Relations* 11 (1948), pp. 512–532.
14. John R. Galbraith, "Influencing the Decision to Produce," *Industrial Management Review* 9 (1967), pp. 97–107.
15. Hersey and Blanchard; see also Jerald Greenberg and Robert A. Baron, *Behavior in Organizations: Understanding and Managing the Human Side of Work* (Englewood Cliffs, NJ: Prentice Hall, 1995), pp. 516–517.
16. Greenberg and Baron, p. 517.
17. Lee Iacocca and William Novak, *Iacocca: An Autobiography* (New York: Bantam, 1984).
18. Although there are many transformational theories, Bernard Bass has developed and researched his in more detail. See Bernard M. Bass, *Leadership and Performance Beyond Expectations* (New York: Free Press, 1985); and Bernard M. Bass and Brice J. Avolio, "Transformational Leadership: A Response to Critiques," in *Leadership Theory and Research*, M. M. Chemers and R. Ayman, eds. (San Diego: Academic, 1993), pp. 49–80.
19. Barge, p. 52.
20. Greenberg and Baron, p. 510.
21. Richard L. Daft, *Organization Theory and Design*, 5th ed. (St. Paul: West, 1995), p. 501.
22. J. A. Conger, "Inspiring Others: The Language of Leadership," *Academy of Management Executive* 5 (1991), pp. 31–45.
23. Gary L. Kreps, *Organizational Communication*, 2nd ed. (New York: Longman, 1990), p. 189.
24. Kenneth Thomas, "Conflict and Conflict Management," in *Handbook of Industrial and Organizational Psychology*, Marvin Dunnett, ed. (Chicago: Rand-McNally, 1976).
25. Robert R. Blake and Jane Syrgley Mouton, "The Fifth Achievement," *Journal of Applied Behavioral Science* 6 (1970), pp. 413–418.
26. Charles Conrad, *Strategic Organizational Communication*, 2nd ed. (New York: Holt, Rinehart & Winston, 1990), pp. 285–319.
27. Excerpt from p. 247 of Charles Conrad, *Strategic Organizational Communication*. Copyright © Holt, Rinehart & Winston, Inc. Reprinted by permission of the publisher.
28. Richard L. Weaver, II, *Understanding Business Communication* (Englewood Cliffs, NJ: Prentice-Hall, 1984), p. 120.
29. Dennis King, "Three Cheers for Conflict!" *Personnel* 58 (January–February 1979), pp. 13–22.

30. Jay Hall, "Decisions, Decisions, Decisions," *Psychology Today* 5 (November 1971), pp. 51–54, 86–88.
31. Jerry Ball, "Chabot College: The Pentagonal Principle for Self-Oriented Classes," *Small Group Behavior* 4 (February 1973), pp. 64–68.
32. Panayiota A. Collaros and Lynn R. Anderson, "Effect of Perceived Expertness upon Creativity of Members of Brainstorming Groups," *Journal of Applied Psychology* 53 (1969), pp. 159–163.
33. Alfred Jacobs et al., "Anonymous Feedback: Credibility and Desirability of Structured Emotional and Behavioral Feedback Delivered in Groups," *Journal of Counseling Psychology* 21 (March 2, 1974), pp. 106–111.
34. Jack R. Weber, "Effects of Videotape Feedback on Task Group Behavior," *Proceedings of the 79th Annual Convention of the American Psychological Association* 6 (Pt. 2, 1971), pp. 499–500; "Effects of Process Feedback, Consultation, and Knowledge of Results on Perceptions of Group Process," *Proceedings of the 80th Annual Convention of the American Psychological Association* 7 (Pt. 1, 1972), pp. 459–460.
35. Marshall Scott Poole, Robert D. McPhee, and David R. Seibold, "A Comparison of Normative and Interactional Explanations of Group Decision-Making: Social Decision Schemes Versus Valence Distributions," *Communication Monographs* 29 (March 1982), pp. 1–19.
36. A. Paul Hare and Robert F. Boles, "Seating Positions and Small Group Interaction," *Sociometry* 26 (December 4, 1963), pp. 480–486; Bernard G. Rosenthal and Alton J. DeLong, "Complementary Leadership and Spatial Arrangements of Group Members," *Group Psychotherapy and Psychodrama* 25 (1972), pp. 34–52; Robert V. Heckel, "Leadership and Voluntary Seating Choice," *Psychological Reports* 32 (February 1973), pp. 141–142.
37. A. Paul Hare, "Small Group Discussion with Participatory and Supervisory Leadership," *Journal of Abnormal and Social Psychology* 48 (1953), pp. 273–275; Leonard Berkowitz, "Sharing Leadership in Small Decision-Making Groups," *Journal of Abnormal and Social Psychology* 48 (1953), pp. 231–238.
38. A. Paul Hare, *Handbook of Small Group Research* (New York: Free Press, 1976), p. 274.
39. Bass, *Bass and Stogdill's Handbook of Leadership*, p. 598.

11 Informative Presentations

You can have brilliant ideas, but if you can't get them across, your brains won't get you anywhere.[1]

LEE IACOCCA,
Iacocca: An Autobiography

On a short flight from Washington to Yale, where he was to give a significant economics speech, President Kennedy decided to make some major last minute changes. Air Force One arrived at the airport with papers everywhere, coffee spilled on some of them. The president's speech writer was concerned about the short time remaining until the scheduled speech. The president said confidently, "You'll make it!"

They set up a typewriter under the bleachers where the president was to speak and handed up the finished typed pages to him one at a time during the speech.

Fortunately, all went well.[2]

Don't you wish you could view speaking in such a positive manner? However, men and women who are just starting their careers tend to prepare themselves for every area of business except one—making oral presentations. Somehow, they feel certain that they will be able to escape making oral reports.

If you are one of these people, we suggest you find *The Guide to Business Periodicals* at a library and look for articles written by people in your business or profession. You will be amazed at the number of articles dealing with formal and informal oral communication skills—regardless of the size of the organization and whether it is a profession or a business. Most of us expect large businesses, such as IBM, General Motors, and McDonnell Douglas, and professionals, such as lawyers and educators and presidents, to give oral presentations. However, small organizations also need employees who are skilled in oral presentations: the high school coach who must sell the board on purchasing new equipment and motivate the team, dentists and dental technicians who must deal with patients and supply companies, salespeople who must present their products and ideas to customers, nurses and doctors, fire and police personnel, paralegal and parafinancial personnel, and so on. Even assembly-line workers at General Motors participate in decision making and formally present group ideas to management. If you move even one step upward in your organization, you will need the oral skills presented in Chapters 11 through 13.

In the business world you will be expected to give *informal* as well as *formal* presentations. You give informal presentations to only one or two persons, while you usually give formal presentations to a much larger group. You typically give informal presentations sitting down, while you are required to stand to give formal presentations. Both formal and informal oral presentations require prior research, careful planning, and proper organization, all of which must relate to the needs of your listeners to be effective. Because you will have to give informal oral reports anyway, why limit your flexibility as a communicator and maybe even your chances for advancement by failing to learn how to make a good, relaxed oral presentation?

When you first begin working in a firm or organization, most of your oral presentations will be in-house unless you are in sales. As an employee, you will be expected to present informational reports, proposals, and recommendations to supervisors. As a supervisor, you will be expected to give instructions, to brief employees on various policy decisions or procedures, and even to inspire or motivate employees when necessary. Both employees and supervisors are expected to give informal briefings and present reports to their colleagues within the company.

The longer you are with the organization and the higher you climb up the organizational ladder, the more likely you are to be asked to speak not only within the organization but also to the general public.

> From the chairman of the board to the assistant manager of the most obscure department, nearly everyone in business speaks in public or makes a speech at some time or other.[3]

Many companies and industries rely on the *speakers' bureau* as a public relations tool. A company speakers' bureau is made up of ordinary employees who have expertise in some aspect of the company and are willing to share it with interested persons. Bell Telephone, Dow Chemical, Xerox, and the United States Army and Navy are a few of the diverse organizations that communicate with the general public through speakers' bureaus.

This chapter will discuss the information needed by both the employee and the manager who wish to prepare and give informative presentations in the following formal or informal situations:

- Supervisors to employees (downward communication)
- Supervisors or employees to management (upward communication)
- Supervisors or employees to fellow workers (horizontal communication)
- Supervisors or employees to customers, clients, or the community (external communication)

BASIC TYPES OF ORAL PRESENTATIONS

Although there are many different types of oral presentations, they can be divided into three general categories: presentations to inform, to persuade, and to entertain. Because entertainment is rarely the purpose of speeches by entry-level employees and supervisors, we will discuss only informative and persuasive presentations.

If your intent is to make the listeners aware of a subject or to present some new ideas or information, then the presentation is an informative

Employees who can give effective presentations are highly valued by business and professional organizations. (© *Charles Gupton/Tony Stone Images*)

one. **Informative presentations** (illustrated by the following sample topics) promote understanding of an idea or convey a body of related facts:

- Nonverbal differences between Japanese and Americans
- How stress affects employee productivity
- How to write an effective memo
- Sales techniques that work
- Potential dangers in using E-mail

If your purpose is to get your listeners to change their beliefs, then your presentation is a persuasive one. **Persuasive presentations** (illustrated by the following sample topics) influence choices or opinions:

- Volunteer work is everyone's responsibility
- Mandatory drug testing benefits all
- Stop using sexist language at work
- E-mail should not be restricted
- Exercise to improve your creativity

As a speaker, be sure to determine whether your presentation is informative or persuasive before you begin preparing because the two types require very different approaches (see Chapter 13 for a discussion of persuasive). However, although their approaches differ, only a thin line divides informative and persuasive presentations. For example, persuasive presentations must inform as well as persuade. How can a speaker persuade listeners unless they are informed of the facts?

To better understand the distinction between informative and persuasive presentations, assume you are an executive at a large aerospace corporation that must lay off workers because of government defense spending cutbacks. The rumor mill is working overtime, sending out rumors about which area will receive layoffs next. Company morale begins to drop. Production also drops as the workers take the attitude, "I'm going to get laid off anyway, so why work so hard?" Attendance becomes so poor that production has to shut down entirely in some areas. Finally, overall production drops to 30 percent. To make matters worse, the employees are still unaware of the truth: No more layoffs are scheduled for six months! The problem here is, What can be done to stop the rumors, increase employee morale, and, as a result, increase production to an acceptable level? How would you handle this problem?

Here is how one farsighted executive used oral presentations in a similar situation. First, the executive called a meeting of all production managers. In an informative presentation using graphs and charts, he briefed them on the company's projected layoffs, dates for the projected layoffs, and the number of layoffs in each department. The managers expressed gratitude for the briefing and noted that they would now be able to give authoritative answers to their employees' questions.

Second, the executive called a meeting of supervisors, discussed the same materials with them, and then gave them a pep talk on the importance of employee morale and of getting accurate information to their employees. The supervisors left the meeting greatly inspired and determined to improve their communication effectiveness.

Third, the executive had each foreman halt production and bring all the line workers to a meeting, where he again presented all the facts and figures on projected layoffs and added that high productivity could cut down the number of layoffs even further. His purpose was to persuade the workers to improve their attendance and productivity. The workers seemed impressed that the executive had taken the time to talk to them, and they were relieved to know that their jobs were relatively secure. The executive must have done a good job: The following week, production jumped 140 percent and remained at a high level.

The basic type of presentation the executive gave to each group can be summarized as follows:

- *Production managers.* The executive needed to *inform* the managers on current projected layoffs so they could answer questions from their employees.

- *Supervisors.* The executive needed to *persuade* the supervisors to continue their efforts to communicate needed information and to build the morale of their employees.
- *Foremen.* The executive needed to *persuade* the foremen that there were no more scheduled layoffs for the next six months, and that those to come later would be minimal (foremen are in excellent positions to squelch rumors).
- *Line workers.* The executive needed to *persuade* the line workers to change their behavior by improving both their attendance and production records.

The remainder of this chapter focuses on informative presentations. Chapter 13 focuses on persuasive presentations.

INFORMATIVE PRESENTATIONS: TYPES AND CHARACTERISTICS

Informative presentations occur continually in business and professional organizations. Although there is some overlap between informative and persuasive presentations, informative presentations are intended to *increase understanding*, not to change an attitude. The majority of informative presentations are informal in nature; most employees are expected to organize and present informal briefings and report to colleagues and supervisors as a normal part of their jobs.

Types of Informative Presentations

Many types of informative presentations are used in business situations. Although the names given to various informative presentations differ greatly from company to company, we will briefly discuss the two types of informative presentations that occur most often in entry-level positions—the oral briefing and the oral report.

An **oral briefing** is designed to present a summary of facts in a short period of time (usually 15 minutes or less). A briefing may be given to an individual (such as an employee, supervisor, or client) or to a group (such as a group of employees, a group of supervisors, several clients, or, on rare occasions, an entire department). Many briefings are informal, as when the supervisor says, "Drop by my office later this afternoon and fill me in on the latest developments of the Walton project," or when an employee or supervisor informally presents information to colleagues at a weekly meeting. Other briefings are more formal, such as a briefing on the status of a particular project given to an entire department. Because briefings last only a short time, few visuals are required.

An **oral report** is designed to present complete details and so requires a longer period of time (usually more than 15 minutes). A report may be a *research report* on the feasibility of producing a new item, an *analytical report* examining various ingredients such as those used to strengthen a type of plastic, a *demonstrative report* explaining how to use a new machine or company product, or an *investigative report* examining a problem area. Often decision-making groups are required to prepare both written and oral reports on a problem and their recommendations for solving it. As with the briefing, reports may be informal or formal but tend to be more formal than most briefings. If the report includes recommendations, the recommendations should be presented in an informative (not persuasive) manner and include both advantages and disadvantages. The detailed information presented in a report can be greatly simplified by the use of visual aids (refer to Chapter 12).

Briefings and reports play an important role in the business communication of both supervisors and employees. It is impossible for supervisors to observe all events or situations themselves. Consequently, informative briefings and reports presented by their employees are the only way supervisors can stay up-to-date on the tremendous amount of information they need to make sound decisions. Supervisors also use briefings and reports to communicate company policies and operational procedures downward to employees. Employees use briefings and reports to communicate ideas and proposals upward to supervisors and horizontally to fellow workers, and to present information or demonstrate product use to clients.

Characteristics of High-Quality Informative Presentations

In one survey, 450 managers reported that they prefer business communications to be brief, clear, and direct.[4] Eighteen organizations that used oral briefings were asked to list reasons for poor briefings. Their lists include confusing organization, poor delivery, too much technical jargon, too long, and lack of examples or comparisons.[5]

According to the director of a communication consulting firm, business speaking should be "plain, straightforward and objective."[6] In addition, the director considers the following characteristics to be important:

- *Accuracy.* Reporting the situation or event as it actually is or was.
- *Objectivity.* Reporting the facts of the situation or event rather than one's biases or feelings about the facts.
- *Completeness.* Reporting all the facts that are relevant.
- *Selectivity.* Reporting only the facts that are relevant.

BASIC OUTLINE FOR INFORMATIVE PRESENTATIONS

Introduction
Capture attention, show benefit to audience, state qualifications, preview purpose and main points

Body

I. Main Point
   A.
   B. } Supporting material: explanation, examples, statistics, quotes, visuals (discussed in Chapter 12)
   C.

II. Main Point
   A.
   B. } Supporting material
   C.

III. Main Point
   A.
   B. } Supporting material
   C.

Conclusion
Summarize purpose and main points, and give closing thoughts

- *Impartiality.* Reporting all or both sides. (This differs from objectivity because one can be objective in reporting only one side.)
- *Interpretation.* Providing background meaning where necessary for the reader's [or listener's] comprehension, or drawing legitimate conclusions to show what it "all adds up to."
- *Clarity.* Explaining the situation or event in terms clear to the reader [or listener].[7]

Now that you know what informative briefings and reports should contain, we will discuss the steps to follow in preparing these presentations.

INFORMATIVE PRESENTATIONS: BASIC OUTLINE

Earlier in this chapter we said that most oral presentations in business can be classified as informative or persuasive. Although each category is unique in certain ways, the basic organization of any presentation is the same—

an introduction, a body, and a conclusion. In the preparation of a presentation, the body is planned first, then the introduction and conclusion.

INFORMATIVE PRESENTATIONS: PREPARATION STEPS

Although there are many different ways to prepare an informative presentation, the following six steps will ensure that your presentation will be high quality.

Step 1: Carefully Analyze Your Potential Listeners

Once the topic has been assigned, all preparation must be guided by the characteristics of your specific listeners. To determine the frames of reference of your listeners, find out as much as possible about them. The executive in our previous example was obviously aware of the importance of audience analysis. Although he presented the same basic information to the managers, supervisors, foremen, and line workers, his basic purpose and supporting material varied depending on the needs and interests of the particular group. Therefore, if you want your listeners (one person or a large group) to listen carefully to your informative report and to understand your ideas, you must be able to relate your presentation to their interests and needs.

When Speaking Outside the Organization ■   If you are asked to make a presentation for a civic group or club outside your organization or to representatives of another company, it will be helpful for you to know the following information about your listeners:

- Specific type of group
- Goal or purpose of the group
- Size of the group
- Characteristics of the members:

    Ages
    Occupations
    Economic status
    Beliefs and values
    Interests

- What knowledge they have about:

    The topic
    The company you represent

> ## PREPARATION STEPS FOR INFORMATIVE PRESENTATIONS
>
> 1. Carefully analyze your potential listeners.
> 2. Determine the general topic.
> 3. Write down your exact purpose in one clear and simple sentence.
> 4. Plan the body of the presentation.
> 5. Prepare the conclusion and introduction.
> 6. Practice using your notes and visual aids.

You can usually discover this information by talking to the group leader or president or to one or more members of the group.

When Speaking Within the Organization ■ If you are asked to make a presentation to a person or group within your organization, find out as much as you can of the following information about your listeners:

- How many people will be present?
- Are they coming by choice? If so, why? What do they hope to get out of the presentation?
- Who are they?

> Names, if possible
> Positions and ranks (Who are the key decision makers?)
> Departments and responsibilities
> Feelings about the company
> Relationships with others present

- What knowledge do they have about your topic?
- What do they know about you, and what general opinions do they have of you?

Another way to analyze how receptive an audience will be is to place them into one of four basic types: (1) friendly, (2) neutral, (3) uninterested, or (4) hostile.[8] Although you need to be careful not to stereotype an audience, it is easier to organize your speech, select supporting materials, and plan your delivery when you can place your audience into a general category. Table 11.1 outlines strategies for dealing successfully with each audience type.

Table 11.1 Strategies for Dealing Successfully with Four Types of Audiences

	Strategies		
	---	---	---
Audience Types	*Organization*	*Delivery*	*Supporting Material*
Friendly (predisposed to like you and your topic)	Any pattern; try something new; ask for audience participation	Warm, friendly, open; lots of eye contact, smiles, gestures, and vocal variety	Humor, examples, personal experiences
Neutral (consider themselves calm and rational; have minds already made up, but think they are objective)	Present both sides of issue; pro–con or problem–solution patterns; save time for audience questions*	Controlled, even, nothing showy, confident, small gestures*	Facts, statistics, expert opinion, comparison and contrast; avoid humor, personal stories, and flashy visuals*
Uninterested (short attention span; present against their will)	Brief—no more than three points; avoid topical and pro–con patterns that seem long to audience	Dynamic and entertaining, move around, large gestures	Humor, cartoons, colorful visuals, powerful quotations, startling statistics
	Do not: Darken the room, stand motionless behind the podium, pass out handouts, use boring viewgraphs, or expect audience to participate		
Hostile (looking for chances to take charge or ridicule speaker; emotional)	Noncontroversial pattern such as topical, chronological, or geographical	Calm and controlled, speak slowly and evenly	Objective data and expert opinion; avoid anecdotes and jokes
	Avoid: Question–answer period if possible; otherwise, use a moderator or accept only written questions		

*Also suggested for a mixed audience.
Source: Compiled from Janet G. Elsea, "Strategies for Effective Presentations," *Personnel Journal* 64 (September 1985), pp. 31–33.

The success of any speech depends on how well the speaker relates the topic to the frames of reference of the audience members. Effective speakers spend a great deal of time analyzing their audiences.

Step 2: Determine the General Topic

Unless you are asked to speak to a group outside the organization and are told to choose any topic you want, the general topic is usually predetermined. Your supervisor may ask for a briefing on a certain project or idea, an engineer may request a technical report on a specific topic, you may wish to represent a new idea or discovery to your colleagues or supervisor, or you may wish to demonstrate a product for a new customer. In all of these cases, the general topic would be obvious.

Step 3: Write Your Exact Purpose in One Sentence

Once your general topic is clear and you have carefully analyzed the potential listeners, you are ready to focus or narrow down the topic for this specific audience's needs and interests. An **exact purpose** should be written in one clear and simple sentence beginning with, "After hearing my presentation, the audience will . . ."

This step is often more difficult than it sounds. Suppose your department has just received a new computer that will greatly increase the capabilities of your information-processing system. You have been asked to introduce the computer to twenty employees whose jobs will necessitate use of the computer. You have been allotted 20 minutes for your presentation. Which of the following statements would best express your exact purpose?

Exact purpose: After hearing my presentation, the audience will . . .
Explain the various uses of the new computer.
Understand how to retrieve information stored in the computer.
Understand how to input new information to the computer.
Realize how the new computer will benefit the company.
Understand how to correct any errors they make while using the computer.
Demonstrate how to use the computer's printer to make copies of important information.
Identify the correct people to contact when they need help in using the computer.

If this is your first presentation, you are probably thinking, "There is no way I can cover all the necessary information about the new computer in 20 minutes! I could speak for hours on the topic!" However, don't forget that your presentation will be given to a specific group of listeners. Organize your topic specifically for them.

Suppose that a careful analysis of the listeners in this situation reveals that none of them have ever directly used a computer before. No computer was previously available to them, so they had to request information from the computer center—a costly and time-consuming process. Although the listeners do not know anything about computers, they are eager to learn. However, you decide that trying to teach specific computer operation techniques in 20 minutes would only cause confusion. Therefore, you decide to state your exact purpose as follows:

> After hearing my presentation, the audience will understand the potential uses of the new computer and who to contact for private computer instructions.

If your listeners had been fairly knowledgeable about computers, obviously your exact purpose would have been completely different.

Step 4: Plan the Body of the Presentation

In planning the body of your presentation, there are four main things to do:

1. Decide on your main points.
2. Determine how to organize those main points.
3. Expand your main ideas into an outline or several storyboards.
4. Add needed verbal and visual supportive materials.

Let's look at each in more detail.

First, decide on the main points to include. We suggest that you brainstorm a list of possible main points that relate to your exact purpose. Then consider each one, selecting those that would most benefit your audience. Most speakers cover two, three, or four main points in their presentations. If you include too many main points, you may lose listeners. Research on memory suggests that five bits of information is about all the average person can remember with accuracy at one time.[9] Therefore, organize your information into five or fewer key ideas or main points. The number of main points you select should depend on (1) the number of points needed to adequately develop your topic, (2) the time limit, and (3) the knowledge and interests of your audience. For most speeches, five topics is maximum; three topics is more common.

Second, select the best method for organizing your main points. The main points can be organized by a variety of methods. The arrangements that seem to be most relevant to business and professional situations are topical, geographical, chronological, and causal.

Topical Arrangement ■   This arrangement is used to break a topic into clusters, divisions, or parts. No spatial, chronological, or causal relationship exists among the main points in a topical arrangement; each is merely one of several topics pertaining to the same subject. Topical arrangement is probably the easiest and, therefore, the most popular method of arrangement. It is the most effective when arranged in one of the following ways:

1. From the most to the least important
2. From the most to the least impressive
3. From the known to the unknown
4. From the familiar to the unfamiliar

The director of research and development of a large corporation presented suggestions to her research team, using the following topical arrangement:

Purpose: After hearing my presentation, the research team will appreciate the guidelines needed for a successful research project.

Main Points:
   I. Obtain top management support.
   II. Define research objectives carefully and fully.
   III. Be realistic when preparing the budget.
   IV. Be prepared to be flexible.

Spatial or Geographical Arrangement ■   This arrangement organizes main points according to their spatial location, such as front to rear, north to south, bottom to top, left to right. The layout of a manufacturing plant could be described by its left, center, and right wings; the layout of a park may be explained by proceeding from entrance to exit; the different functions of a hospital could be explained by progressing from the bottom to the top floor.

A sales manager gave an informative briefing at a sales meeting, using the following spatial or geographical arrangement:

Purpose: After hearing my briefing, the audience will be aware of the company sales increases in the United States.

Main Points:
   I. New England sales have increased 10 percent.
   II. Midwestern sales have increased 5 percent.
   III. West Coast sales have increased 30 percent.

Chronological or Time Arrangement ■ This arrangement is used to present events in the order (or by the date) of their occurrence, and to present steps in the order in which they occur or in the order in which they should be followed. For example, the steps to follow in evacuating an office building during a fire would be presented from first to last step; the history of nuclear power could be presented in chronological order from the date when it was discovered to the present.

A building contractor presented a report to area realtors, using the following time arrangement:

> *Purpose:* Afer hearing my report, area realtors will be familiar with the procedures followed by building contractors in locating land for building.
>
> *Main Points:*
>
>   I. First, the blueprints for the development are drawn.
> II. Second, possible sites are selected.
> III. Third, cost and marketing surveys are conducted for each site.
> IV. Finally, land is purchased and cleared.

Causal Arrangement ■ When your main points have a cause–effect or effect–cause relationship, you are using the causal pattern of arrangement. In this type of organization you would have only two main points: One would be the cause and the other would be the effect. In cause–effect, you discuss a problem or condition and then follow with the result or effects of the condition. In effect–cause, you present the result first and then discuss the problem or condition that caused it.

A supervisor's presentation on E-mail misuse, resulting in a new company limitation policy, might use the following cause–effect arrangement:

> *Purpose:* After hearing my presentation, employees will realize why the company has decided to restrict employee use of E-mail.
>
> *Main Points:*
>
> I. Many employees use the company E-mail system for social and personal business.
> II. The company needs to put restrictions on when and how employees use E-mail.

Third, expand your main ideas into an outline or into several storyboards. Unless you are giving a manuscript presentation, do not write out the speech word for word. It takes twice as long to organize your thoughts this way. It is much faster and easier to work with a simple sentence outline. Or, if you really dislike making outlines, try using storyboards instead. Storyboards don't require the structure or use of symbols found in regular outlines plus they provide space to sketch visual aids (thus stimulating right-brain thinking and creativity). Let's look in more detail at both outlines and storyboards.

Outlines ■ When used correctly, an outline is an effective *planning tool.* When you look at a presentation written in manuscript form, can you tell at a glance how the main points are organized? Can you tell which of your main points have too much supporting material and which don't have enough? Can you be sure that you have used a variety of supporting material? When you can't see your presentation in outline form, it's difficult to see the big picture and to know what changes are needed.

To be effective outlines need to follow a few basic guidelines:

- *Use standard numbering.* Roman numerals, capital letters, and standard numbers are recommended. The different levels most typically used in speech outlines are:

  I. First main point
     A. Subpoint or supporting material
        1. Supporting material

- *Indent for faster comprehension.* When each main point and level is indented (instead of left aligned or centered), you can grasp your general ideas quickly to find needed information.
- *Include at least two items per level,* when possible. In other words, if you have an "A," you need a "B"; if you have a "1," you need at least a "2." However, don't force an unnatural division just to have two parts. On rare occasions, you might use a single item.
- *Use parallel elements in each level.* Therefore, if the item in "A" is a sentence, then "B" should also be a sentence (both could be phrases as well). Both sentences and phrases need to have similar structure and the same voice (either active or passive). For example, in a speech on the common cold, the following main points are not parallel:

    I. Many remedies have been tried
   II. Modern therapy is best
  III. Curing the cold with vitamin C

  The first two points are sentences (one is passive voice and one is active voice) and the third one is a sentence fragment. To make them parallel, you could use the following noun phrases: Ancient remedies, Modern therapy, and Vitamin C cure.
- *Capitalize the first word in each level.* It only takes a glance to know where a new level begins when the first word in each level is capitalized.

Does the following speaker's outline follow the guidelines listed above?

After hearing my presentation, my colleagues will realize that direct access to our new Xanus-2 computer will make our lives easier.

I. It will save us time
    A. Average report preparations should drop from seven days to one day
    B. Less time must be spent on paperwork
    C. Long lead time required by computer center is eliminated
II. It will allow us to impress customers
    A. Instant status checks can be obtained on customer or in-house requests
    B. General reports can be personalized for each customer
III. It will allow us to prepare better reports
    A. Data can be updated before printing
    B. Revisions can be made any time they are needed
    C. Color computer graphics can be added

If you follow the informative outline format (Figure 11.1), you will also include transitions, sources (including page numbers) where you found your information, and a list of your references.

Storyboards ■ Storyboards, like outlines, are planning tools that help you avoid the pitfalls of writing a word-for-word presentation in manuscript style. For some, storyboards are less tedious and more helpful than outlining. Normally, you use a separate storyboard for the introduction and conclusion and one for each of your main points. Using the storyboard format (shown in Figures 11.2a and 11.2b) has the following advantages:[10]

- Does not require the structure or use of symbols found in regular outlines; bullets or dashes work just as well.
- Is an excellent way to tell if the supporting points and information are adequate.
- Allows for a rough sketch of visuals.
- Encourages you to develop transitions.
- Makes it easy to tell if your arguments flow smoothly.
- Makes it easy for others to read and evaluate your ideas, which is especially important if you are giving a team presentation.

Once storyboards for each main point have been completed to your satisfaction and checked by a friend, colleague, or supervisor, you are ready to prepare the actual visual aids and your notes for use during the speech.

Figure 11.1 Informative outline format.

Informative Outline Format	Type of Source:

Topic or Title:
Exact Purpose:

	Type of Source:
INTRODUCTION:	(Personal
☐ Attention getter:	observation,
☐ Audience motivation:	interview,
☐ Qualifications:	media or
☐ Purpose statement:	reference)
☐ Preview of main points:	

BODY with SUPPORTS:

   I.   **Main point #1:**
       A.   Subpoint or supporting material
          1.   Supporting material
          2.   Supporting material
       B.   Subpoint or supporting material

       [Transition]

   II.   **Main point #2:**
       A.   Supporting material
       B.   Supporting material

       [Transition]

   III.   **Main point #3:**
       A.   Subpoint or supporting material
       B.   Subpoint or supporting material
          1.   Supporting material
          2.   Supporting material

CONCLUSION:
   ☐ Summary:
   ☐ Closing thought:

References:
(Books, magazines, newspapers, etc.)

Fourth, add needed verbal and visual supporting materials. Supporting materials are any type of verbal or visual information used to clarify, prove, or add interest to the main points of your presentation. Verbal supporting materials (covered in detail in Chapter 12) include explanations,

Figure 11.2a Storyboard. *(Source: Marya W. Holcombe and Judith K. Stein, Presentations for Decision Makers, by permission of Lifetime Learning Publications. Copyright 1983 by Wadsworth Publishing Company.)*

Storyboard Format		
Topic or Title: **Exact Purpose:**		
Step or Main point:		
Supporting statements:	**Type of Source:** (Personal observation, interview, media or reference)	**Data: charts, tables, etc.**
Transition sentence:		
References:		

comparisons, illustrations, examples, statistics, and expert opinions. Look for supporting materials in printed materials, computer databases, and interviews and personal experiences. Printed materials include:

Figure 11.2b Sample storyboard (compare to traditional outline on p. 344).

Storyboard

Topic or Title: XANUS -2 computer

Exact Purpose: After hearing my presentation, my colleagues will realize that direct access to our new XANUS -2 computer will make our lives easier.

Main point #1: Access to department's new XANUS -2 computer will SAVE US TIME.

Supporting statements:	Sources:	Data: charts, tables, etc.
Average report preparation time will be substantially cut.		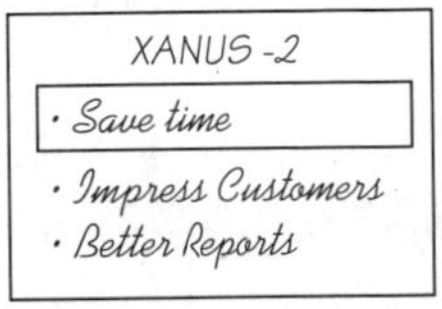
– Last year's total dept. hrs. preparing reports was 3,700 hrs.		Total Report Hours
– With XANUS -2, ave. single prep. time should drop from 7 days to 1 day.		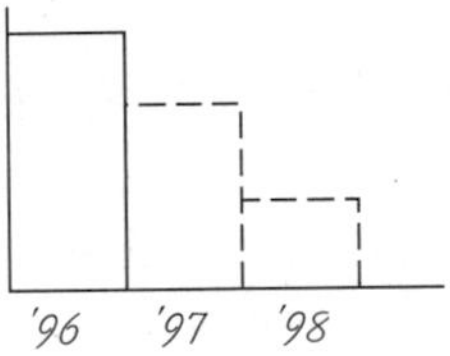
– Next year, prep. time estimated to drop by 50% more!	Ref. #1 p.3	
Lead time required by computer center eliminated.		Total Hours
Less time spent on paperwork.	Ref. #1 p.10	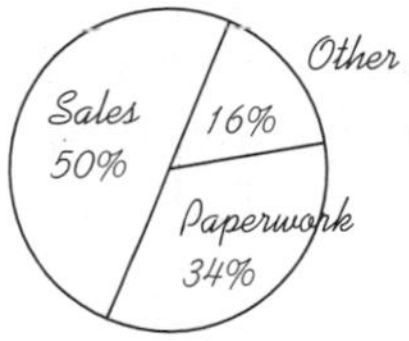

Transition sentence: More time isn't the only advantage to our new XANUS -2 computer.

References: 1996 End of Year Report

- Pamphlets
- Books
- Magazines (especially check the *Readers' Guide to Periodical Literature* and such specialized indexes as *Business Periodicals Index*, *Education*

> *Index, Index to Journals in Communication Studies,* and *Social Science Index*)

- Newspapers (major newspapers are indexed in the *National Newspaper Index*)
- Specialized dictionaries and encyclopedias (such as *Dictionary of American History* or the *Physician's Desk Reference*)
- Quotation books (such as *Bartlett's Familiar Quotations* or the *Toastmaster's Handbook*)
- Yearbooks (especially note *The Book of Lists, Facts on File Yearbook,* and *The Statistical Abstract of the United States*)

There are also many helpful computer databases. Especially helpful are *InfoTrac, Periodical Abstracts on Disc, Education Index, Comm Index, ERIC, Medline,* and *Psylit.*

We discuss making effective visual aids in Chapter 12.

Step 5: Prepare the Conclusion and Introduction

Many good presentations have failed because of dull introductions and less than memorable conclusions. Just because people show up at your presentation does not mean they plan to listen—unless you make it impossible for them not to. And if you want them to continue thinking about your ideas even after they return to their offices, you must make it impossible for them to forget. The ideas in this section will help you focus and keep your listeners' attention on your presentation. Although the conclusion comes after the introduction in a presentation, ideally it is prepared first; so we will discuss them in that order.

The Conclusion ■   No oral presentation is complete without a conclusion. Even if you began with your concluding point—your proposal or solution, for example—you will need to repeat it again. The conclusion normally contains two parts: (1) a summary and (2) a closing thought or statement. The summary can be general (referring to the overall topic of the presentation) or specific (listing the main points covered). The intent of the summary is to clarify for the listeners any confusion about the purpose and main points of your presentation.

The closing thought or statement serves as a final attention getter. Its purpose is to give the audience a thought or challenge that will keep them thinking about your presentation long after it is completed.

Linda Reivity, secretary of the Department of Health and Social Services for the State of Wisconsin, concluded her speech "Women's Achievements Toward Equality" with this thought-provoking statement:

I would like to close today with a salute to former President Grover Cleveland who in 1905 said, "Sensible and responsible women do not want to vote."

May all those who display equal enlightenment as [his] attain an equal place in history.[11]

Examples and stories are also effective ways to end presentations. Stephen E. Ewing, president and chief operating officer for MCN Corporation and MichCon, concluded his presentation "Marble and Mud: Shaping the Future of the Natural Gas Industry" with this challenging story:

> Many of you are golfers, so I have a story that sums up my point—a story told at one time by Glenn Cox, president of Phillips Petroleum.
>
> At the 1925 U.S. Open, golfer Bobby Jones insisted on penalizing himself a stroke when his ball moved slightly in the rough when the blade of his iron touched the turf. Nobody else could possibly have seen the ball move. The penalty dropped Jones into a tie with golfer Willie McFarlane, who went on to win the playoff.
>
> Tom Kite did the same thing 53 years later in 1978. The self-imposed penalty caused him to lose the Hall of Fame Classic at Pinehurst by one stroke.
>
> Reporters asked both men why they took the penalties. And both said essentially the same thing—"There's only one way to play the game."
>
> Ladies and gentlemen, there is only one way to play our game—and that's with a high ethical sense—even in the fiercely competitive businesses we are in.[12]

Any attention getters that can be effective in your introduction can also be used successfully to conclude your presentation. One method is to refer back to your opening remarks. For example, if you began with a rhetorical question, you can end by answering or re-asking the question; if you began with a quote, mention it again or end with another quote. Other effective ways to close are issuing a challenge or appealing for action.

Ending your presentation without a closing thought is like giving a birthday gift in a brown paper bag: Neither the audience nor the person feel like they received anything special. However, a clever conclusion is like wrapping paper and bow; it dresses up the presentation and leaves the audience feeling like they received a gift.

The Introduction ■ The introduction of an oral presentation should

1. Capture the attention of your listeners.
2. Motivate them to listen by showing the importance or benefit your presentation will have for them.

3. Convince them that you are qualified to speak on the subject.
4. Explain the purpose of your presentation.

Let's look at each step in more detail.

First, capture the attention of your listeners. As you begin your presentation, listeners' attention may be focused on many other things. One person may be worrying about a car payment that is due. Another may be reviewing a big business deal that fell through that afternoon. Others may be wishing they were home eating lunch. The purpose of step 1 is to direct attention from individual concerns and thoughts to your presentation. Some common techniques for gaining attention:

- *Reveal one or more startling facts.*
- *Ask a rhetorical question* (a question that causes the audience to think rather than respond) *or an actual question* (listener response is usually obtained by a show of hands).
- *Tell a joke or humorous story relating directly to the topic.* Poorly told jokes do not impress listeners. If you are not good at humor, try something else.
- *Briefly cite two or three specific incidents or examples that relate to the topic.*
- *In detail, recount an actual or hypothetical event* (often called an *illustration*).
- *Refer to the specific occasion or event for which you are speaking* (such as a company's fiftieth anniversary).
- *Quote or paraphrase a well-known publication or expert.*
- *Briefly demonstrate the item or skill you will be discussing in your presentation.*

American Robert L. Clarke, while speaking in London, used humor in his introduction to capture audience attention and to establish a common ground with his audience:

> . . . I will in my remarks tonight remain ever mindful of the linguistic ocean that separates the United Kingdom and the United States.
>
> Though I hope you will forgive me if you discover I have lost my bearings between the two shores.
>
> The waters are treacherous even for those with much greater experience with them than I have.
>
> Even Winston Churchill—whose mother, as you know, was American—found himself adrift at times.
>
> During a visit to the United States, Churchill was invited to a buffet luncheon at which cold chicken was served.
>
> Returning for more, he asked politely: "May I have some breast?"

His hostess replied: "Mr. Churchill, in this country we ask for white meat or dark meat."

Churchill apologized profusely.

The following morning, the hostess received a magnificent orchid from her guest of honor.

The accompanying card read: "I would be most obliged if you would pin this on your white meat."[13]

Speaking this time on the topic of bank failures to the Exchequer Club of Washington, D.C., Clarke used this attention getter:

In the old *Andy Griffith Show* on television, Deputy Barney Fife once asked Sheriff Andy why he had good judgment. "Well," said Andy, "good judgment comes from experience." Barney then asked: "Then where does experience come from?"

Andy's answer was: "Experience comes from bad judgment."

I've been thinking a lot lately about experience and judgment—good and bad.[14]

Although humor can be very effective in a presentation, a recent study found that self-disparaging humor (where the speaker uses him- or herself as the brunt of a joke) has a negative effect. More specifically, Michael Hackman found that when either high- or low-status informative speakers used humor that focused on their personal shortcomings, audiences judged the speeches to be more humorous; however, at the same time, audiences rated the speakers as being less competent, less interesting, and less desirable to associate with.[15] But C. R. Gruner found that "humor directed at one's occupation or profession does not harm a speaker's image."[16]

Second, convince the audience of the benefit to them. Capturing the initial attention of your listeners does not guarantee that they will listen to the remainder of your presentation. To keep their attention, you must convince them that the presentation will benefit them in some way—that is, will help them satisfy personal or job-related needs. For more on determining which needs will motivate your listeners, read the section in Chapter 13 on needs that motivate employees and needs that motivate managers.

Third, assure the audience that you are qualified to speak on the subject. Unless they are convinced that you know what you are talking about, very few business or professional people will even take the time to listen to your ideas or proposals, let alone be persuaded by them. You can demonstrate your qualifications to speak on the topic by referring to your personal experience, the detailed research you have done on the topic, the interviews you have conducted with knowledgeable people, or the articles and books you have read that were written by experts.

Fourth, explain the purpose of your presentation. In this step, you should include a general statement of purpose and a summary of the main points to be covered. The average listener finds it much easier to follow and remember the ideas contained in your presentation when your introduction lists the key points that will be covered.

Many business speakers also suggest that you "start your presentation with your recommendations or conclusions unless you have a compelling reason not to."[17] This method helps you keep the attention of the typically rushed, tired, and stressed-out business audience. It also helps you determine what background material to leave out; include only the points needed to support your conclusions. However, if your conclusion is bad news, sensitive information, or a controversial proposal, it would be better to report the background data and events *before* stating what you hope is the obvious conclusion or recommended action. Your audience is more likely to listen objectively and less likely to interrupt with questions if such conclusions are presented last.

Although we suggest that you include all four steps of the introduction in any practice presentation you give in a training seminar or classroom, the presentations you give in business and professional situations may not need to include all four steps. Which steps to include depend on your listeners. For example, step 1 may be omitted when your audience is obviously already interested in your specific topic. Step 2 may be omitted when your listeners are already motivated to listen or if the benefit to them is too obvious to mention. Step 3 may be omitted when your listeners are already aware of the experience, knowledge, or training that qualifies you to speak on your subject. Even step 4 may be omitted if you are trying to build suspense or if, as mentioned earlier, you know that the audience you are trying to persuade is against your proposal. In this case, you should make the specific ideal or proposal clear in the conclusion of the presentation, rather than in the introduction—the backdoor approach. Check your understanding of when to omit certain steps of the introduction by analyzing the following situations:

EXAMPLE 1

Imagine that you are asked by your supervisor to present an informative report on the uses of a new piece of machinery. Your audience will consist of your supervisor and her assistant. Which steps should you include in your introduction?

Obviously, your listeners are already interested, so step 1 could be omitted. They specifically asked you to give this report, so they are definitely motivated to listen; step 2 could be omitted. Because you work for them, they already know you are qualified to speak on this topic; step 3 could also be omitted. Your audience is aware of your general purpose but does not know what main points you plan to cover. Therefore, in this situation you should omit steps 1, 2, and 3 and get right to the point by explaining your specific purpose (step 4): "This new copy machine can save us time and ease our work load by performing four much-needed tasks for us. These four tasks are . . ."

EXAMPLE 2

Suppose you were giving the same report to a large group of foremen and supervisors. Most of the foremen have no idea what your report will be about, several of your listeners have no idea who you are, and three of the supervisors feel that this meeting and the new piece of equipment will be a complete waste of time. Which steps should you include in your introduction?

This time you will need to include all four steps! Step 1 is needed to direct the attention of this diverse group to your topic, especially those foremen who are unaware of the nature of your report. Step 2 is needed to show the listeners how your topic will benefit them. The difference in the personal needs of the uninformed foremen and the supervisors who have already decided that the machine is worthless should be taken into consideration when planning how to motivate the listeners. Step 3 is needed because many in your audience are unaware of your qualifications. Step 4 is needed to make the purpose of your presentation clear.

Before we move to the body of the oral presentation, we need to make one more observation about the introduction: As long as you include the necessary steps, the arrangement of the steps can vary. If an attention getter is needed, it should come first. But the placement of the other three steps depends on you, your topic, and your audience.

Step 6: Practice Using Your Notes and Visual Aids

"Outlines and notes are not the same. The outline is a planning tool; notes are a delivery tool."[18] It takes practice to use notes and visual aids smoothly and to feel confident while speaking. Feeling confident while speaking is one of the advantages of rehearsing. The best results are obtained when you prepare two ways: by visualizing yourself giving a successful presentation and by actually practicing the presentation aloud. The following suggestions will help you as you practice:

- *Prepare a key-word outline and copy it onto one or two note cards.* If you have any quotes, put each one on a separate note card—typed and double-spaced for ease of reading. If you are using transparencies, decide what notes, if any, to put on each transparency frame.

- *Practice your presentation.* Tape record yourself to get feedback on your vocal delivery or practice in front of a mirror. If possible, practice in a room similar to the one in which you will be speaking. After you begin to feel comfortable with your speech, practice it in front of a friend or family member. Ask them for specific comments on your presentation. Practice making direct eye contact and using gestures.
- *At least once before the actual speech* (two or three times would be better), *practice using your visual aids with all the needed equipment.* Videotape yourself if possible or ask a friend to observe one of your final practices.

In the following section we discuss specific delivery techniques that will work for you. To be effective, however, you must practice using them.

INFORMATIVE PRESENTATIONS: IMPROVING DELIVERY

If you have prepared a clearly organized presentation with a good introduction and conclusion, you are on the road toward an effective oral presentation. However, two things are still missing: verbal and visual supporting material (to be discussed in Chapter 12) and an effective delivery. In our discussion in Chapter 1, we learned that all three codes—language, paralanguage, and nonverbal—occur in the communication process. Your words, your tone of voice, and your gestures, eye contact, and appearance must reinforce each other for your presentation to be most effective. Let's look at each of these codes and its role in effective delivery.

Delivery and Nonverbal Behavior

As a speaker, you should appear relaxed, enthusiastic, and natural. You should not become a different person when you give an oral presentation; you should not step into a speaker's disguise. You should simply be yourself, presenting your ideas in a natural yet enthusiastic manner. Much of this manner depends on your nonverbal behavior.

To appear natural and relaxed, you need to look directly at your listeners and even smile occasionally. Don't look over the heads of or between listeners; look them directly in the eye so that you can get valuable feedback. An audience knows when you are avoiding direct eye contact; they may very well decide that you are nervous and lack authority. If you want your listeners to have confidence in what you are saying, you must appear confident! Dressing up for the presentation is one way to feel more confident and a good way to indicate nonverbally that what you have to say is important.

Gestures and a certain amount of movement not only help you appear natural but also add enthusiasm and authority to your presentation. Of course, neither your gestures nor your movements should distract the audience's attention from what you are saying, but too little movement can cause your audience to lose interest. Used correctly, gestures add excitement and reinforce main ideas. The best way to gesture is to get so involved in the topic that the gestures come naturally without conscious effort. Movement, such as stepping forward or backward or to either side, is also an effective way to show enthusiasm, to emphasize a point, or to progress from one idea to another. For the best effect, try to move either at the beginning or the end of a sentence or an idea.

Delivery and Voice

The best speaking voice is one that sounds conversational, natural, and enthusiastic. People are more likely to listen closely to your presentation and therefore to understand your ideas more clearly if you speak much as you do in ordinary conversation. Most people speaking with a friend automatically use excellent vocal variety. Vocal variety, the key to a conversational voice, is achieved by varying volume, pitch, emphasis, and rate in a natural manner.

Volume, the loudness and softness of your voice, is important in several ways to your success as a speaker. First, a good speaker must be loud enough to be heard easily from all parts of the room. Second, a speaker also needs to vary the volume of the voice to make the presentation interesting. Third, an effective speaker uses increases and decreases in volume to emphasize words or phrases.

Pitch, the highness and lowness of vocal tones, is also important to vocal variety. Too little variety in pitch can make your voice a dull and uninteresting monotone (like a piano repeating only one note). However, extreme changes in pitch can make you sound unnatural and insincere. Effective speakers use step changes in pitch (changes between high, medium, and low pitches) and pitch inflection (gradually rising or falling pitch) to add interest and enthusiasm to their voices and to communicate subtle or implied meanings.

Emphasis, stressing a word with your voice to give the word significance, is another important ingredient of vocal variety. In emphasizing a word, two things happen: Your pitch goes up (usually followed by a downward slide) and your volume increases. Lawyers certainly know the value of emphasis. They can repeat the exact words of a witness, yet make the sentence sound entirely different. For a demonstration of this point, say the following sentence five times, each time emphasizing a different word as shown. Listen to your pitch and volume as you speak. You should be able to give five different meanings to the sentence.

Why did you fire him?

Why *did* you fire him?

Why did *you* fire him?

Why did you *fire* him?

Why did you fire *him*?

Rate, how fast or how slowly you speak, is especially important in maintaining listener attention. Constantly speaking at the same rate can lull your listeners to sleep. An effective speaker usually speaks faster to show excitement, to build suspense, or for emphasis. A slower speaking rate can also be used for emphasis to show the importance of an idea; combined with low pitch, a slow rate can indicate inappropriate or boring ideas. Be sure to pause after important phrases or ideas to let the listeners absorb them.

Delivery and Language

Listeners expect speakers to use a more informal style than that of written reports. For example, in oral communication it isn't always necessary to use complete sentences, but it is important to use short, simple sentences. It is fine to use personal pronouns such as *I, we, you, us,* and contractions such as *I've* or *won't*—forms often avoided in formal written English.

One of the most serious mistakes a speaker can make is to try to impress listeners by using long or extremely technical words or jargon. Do not assume that upper management, employees in other departments, or the public will understand the technical terms and jargon used in your own department—they probably won't. The best language is *vivid* (paints a picture for the listener), *specific* (gives details), and *simple* (easy to understand). Oral presentations are not like football games—there is no instant replay. Your listeners need to understand you the first time.

Here is a sample of the type of language to avoid. This government memo so upset President Franklin Roosevelt when he read it that he immediately rewrote it and sent it back to the author:

Such preparations shall be made as will completely obscure all Federal buildings and non-Federal buildings occupied by the Federal Government during an air raid for any period of time from visibility by reason of internal or external illumination. Such obscuration may be obtained either by blackout construction or by termination of the illumination.[19]

Here is President Roosevelt's rewritten version:

> Tell them that in buildings where they have to keep the work going, to put something over the windows; and, in buildings where they can let the work stop for a while, turn out the lights.[20]

More recently, Alexander Haig, who combined the language of diplomacy with the language of his previous job as general, confused people with such phrases as "'careful caution', 'caveat my response', 'epistemologicallywise', 'nuanced departures', 'definitizing an answer', and 'saddle myself with a statistical fence'."[21]

Putting your ideas into simple, easy-to-understand language that fits the frames of reference of your listeners and is vivid and specific can be more difficult than you may suspect. But which is more important: impressing your listeners with your technical language or impressing your listeners with your ability to communicate?

Speakers also need to be aware that certain words may cause listeners to have either positive or negative reactions. Try to make words work for you, not against you. For example, see the "sweet and sour" words listed in the box on page 358.

Controlling Nervousness

Feeling nervous prior to a new communication situation is perfectly normal. We all experience a butterfly-in-the-stomach, anxious feeling at times—your friends do, your boss does, top-level managers do, and so do the vice president and the chief executive officer of your organization. Because speaker anxiety is so prevalent, we included it as an obstacle to communication in Chapter 6. Reread the section "Communicator Anxiety" in Chapter 6 and determine whether your anxiety is more situational or trait in nature. Then follow the guidelines for how to manage that type of anxiety.

If all else fails, *fake confidence!* It doesn't matter how nervous you are inside—don't admit it to your listeners. *Never apologize.* If your nervousness causes you to leave out a crucial idea, summarize what you have covered so far and insert the idea by saying, "Another topic that needs to be considered is . . ." After all, the listeners don't have a script of your presentation, so how will they know you left something out or changed the order of topics? If you do make an obvious error, don't call attention

Words: Sweet and Sour

Whether you're trying to win an argument, close a sale, or just be personable on paper, the words you use can help, or hinder, your cause. Research has uncovered the words to which most people react favorably—and unfavorably. Here they are:

Most People Like These Words

advantage	ease	integrity	responsible
appreciate	economy	justice	satisfactory
benefit	effective	kind	service
capable	efficient	loyalty	success
confidence	energy	please	superior
conscientious	enthusiasm	popularity	useful
cooperation	genuine	practical	valuable
courtesy	helpful	prestige	vigor
dependable	honesty	progress	you
desirable	honor	reliable	yours

Most People Dislike These Words

abuse	decline	ignorant	squander
alibi	discredit	imitation	superficial
allege	dispute	implicate	tardy
apology	exaggerate	impossible	timid
beware	extravagance	misfortune	unfair
blame	failure	negligent	unfortunate
cheap	fault	opinionated	unsuccessful
commonplace	fear	prejudiced	waste
complaint	fraud	retrench	worry
crisis	hardship	rude	wrong

Source: Ted Pollock, "A Personal File of Stimulating Ideas and Problem Solvers," *Supervision,* Vol. 46, No. 2 (February 1984), p. 25. Reprinted by permission. © by the National Research Bureau, Inc., 424 North Third Street, Burlington, IA 52601.

to it. All speakers make a few minor errors—listeners expect it. To look confident, avoid toying with pencils, paper clips, or other small items that will distract the listener and make you look nervous and unprofessional. Remember, if you want your listeners to have confidence in what you are saying, you must *appear* confident. Luckily, imitation confidence has a way of turning into real confidence without your even being aware of it.

Selecting the Best Method for Delivery

Often the success of your presentation depends on the method of delivery you select: speaking from memory, from outlined notes, from written manuscript, or completely impromptu. We will briefly discuss each of these methods.

Speaking from Memory ■ This method of delivery is seldom selected by business and professional speakers. First, it takes a great deal of time to memorize a manuscript word for word, and few people have this luxury. Second, speaking from memory makes it difficult or impossible to react to listener feedback. A question from a listener can make the speaker forget the next sentence or maybe even the entire topic. Even if the listeners make no verbal comments, they make plenty of nonverbal ones. How can a speaker, who sees from facial expressions that a certain idea is not understood, correct the problem when speaking from memory? Any deviation from the practiced speech could cause the speaker to lose concentration and forget the memorized material.

Speaking from Outlined Notes (Extemporaneous Speaking) ■ *This is the preferred method of delivery for most business speakers.* An extemporaneous presentation is not memorized or even written out word for word. Instead the speaker lists the main ideas to be covered. Then the speaker decides what verbal and visual supporting materials to use to prove and clarify each of the main ideas and lists these in outline fashion on note cards. An introduction and conclusion are then added. When the presentation seems to be ready, the speaker practices aloud using only the note cards for guidance until he or she feels comfortable using them. Each time the presentation is given, it will be a little different unless it has been memorized. Speaking from outlined notes allows the speaker to sound conversational, to maintain good eye contact with the listeners, and to alter the speech if listener feedback indicates confusion.

Speaking from a Manuscript ■ This method is much more difficult for most people than speaking from outlined notes. The speaker must read a prepared presentation word for word but make it sound conversational and personal by using good vocal variety and maintaining fairly direct eye contact with the audience. However, unless the speaker deviates from the manuscript occasionally, he or she cannot respond to listener feedback any more than in a memorized presentation.

Nevertheless, for the *experienced* speaker, there are certain advantages to a manuscript presentation. For example, when the speaker is given a very strict time limit, speaking from manuscript helps to ensure that the presentation will not be too long. For people who speak to audiences outside the company, speaking from the manuscript has the advantage of allowing upper management to read and okay the presentation before it is given. This method also protects the speaker from saying something unintentionally and from blatant misinterpretation. Top-level managers and executives, state governors, and the president of the United States often use manuscripts for protection.

If you must use a manuscript sometime in the future, be sure to practice reading it until your pitch, rate, volume, and emphasis make you sound authoritative yet conversational and you are able to glance up and make eye contact with your listeners often enough to look natural. To communicate your exact meaning to your listeners, one business specialist suggests that as you read, you visualize in your mind the exact thoughts and feelings you had when you first wrote the manuscript. For example:

> For the term "business" you should have a mental visual image of a specific business establishment in operation at a given time. Details in the picture should be complete as to specific people, happenings and background setting—all drawn from the speaker's experience.... If, from your own experience, you create a mental picture which is as complete as possible in every one of those specific details, then you have developed a base which will give each word or phrase its authenticity and believability.[22]

Impromptu Speaking ■ This method, speaking without prior preparation and without notes or manuscript, is obviously a hazardous way to give a major presentation. However, every time your manager, a client, a newspaper reporter, or a job interviewer asks you a question or asks for your opinion, your response is an impromptu presentation that must sound intelligent, authoritative, and confident! A hesitant, apologetic, or stumbling answer does not project the professional image you want. When asked to speak impromptu, try the following:[23]

1. Appear confident (even if you must pretend).
2. Decide on your conclusion first, so that everything you say can lead up to the conclusion in an organized manner.
3. Begin with a general statement or background information to give you time to think of one, two, or three supporting reasons for your conclusion.
4. Introduce your supporting reasons with the word *because* until you can stay organized without it. For example:

   Q: Do you think speech training should be a requirement for promotion of area managers?

A: *Because* the average area manager is called on to make at least four formal presentations to the public a year, and *because* they make weekly informal presentations to their employees, I certainly see speech training as a necessary requirement for promotion.

5. Answer the question directly and honestly. However, in those rare instances when you are asked a question you don't wish to answer, or one for which you don't have an answer (and you feel it would be unacceptable to say, "I don't know"), it may be justifiable to change the topic to one you do want to answer. Politicians are very good at changing subjects with such comments as:

> "That's an important question—almost as important as . . ."
>
> "I was hoping someone would ask me that question because it gives me an opportunity to talk about . . ."
>
> "Could I come back to that question? I've been wanting to reply to the remark this gentleman made earlier. He said . . ."
>
> "I think we need to look at the problem from a different angle . . ."

Although there are times when speaking from memory, speaking from a manuscript, and impromptu speaking are appropriate, remember that most successful business speakers do not memorize, or read word for word, or speak without prior preparation. *The preferred method of delivery for most business speakers is speaking from brief, outlined notes.*

SUMMARY

In this chapter, we have discussed basic information that applies to any formal or informal informative presentation that you may give within an organization or to the public. Effective speakers start by determining the topic and then carefully analyzing the audience. If your presentation does not fit the frames of reference of your audience, you are much less likely to communicate with them successfully.

Once you have determined your listeners' frames of reference, you should determine your topic and write your exact purpose in one simple sentence. When your topic is narrowed, plan the body, and finally the conclusion and introduction of your presentation. This chapter covered several effective ways to organize these basic parts of an informative presentation. Of course, how you organize your presentation will depend on your listeners' needs, interests, and knowledge; the situation; the time limit; and your own speaking style.

Before the presentation, unless absolutely impossible, effective communicators *practice* the presentation until they feel comfortable with it. The best delivery is an enthusiastic and conversational one.

Chapter 12 will discuss the use of verbal and visual supporting materials to prove, clarify, and add interest to your presentations, and Chapter 13 will cover persuasive presentations—as an individual or in a team.

CHECKPOINT

Before continuing to the next chapter, check your understanding of Chapter 11 by completing the following exercises:

1. Discover which organizations in your community have a speakers' bureau. Maybe your own company has one. Phone and get the name of a speaker (preferably one who is similar in rank and position to you). Ask the person how he or she analyzes the audience before each presentation. Compare the answer with the suggestions made in this chapter.

2. Outline a technical report or briefing. Clip the outline into sections making sure no numerals or letters are visible. Give the pieces to a friend to see if he or she can reassemble them into the original sequence. If your friend is unable to reassemble the outline into the original sequence, the chances are good that you have a confusing outline. If so, revise the outline and try the procedure again.

3. To get an idea how your voice sounds to others, leave a detailed message on your answering machine or voice mail system. Do this regularly until your vocal variety and tone project the warmth or enthusiasm or authority you desire.[24]

4. Do you get nervous when you have to make a report to your boss or a group of fellow workers? If so, make a list of the items that contribute to your nervousness. Beside each item write one or two possible cures (check Chapter 6 for additional suggestions). Before future presentations, review your list and work to get your nervousness under control.

5. Prepare an oral briefing 3 to 4 minutes long. Select any subject you wish, prepare the presentation according to suggestions in Chapters 11 and 12, and then record the briefing. Replay the tape several times for self-evaluation and criticism.

6. Read and analyze one of the presentations included in Appendix D. What are its strengths? What are its weaknesses? How would you change it if you were the presenter?

NOTES

1. Lee Iacocca and William Novak, *Iacocca: An Autobiography* (New York: Bantam, 1984), p. 16.
2. From a television documentary, "Air Force One: The Planes and the Presidents," aired by Public Broadcasting Service January 1985 and based on *Flying White House: Story of Air Force One* by Jerald F. ter Horst (Des Plaines, IL: Bantam, 1980).
3. "The Science of Speechmaking," *Dun's Review and Modern Industry* (December 1962), p. 32.
4. Mary C. Bromage, "Defensive Writing," *California Management Review* 13 (1970), pp. 45–50.
5. J. E. Hollingsworth, "Oral Briefings," *Management Review* 57 (August 1968), pp. 2–10.
6. Roger P. Wilcox, *Communication at Work: Writing and Speaking* (Boston: Houghton Mifflin, 1977), p. 11.
7. Wilcox, p. 373. Although Wilcox intended these characteristics to apply to the written report, they apply equally well to the oral report and the oral briefing. See also Norman B. Sigband and Arthur H. Bell, *Communication for Management and Business*, 5th ed. (Glenview, IL: Scott, Foresman, 1989), pp. 151–152.
8. Janet G. Elsea, "Strategies for Effective Presentations," *Personnel Journal* 64 (September 1985), pp. 31–33.
9. In 1956, Miller declared that the human memory span was seven, plus or minus two. However, in 1967, Mandler argued that a more realistic number was five. Finally, in 1975, Broadbent argued that even five was too high; a more accurate number was three. For more specific information read G. A. Miller, "The Magical Number Seven, Plus or Minus Two: Some Limits on Our Capacity for Processing Information," *Psychological Review* 63 (1956), pp. 81–97; G. Mandler, "Organization and Memory," in *The Psychology of Learning and Motivation: Advances in Research and Theory*, Vol. 1, K. W. Spence and J. T. Spencer, eds. (New York: Academic, 1967), pp. 327–372; and D. E. Broadbent, "The Magic Number Seven After 15 Years," in *Studies in Long-Term Memory*, A. Kennedy and A. Wilkes, eds. (London: Wiley, 1975), pp. 3–18; George A. Miller, *The Psychology of Communication* (Baltimore: Penguin, 1969), pp. 15–43.
10. Marya W. Holcombe and Judith K. Stein, *Presentations for Decision Makers: Strategies for Structuring and Delivering Your Ideas* (Belmont, CA: Lifetime Learning Publications, 1983), pp. 63–72.
11. Linda Reivity, "Women's Achievements Toward Equality," *Vital Speeches* 52 (December 15, 1985), p. 153.
12. Stephen E. Ewing, "Marble and Mud: Shaping the Future of the Natural Gas Industry," *Vital Speeches* 57 (June 1, 1991), p. 491. Used by permission.
13. Robert L. Clarke, "Hard Times and Great Expectations: The Condition of the National Banking System," *Vital Speeches* 54 (July 1, 1988), p. 548.
14. Robert L. Clarke, "Bank Failures: Poor Policies, Planning, and Management," *Vital Speeches* 54 (March 1, 1988), p. 290.
15. Michael Z. Hackman, "Reactions to the Use of Self-Disparaging Humor by Informative Public Speakers," *The Southern Speech Communication Journal* 53 (Winter 1988), pp. 175–183.
16. C. R. Gruner, "Advice to the Beginning Speaker on Using Humor—What the Research Tells Us," *Communication Education* 34 (1985), pp. 142–147.
17. Richard Wiegand, "It Doesn't Need to Be Dull to Be Good: How to Improve Staff Presentations," *Business Horizons* 28 (July–August 1985), p. 36.
18. Thomas Leech, *How to Prepare, Stage, and Deliver Winning Presentations* (New York: AMACOM, 1982), p. 105.
19. John O'Hayre, *Gobbledygook Has Gotta Go*, U.S. Department of the Interior, Bureau of Land Management (Washington, DC: U.S. Government Printing Office, 1966), p. 39.
20. O'Hayre, p. 39.
21. Robert B. Rackleff, "The Art of Speech Writing," *Vital Speeches* 54 (March 1, 1988), p. 312.
22. Harold O. Haskitt, Jr., "When Speaking from a Manuscript: Say It and Mean It," *Personnel Journal* 51 (February 1972), pp. 108–112.
23. Adapted from Janet Stone and Jane Bachner, "Speaking Impromptu," in *Speaking Up: A Book for Every Woman Who Wants to Speak Effectively* (New York: McGraw-Hill, 1977), pp. 153–161.
24. Suggested by Bert Decker, *You've Got to Be Believed to Be Heard* (New York: St. Martin's, 1991), p. 226.

12

Verbal and Visual Supporting Materials

Some of the world's greatest communicators have been known to use humor to make a serious and important point. Ever notice in conferences and meetings you attend the way in which skilled communicators are able to go right to the heart of an issue with a humorous comment? Humor is a vital tool in capturing or refocusing attention. People like Will Rogers, Abraham Lincoln and Mark Twain could say more with a little humor than most of us could say in a serious dissertation.[1]

EDGAR B. WYCOFF,
Communications Consultant

Y ou have just walked out at the end of a meeting and you hear people commenting: "Wasn't that a fantastic talk?" "What a voice!" "Really impressive!" "I could listen to Jones all evening!" "I felt like Jones was talking directly to me!" "I wish I could speak with half that authority." "It won't be long before Jones gets promoted."

But, when you begin to think about the talk, you realize that the speaker's central idea and main points were not clear, that the reasoning used by the speaker had several serious gaps in it, and that the supports for the speaker's arguments were so weak they were almost nonexistent. Does this sound familiar?

A similar experience happened to Carolyn, a supervisor for a large toy company. She and several other supervisors were asked by upper management to present their ideas for a new sales campaign. Carolyn had an idea that she was sure would work. She organized her thoughts very carefully and even found time in her busy schedule to practice her presentation several times. She was the last supervisor to speak—everyone was tired and ready to go home. However, when Carolyn began to speak, everyone listened. At the end of her speech, the applause was very enthusiastic. Several supervisors complimented her on her superb presentation, and she overheard several others expressing amazement at her authoritative delivery. Carolyn felt sure that her plan had a very good chance of being accepted.

The next morning, however, she was disappointed to find that her ideas received very little comment. What happened? Well, when the other supervisors thought about her key points, they found it very easy to disagree with them because Carolyn had failed to clarify or prove her ideas sufficiently with concrete supporting materials—verbal supports (such as examples, statistics, quotes, and comparisons) or visual aids.

An effective delivery is certainly important to gain your listeners' careful attention and sympathy, but a good oral presentation includes more than just delivery. Your ideas must also be supported by concrete data and facts if you want your listeners to remember the information they hear in your informative presentations and to remain convinced by your persuasive presentations even after hearing opposing arguments. This chapter, therefore, will cover both verbal and visual supporting materials.

SUPPORTING MATERIALS DEFINED

The key to understanding what is meant by supporting materials is the verb *support*. One of its dictionary definitions is "to hold up or serve as a foundation or prop for."[2] Therefore, **supporting materials** are informative materials that serve as a foundation for our assertions, ideas, or statements. An idea is supported in the same way a building is supported by its foundation. Neither the building nor the idea can stand for very long unsupported: The building is weakened by shifting ground and crumbling piers; the idea, by opposition and counterarguments. Supporting materials have several purposes:

- *Clarify.* If your listeners do not understand your ideas or statements, your presentation will fail. The effective speaker uses visual supports (such as charts, graphs, and pictures) and verbal supports (such as examples, comparisons, and explanations) to clarify ideas.
- *Prove.* Often, statements must be proved or substantiated before they are accepted. The effective speaker uses verbal supports (such as statistics, quotes, and illustrations) as evidence for ideas and statements.
- *Add interest.* Because every person has a different frame of reference, not everyone will view a particular support as interesting. An effective speaker uses a variety of supports for each idea or assertion.

VERBAL SUPPORTING MATERIALS

The verbal supporting materials most often used by business and professional speakers can be divided into six categories:

1. Explanation
2. Comparison (including figurative comparison and literal comparison)
3. Illustration (including hypothetical illustrations and factual illustrations)
4. Example
5. Statistics
6. Expert opinion

Explanation

In an **explanation,** the speaker simply describes the relationship between certain items, makes clear the definition of a term or word, or gives instructions on how to do something or how to get somewhere. For example, a speaker might describe the relationship between the sales and purchasing departments, give the official company definition of compensation time, or describe how to operate a new piece of machinery.

In a speech on employee involvement, Allen A. Schumer, senior vice president of operations of Miller Brewing Company, used this explanation to clarify the company's concept of employee involvement:

REMEMBER, EXPLANATIONS . . .

- Should be specific, but brief.
- Should be used only for clarification, not for proof.
- Are generally used too often by beginning speakers. If the only support you use is explanation, your presentation will not only lack proof but will most likely lack interest as well. As often as possible, replace or reinforce the explanation you planned to use with some other type of support.

Now, let's get back to MAKING EMPLOYEE INVOLVEMENT HAPPEN! To begin, let's make sure we agree on just what Employee Involvement *is*. . . .

Employee Involvement—and its twin, Participative Management—is simply the idea of treating employees in a responsible, dignified manner. It's a way of life—it's who we are and how we do things. And it's a style of management, of operation, that becomes second-nature—a part of the culture of the company and our people.

At Miller, we are trying to create a work environment where our people feel committed to doing their best, so that they will go that extra mile to achieve company goals.[3]

In a speech entitled "Television: How Far Has It Come in 30 Years," Newton N. Minnow, director of The Annenberg Washington Program in Communications Policy Studies of Northwestern University, used the following explanation to show the importance of television as an educator:

Suppose you were asked this multiple-choice question: Which of the following is the most important educational institution in America? (a) Harvard, (b) Yale, (c) Columbia, (d) the University of California, (e) none of the above. The correct answer is e. The most important educational institution in America is television. More people learn more each day, each year, each lifetime from television than from any other source. All of television is education: the question is, what are we teaching and what are we learning?[4]

Comparison

Speakers use **comparisons** to show the similarities or differences between something the listeners know and something they do not know. Suppose, for example, you are speaking to a group of supervisors about an often used but ineffective way of motivating workers—the "dangling carrot" approach. To clarify your point, you could compare this method of motivating workers to a parent motivating a teenager to clean up his room by promising the use of the family car.

There are two types of comparisons: literal and figurative. A **literal comparison** shows similarities or differences between two or more items from the *same* class or category. The following are examples of literal comparisons: two styles of management, sales of two competing companies, two advertising campaigns, and monthly travel expenses of five top salespersons. Although comparisons are not used as absolute proof, a literal comparison can offer solid evidence for your point if the items being compared are almost identical. For example, saying that because company X uses the democratic style of management successfully, it would also work for your company would be unconvincing if the two companies were different in size, organizational structure, employee desires, and management abilities. But if the two companies were very similar, listeners would have good reason to believe the assertion.

Richard D. Lamm, former governor of Colorado, used a literal comparison when he compared affordable housing in his generation with affordable housing for today's generation:

> Let's look at housing. My wife and I bought our first house in 1963 for $11,900. Our first house payments were $49 a month. Virtually everyone in our generation could afford to buy a house. Yet a recent congressional study estimated that significantly fewer of those under 30 would ever be able to buy their own homes. My generation only had to spend 14 percent of our income to buy a median-priced house, where today's average 30-year-old must spend 44 percent of his income to buy a median-priced house. We passed laws that gave ourselves big tax breaks for owning our

own homes and government subsidized mortgages on top of that. Yet many of our children will never in their lives be able to own their own homes.[5]

A **figurative comparison** shows similarities or differences between two or more items from *different* classes or categories. A speaker who compares a salesperson's competitive drive to the drive of a hungry bear is using a figurative comparison. An example:

> But just as our fast-food industry has become our "junk food" industry, so have our fast-fact industries—television and advertising—become our junk-fact industries.[6]

Figurative comparisons are never used for proof, but they do add interest and clarify ideas.

The Japanese ambassador to the United States, Takakazu Kuriyama, in a speech delivered at George Washington University, clarified the state of Japanese–American relations by using a figurative comparison:

> Conceptually, the Japanese–U.S. relationship has been compared to the three legs of a stool. The three legs are security, global cooperation and economic relations. The first two legs are strong. Our security ties remain close. We cooperate on a number of global issues. . . . It is the third leg of economic relations that makes the whole stool seem a little wobbly right now.[7]

Illustration

An **illustration** is a narrative or story told in vivid detail to paint a picture for the listener. A speaker recommending that the company provide more conference rooms might present an illustration about a buyer who, when an important client arrives, has no conference room available. A good speaker would give such a vivid picture of the event that the listeners would feel the embarrassment and anger of the buyer trying to negotiate an important purchase in the middle of ringing telephones and competing conversations.

Illustrations can be factual or hypothetical. A **factual illustration** is a detailed narrative about someone, something, or some event that actually happened. Discussing the second key to becoming truly successful—believing in yourself even when no one else does—Harvey B. Mackay used the following factual illustration in a commencement address at Penn State University:

> A few months ago I was in New York and hailed a taxi. It turned out to be one of the most memorable rides of my life.

In my personal opinion, the majority of New York cab drivers are unfriendly, if not downright rude. Most of the cabs are filthy, and almost all of them sport an impenetrable bullet proof partition. This time, I jumped into a cab at LaGuardia Airport and guess what? It was a *clean* cab. There was beautiful music coming out of the sound system and believe it or not, no bullet proof partition.

I said to the driver, "Park Lane Hotel please." He turned around with a big broad smile and said, "Hi, my name is Wally," and he handed me a mission statement. That's right, a *mission statement!* It said he was going to get me there safely, courteously, and on time.

As he pulled away from the curb he held up copies of *The New York Times* and *USA Today* and said "Be my guest." A few minutes into the ride he motioned to me not to be bashful and to help myself to some of the fruit in the basket on the back seat. He then promptly asked if I preferred to listen to rock and roll or classical music from his audio tape collection. About ten minutes into the ride he held up a cellular telephone and said, "It's a dollar a minute if you would like to make a call."

Somewhat shocked, I blurted out, "Where did you learn this?" He answered, "On a talk show." I then asked, "How long have you been practicing this?" And he answered, "Three or four years." I then said, "I know this is prying, but would you mind sharing with me how much extra money you earn in tips?" He responded proudly, "Twelve to fourteen thousand dollars a year!"

He doesn't know it but he's my hero. He's living proof that you can always shift the odds in your favor if you believe in yourself.[8]

The **hypothetical illustration,** the second type of illustration, is a detailed narrative about someone who could exist or some event that could or probably will happen in the future. In other words, the hypothetical illustration is created or made up by the speaker to fit a particular situation. To be effective, the hypothetical illustration must be possible or likely. Hypothetical illustrations usually begin with "What would you do if . . . ," "Suppose for a moment . . . ," "Imagine . . . ," "Put yourself in this situation . . . ," and other similar phrases.

During the Civil War, Abraham Lincoln used a hypothetical illustration combined with a figurative comparison to silence critics of his war policy:

Gentlemen, I want you to suppose a case for a moment. Suppose that all the property you were worth was in gold, and you had put it in the hands of Blondin, the famous rope-walker, to carry across the Niagara Falls on a tightrope. Would you shake the rope while he was passing over it, or keep shouting to him, "Blondin, stoop a little more! Go a little faster!" No, I am sure you would not. You would hold your breath as well as your tongue, and keep your hands off until he was safely over. Now the government is in the same situation. It is carrying an immense weight across a stormy ocean. Untold treasures are in its hands. It is doing the best it can. Don't badger it! Just keep still, and it will get you safely over.[9]

> ### REMEMBER, ILLUSTRATIONS . . .
>
> - Should be detailed and vivid, painting a picture for your audience.
> - Should relate clearly to the point you are supporting.
> - If factual, are used both to clarify and to add proof; the more illustrations you use, the stronger the proof.
> - Are used by speakers in introductions to get the attention and personal involvement of the audience.
> - If hypothetical, are sometimes more effective than factual illustrations, because they involve listeners more personally by urging them to picture themselves taking part in a particular situation.

Example

Examples are brief references to specific items or events. Examples can be presented either as lists of items with no detail or as items that are described with a few brief facts.

A facilities manager making a case for a company smoking policy gave the following statement supported by examples:

> It costs employers an average of $4,600 more per year to keep a smoker, rather than a nonsmoker, on the average payroll. The cost breakdown is as follows:
>
> $1,820 in lost productivity.
> $1,000 in damage and extra maintenance.
> $765 in time lost to illness and early death.
> $230 in medical care.
> $220 in absenteeism.
> $86 in nonsmoker illness due to second-hand smoke.
> $45 in smoke related accidents.
> $45 in increased fire insurance.[10]

In a speech entitled "How Women and Minorities Are Reshaping Corporate America," Linda Winikow, vice president of Orange and Rockland Utilities, Inc., used these two examples to illustrate how simply being a woman creates barriers to advancement:

> When I first became involved in politics, back in the early 1970's, men found it difficult to swallow that I could be a member of the Zoning Board of Appeals and be pregnant simultaneously!

> And when I was a New York State Senator, I was stopped by the State Police on the New York State Thruway because they thought my car—with its Senate license plate—must be stolen, since a woman was in it![11]

In his speech entitled "Our Kids Deserve Better!" Michigan Governor John Engler used a series of examples to support his point that our schools aren't working:

> We've all heard the stories. About the mom in Detroit who broke the law and was sentenced to probation. Her crime? Sending her daughter to a higher-quality school in the suburbs where she didn't live.
>
> Or how about the Eaton Rapids kindergartner who has to ride a bus two hours a day because his school district won't release him to attend a school 10 minutes down the road.
>
> Or the story about a mother who went to court and gave up custody of her son so he could live with relatives in order to attend a higher-quality school.
>
> Or the stories about school districts hiring "family police" at taxpayer expense to investigate where children live![12]

Statistics

Statistics are numbers used to show relationships between items. Used correctly, statistics can clarify and add proof to your ideas; used incorrectly, they can confuse and bore your listeners. Statistics can work for you if you follow these important rules.

Make Your Statistics Meaningful by Relating Them to the Listeners' Frames of Reference ■ This is the most important rule in using statistics. Compare the statistics to something familiar to the listeners. For example, a speaker might say, "The business community spends more than $100 billion per year to fill out federal government forms." How many people have any real idea how much money $100 billion is? If the audience contained small-business owners, the speaker might say, "This money, if divided among 500,000 small businesses owned by women or minorities, would give them $200,000 each."

Instead of just telling his Indiana University audience that tobacco kills close to 500,000 Americans each year, Lonnie Bristow, chair of the board of trustees of the American Medical Association, made the statistic more meaningful in the following way:

> I ask you to check your watches. Because in this hour, by the time I'm done speaking, 50 Americans will die from smoke-related diseases. By the time you sit down to breakfast in the morning, 600 more will

---

REMEMBER, EXAMPLES . . .

- Are brief references to specific items or events. Don't forget that illustrations mention items in detail, while examples use very little detail.
- Are used for both clarification and proof.
- May contain no detail (such as lists of items) or may include a few brief facts.
- Are usually found in groups of two or more. It is possible to use a single example, but most speakers find that examples work better to clarify and prove when several are used.
- Are often included immediately following a factual illustration to add additional proof to the illustration. Time limits usually do not allow for enough detailed illustrations to prove an idea completely. By following the illustration with a series of examples, you are saying to your audience, "And I could include even more facts if I only had the time."

---

have joined them; 8,400 by the end of the week—every week, every month, every year—until it kills nearly half-a-million Americans, year in, year out.

That's more than all the other preventable causes of death combined. Alcohol, illegal drugs, AIDS, suicide, car accidents, fires, guns—all are killers. But tobacco kills more than all of them put together.[13]

Eliminate Any Statistics That Are Not Absolutely Necessary ■ Listeners generally do not pay attention when long lists of statistics are read. If you still want to use several statistics, use a chart or graph to simplify them and make them much easier to understand.

Round Off Statistics to an Easy Number for Listeners to Remember ■ Say, "The amount approaches 25,000," or "approximately 25,000" instead of saying, "The amount is 24,923.002."

Demonstrate the Credibility of Your Statistics ■ Show credibility by citing the source, the expertise of the source, and the size of the population from which the statistics were compiled. Consider this statistic: "Four out of five managers recommend using employee appraisals." How many managers had to be interviewed to make that statement? Only five! Reporting the statements of only five managers out of the thousands that exist is obviously not a very good recommendation. However, suppose we knew that a survey of 5,000 mid-managers from companies of various sizes was

REMEMBER, STATISTICS . . .

- Are figures used to show relationships between items.
- Are made more meaningful when directly related to the listeners' interests and knowledge.
- Should be used sparingly.
- Are easier to understand and remember when displayed as a line graph, bar graph, or circle graph.
- Should be rounded off.
- Are more credible when cited along with a source and the source's qualifications.

conducted by the Independent Business Polling Corporation and that four out of five of the 4,000 managers who replied to the survey (that is, 3,200 managers) recommended the use of employee appraisals. We would then be much more likely to consider the statistic seriously.

In a speech about computer on-line information technology, Brent Baker, dean of the College of Communication at Boston University, clarified the credibility of his statistics as follows:

Let's look at the citizen information capabilities: Late last year the Congressional Office of Technology Assessment (OTA) issued a report on "Electronic Delivery of Federal Services." In that report were some interesting facts:

- Only 17 percent of U.S. households own personal computers and only a fraction have modems for on-line services. . . .
- 94 percent of U.S. households have telephone service.
- 96 percent of U.S. households have television sets and 72 percent have VCRs.
- 61 percent of U.S. households subscribe to cable television and 97 percent have the technical capability to be connected.[14]

Expert Opinion

Expert opinion refers to the ideas of another person (an expert in the field), either paraphrased or quoted directly by the speaker. Supporting your ideas with expert opinion is an excellent way to add both clarification and proof to your presentation. To prove an idea with expert opinion be sure to (1) state the name of the expert, (2) briefly describe the qualifications of the expert unless you are sure the listeners are already familiar with the person, and (3) briefly cite where and when the expert reported this information—in a personal interview conducted last Wednesday, in the last issue of the *Harvard Business Review*, and so on.

When paraphrasing—putting the expert's ideas into your own words— make sure that you don't misrepresent the expert's ideas. Here is a sample of how to introduce a *paraphrase:*

> In her new book, *Talking from 9 to 5*,[15] Deborah Tannen, university professor and well-known authority on male–female communication, makes the point that . . . [put information in your own words]

Here is an example of how to introduce a *direct quote:*

> In response to a question asking whether men or women tend to be the most indirect in their communication at work, Dr. Tannen, a well-known authority on male–female communication and author of the popular book, *Talking from 9 to 5*, answered, "[insert quote]"

Make sure as you read direct quotes that your delivery is lively and convincing; avoid a dull or monotone presentation.

When your audience is unfamiliar with your experts, you will need to introduce them thoroughly, as Jenny Clanton did in her speech entitled "Plutonium 238: NASA's Fuel of Choice." In her attempt to inform the audience of the danger of Plutonium 238, she used the following paraphrase:

> Last July, *Common Cause* magazine contacted Dr. Gofman at Berkeley and asked him to place Plutonium 238 in perspective. Before I share Dr. Gofman's assessment, please understand he's no poster-carrying "anti-nuke." Dr. Gofman was co-discoverer of Uranium 233, and he isolated the isotope first used in nuclear bombs. Dr. Gofman told Karl Grossman, author of the article "Redtape and Radio-activity," that Plutonium 238 is 300 times more radioactive than Plutonium 239, which is the isotope used in atomic bombs.[16]

If your expert is well-known to your audience, it is not necessary to cite the expert's qualifications. For example, Max D. Isaacson, vice president of administration for Macmillan Oil Company, used the following quote, which needed no detailed introduction:

> But I've always been fond of quoting Eleanor Roosevelt on the subject of self-confidence, and it was she who said, "No one can make you feel inferior without your consent." Think about that for a moment. "No one can make you feel inferior without your consent." Isn't that a remarkable statement?[17]

REMEMBER, EXPERT OPINIONS . . .

- May be paraphrased or quoted directly.
- Should be kept brief to keep listener interest.
- May be used for both clarification and proof.
- Should be quoted as though the expert were actually speaking—not read in a dull or monotone voice.
- Should usually include the names and qualifications of the expert and when and where the information was reported.
- Should, in many cases, be followed by an explanation. Don't assume that the listener understood either the content of the quote or your reason for citing it.

Whether you are paraphrasing or using a direct quote, make sure your audience understands what the expert is saying. If you feel there is any chance of confusion, follow the paraphrase or quote with such comments as: "In this quote, _____ is making the same argument I made earlier"; or "What is _____ saying? He or she is telling us . . ."; or "I cited _____ because . . . ."

The six types of verbal supporting materials often overlap. For example, you may quote an *expert* who is *explaining* an idea by *comparing statistics!* The effective speaker uses a variety of supports to keep the listeners interested. However, do not forget which supports are used only to clarify and which supports are used both for clarification and for proof. An employee who approaches the boss about implementing job rotation as a means of employee development but uses only clarification supports shouldn't be surprised to find the request rejected. Supports that add proof would be needed in this type of presentation. Here is a quick review of the verbal supports:

VERBAL SUPPORTS USED ONLY FOR CLARIFICATION	VERBAL SUPPORTS USED FOR BOTH CLARIFICATION AND PROOF
■ Explanation	■ Literal comparison (but this is very weak proof)
■ Figurative comparison	■ Factual illustration
■ Hypothetical illustration	■ Examples
	■ Statistics
	■ Expert opinion

VISUAL SUPPORTING MATERIALS

Have you ever tried to give instructions orally on how to get somewhere and finally, frustrated, said, "Here, let me draw you a map"? Such a situation demonstrates the value of visual supporting material. It is easier for people to understand when they can see and hear instructions at the same time. A **visual aid,** therefore, is anything presented in a form that the listener can *see* to supplement the information the listener *hears.*

Benefits of Using Visual Aids

Effective visual aids are helpful to the business and professional speaker (especially the technical speaker) in the following ways.

Visual Aids Save Time and Add Interest ■ The old saying "A picture is worth a thousand words" is usually true. A single visual aid may save you many words and, therefore, time. There is a scientific reason why visuals take less time to comprehend:

> The human mind is divided into two halves that "think" differently. The left side of the brain controls logical thought. When you hear words, it is your left brain that understands what you hear. The right brain, the creative side, controls conceptual thought. It enables you to comprehend complex information with blinding speed . . . in fact, in as little time as it takes you to just glance at a picture.[18]

If you include no visuals or only data charts loaded with statistics, you are asking the left side of the brain to do all the work. After a while, you run the risk of mistakes in reasoning, information overload, and boredom. In computer terminology, the system shuts down. On the other hand, in only one glance the right brain can understand complex ideas presented in graphic form. Speaking to both sides of your audience's brain is a good way to increase understanding, add interest, and save time. For example, look at the data in Table 12.1. Can you quickly tell which alternative would be the cheapest? Now look at the same data presented in graph form (Figure 12.1). At a glance, you can tell that although its initial cost is greater, by the end of the second year the personal computer would cost the least money.

Visual Aids Improve Listener Understanding ■ Listeners interpret the meaning of your words from their own frames of reference. Even if you use specific, simple language and effective verbal supports, each listener's image of your ideas will differ in certain ways from your own. A visual aid,

Table 12.1 Data Can Often Be Difficult to Grasp

Cost–Benefit Analysis

	Current System	Alternatives	
		Terminal	Personal Computer
Initial development costs			
Hardware	$ 0	$1,500	$7,000
Software	0	0	500
Total	$ 0	$1,500	$7,500
Yearly operating costs			
Phone lines	$ 0	$3,500	$ 500
Supplies	250	1,000	500
Labor (overtime)	2,000	0	0
Maintenance	0	50	250
Lost Sales	4,000	0	0
Total	$6,250	$4,550	$1,250
Annual cost savings	$ 0	$1,700	$5,000

Source: *Living with Computers*, 2nd ed., by Patrick G. McKeown, copyright © 1988 by Harcourt Brace Jovanovich, Inc. Reprinted by permission of the publisher.

such as an actual object, a chart, a picture, or a graph, improves understanding by giving the listeners something concrete to see and therefore makes their mental image more exact and more like the image you have in mind. A good visual aid also improves understanding by helping to focus the listeners' attention on the ideas you are presenting. Without such help, some listeners will misunderstand your message because their attention wanders.

Visual Aids Improve Listener Retention ■ Research on listening indicates that a few days after a presentation, most listeners will remember only about 10–25 percent of your presentation.[19] And because of frame of reference differences, part of the 25 percent they do retain may be inaccurate. Don't fool yourself into thinking that better organization, more interesting examples, and more dynamic delivery will greatly improve these statistics. *However, visual aids can definitely improve what the audience remembers.* Research by the University of Minnesota and 3M found that presentations using visual aids (especially color visuals) improved audience retention.[20]

Figure 12.1 Cost comparison of alternatives. *(Source:* Living with Computers, *2nd ed., by Patrick G. McKeown, copyright © 1988 by Harcourt Brace Jovanovich, Inc. Reprinted by permission of the publisher.)*

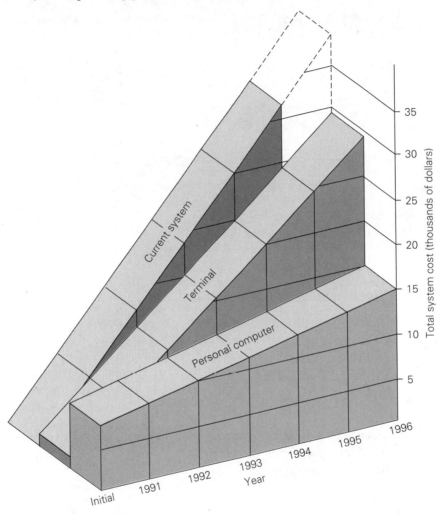

Studies by the Industrial Audio Association indicate that average listeners remember 20 percent of what they *hear,* 30 percent of what they *see,* and 50 percent of what they *see* and *hear!*[21] Summarizing research in instructional media, one author's statistics in Figure 12.2 show that verbal and visual information together are more effective than either verbal or visual information alone.[22] Although research statistics differ somewhat, the message is the same: *Presenters should no longer consider visual aids as optional but as absolute necessities!*

Figure 12.2 Audience recall is greater when speakers use visual aids.

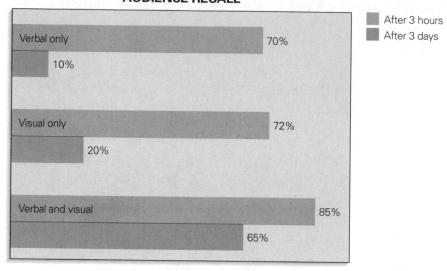

AUDIENCE RECALL

After 3 hours
After 3 days

Verbal only — 70%
10%

Visual only — 72%
20%

Verbal and visual — 85%
65%

Types of Visual Aids

Now that we know the benefits of using visual aids, let's take a quick look at the types of visual aids used most often in presentations: overhead transparencies; slides; flip charts and posters; objects, models, and handouts; markerboards and chalkboards; and computer-generated visuals and audiovisual aids.

Overhead Transparencies ■   As your career progresses, you will probably discover that **transparencies** (or **viewgraphs**) are used more than any other visual aid. They are popular because:

- *They can be projected in normal room light.* This allows the speaker to maintain eye contact with the audience (necessary in establishing rapport and interpreting nonverbal reactions) and still glance down at the transparency on the overhead projector when needed. Don't turn to look at the screen, placing your back to the audience. If you wish to point to the screen instead of the transparency, back up within a few inches of the screen so that you are parallel with it. This way, you can point to an item on the screen and still maintain eye contact with your audience.
- *Notes and personal reminders can be placed on the frames around each transparency.* Frames are also good for **overlays**—pieces of clear or

Figure 12.3 Slide of a text visual.

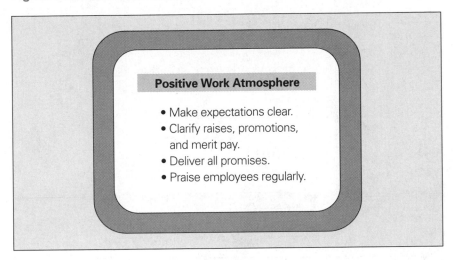

colored acetate that are taped to the frame and folded back until needed (see Visual 1 on p. 387).

■ *They can be made with minimal effort.* With computer software (such as WordPerfect, PowerPoint, PageMaker, or Harvard Graphics), a variety of typefaces, and some clip art (ready-to-use drawings and pictures), you can create professional-looking text and graphics for your transparencies. With the appropriate acetate (film), transparencies can be produced on laser printers, color plotters, copy machines, thermofax machines, or at a local copy shop.

■ *They can be shown effectively to any size audience.*

Slides ■ Slides (Figure 12.3) are popular because they can have dark and even black backgrounds, can use intense colors, are easy to transport, and can be shown to any size audience. However, the time required to produce them is a major disadvantage and the room must be darkened for projection, which makes interaction with your audience difficult and reference to your notes impossible. Be sure to practice using the remote control and coping with a dark room. Bring a long cord for the remote control unit so you can control the slide projector from the front of the room. You may wish to bring a pencil flashlight to place on the lectern so you can see your notes.

Flip Charts and Posters ■ Posters and **flip charts** tend to set an informal mood, are simple to prepare, and can add a feeling of spontaneity to your

Figure 12.4 Poster.

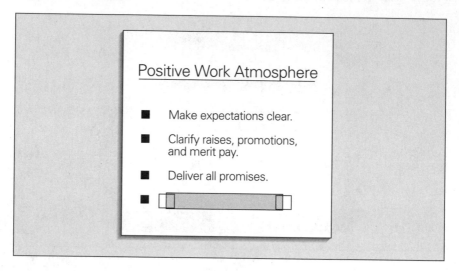

presentation if you write on them as you speak. However, they have several disadvantages:

- They are awkward to transport and even more awkward to store.
- Markers tend to bleed through newsprint. Either leave a blank page between each page you plan to write on or use water-based markers, which will not bleed.
- They can be used only with small groups (fewer then thirty people).

When several key ideas are included on a poster, you may wish to have each idea covered with a strip of paper that can easily be removed as you reach that idea or point in your talk (Figure 12.4). Or, briefly give an overview of all the items on the chart and then go back and discuss each one in detail.

You may prefer to use a flip chart and include only one idea per page (Figure 12.5). When you have finished one idea, simply flip the page to the next idea. The final page should include all your key ideas to refresh the listeners' memory during your summary.

Posters and flip charts are also used to call attention to single words or phrases (technical words, new or seldom-used words, foreign words or phrases).

Objects, Models, and Handouts ■ **Objects** can be very effective visual aids as long as they are large enough to be seen yet small enough so you can

Figure 12.5 Flip chart.

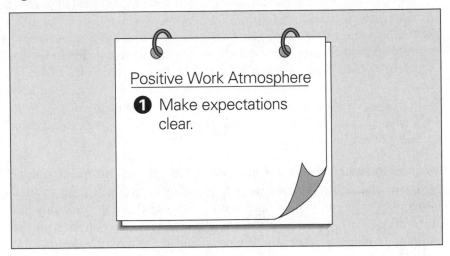

display them easily. To keep from distracting audience members, wait until your presentation is completed before passing objects around the audience for a closer view. If an object is either too small, too large, or too dangerous to be used as a visual aid, you might want to use a **model** instead. For example, a model car, a model office layout, or a model of an atom would all be effective visual aids. **Handouts** can be both a help (they limit the audience's need to take notes) and a distraction (the audience may read the handout instead of listening to you). So, unless you need the audience to do something with the material while you are speaking (like answer a survey or a checklist), it's better to give handouts at the conclusion of your speech.

Markerboards and Chalkboards ■ **Markerboards** are usually preferred over **chalkboards** because the glossy white of the markerboard is more attractive and there is no messy chalk residue. Also, small markerboards are often placed on easels so they can be moved closer to the audience for a more personal feel. However, both markerboards and chalkboards have several drawbacks, thus they should be used only as a last resort:

■ *Practice is vital for success in using markerboards and chalkboards.* Unless you practice ahead, your information may be either too small to see or so large that you run out of space; or you'll need to erase your sketch or repeat it several times to get the proportions correct; or you might forget the spelling of a key word.

- *Because drawing on the board uses valuable speaking time, you must be able to speak and draw at the same time.* You will need a great deal of practice to do this well.
- *While writing on the board, your back is toward the audience.* This not only affects audience interest and denies you valuable audience feedback, but also makes it difficult for you to project your voice to the back of the room. A markerboard is somewhat better because you can stand beside it and still look at the audience occasionally.
- *Using the chalkboard makes you look less prepared and less professional than using other types of visuals.*

Computer-Generated Visuals and Audiovisual Aids ■ Affordable computer hardware and software now make it possible to produce sophisticated shows with color, animation, and sound. In a small group (probably not more than eight), your **computer visuals** can be viewed directly on the computer screen. In larger groups you will need to project the images onto a larger screen, using a portable LCD flat-panel, which sits on top of a regular overhead projector.

Audiovisual aids, if used with care, can also add interest to your presentation. For example, if a VCR (videocassette recorder) is available, you could use a videotape to show a brief segment of a rafting trip down the Colorado River. To point out something of special interest, you could put the tape on slow motion, pause it, or replay a segment. Normally the sound should be turned off, so you can talk during the tape as you would with other visuals. Audiotapes and CDs (compact discs) can also enhance your presentation. For example, a presentation on types of jazz would be much more informative if the audience could hear brief cuts from well-known jazz selections.

Using the Correct Type Size and Typeface

Now that we have discussed the types of visual aids, let's look at one of the most common mistakes that speakers (even experienced speakers) make in preparing visuals: *using text that is too small for easy audience viewing.* To make sure your posters, flip charts, chalkboards, and markerboards are easy for your audience to read, we recommend that

- *Titles* should be approximately 3 inches high.
- *Subtitles*, if used, should be 2 to 2½ inches high.
- *Text* should be 1½ inches high.

When you use these size recommendations, the text may seem too large at first. However, these guidelines will ensure that even the people in the back row can see your message clearly.

Figure 12.6 Determining type sizes in points or inches (measure only capital letters).

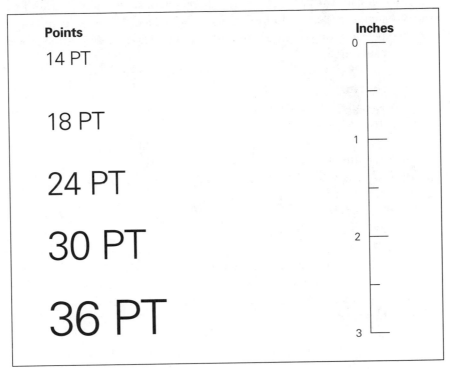

When you use slides, transparencies, and projected computer visuals, your listeners will have no problems if you use the following suggested minimum point sizes (see Figure 12.6):

	Title	*Subtitle*	*Text*
Transparencies	30–36 pt.	24 pt.	18 pt. (24 pt. if no subtitle)
Computer visuals	30–36 pt.	24 pt.	18 pt. (24 pt. if no subtitle)
Slides	24 pt.	18 pt.	14 pt. (18 pt. if no subtitle)

Remember, you can always use larger point sizes, but no type should be smaller than those recommended. Obviously, regular typewriter and computer print sizes will *not* work!

When using slides, transparencies, and projected computer visuals, you will also need to select the typeface or fonts to use. There are over 10,000 different typefaces in existence and over 1,000 readily available typefaces for personal computer users.[23] Keep in mind that typefaces can affect the readability of your visuals and will either harmonize with or distract from the overall tone or style of your speech. Imagine your audience's confusion if you were giving a serious business presentation but your visuals used Poster Bodoni, a playful typeface. Here are some suggested typefaces for visuals along with the images or connotations they project to audiences:

- Helvetica (urban)
- Times Roman (official)
- Century (friendly)
- Garamond (sophisticated)
- Palatino (upbeat)
- Optima (elegant)
- Bodoni (trendy)
- Futura (modern)
- Poster Bodoni (playful)[24]

Generally use no more than two different typefaces per visual, and be consistent in your use of typefaces for all visuals used in a particular presentation. For business presentations, the following typeface combinations are very effective:[25]

- For a classical business look, use a Helvetica title with Times Roman text.
- For an official, confidence-inspiring look, use Times Roman for both title and text.
- For a corporate look, try a Futura title with Garamond text. Change the text to Bodoni for a collegiate or athletic look.
- For a reassuring, friendly look, use Century or Century Schoolbook for both title and text.

Sometimes the only way to ensure that your visuals are sending the message you desire is to see them projected on a screen—once they are enlarged, the tone is more obvious.

Preparing Text Visuals

Visual aids can be divided into two basic groups: text visuals and graphic visuals. **Text visuals** include mainly text or printed words with one or two clip art drawings or pictures. This is different from **graphic visuals,** which include charts, diagrams and schematic drawings, graphs, maps, or pictures—with just enough words to clarify the visual. (The following two pages contain text and graphic visuals produced by seminar students.)

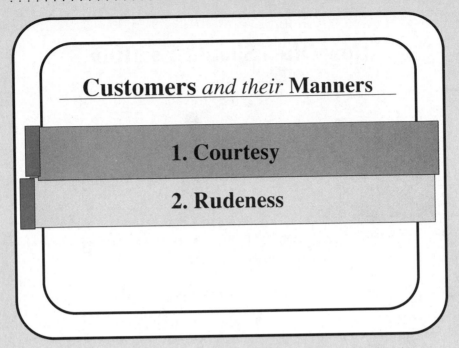

Customers *and their* **Manners**

1. Courtesy

2. Rudeness

VISUAL 1 **Text visual** with color acetate overlays to highlight main points.

Employee Creativity

- Keep channels open

- Encourage new ideas

- Reward creativity

- Promote participation

VISUAL 2 **Text visual** with clip art.

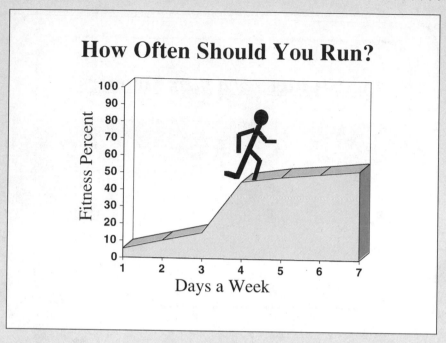

VISUAL 3 **Graphic visual** with 3-D filled line graph and pictograph.

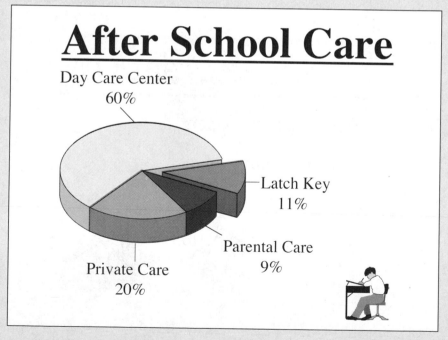

VISUAL 4 **Graphic visual** with 3-D pie chart and clip art.

Figure 12.7 How many of these design rules are broken by this visual?

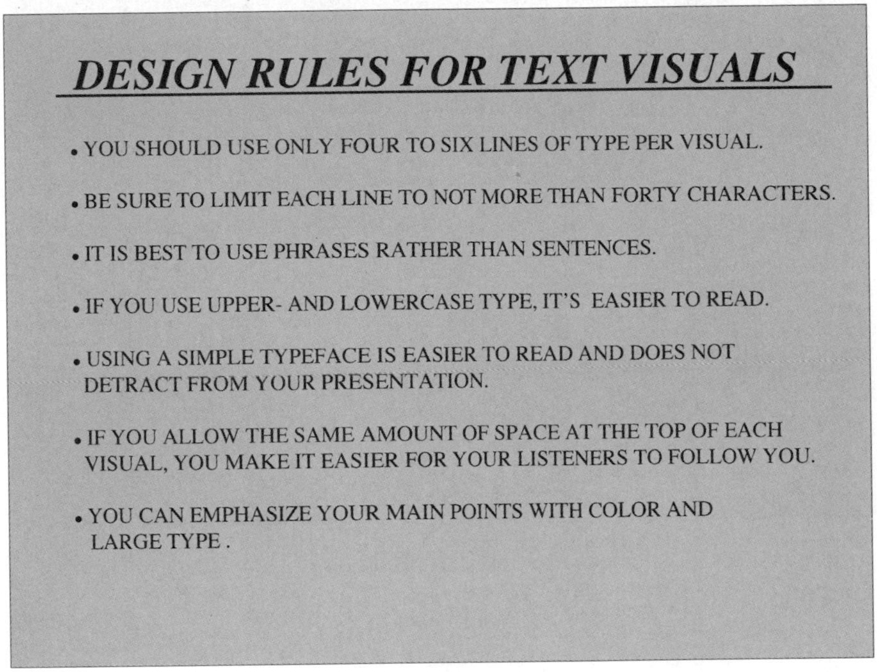

DESIGN RULES FOR TEXT VISUALS

- YOU SHOULD USE ONLY FOUR TO SIX LINES OF TYPE PER VISUAL.

- BE SURE TO LIMIT EACH LINE TO NOT MORE THAN FORTY CHARACTERS.

- IT IS BEST TO USE PHRASES RATHER THAN SENTENCES.

- IF YOU USE UPPER- AND LOWERCASE TYPE, IT'S EASIER TO READ.

- USING A SIMPLE TYPEFACE IS EASIER TO READ AND DOES NOT DETRACT FROM YOUR PRESENTATION.

- IF YOU ALLOW THE SAME AMOUNT OF SPACE AT THE TOP OF EACH VISUAL, YOU MAKE IT EASIER FOR YOUR LISTENERS TO FOLLOW YOU.

- YOU CAN EMPHASIZE YOUR MAIN POINTS WITH COLOR AND LARGE TYPE.

Posters, flip charts, slides, and transparencies are all examples of visual aids that display text visuals well. The most effective text visuals include one or two clip art drawings or pictures that *anchor* the audience to the fact, concept, or idea you are presenting.[26] For example, in a presentation about the steps realtors follow in selling homes, you could have a picture of a house with a "For Sale" sign in front. Later, when audience members try to remember the steps in your talk, they will recall the house (the anchor), which will help them remember the specific points.

Effective text visuals also follow specific design rules discussed by Marya Holcombe and Judith Stein in *Presentations for Decision Makers*.[27] These rules are summarized in Figure 12.7. Before reading further, look at Figure 12.7 to see how many of the rules listed in the visual are violated in this figure. Then continue reading and see if you were correct. Remember, if visuals require effort to read, the audience is forced into a reading mode rather than a listening mode. Listeners can't pay attention to what you are saying while they are reading your visual. Therefore, a good visual should make sense in 6 seconds or less.

Use No More Than Four to Six Lines of Text ■ Not counting the title and subtitle(s), when a visual contains more than six lines of text, it takes too

Effective business speakers use well-designed visuals that their listeners can grasp in 6 seconds or less. (© *Charles Gupton/The Stock Market*)

long for your audience to grasp. Of course, if the text is a list containing single words, seven or eight lines might be fine. In general, if you need more than six lines of text, you probably should split the information into two visuals or narrow and simplify your text.

Limit Each Line to Forty Characters ■ If your text contains more than forty characters per line (count letters and spaces), you aren't leaving enough *white space* (space that contains no text or graphics). White space is essential for fast comprehension and prevents your visual from looking cluttered and unorganized.

Use Phrases Rather Than Sentences ■ Eliminate unnecessary words so listeners can grasp the content of your visual in 6 seconds or less. Figure 12.7 shows how sentences slow down comprehension. The same information using phrases is displayed in Figure 12.8. Which visual would you rather have an instructor use in a lecture?

Use Upper- and Lowercase Type ■ Although speakers often put their titles and text into all caps because they think it will look larger and therefore be easier to read, research has shown that text in all capitals is more difficult to read and comprehend.[28] To illustrate why this is true, try a brief

Figure 12.8 Which visual takes less time to read—this one or Figure 12.7?

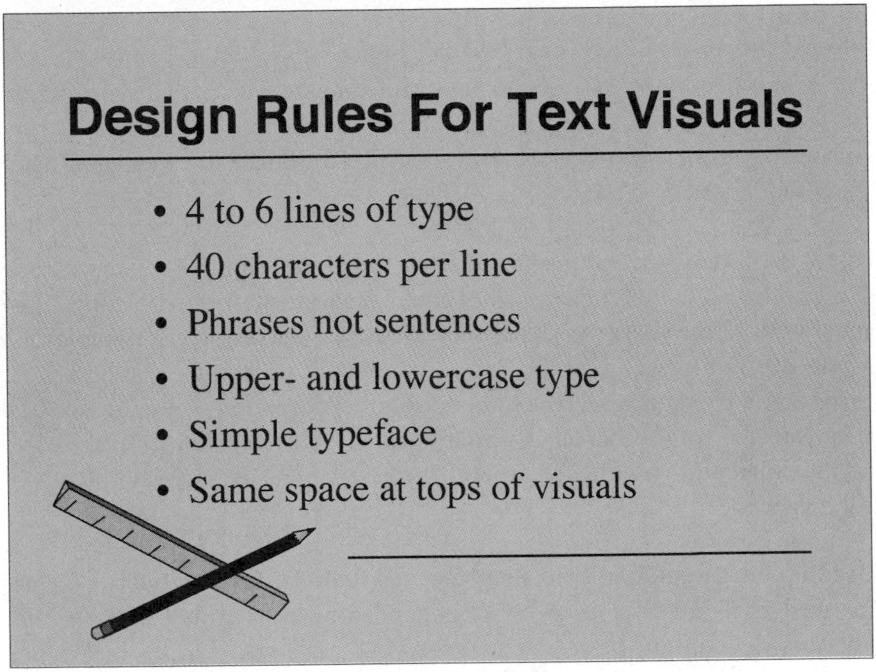

Design Rules For Text Visuals

- 4 to 6 lines of type
- 40 characters per line
- Phrases not sentences
- Upper- and lowercase type
- Simple typeface
- Same space at tops of visuals

Figure 12.9 Word recognition experiment. *(Source: J. Michael Adams, David D. Faux, and Lloyd J. Rieber, Printing Technology, 3rd ed. [Albany, NY: Delmar, 1988], p. 48.)*

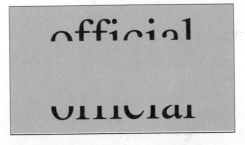

experiment using Figure 12.9. The word *official* has been divided into two lines. Hold your hand over the top line and ask at least four people to read the bottom line. Now hold your hand over the bottom line and ask four other people to read the top line. Which line were more people able to read correctly? The reason that the top line is easier to read is that word recognition comes mainly from the upper half of lowercase letters. However, when the word *official* is put in all capitals (OFFICIAL), it becomes a shapeless box that cannot be instantly recognized.[29] Therefore, use all caps only for special emphasis.

Use a Simple Typeface ■   Avoid script and fancy typefaces that are difficult to read. The typefaces suggested earlier in this chapter have stood the test of time and are known to work for visual aids. Feel free to experiment, but just don't get carried away.

Allow the Same Space at the Top of Each Visual ■   Many speakers incorrectly center the content on each of their visuals from top to bottom. This means that some visual aids have only a few lines in the middle of the page, while others utilize the entire page. As a result, each time you project a transparency or slide onto the screen, or hold up a poster, the audience has to locate the title—this takes valuable time. Your visuals will look more professional and be easier to view if the text begins at the same place on each visual.

Use Clip Art, Large-Sized Type, Boldface, and Color for Emphasis ■   *Clip art* (as well as pictures, photos, and freehand drawings) adds emphasis and anchors the content of your visual for your audience. Large-sized type, boldface, and color are excellent ways to direct the eye to areas you wish to emphasize. The largest and boldest type will usually be noticed first unless you have also used color. If you want to direct your audience's attention to a portion of a complicated diagram, color is the way to do it. Even on a color visual, a bright, contrasting color will draw your audience's attention.

Preparing Graphic Visuals

The most commonly used types of graphic visuals are charts, diagrams and schematics, maps, and graphs. *Organization charts* and *flowcharts* are used constantly by business and professional presenters. Figure 12.10 is a flowchart of the process followed by a systems analyst, whether solving problems in an existing system or in developing a new system.

Diagrams and *schematic drawings* also make effective graphic visuals. It doesn't take an artist to draw the diagrams or schematics needed in most presentations—you can do them yourself. With the help of computer clip art, any speaker could compile Figure 12.11, which is a simple schematic. If more complicated diagrams are needed, such as the cutaway diagram in Figure 12.12, you may ask for assistance from the graphic arts department or from an engineer or draftsperson where you work.

Figure 12.10 Flowchart. (*Source:* Living with Computers, *2nd ed., by Patrick G. McKeown, copyright © 1988 by Harcourt Brace Jovanovich, Inc. Reprinted by permission of the publisher.*)

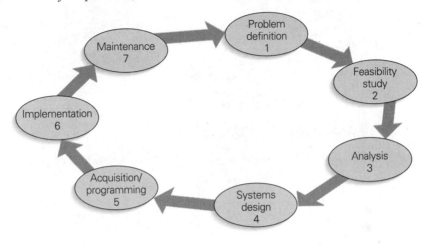

Figure 12.11 Schematic. (*Source:* Computer Currents, *by George Beekman, copyright © 1994 by Benjamin/Cummings Publishing.*)

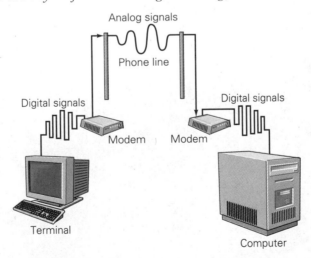

Maps are another type of graphic visual. A presentation on the graying of America might include a map of the United States to show which states have more people over the age of 65 (Figure 12.13).

Graphs have traditionally been used in industry to display complicated, difficult-to-interpret data in simplified, visual form. Now that the cost of

Figure 12.12 Cutaway diagram showing construction of a fiber optic cable. *(Source: June J. Parsons and Dan Oja,* New Perspectives on Computer Concepts, *copyright © 1995 by Course Technology, Inc., p. 175.)*

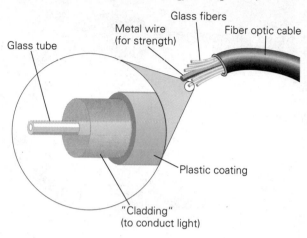

Figure 12.13 Map of the United States showing the percent of the population over 65 years of age. *(Source: Mark T. Mattson,* Atlas of the 1990 Census, *copyright © 1992 by Macmillan, p. 39.)*

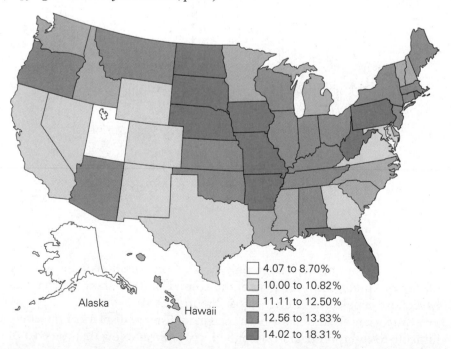

computer-generated graphics is within the range of most companies and individuals, graphs are being used even more extensively.

To business and professional people who give oral presentations to employees or management, a graph is certainly worth a thousand words! Graphs have many uses in oral presentations:[30]

- Graphs show trends over a specified period of time.
- Graphs show relationships among various data.
- Graphs make it easy to compare actual figures with projected or "what if" figures.
- Graphs greatly reduce misinterpretation of data.

A district sales manager for a fast-food franchise certainly discovered the value of graphs. Most of the eleven stores in the district were below their estimated sales potential for some unknown reason. The computer printouts, which each store manager received every month, plus the pep talks from the district manager, should have motivated the store managers, but sales continued to lag. At the suggestion of a friend, the district manager decided to call all eleven store managers to a meeting and to present the problem to them once more, this time using various graphs. As a result, the store managers were able to determine clearly and easily (1) each store's sales trends over a certain period of time, (2) how each store compared in sales to the other stores, and (3) how closely the sales of their individual stores matched estimated potential sales. The managers all seemed surprised and even embarrassed at the information and expressed their appreciation for the graphs. The district manager was pleasantly surprised that sales began to increase shortly after the meeting.

There are many types of graphs that the district manager could have used. Examples of the principal types—line graph, vertical bar graph, horizontal bar graph, stacked bar graph, pictograph, and circle graph—are discussed briefly here. In general,

- To show *trends or patterns over time*, use the line graph, the vertical bar graph, or a combination of the two.
- To show *relationships and comparisons between data*, use the vertical bar graph, horizontal bar graph, grouped bar graphs, or a simple data chart.
- To *compare parts to the whole* when there is no time factor to the relationship, use the circle graph (called a pie chart) and stacked bar graph.
- To show *percentages*, try a pictograph.

Color, small clip art illustrations, and background images (if used sparingly) can add eye-catching appeal. To be successful, graphic aids should

Figure 12.14 Limit data to what is needed to support your verbal point and eliminate distracting grid lines.

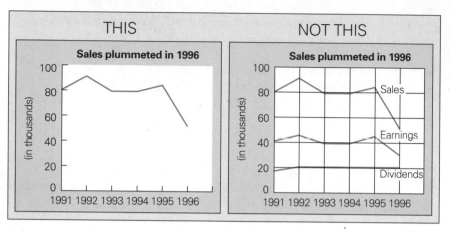

Figure 12.15 Group distracting data under a general heading.

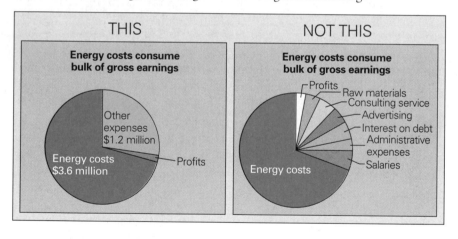

follow the design rules discussed by Holcombe and Stein in *Presentations for Decision Makers* (see Figures 12.14 through 12.17):[31]

Limit Data to What Is Absolutely Necessary ■ Figure 12.14 illustrates the importance of using only the data needed to support your verbal points. Because the speech deals with sales, the line graphs for earnings and dividends (as well as the distracting grid lines) are not necessary and actually obscure the seriousness of the sales decline. It is always a good idea, how-

Figure 12.16 For viewing ease, the space between bars should be eliminated or be narrower than the bars.

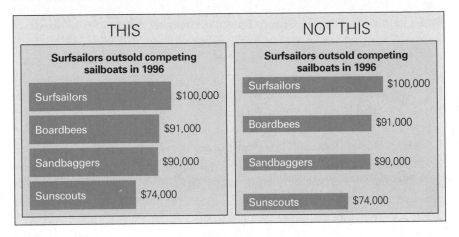

Figure 12.17 For viewing ease, eliminate data points.

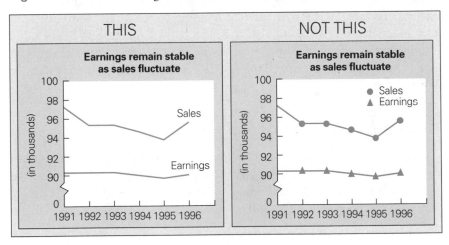

ever, to have additional materials ready in case of audience questions. For example, the earnings and dividends line graphs would make excellent overlays, which, if used to answer a question, would certainly be impressive.

Combine Data When Possible ■ Figure 12.15 illustrates the principle of grouping data. When seven small categories of costs were grouped under the general heading of "Other Expenses," we greatly reduced the amount of time needed to get the point of the pie chart. You could follow this visual with a second one that lists the content of "Other Expenses."

Make Bars Wider Than the Spaces Between Them ■   When the white space between the bars is wider than the bars themselves as in Figure 12.16, the trapped white space visually pushes the bars apart, making them seem unrelated.[32] Therefore, for easier audience viewing, make sure that the bars are wider than the spaces between them, regardless of whether the bars are placed horizontally or vertically.

Keep Background Lines and Data Points to a Minimum ■   In most cases, grid lines (like those used in Figure 12.14) and data points (like those in Figure 12.17) should be eliminated from your visuals. Grid lines and data points are distracting, take too much time to interpret, and are not necessary for understanding. If you know your audience expects grid lines and data points, then use them, but include only essential data points and make the grid lines lighter than the data lines.

Always Use Headings ■   Whether your graphic visual is a chart, graph, map, or picture, always use a title or heading to reinforce your point. For example, a hand-drawing of a skier in the correct position to begin water skiing might seem obvious to you as the speaker, but without a title or heading, the exact purpose of the visual wouldn't be immediately clear to your audience.

General Design Principles[33]

Before we conclude this section on visual supporting material, let's look at four general design principles that apply to all visuals, whether text or graphic. A summary of these design principles, discussed by R. Williams in *The Non-Designer's Design Book*,[34] follows:

Contrast

The idea behind contrast is to avoid elements on the page that are merely *similar*. If the elements (type, color, size, line thickness, shape, etc.) are not the *same*, then make them **very different**. Contrast is often the most important visual attraction on a page.

Repetition

Repeat visual elements of the design through the piece. You can repeat color, shape, texture, spatial relationships, line thicknesses, sizes, etc. This helps develop the organization and strengthens the unity.

ALIGNMENT

Nothing should be placed on the page arbitrarily. Every element should have some visual connection with another element on the page. This creates a clean, sophisticated, fresh look.

PROXIMITY

Items relating to each other should be grouped close together. When several items are in close proximity to each other, they become one visual unit rather than several separate units. This helps organize information and reduces clutter.[35]

Analyzing Figure 12.18 Using Design Principles ■ Let's illustrate how these four design principles can really improve the quality of a visual aid. Look at Figure 12.18. First, what's right about this transparency? The speaker has chosen Century as the typeface (a typeface that gives a caring, friendly impression), which seems appropriate for the topic. The type is large enough for easy audience viewing (the title is 36 point and the main ideas are 30 point), and only necessary words have been used on the visual. Also, a two-line underline separates the title from the main points, which helps the audience grasp the organization of the visual. This visual, then, is basically good.

So, what's wrong? It's bland, isn't it? Nothing attracts the eye. This transparency does not follow the four design principles presented by Williams:

1. Even with the title in boldface, there isn't enough *contrast*. The type sizes of the main points and the titles are too similar for contrast.
2. There isn't enough *repetition* throughout the transparency. The bullets (squares in front of the main points) do repeat, but are too bland to be noticed. The bold of the title needs to be repeated some-where—maybe the bullets could be filled in or the underline could be made bold.
3. The main points on the page are in *alignment*, but they don't line up with anything else. If the main points were centered (normally, not a good idea), they would align with the title and underline, which are already centered. Williams says that "every item should have a visual connection with something else on the page."[36] Right now, neither the title nor the underline do.
4. There is too much space between the title and the first main point and between each of the main points. It almost looks like there are five separate items on the page. Closer *proximity* between items is needed so they become a visual unit.

Figure 12.18 How would you improve this visual?

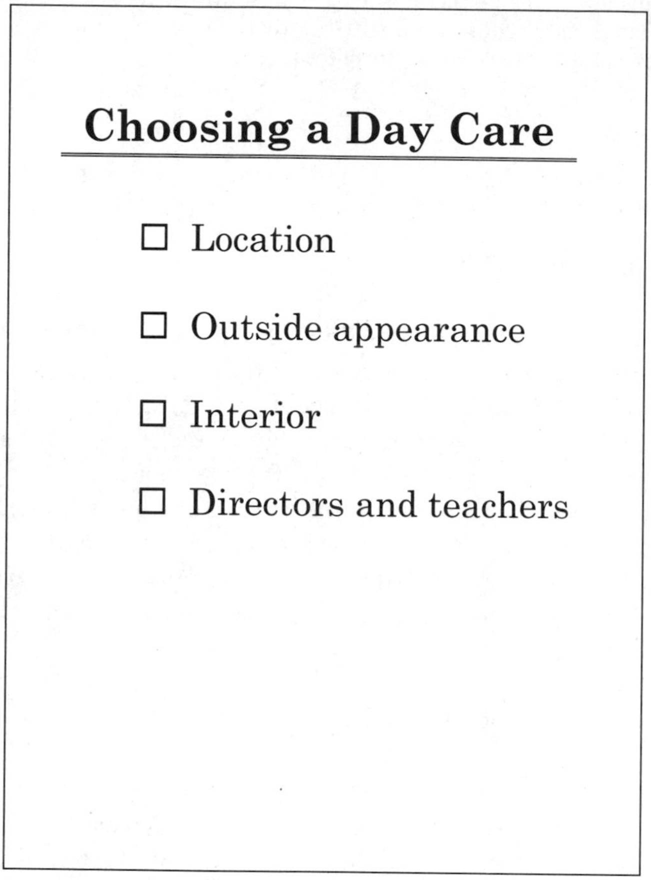

> # Choosing a Day Care
>
> ☐ Location
>
> ☐ Outside appearance
>
> ☐ Interior
>
> ☐ Directors and teachers

Redesigning Figure 12.18 Using Design Principles ■ How can we redesign the day-care visual to incorporate the four design principles? Figure 12.19 shows one approach:

1. To show *contrast*, the type size of the title is larger (40 points) while the type size of the list is smaller (24 points).
2. To establish *repetition*, the boldface of the title is repeated in the solid bullets (the dark squares) and the two dark lines.
3. To achieve *alignment*, the title, underline, and bullets line up on the left while the title, underline, graphic, and bottom line all align on the right. Besides adding alignment, the graphic adds warmth and visual interest.

Figure 12.19 One approach to redesigning the visual in Figure 12.18.

Choosing a Day Care

- Location

- Outside appearance

- Interior

- Directors and teachers

4. To maintain *proximity*, the main points in the list are grouped together as a visual unit.

This is only one of many possible ways to redesign the day-care visual. What method would you suggest?

SUMMARY

We began this chapter talking about Carolyn, a supervisor for a large toy company. She and several other supervisors presented their ideas for a new sales campaign to upper management. Carolyn was a good speaker. She was well organized and found time to practice her presentation. Her delivery was authoritative yet conversational—definitely above average. How-

---

Remember, Visual Aids . . .

- Are used to supplement, not to replace, verbal messages; use them sparingly.
- When used correctly, can improve understanding, create interest, save time, and aid memory.
- Should require no more than 6 seconds for the audience to grasp.
- Must be large enough to be seen easily by all listeners.
- Generally should contain only one idea per visual, so that the idea is immediately obvious.
- Should be as simple and uncomplicated as possible. If you use color, select only two or three colors per visual.
- Should look neat and professional.
- Should be accompanied by a brief explanation designed specifically for your listeners. Some people will need more explanation than others, but be careful not to talk down to them or to explain the obvious.
- Require practice to be handled effectively. Moving from one visual to the next quickly and smoothly, standing so your body does not block the visual, using a pointer to locate various aspects of the visual, selecting the right words to explain the visual, keeping most of your attention on the listeners, and working without light when using slides— these all require about the same amount of practice as the verbal part of a speech.
- Should be shown only while you are referring specifically to them. Keep them covered or hidden until you are ready to use them, and remove or recover them when finished.
- Usually should not be passed around because listeners will be distracted from what you are saying.

---

ever, Carolyn made a very serious mistake. She failed to use sufficient supporting materials. As a result, some of her ideas were not clear and others lacked necessary proof.

To change the outcome of her presentation, Carolyn should have used many of the verbal supporting materials discussed in this chapter. For example, to clarify her ideas, she could have used these verbal supports: explanation, figurative comparison, or hypothetical illustration. To add proof to her arguments, she could have used several of these verbal supports: literal comparison, factual illustration, examples, statistics, and expert opinion. To add additional interest to the presentation, she needed to use a variety of supporting materials.

To improve the outcome of her presentation, Carolyn should also have used several visual supporting materials—either text visuals, graphic visuals, or both. *Visual aids are not optional.* Effective speakers know that audience attention and retention are enhanced when visuals are included. Follow the four design principles described here as you create your visual aids.

As you prepare your presentations, regardless of whether they are formal or informal, avoid the mistakes Carolyn made. Do not overlook the importance of supporting materials. They can be the difference between a successful and an unsuccessful presentation.

CHECKPOINT

Before continuing to the next chapter, check your understanding of Chapter 12 by completing the following exercises:

1. At the next formal or informal presentation you attend, identify the types of supporting materials used by the speaker. Determine whether the supports are adequate for clarity, proof, and interest. If you were giving the presentation, what changes would you make?
2. Construct a chart or graph to represent the following sources of income expected by the Draper Piano & Organ Company:

    > Sale of new pianos—43 percent
    > Sale of new organs—26 percent
    > Private lessons—20 percent
    > Used merchandise—7 percent
    > Piano tuning—4 percent

    Ask two or three friends to help you think of ways that your chart or graph might be improved.
3. Look at the text and graphic visuals on pages 387–388. Compare them to the guidelines for effective visuals discussed in this chapter. Which visuals are the most effective? Why? Which are the least effective? Why? What one change would make the most improvement in each visual?

NOTES

1. Edgar B. Wycoff, "Canons of Communication," *Personnel Journal* 60 (March 1981), p. 212.
2. *Webster's New Collegiate Dictionary*, 8th ed. (Springfield, MA: Merriam, 1980), p. 1162. Reprinted by permission of G. & C. Merriam Company, publishers of the Merriam-Webster dictionaries.

3. Allen A. Schumer, "Employee Involvement: The Quality Circle Process," *Vital Speeches* 54 (July 1, 1988), p. 564.

4. Newton N. Minnow, "Television: How Far Has It Come in 30 Years," *Vital Speeches* 57 (July 1, 1991), p. 554. Used by permission.

5. Richard D. Lamm, "The Ten Commandments of an Aging Society," *Vital Speeches* 54 (December 15, 1987), p. 135.

6. Gerald M. Goldhaber, "Warm Flesh Beats Cold Plastic," *Vital Speeches* 45 (September 1, 1979), p. 683.

7. Takakazu Kuriyama, "U.S. and Japan Trade Relations," *Vital Speeches* 60 (May 1, 1994), p. 422.

8. Harvey B. Mackay, "How to Get a Job: How to Be Successful," *Vital Speeches* 57 (August 15, 1991), p. 658. Used by permission.

9. *Town Meeting* 11 (October 11, 1945), p. 24; quote and source reported by Raymond S. Ross, *Speech Communication*, 5th ed. (Englewood Cliffs, NJ: Prentice-Hall, 1980), pp. 181–182.

10. William M. Timmins, "Smoking Versus Nonsmoking at Work: A Survey of Public Agency Policy and Practice," *Public Personnel Management* 16 (Fall 1987), pp. 221–234.

11. Linda Winikow, "How Women and Minorities Are Reshaping Corporate America," *Vital Speeches* 57 (February 1, 1991), p. 243. Used by permission.

12. John Engler, "Our Kids Deserve Better!" *Vital Speeches* 60 (November 15, 1993), pp. 73–74.

13. Lonnie R. Bristow, "Protecting Youth from the Tobacco Industry," *Vital Speeches* 60 (March 15, 1994), p. 333.

14. Brent Baker, "Damn the Consumers—Full Speed Ahead: The Electronic Highway," *Vital Speeches* 60 (May 1, 1994), p. 445.

15. Deborah Tannen, *Talking from 9 to 5: How Women's and Men's Conversational Styles Affect Who Gets Heard, Who Gets Credit, and What Gets Done at Work* (New York: Morrow, 1994).

16. Jenny Clanton, "Plutonium 238: NASA's Fuel of Choice," *Vital Speeches* 55 (April 1, 1989), p. 375.

17. Max D. Isaacson, "Public Speaking and Other Coronary Threats," *Vital Speeches* 46 (March 15, 1980), p. 352.

18. In a brochure advertising *Picture Perfect* and *Diagraph*, business graphics software by Computer Support Corporation, Dallas, Texas 75244. Picture Perfect is a registered trademark of Computer Support Corporation. Diagraph is a registered trademark licensed to Computer Support Corporation.

19. Ralph G. Nichols and Leonard A. Stevens, *Are You Listening?* (New York: McGraw-Hill, 1957).

20. Douglas R. Vogel, Gary W. Dickson, and John A. Lehman, "Persuasion and the Role of Visual Presentation Support: The UM/3M Study," *3M Corporation* (1986), pp. 1–20.

21. Research results available from Audio Visual Management Association, P.O. Box 821, Royal Oak, MI 48068.

22. E. P. Zayas-Baya, "Instructional Media in the Total Language Picture," *International Journal of Instructional Media* 5 (1977–1978), pp. 145–150.

23. Steve Byers, *The Electronic Type Catalog* (New York: Bantam, 1992), p. xii.

24. These typeface connotations were compiled from the following sources: Carol Buchanan, *Quick Solutions for Great Type Combinations* (Cincinnati: North Light Books, 1993) and Don Dewsnap, *Desktop Publisher's Easy Type Guide: The 150 Most Important Typefaces* (Rockport, MA: Rockport Publishers, 1992).

25. See note 24.

26. Allan Paivio, *Imagery and Verbal Processes* (New York: Holt, Rinehart & Winston, 1971).

27. Marya W. Holcombe and Judith K. Stein, *Presentations for Decision Makers: Strategies for Structuring and Delivering Your Ideas* (New York: Lifetime Learning, 1983), p. 79. Reprinted by permission of Van Nostrand Reinhold.

28. J. Michael Adams, David D. Faux, and Lloyd J. Rieber, *Printing Technology*, 3rd ed. (Albany, NY: Delmar, 1988), p. 48.

29. Revised from Floyd K. Baskette, Jack Z. Sissors, and Brian S. Brooks, *The Art of Editing*, 5th ed. (New York: Macmillan, 1992), p. 267.

30. Adapted from Walter J. Presnick, "Helping Managers See the Trends," *Administrative Management* 41 (April 1980), pp. 35–48.

31. Holcombe and Stein, p. 97.

32. Robin Williams, *The Non-Designer's Design Book: Design and Typographic Principles for the Visual Novice* (Berkeley: Peachpit Press, 1994), p. 14.
33. This section is taken from Cheryl Hamilton, *Successful Public Speaking* (Belmont, CA: Wadsworth, 1996), pp. 161–164.
34. Williams, p. 14.
35. Williams, p. 14.
36. Williams, p. 27.

13 Persuasive Presentations: Individual or Team

O f the many types of communication prevalent in business and industry, none is more important than public speaking. Through presentations made to large and small groups, speakers attempt to persuade people, inform them, impress them, and entertain them. Unfortunately, public speaking is also the most frequently mishandled form of communication. Because of inadequate speaker performance, attempts to influence misfire, misunderstandings occur, images suffer, and ceremonies collapse.[1]

JOHN E. BAIRD, JR.,
Modern Management Methods, Inc.

A twenty-year study of MBA graduates from Stanford University has concluded that no skill is more important to business success than good communication (especially the desire and ability to persuade, which is a speaking skill).[2] As we cautioned earlier, to overlook the importance of speaking skills is to limit your flexibility as a communicator and perhaps even your chances for advancement.[3]

PERSUASIVE PRESENTATIONS: DEFINITIONS AND TYPES

Although persuasion is one of the most often used business communication skills, it may very well be one of the *least effectively used*. To learn to use persuasion, speakers first need to know exactly what persuasion is and what the various types of persuasion are.

Persuasion Defined

Many people either think persuasion is giving information or confuse it with coercion. Simply giving a list of options does not mean your audience will select the one you want them to select. This approach is similar to a child trying to sell magazines with the line, "You don't want to buy any magazines, do you?" Some businesspeople use a similar approach when they take a middle-of-the-road stance. Middle-of-the-road speakers cover several possible alternatives, but refuse to take a stand or argue for any particular view. They apparently believe that their listeners will do the "right" thing. Other businesspeople view persuasion as coercion. They think that the only way to get people to do what they want is by force or trickery.

Neither of these methods is effective, and neither is truly persuasion. "Persuasion is communication intended to influence choice,"[4] but it is not the same as coercion. To *coerce* is to eliminate or exclude options. To *inform* is to increase the number of a person's options or choices (the more you know, the more choices you have). To **persuade** is to limit the options that are perceived as acceptable.[5]

There is no force or trickery in persuasion. The receivers of the persuasive message must weigh the logic and evidence and make their own decision. Once that decision has been made, they alone are responsible for it, although the sender helped influence the decision.

Types of Persuasive Presentations

There are two basic types of persuasive presentations: the presentation to convince and the presentation to actuate. The two speeches differ in the degree of audience reaction sought: The presentation to convince seeks intellectual agreement from listeners, while the presentation to actuate asks listeners for both intellectual agreement as well as action of some type.

Presentation to Convince ■   In a presentation to convince, you want your audience to agree with your way of thinking. You aren't asking them to do anything—just believe you or agree with you. This approach is especially good when your audience initially disagrees with your position and you realize that moving them to action is unlikely—getting agreement is a more realistic goal.

Presentation to Actuate ■   In a presentation to actuate, you want your audience to go one step past agreement to take a particular action. First you must *convince* them of the merits of your ideas; then you want to *actuate* them—move them to action. Most speakers try to persuade the audience to do something they haven't been doing (like join a work team). However, there are three other approaches you can use:[6] You can urge the audience *to continue* doing something (like continue eating balanced meals), *to stop* doing something (like stop waiting until the last minute to prepare reports), or *to never start* doing something (like avoid smoking cigarettes). Depending on your topic and your audience, you may want to include more than one action request. For example, in a speech on alcohol you might urge audience members who drink to use a designated driver, those drinkers who have used designated drivers to continue to do so, and those who don't drink to never start.

The type of persuasive presentation you pick may depend on the topic itself (some topics lend themselves to a particular approach). For example, if your topic is the cultural bias of standardized interview screening tests, your persuasive presentation will convince rather than actuate. This topic lends itself to *believing* rather than *doing*. On the other hand, topics like the need for volunteers in local schools or the health problems resulting from recycled cabin air in commercial airliners lend themselves to listener action. In the first case, you might urge your listeners to spend at least 1 hour a week as a volunteer at a local school; for the second topic, you might recommend that your audience write to commercial airlines, state and national government officials, and the Federal Aviation Administration urging that cabin air be continually replaced with fresh air, not recycled.

Persuasive Presentations in Business

As with informative presentations, the types of persuasive presentations in business and what they are called vary from company to company. Some companies label the persuasive presentation a "pitch," others a "proposal," and still others a "presentation." Because the differences among these types are subtle, we will simply use the term *persuasive presentation*.

Many persuasive presentations are informal and are given within the organization by supervisors to their employees or by employees to their supervisors. Topics might include convincing employees of the need for a new reorganization plan, urging compliance with a company regulation, advocating a new piece of machinery, policy change, or postponement of a deadline.

Other persuasive presentations are given to an individual or group from outside the organization. Such presentations are more formal. For example, the engineers from one company might plan a formal presentation about a new product for visiting engineers from another company. International business meetings definitely require one or more formal presentations. For these meetings, visual aids are prepared in the language of the guest country. Many companies also give persuasive presentations to the general public in an attempt to create a good public image or to change a negative one. A power company, for example, might decide to have company representatives deliver persuasive presentations to various clubs and organizations in an attempt to change public opinion on the use of nuclear power. And, of course, salespersons give sales presentations to customers about products.

PERSUASIVE PRESENTATIONS: THEORY

We asked a large number of businesspeople, about half of whom were in low-level supervisory positions, to think back to the last really good persuasive presentation they had heard and to tell us what part of the presentation most influenced them. Many answered that the evidence in the presentation was the most important factor; some mentioned that they were persuaded because the speaker's suggestion was really needed; others admitted that they were influenced by the qualifications and expertise of the speaker. These three factors (evidence, need, and expertise) were more often cited as reasons for being persuaded than were any other factors.

Unconsciously, these businesspeople were probably influenced to some degree by all three factors plus one other. Persuaders have found that persuasion in business (and in other environments as well) depends on four main factors:

1. The evidence and logic of the message
2. The credibility (which includes expertise) of the persuader

Figure 13.1 Factors that lead to persuasion in business.

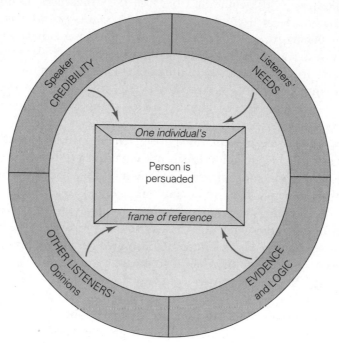

3. The psychological needs of the listeners who are being persuaded
4. The opinions held by key people in the audience

Study the model of persuasion in Figure 13.1 as we look at each of these factors in more detail.

Evidence and Logic of the Message

Of the four factors leading to persuasion, evidence is the most confusing. Americans like to think of themselves as logical people who make logical decisions. They expect speakers to use logic and evidence in their presentations. And, of course, when the listeners are persuaded, they attribute the persuasion to the superior logic and evidence used by the speaker.

Evidence is defined as factual statements and opinions originating, not from the speaker, but from another source.[7] Evidence forms the basis for the logical arguments a speaker develops. (See Chapter 12 for supporting materials that can serve as evidence.) **Logic** has been defined as "the study of orderly thinking, the sequence and connection of thoughts and ideas as they relate to one another."[8] In other words, it is logic that connects the various pieces of evidence in a meaningful and persuasive argument.

Researchers have begun to realize that evidence and logic may not be nearly as effective as previously thought and that certain uses of evidence may even be harmful to persuasion. Note the following research findings:

- Listeners have difficulty in identifying evidence and intellectual appeals, in distinguishing between logical and illogical messages, and between high-quality evidence and low-quality evidence.[9] Apparently, even though listeners think logic and evidence are important, they can't necessarily identify them in speeches.
- Low-ability listeners who are not personally involved with the topic will tend to be persuaded when a large amount of evidence is presented (even if the evidence is poor quality).[10]
- Evidence and arguments that are novel or "new" to an audience are more persuasive.[11]
- Logical-sounding phrases (such as "therefore," "as a result," "it is only logical that," and "it is possible to conclude") may cause listeners to judge a presentation as more logical than a presentation without such words.[12] This finding explains how unethical speakers who use logical-sounding words are sometimes able to fool their listeners.
- Listeners who are in favor of the speaker's proposal or who consider the speaker to be credible are more likely to rate the speech high in evidence even if no evidence is presented.[13] However, for a less credible speaker, use of evidence may increase his or her perceived credibility, thereby increasing persuasiveness.[14] In most cases, it seems that speaker credibility and listener attitude toward a topic are more important persuasive factors than evidence.
- When evidence is used, mentioning the source of the evidence without explaining who the expert is does not make the presentation more persuasive. In fact, unless the source's qualifications are also explained, citing the source of the evidence actually makes the presentation *less* persuasive.[15]
- When giving a source, it is more effective to cite the source and his or her qualifications *after* the evidence is presented. Cite the source *before* the evidence only if you know the listeners consider the source a highly credible one.[16]
- "Self-reference" speakers (who support their assertions by citing firsthand experiences) are rated higher in trustworthiness and are more persuasive than speakers who refer only to high-prestige sources.[17] Personal examples and experiences also tend to be more persuasive than statistical or numerical data[18] and to have a longer-lasting persuasive effect.[19]

Figure 13.2 Persuasiveness of evidence presented in four different methods.

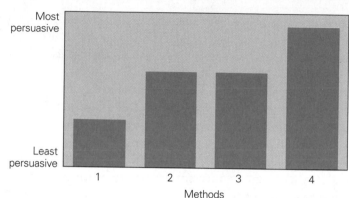

Figure 13.2 summarizes research findings on the following methods of using evidence:

- *Method 1: Assertion plus evidence plus source.* "We need to paint our workroom walls orange [assertion]. Productivity normally increases by 20 percent when walls are painted orange [evidence] according to Kenneth Johnson [source]."
- *Method 2: Assertion plus evidence.* "We need to paint our workroom walls orange [assertion]. Productivity normally increases by 20 percent when walls are painted orange [evidence]." (Note that here the evidence is not linked to a source or documented in any way.)
- *Method 3: Assertion plus evidence plus source plus qualifications of source.* "We need to paint our workroom walls orange [assertion]. Productivity normally increases by 20 percent when walls are painted orange [evidence], according to Kenneth Johnson [source], the research director for Business Color, Inc. [qualifications of source]."
- *Method 4: Assertion plus firsthand experience.* "We need to paint our workroom walls orange [assertion]. Twice I have been in departments that painted their work areas orange and both times productivity increased approximately 20 percent [firsthand experience]."

Notice that method 1, the method that many of us use, is the least persuasive of all four methods. As discussed earlier, citing a source without giving the qualifications of the source is even less persuasive than presenting evidence with no source at all. As Figure 13.2 shows, the most persuasive type of evidence is often firsthand experience. Let's discuss when to use each method.

For Persuasive Presentations _Within_ the Organization ■ When speaking _inside_ the organization to people who know you well, _method 2_ (assertion plus undocumented evidence) and _method 4_ (assertion plus firsthand experience) are the two best methods for presenting evidence. Method 2 is often used for several reasons. First, in the business world, time is extremely precious to everyone, particularly to management. As a result, individuals rarely have more than 20 to 30 minutes to present their ideas and answer questions. If the topic is very important, they might have as much as an hour. Because of such pressure, management and other listeners tend to view extensive documentation as a waste of time. If they need further verification of a point, they ask for it.

Second, extensive documentation is unnecessary for presentations within the organization because those listening to the presentation are usually already somewhat familiar with the topic being discussed. Even if the presentation concerns a new concept or product, they will normally have enough general knowledge in the field to determine whether the speaker's figures or evidence are reasonable.

Third, the person giving the presentation is usually an acquaintance of the listener, so his or her credibility and expertise are already known. If the speaker is relatively unknown or of lower rank than most of the listeners, his or her boss will attend the meeting to add credibility and to answer any problematic questions. Even when a team of speakers from one company travels to another company to present a proposal to people they have never met, each team judges the credibility and expertise of the other by the titles and ranks of the members. This is one reason why titles and positions are so important in business negotiation.

Some speakers who wish to add to their credibility include an abbreviated version of the source (prestigious sources only) on the transparency they show their audience. For example, at the bottom of a transparency demonstrating the results of a business survey, they might simply print, "Dun & Bradstreet."

Method 4 (assertion plus firsthand evidence) is also a common method of presenting evidence in a persuasive presentation. To whom would you rather listen—a person urging adoption of a method devised by a well-known business inventor or the actual inventor who could discuss the method firsthand? Would you rather hear about a new way to conduct employee appraisals from a manager who quotes from a book on the subject or from a manager who has firsthand knowledge of how the method works? Suppose that during the last company appraisal, this manager had appraised one-half of the employees using the old method and the other half using the new method. This manager could tell you firsthand whether the theory in the book worked well enough to adopt.

Method 4 should be used only if you have considerable firsthand experience and are an authority on the topic (know more than most of the listeners). Otherwise, method 2 would be the best. However, method 4 speakers should come prepared with more than just personal experience. They should have made an objective and complete search for relevant evidence (both for and against their idea) before preparing for the talk. They must be sure that their experiences are not exceptions to the rule and that the proposals they are recommending are the best ones for the company. If someone asks for additional evidence, they must be prepared to present it.

For Persuasive Presentations *Outside* the Organization ■   When speaking outside the organization—at conventions, to educators, to customers, or to the general public—the best methods of using evidence are *method 3* (assertion plus evidence plus source plus qualifications of source) and *method 4* (assertion plus firsthand experience).

There are several reasons for using method 3. First, because these listeners do not know you personally, you enhance your credibility by citing sources that these listeners consider prestigious. Also, these listeners will expect knowledgeable speakers to include documented evidence in their presentations. To appear credible (and to improve your persuasiveness), you must meet the expectations of your listeners.

A second reason for using method 3 when speaking to the general public is that documented evidence may counteract opposing arguments that the listeners hear from other speakers. Communications researcher James McCroskey found that audiences were less affected by the opposing view (counterpersuasion) of a second speaker if the first speaker's message contained documented evidence.[20] Although undocumented evidence can be persuasive, once the listeners leave the speech environment, they may begin to think about the arguments, realize that no sources were cited, and begin to doubt the speaker. Later, when they are exposed to opposing views, they may be dissuaded from the speaker's viewpoint. However, if the speaker supports arguments with carefully documented, prestigious sources, the listeners may feel more confident in these arguments and consequently be less likely to be dissuaded by later opinions.

If you are already known as an authority, or if the person introducing you presents you to the audience as an authority, then method 4 (assertion supported by firsthand experience) will be effective. You can also combine methods 3 and 4.

Presenting One or Both Sides of Your Position ■   Before we conclude this section on evidence, there is one more question we need to discuss: Should business speakers present only the arguments that support their proposal, or should they introduce and then refute opposing arguments (counter-arguments)?[21]

- *Present only your side of the argument when the listeners already agree with your proposal.* Presenting negative arguments that they had not thought of (even if you refute them well) may create some doubt in the listeners' minds and sabotage your attempt at persuasion (boomerang effect).
- *Present only your side of the argument when your listeners know nothing about your topic* (too many arguments would cause confusion), *when you want them to take an immediate action* (such as donating money at the door as they leave), *or when there is very little chance that they will hear the other side from another speaker or the news media.*
- *Present both sides of the argument when the listeners are fairly knowledgeable on your topic, when they already disagree with your proposal, or when there is a good chance that they will hear the other side from another speaker or the news media.* Knowledgeable listeners, especially when they disagree with the speaker, are suspicious of speakers who present only one side of the topic. Presenting both sides also serves to "inoculate" the listeners against later opposing arguments.

According to William McGuire's "inoculation theory," inoculating a listener against opposing ideas is similar to inoculating a person against a disease.[22] The person who has never heard any negative arguments on a certain topic will be very susceptible to opposing arguments just as the person who has lived in a germ-free environment is susceptible to catching a disease. We can create immunity by giving a shot containing a weakened form of the disease, or in the case of a presentation, by presenting a brief look at opposing arguments along with their refutation (facts and logic disproving the arguments). Then, when the listener hears opposing arguments, he or she can say, "Oh, yes, I knew that. However, it's not important because research shows that . . ." Presenting both sides also seems to make listeners more resistant to additional new arguments that the speaker did not even cover.[23] Apparently, inoculating listeners gives them the immunity needed to continue building their own counterarguments. For example, when hearing a new argument the listener says, "I haven't heard this specific argument before, but based on the information I know, this argument couldn't be true because . . ."

To summarize, when speaking (formally or informally) to business audiences *within* the organization, you should normally *present both sides*. Regardless of whether your listeners agree or disagree with you, they will normally be well informed and in a position to hear opposing arguments. To show that you have thoroughly researched the problem, you need to discuss briefly the possible disadvantages—such as cost, limitations, or resulting problems—and then show how these disadvantages are minor compared to the many advantages of your proposal.[24]

Remember that presenting both sides does not mean that you give your opposition equal time. Presenting the other side means that you mention one or two objections to your plan (such as high cost) and then (1) show how each objection is based on inaccurate information or faulty reasoning, or (2) if an objection is accurate, show how this disadvantage is minor compared to the many advantages of your proposal. After all, every view has some disadvantages. *The key is to show that any disadvantage to your plan or position is minor.*

Credibility of the Speaker

Another important factor of persuasion is the credibility of the speaker. A **credible person** is someone whom others view as believable—someone in whom they can place their confidence. In general, research has found that the greater your credibility, the more persuasive you are.[25] The important role that speaker credibility plays in persuasion is illustrated by the decision-making practices of 137 executives and purchasing directors from 70 metal-working companies. The study found that when these executives and directors made decisions on awarding contracts, they were more than twice as likely to base their decisions on the credibility of the suppliers than on any other factor. They felt that finding someone with whom they could work well—someone who was honest and dependable—was even more important than finding a good price.[26]

Researchers have discovered that a speaker's credibility depends on such factors as the situation, the audience's involvement with the topic, and the audience's similarity to the speaker. Note the following research findings:

- Listeners who have very low involvement with the topic tend to be more persuaded by the expertise of the speaker than by the quality of arguments or evidence. However, listeners who are very involved with the topic are more persuaded by quality arguments than by the credibility of the speaker.[27] One explanation for this finding is that involved listeners are more likely to pay attention to and evaluate the arguments presented by the speaker, while listeners who are not involved with the topic are less interested in evaluating arguments and more likely to be influenced by impressions they have formed of the speaker.[28]
- When a persuasive message uses an audio or video mode, the level of listener persuasion is likely to be determined by the credibility of the

speaker; however, when the message is in the print mode, the level of listener persuasion is more likely to be determined by the data and quality of evidence.[29] This may be because print allows time for careful analysis of data, while audio and video do not—listeners must base their evaluation of a speaker's evidence on speaker credibility factors such as sincerity and trustworthiness.[30]

- Perceived similarity between audience members and the speaker may enhance persuasion in two basic ways.[31] Audience members may perceive attitudinal similarities between themselves and the speaker. Attitudinal similarities (even when these similarities don't relate specifically to the topic of the speech) result in increased audience liking for the speaker and a higher rating of *trustworthiness*.[32] Suppose you have a positive attitude toward pet ownership and discover from the speaker's attention getter that she has two pets at home. Would this similarity of attitude cause you to increase your liking of the speaker? Even if the speaker's topic happened to be on recycling? Research indicates that this occurs. However, speakers tend to be judged as more *competent* only when perceived similarities are *relevant* to the topic.[33]

A speaker's credibility seems to be the result of five basic elements: trustworthiness, competency, dynamism, objectivity,[34] and organizational rank.

Trustworthiness ■ Most listeners determine the credibility of various speakers by observing all five elements and averaging them together. However, when speakers appear untrustworthy, their credibility is questioned regardless of their other qualities.[35] Therefore, trustworthiness (honesty, fairness, integrity) is the most important of the five elements. Several factors seem to affect whether listeners perceive speakers as untrustworthy. For example, speakers who avoid eye contact, shift their eyes rapidly from place to place, or always look over the listeners' heads appear to be ashamed or to have something to hide and, as a result, may be judged untrustworthy. Speakers with poor articulation, breathy or nasal voices, or who speak either in a monotone or too rapidly are also perceived as less trustworthy.[36] In addition to having an effective delivery style, speakers can improve their perceived trustworthiness by presenting both sides of an argument and by appearing friendly and likeable.[37]

Competency ■ Another major factor of credibility is competency. Listeners are more likely to judge a speaker credible if they perceive the speaker as competent (knowledgeable, experienced, expert) on the topic. However, speakers who use "nonfluencies" while speaking are often judged as low on competence. **Nonfluencies** include such things as inaccurate articulation, vocalized pauses (like "uh," or "and uh"), and unnecessary repetition of words.[38] In addition to avoiding nonfluencies, you can appear competent by citing personal experiences that relate to the topic, by citing sources the listeners feel are prestigious, by speaking confidently, and by using high-quality visual aids.

Dynamism ■ Dynamism is another element of credibility. A dynamic speaker is one who is forceful, enthusiastic, and uses good vocal variety (discussed in Chapter 11). Can't you often distinguish the boss from the employee simply by the forcefulness of their deliveries? Speakers who avoid direct eye contact, are soft-spoken, use very little vocal emphasis, and appear hesitant give the impression that they are uncertain about what they are saying (incompetent) or that they are trying to deceive the listeners (untrustworthy). As a result, the listeners are less likely to be persuaded.

Also, at the same time, the dynamic speaker must also remain conversational. Researchers found that as speakers move from low to moderate levels of dynamism, they are perceived as more credible (moderately dynamic speakers are still considered conversational). However, as speakers move from moderate to extreme levels of dynamism, they are perceived as less conversational, less trustworthy, and less credible.[39] Speakers with more than moderately dynamic deliveries are perceived as unnatural and phony.

Objectivity ■ The fourth element of speaker credibility is objectivity. An objective speaker is one who is open-minded, impartial, and appears to view evidence and arguments in an unbiased manner. Speakers usually seem objective when they discuss all viewpoints of the proposal (of course, they must conclude by showing why their arguments are best).

Organizational Rank ■ In business, the formal position or rank of the speaker within the organization is another element of credibility—although perhaps less important than the others. More people would be impressed by a presentation given by the company's president or assistant vice president than by someone of lower rank. Therefore, "all other things being equal, the higher the organizational status of the speaker the higher his credibility and the greater the effect upon the audience."[40]

If the listeners don't know you and are unaware of your credibility, or if you have low credibility, some of the following suggestions might prove helpful:

■ Have a highly credible expert on the topic (or someone of higher rank) introduce you and establish you as a competent and trustworthy speaker. If you have low credibility, identify yourself *after* your presentation so that your listeners will be less likely to tune you out or ignore your message.

- Support your assertions with up-to-date, carefully documented evidence and sources that the listeners consider prestigious.[41] Identifying your views with those of a respected person or institution will increase your credibility considerably.

- Present both sides of an issue (the disadvantages as well as the advantages) to improve your credibility by showing your willingness to be fair and honest.

- Present your ideas in a smooth, forceful, and self-assured manner, while maintaining good eye contact with the listeners; this will help you appear more credible.[42] Careful preparation and practice help make a self-assured delivery.

- Establish a common ground with your listeners by identifying beliefs, organizations, or problems you share. Listeners are more likely to consider you credible if you are similar in some important way to them.[43] You may also demonstrate similar group membership by your dress and use of jargon.

- Be sure to recognize (in content or delivery) the formal status and knowledge of the listeners.[44] Suppose a speaker scheduled to present a proposal to a group of important managers shows up late, takes time to set up the overhead projector, presents roughly drawn charts, and discusses the proposal at a very elementary level. How much credibility would this speaker have by the end of the presentation? People do not like to be treated as though they are less important than their positions in the organization indicate. These managers would undoubtedly be insulted and less likely to be persuaded. Also, male speakers often lose their credibility with female listeners by referring to women as "girls," "gals," "honey," or other terms that disregard the formal status of women.

Psychological Needs of the Listeners

To be successful at persuasive speaking, you need more than credibility and a presentation that includes evidence plus sources plus qualifications; you also must adapt your arguments to the psychological needs of your listeners.[45] In fact, your audience may choose not to believe your evidence no matter how good it is. For example, remember a time when you had an argument with someone and you knew that the arguments and evidence you presented were correct. Yet when you presented these facts, their response was, "I don't care. I don't believe it." Frustrating, isn't it? As persuasive speakers, we need to remember that *it isn't evidence unless the*

Figure 13.3 Maslow's hierarchy of needs.

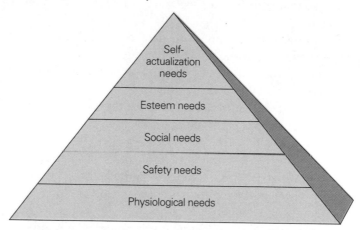

audience thinks it's evidence. However, if you can get your audience to relate personally to your evidence—to decide that your topic is important to them and their specific needs—they are more likely to consider your evidence as logical and reasonable.

The importance of relating to personal needs is illustrated by the following example:

> An excellent vice president had decided to retire early, much to the disbelief of his coworkers. All kinds of inducements (such as a substantial salary increase, more office help, and a new car) were offered to convince him to stay with the company. When inducements didn't work, his colleagues pointed out how much he was needed. Nothing was successful. On his last day with the company, he was having lunch in the executive dining room with the president and two other executives. The president began to discuss a completely new and risky project that the company was contemplating. Almost in jest, the president suggested that the vice president stay and head the new project. He accepted! None of the other appeals had related to his personal need for achievement. The challenge presented by the new project was something he could not resist.

Hierarchy of Needs ■ Discovering your listeners' basic needs and motives is an essential part of your audience analysis. Abraham Maslow tells us that all people have the same basic needs or drives, which are shown in Figure 13.3.[46] Think of these needs as the rungs of a ladder. Although people may be motivated by several levels at one time, generally a lower rung must be satisfied before the next rung becomes important. As each goal is fulfilled, it is replaced with another. Let's look at each of these basic needs:

- *Physiological needs.* Food, shelter, clothing, air, water, and sleep.
- *Safety needs.* A job and financial security; law and order; protection from injury, poor health, or harm; and freedom from fear.
- *Social needs.* Love, companionship, friendship, and a feeling of belonging to one or more groups.
- *Esteem needs.* Pride, recognition from others, status and prestige, and self-recognition.
- *Self-actualization needs.* Becoming the best person one can—developing to one's fullest capabilities and achieving worthwhile goals.

Because most of the presentations you will give will be within the organization, let's look specifically at the basic needs of employees and managers.

Needs That Motivate Employees ■ You will most likely be a manager at some time during your life, and as a manager you will want to inform as well as to persuade your employees. Even if you are not a manager, you may be asked to present certain information or ideas to your fellow employees. To be a successful communicator in either of these situations, you should know what needs motivate employees.

First, employees are motivated by *personal needs,* the five basic drives outlined by Maslow. Communication with employees who have unsatisfied personal needs is very difficult—their reactions serve as roadblocks to successful communication.[47] These reactions—anxiety, boredom, self-doubt, frustration, and bitterness—keep employees from paying careful attention or from showing an interest in your ideas or information (see Table 13.1). You cannot communicate successfully with people who do not want to listen to you. Such reactions also keep employees from believing you or from acting on your proposals.

Although employees are basically motivated by personal needs, they do have a second type of need—the *job-reward need.*[48] A job-reward need is the specific reward the employee gets for completing a specific goal or assignment in the organization. (Obviously, personal and job-reward needs overlap.) Consider the following example. Your company announces that a new position of troubleshooter is open for applications. The troubleshooter will have the responsibility of traveling to the various branch plants to fix the production problems that occur. Three people apply for the position: Jones, Harper, and Williams. All three are hard workers and are capable of handling the job. Although each wants the same job, their personal and job-reward needs differ, as shown in Table 13.2. Regardless of who is selected for the job, management needs to be aware of the person's job-reward needs in order to plan effective motivational appeals.

Table 13.1 Roadblocks to Successful Communication

Unsatisfied Personal Needs	→ Result in →	Roadblocks to Successful Communication*
Physiological needs		Pain, physical discomfort or impairment, illness
Security needs		Tension, anxiety, worry, fear, panic, danger
Social or love needs		Loneliness, boredom, feelings of being unloved or unloveable, low self-image
Esteem needs		Loss of confidence, low self-image, self-doubt
Self-actualization needs		Feelings of futility, alienation, bitterness, wasted chances, being at a "dead-end"

*Compiled from Robert E. Lefton et al., *Effective Motivation Through Performance Appraisal* (New York: Wiley, 1977), p. 79.

Table 13.2 Personal and Job-Reward Needs of Applicants

Applicant	Personal Needs	Job Reward Sought
Jones	Esteem needs (does not feel that current job carries enough status or prestige)	Wants the prestige and possible promotion that will come with the job
Harper	Achievement needs (feels that it is time to move into a new job for personal growth)	Wants the challenge and chance of achievement the job promises
Williams	Security needs (wants to take early retirement so needs to increase savings)	Wants the salary and overtime pay that will come with the job

Needs That Motivate Managers ■ For many employees, getting along with the boss consumes both time and energy. Chapter 3 described ways to communicate with the open, closed, blind, or hidden boss. We suggest you review those techniques. In addition, to communicate successfully, you will need to know what primary needs motivate managers (regardless of their level in the organization).

Maslow's five categories of needs relate to managers as well as to employees. Under normal business circumstances, managers' motives

REMEMBER, IF YOU ARE A MANAGER . . .

- Determine what personal needs employees are trying to satisfy.
- Discover what job rewards employees feel will help them satisfy their personal needs.
- Decide which employee needs can be satisfied without impeding organizational objectives.
- Explain the available opportunities for need satisfaction to employees and show how your information, ideas, or proposals can help them achieve the job rewards that will satisfy their personal needs. In an informative talk, this occurs only in the introduction; *in a persuasive talk, it occurs throughout.*[49]

REMEMBER, IF YOU ARE AN EMPLOYEE . . .

- Select two or three personal needs that your audience considers important. Ideally, every member of the audience should be trying to satisfy at least one of these personal needs.
- Establish a common ground with your audience by showing them that you have the same or similar gripes, complaints, concerns, or worries (these are really personal needs) about the job.
- Show how your ideas, information, or proposal will solve one or more of these gripes, complaints, concerns, or worries (you are actually showing them how your presentation will help satisfy their personal needs). In an informative presentation, this is usually done in the introduction; *in persuasive talks, it continues throughout the speech.*

seem to fall into three of the basic need categories—safety, esteem, and self-actualization. In fact, most managers fit into either of two categories: achievement seekers (achievement is a primary ingredient of self-actualization) and security and status seekers (need for security is part of Maslow's safety category and status is a major ingredient of esteem).[50]

REMEMBER, WHEN PRESENTING IDEAS
TO MANAGERS . . .

- For achievement-seeking managers, show how your idea or proposal will help the department, manager, or company achieve a particular goal.
- For security- or status-seeking managers, show how your idea or proposal relates to their basic needs of status and security. Perhaps your proposal will bring new work to the department, thereby increasing job security, or perhaps the idea will bring recognition and status to the department and its manager.
- Focus your report or proposal on its practical applications. Include documented proof if possible.
- Get to the point immediately. The manager's time is extremely valuable, so clearly state your main idea and purpose early in the presentation.

Managers who are *achievement seekers* are usually upper-level managers or executives who have deliberately worked to obtain their positions. They feel driven to achieve, want continuing challenges and responsibilities, and strive for creativity and excellence. Like all people, achievement seekers need security and status, but they view both security and status as by-products of their achievements, not major goals.[51]

Security and status seekers often become managers not by intent but through a series of promotions. They may be highly skilled in some technical area but feel somewhat unprepared for handling people. Consequently, they develop primary needs for security and status. Managers in this category are interested in achievement, but they tend to view it as a way to get security and status rather than as a goal in itself.

In addition to their personal needs, managers are motivated by the pressures and needs of the organization. As a consequence, managers tend to be more concerned with the task than with the needs of the people performing the task. This does not mean that managers aren't interested in their subordinates; most of them are. But the organization and related tasks are their primary concern. Furthermore, managers tend to be interested in a proposal only if you can show its practical application.[52]

Although we have given you a general view of manager and employee needs, don't forget that each person is an individual who is different from every other person. Before you prepare your report or proposal, find out the specific likes and dislikes of the manager or employees to whom you are presenting your ideas.

To summarize the section on psychological needs of listeners, remember that workers have two basic categories of needs: (1) personal needs, which include physical, safety, social, esteem, and self-actualization needs; and (2) job-reward needs, which include the specific rewards the worker gets for completing a goal or assignment in the organization. Managers are generally motivated by the need to achieve, the need for security or status, and by the pressures and needs of their organizations. Successful business speakers carefully analyze their listeners to determine their personal and job-reward needs and then relate their persuasive proposals to those needs.

Opinions of Other Listeners

In almost every group, there is a key person (or persons) whom others look to for advice. To persuade the group, the speaker must first persuade these key people or opinion leaders. Sociologists have found that[53]

- Opinion leaders tend to have slightly more formal education and a higher social status than the people to whom they give advice. Therefore, they serve as models to the others in their group.
- "Opinion leaders tend to be better informed in those areas about which they are consulted."
- "Opinion leaders talk to more people than non-leaders."

Opinion leaders are perceived as being more credible in certain areas. Therefore, if the opinion leader is opposed to the speaker's proposal, the group most likely will be opposed also. However, if the opinion leader favors the proposal, the group will tend to favor it. In a business setting, the key opinion leaders in a group may be the supervisors or managers. If you are speaking within the organization, it should be fairly easy to discover who the key people are and what their opinions are likely to be. Direct your arguments toward these people.

PERSUASIVE PRESENTATIONS: PREPARATION STEPS

If you follow the steps described here, you will be able to prepare successful persuasive presentations.

> PREPARATION STEPS FOR
> PERSUASIVE PRESENTATIONS
>
> 1. Analyze your expected listeners and their needs.
> 2. Write your exact purpose as a position statement.
> 3. Determine your initial credibility and plan to increase it if necessary.
> 4. Research your topic and determine the best method for presenting evidence to this audience.
> 5. Decide how to organize your presentation for the best effect.
> 6. Prepare an outline or storyboards to check verbal and visual supports, introduction, and conclusion.
> 7. Review your presentation to ensure it is ethical.
> 8. Practice your presentation to gain confidence.

Step 1: Analyze Your Expected Listeners and Their Needs

In general, you should obtain the same information about your listeners as you would when preparing an informative presentation. In addition, you need to identify the people who are likely to influence the decisions of the other listeners. Plan your presentation for these key people.

If you want to be persuasive, you must show how your proposal will help fulfill one or more of your listeners' needs. Earlier, we compared Maslow's hierarchy of needs to a ladder with rungs. If your listeners have several needs (as most people do), begin with the lowest needs that relate to your topic, and relate your proposal to those needs (see Figure 13.4). For example, during the Vietnam War, American propaganda pamphlets appealing to the high ideals of democracy were found to be ineffective on the typical Vietnamese soldier, who was starving. "Join us and get two chickens and a bag of rice" would have been a more effective appeal, wouldn't it? Similarly, if your listeners were concerned with job security and were worried about having enough money to pay their bills, appealing to their desire for self-actualization or their sense of pride would probably be an ineffective way to motivate them to work harder. However, you would likely have more success if you explained how increased productivity would not only help secure their jobs in the department but would also get them raises at their next evaluation. *The relationship between listener needs and persuasion is very strong. Don't underestimate it.*

Figure 13.4 Relating listeners' needs to a successful persuasive approach.

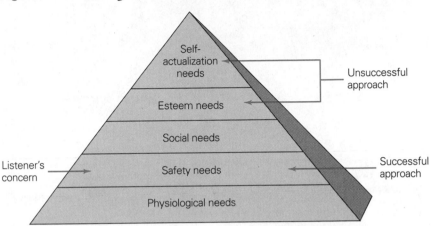

Step 2: Write Your Exact Purpose as a Position Statement

Before writing your purpose, you must determine exactly what reaction you hope to elicit from your listeners. Are you hoping to reinforce a current belief or inspire agreement (presentation to convince), or to request some specific action (presentation to actuate)? Write your exact purpose in the form of a position statement—a simple sentence that states exactly how you feel about the issue you have chosen. A sample position statement for a presentation to actuate might be: "Everyone should take an active role in seeing that cigarette advertising is banned from all sports events."

Step 3: Determine Your Initial Credibility and Plan to Increase It If Necessary

If your listeners have met you previously, or have heard about you, or have heard about your department or company, you already have some credibility with them. If this initial credibility is positive, it will add to your persuasiveness; if it is negative, you will need to supplement your initial credibility in one or more of the ways suggested earlier in this chapter.

One study has shown that 25 to 75 percent of the customers of small businesses less than ten years old come from referrals.[54] Obviously, employee credibility and company credibility are important to sales, both at the time of presentation and after. A salesperson can continue bolstering personal and company credibility even after a sale:

> A telephone call to find out how it's going is worth it; a follow-up session to check on progress; advertising to reassure customers that the purchase

Colin Powell, former Chairman of the Joint Chiefs of Staff, makes emotional contact with listeners when he speaks. *(© Ed Quinn/Saba)*

was a good one; follow-up mailing of thank you [notes]; feedback questions; newsletters to users; free information on related ideas/products/ services; are all statements of "We care."[55]

In a popular book, *You've Got to Be Believed to Be Heard*, Bert Decker advises the speaker that it is essential "to be liked, believed, and trusted. It's a matter of making emotional contact."[56] Once you've made emotional contact with your audience (as do Lee Iacocca, Jane Pauley, and Colin Powell), once they trust and like you, then—and only then—will they really hear you.

Step 4: Research Your Topic and Determine the Best Method for Presenting Evidence to This Audience

Review the methods for presenting evidence discussed earlier in this chapter. Don't forget to use a variety of supporting materials to clarify and add interest, as well as to support your arguments.

Step 5: Decide How to Organize Your Presentation for the Best Effect[57]

Persuasive speakers select from five main patterns when organizing the main points in the body of their presentation: claim pattern (inductive and deductive), causal pattern, problem–solution pattern (problem–solution–

Figure 13.5 Organizational patterns for persuasive presentations.

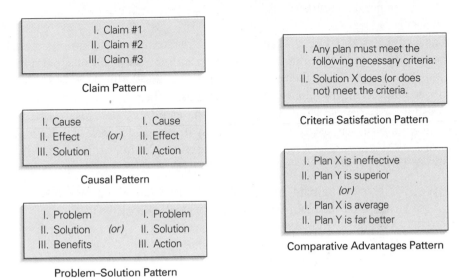

PERSUASIVE PATTERNS

I. Claim #1
II. Claim #2
III. Claim #3

Claim Pattern

I. Cause   I. Cause
II. Effect *(or)* II. Effect
III. Solution   III. Action

Causal Pattern

I. Problem   I. Problem
II. Solution *(or)* II. Solution
III. Benefits   III. Action

Problem–Solution Pattern

I. Any plan must meet the
   following necessary criteria:

II. Solution X does (or does
    not) meet the criteria.

Criteria Satisfaction Pattern

I. Plan X is ineffective
II. Plan Y is superior
        (or)
I. Plan X is average
II. Plan Y is far better

Comparative Advantages Pattern

benefits or problem–solution–action), comparative advantages pattern, and criteria satisfaction pattern (see Figure 13.5).

Claim Pattern ■ In the claim pattern, the problem is reviewed in the introduction step and the reasons for believing (or not believing) a particular fact, for holding (or not holding) a particular value, or for advocating (or not advocating) a particular plan are presented in the body of the presentation. Although the claim pattern is similar to the topical pattern used in informative presentations, the language is definitely persuasive. The claim pattern often involves the use of either inductive or deductive reasoning. **Inductive reasoning** involves presenting the specific evidence first, then building up to the general conclusion; **deductive reasoning** involves presenting the position or general conclusion first, then providing the supporting evidence. For example, a speech advocating prison reform before a potentially hostile audience might use the following inductive claim pattern:[58]

I. Prison spending costs society over $20 billion each year. [**claim 1:** specific evidence]

II. Much of this expense goes to provide recreational equipment and services that even many taxpayers can't afford. [**claim 2:** specific evidence]

III. In addition, civil lawsuits filed by inmates are clogging federal and state courts. [**claim 3:** specific evidence]

IV. It's time to end the resort status of American prisons. [**claim 4:** general conclusion]

Causal Pattern ■ The causal pattern in persuasive presentations uses cause–effect reasoning that is followed by either a solution or an action step (see Figure 13.5). Because you are using cause–effect reasoning to prove your point, it's important that the cause–effect relationship you are presenting is real and not just a chance happening. The causal organization pattern was used by Jeff Davidson in his speech entitled "Overworked Americans or Overwhelmed Americans? You Cannot Handle Everything":[59]

I. The overwhelmed, pressured feeling that Americans have is caused by the complexity of our society. [**cause**]
A. Population growth
B. Expanding volume of knowledge
C. Mass media and electronic growth
D. Paper trail culture
E. Overabundance of choices

II. As complexity increases, these pressured feelings will turn into feelings of overwork and total exhaustion. [**effect**]

III. It's not too late to take control of your life. [**action**]
A. Make choices in what to ignore.
B. Avoid engaging in low level decisions.
C. Learn to enjoy yourself.

Problem–Solution Pattern ■ The problem–solution pattern can take a variety of forms. The two most popular forms are the problem–solution–benefits and the problem–solution–action patterns. Both patterns begin with a detailed discussion of the problem, its seriousness, and its effect on the audience. Next, a solution (or solutions) is presented to solve or improve the problem. Finally, additional benefits resulting from your solution are described or a particular course of action is recommended to the audience. Nevin S. Scrimshaw used a problem–solution–benefit pattern in his speech entitled "The Consequences of Hidden Hunger":[60]

I. The magnitude and consequences of hidden hunger still devastate a large proportion of the world's population. [**problem**]

II. Hunger can be abolished as a public health problem in the world if we are willing to take the required actions. [**solution**]

III. Conquering hunger will release human potential for creating better societies. [**benefits**]

A student's speech on drunk drivers used a problem–solution–action pattern of organization:

I. The high number of auto–alcohol-related accidents indicates a serious problem. [**problem**]
   A. Nationally, 2 of 5 involved in auto–alcohol accidents.
   B. Nationally, 17,000 killed in auto–alcohol accidents.
   C. In our state, 1,800 killed in auto–alcohol accidents.
II. There are several workable solutions to the DWI problem. [**solutions**]
   A. Year-round sobriety checkpoints
   B. Legal blood-alcohol level lowered from 0.1 to 0.08
   C. Stronger penalties for drunk driving
III. Action must be taken now. [**action**]
   A. "Lights-on-for-life" promotion
   B. Letter to senators

Comparative Advantages Pattern ■   The comparative advantages pattern of organization is normally used when your audience already agrees with you on the problem but may not agree on the solution. Only a brief mention of the problem is needed during the speech introduction. The comparative advantages pattern concentrates on the advantages of one course of action over another. Usually, you will want to show that one course of action is greatly inferior over your more desirable plan for a number of reasons. However, it is possible that the current plan is OK, but it just doesn't have the advantages of your plan. In his speech on "Aid to Russia" Lawrence M. Lesser used the comparative advantages pattern:[61]

I. The current method of giving aid to Russia in the form of cash grants, loans, and credit guarantees isn't working. [**current plan is ineffective**]
   A. Russia is in default on $600 million of interest payments on $4.2 billion of U.S. agricultural credit guarantees used to purchase American grain.
   B. Russia has failed to pay $200 million in debts it owes to 57 American companies.
   C. Russia has defaulted on payments on the $4.5 billion it borrowed from international lenders forcing the U.S. to pay $180 million in loan loss claims.
II. Bartering, a concept Russia is very familiar with, is a much better way of providing aid to Russia. [**new plan is superior**]

Criteria Satisfaction Pattern ■   Whether you are dealing with products, services, or ideas, the criteria satisfaction pattern is a successful tool that works well even when audience members oppose your position. First, you establish criteria (guidelines or rules) that should be followed when evaluating possible plans or solutions (We all want our managers to be knowledgeable and fair). Second, you show how your plan meets or exceeds the established criteria (Not only is Manager X knowledgeable and fair, she is also a dynamic speaker). Of course, it's important to carefully consider your audience's values and needs when selecting and explaining why your criteria are important. If you can get your audience to agree with your criteria, the chances are good that they will also agree with your plan. Using the criteria satisfaction pattern, Farah Walters, president and chief executive officer of University Hospitals of Cleveland and a member of President Clinton's National Health Care Reform Task Force, gave a speech called "If It's Broke, Fix It: The Significance of Health Care Reform in America":[62]

I. Any health care plan should be measured against six fundamental principles: [**necessary criteria**]
   A. Provide security for all Americans.
   B. Provide choice of physician.
   C. Provide continuity of care.
   D. Be affordable to the individual, to business, and to the country.
   E. Be comprehensive in terms of coverage.
   F. Be user friendly for consumers and providers.
II. The health care plan designed by the National Health Care Reform Task Force meets all six of these fundamental principles. [**plan meets criteria**]

In addition to the five primary organization patterns just discussed, persuasive presentations may use the motivated sequence.

The Motivated Sequence[63] ■ The motivated sequence was developed by communications professor Alan Monroe more than fifty years ago. It is similar to the problem–solution–action pattern and is especially effective with speeches to actuate using a statement of policy.[64] The motivated sequence is more than just a pattern of organization for your main points—it includes the introduction and conclusion as well. The motivated sequence involves five steps: attention, need, satisfaction, visualization, and action. Let's take a brief look at each step.

■ *Attention step.* In the attention step, you grab your listeners' attention (using any of the methods described in Chapter 11) so that they want to continue listening.

- *Need step.* In the need step, you direct the audience's attention to a specific problem that needs to be solved. Describe the problem using credible, logical, and psychological appeals (earlier in this chapter), and show how the problem relates specifically to your listeners.

- *Satisfaction step.* In this step, you satisfy the need by presenting a solution to the problem. The following basic framework is suggested: "(a) briefly state what you propose to do, (b) explain it clearly, (c) show how it remedies the problem, (d) demonstrate its workability, and (e) answer objections."[65] In demonstrating the workability and feasibility of the solution, as well as answering possible audience objections, be sure to use supporting materials that will support your statements (see Chapter 12).

- *Visualization step.* After you have presented the solution to your problem, vividly picture the future for your audience. Use either positive, negative, or contrast methods. In the positive method, you picture the improved future that the audience can expect when your solution is implemented. In the negative method, you picture the undesirable conditions that will continue to exist or will develop if your solution is not adopted. The contrast method uses both the positive and negative methods, beginning with the negative and ending with the positive. The purpose of this step is to "intensify audience desire or willingness to act—to motivate your listeners to believe, to feel, or to act in a certain way."[66]

- *Action step.* In the action step, you conclude your speech by challenging your audience to take a particular action—you want a personal commitment from them. Say exactly what you want them to do and how they can do it.

Check your knowledge of persuasive organization by taking the quiz in the Awareness Check box.

AWARENESS CHECK: PERSUASIVE PATTERNS[67]

Directions: The following are six mini-outlines, each with a title and main points. Identify how the main points of each outline are organized by selecting one of the following patterns: (a) claim, (b) causal, (c) problem–solution, (d) comparative advantages, or (e) criteria satisfaction.

(continued)

_____ 1. "Youth Violence"[68]
    I. Youth arrested for violent crimes is up 50 percent.
    II. Youth arrested for murder is up 128 percent.
    III. Youth killed by firearms is up 59 percent.
    IV. Neighborhood prevention programs are needed to control youth violence.

_____ 2. "Senseless or Sensible Divorce?"[69]
    I. When divorce is settled in court, it's expensive, lengthy, promotes destructive competition, and clogs the court system.
    II. Divorce settled by mediation solves these problems.
    III. In addition to solving basic divorce problems, mediation has an important benefit: It allows both parties time to stabilize personally.

_____ 3. "Overweight Americans"
    I. Losing weight by dieting has very few advantages.
    II. Losing weight by lowering fat intake has several important advantages.

_____ 4. "Becoming a Blood Donor"
    I. Blood donors are crucial to alleviating America's blood shortage.
    II. Blood donors are essential if new medical treatments (such as heart and bone marrow transplants) are to continue.
    III. Blood donors are paramount in disasters like the Oklahoma City bombing.

_____ 5. "Helping the Homeless"[70]
    I. Any workable solution to helping the homeless must meet the following guidelines:
        A. Respect the rights and dignity of the homeless.
        B. Require that the homeless work for shelter and food.
        C. Offer drug and alcohol prevention programs.
        D. Offer hope.
    II. Our community's attempt to help the homeless by giving them money and housing violates all of the above guidelines.

_____ 6. "Good Mothers Care for Their Children at Home"
    I. Many single mothers with children must put them in day care during work hours.
    II. In several recent cases, the court has taken custody from single mothers who placed their children in day care rather than caring for them at home.
    III. Such decisions are irresponsible and must be reversed.

ANSWERS

1. *a* claim pattern with inductive reasoning.
2. *c* problem–solution–benefits pattern.
3. *d* comparative advantages pattern.
4. *a* claim pattern.
5. *e* criteria satisfaction pattern.
6. *b* causal pattern.

Step 6: Prepare an Outline or Storyboards to Check Your Verbal and Visual Supports, Introduction, and Conclusion

Review Chapter 12 for suggestions on verbal and visual supporting materials. Reread the sections in Chapter 11 on outlines and storyboards as well as introduction and conclusion suggestions. Remember that persuasive conclusions must be *persuasive*. In addition to summarizing your position and ending in a memorable way, you should issue a challenge and/or appeal for action.

Step 7: Review Your Presentation to Ensure It Is Ethical

Ethical problems are more likely to occur in persuasive rather than informative situations. Speakers may be led into unethical behavior when they are deciding which emotional and logical appeals to use and how to establish speaker credibility. In Chapter 1 we defined ethics as "the moral principles that guide our judgments about the good and bad, right and wrong of communication."[71] It is not always easy to see the rightness and wrongness of communication. Does the end ever justify the means? How about a passenger who talks a hijacker into giving up his gun by telling the hijacker lies? How about a union leader who gets union members to vote a certain way by making up statistics? How about an advertising promoter who doubles previous sales by making false promises about a certain product? How about a student who invents the evidence used in his speech because he has no time for research due to a family illness? How about parents who greatly exaggerate a problem to convince their child not to participate in a highly dangerous activity?

What if any of the above people found out they had been lied to? Should the possibility of getting caught determine a speaker's ethical standards? Although we can't deny that ethics may depend at times on the situation, *real persuasion does not involve manipulation, trickery, coercion, or force*. In persuasion, the individual's right to decide cannot be prevented.

According to Joseph De Vito, an *ethical presentation* "facilitates the individual's freedom of choice by presenting the other person with accurate bases for choice."[72] On the other hand, De Vito says that *unethical presentations* "interfere with the individual's freedom of choice by preventing the other person from securing information relevant to the choices he or she will make."[73] With this definition, speakers who lie or twist evidence, or use extreme emotional or fear-threat appeals, would be considered unethical regardless of the rightness or goodness of their purpose.

Because speakers have a great deal of influence *on* their audiences, they also have a great deal of responsibility *to* their audiences. Lena Guerrero is an example of an influential person who abused this responsibility (one of her speeches contained falsehoods) and, as a result, lost a promising career in politics. In 1991, Guerrero was appointed railroad commissioner by Texas Governor Ann Richards. According to her resume, Guerrero had a degree from the University of Texas and was a member of Phi Beta Kappa, a scholastic honor society. In an address to the graduating class of Texas A&M, she told the graduates that she knew just how they were feeling at that moment because she remembered her graduation so well. In actual fact, Guerrero had never graduated (she still needed to complete six courses) and was not an honor student.[74] When she was first asked about the inaccuracies, Guerrero denied them, then later said she was "stunned to learn she had not graduated from UT," and finally, twelve days after the inaccuracies came to light, admitted that she had lied.[75] When she resigned from public office in September 1992, she told reporters:

> I now realize I have been in a hurry all my life. In my haste, I was reckless. . . . I allowed misperceptions, embellishments and errors of fact about my academic record to go uncorrected. . . . I've done a lot of soul-searching about how that happened. And the only thing I can say to you is perhaps you want something to be so much that you begin to believe it is.[76]

Perhaps to Guerrero she was only an "embellishment" away from graduating—she had six more courses to complete. However, to the American public, the embellishment was a falsehood that remained on her resume for twelve years before it was finally challenged.

In addition to researching carefully and reporting the truth, you must be careful not to plagiarize. *If you read an article (or hear an ad or TV program) and then use the information in that article, ad, or program in your speech without citing the source(s), even if you paraphrase the content, you are plagiarizing.* **Plagiarism** is using the ideas of someone else (whether paraphrased or word for word) without giving credit. Although plagiarism is a problem in any type presentation, be especially careful in persuasive presentations. Remember that being ethical is good business. For more on business ethics, read the sample speech entitled "The Right Way" in Appendix D.

Step 8: Practice Your Presentation to Gain Confidence

Work for a dynamic yet conversational delivery. While you practice, videotape your presentation if possible. Practice with your notes and visual aids. Practice makes it easier to manage any situational anxiety that may stifle your forcefulness. As you know, a dynamic yet relaxed delivery improves your credibility and persuasiveness.

TEAM PRESENTATIONS

In some organizations, team presentations of two or more people are more common than individual presentations. The team presentations given by IBM, for example, are well known in the industry. Team presentations are more common in larger organizations where the budgets are large and the stakes are high:

- A manufacturing team bidding on a building contract
- A productivity director and two assistants presenting a new productivity measurement system to the company's middle and upper managers
- A Xerox team presenting the benefits of its copy machine to a multimillion-dollar purchaser
- A cable TV company asking for a city franchise

However, team presentations can be successful with only two or three speakers and a limited budget. For example:

- A team of insurance salespersons explaining a policy to a client
- Two small business partners attempting to get a bank loan to start their business
- A team of educators asking for a grant from the National Endowment for the Humanities
- Employees presenting a new accounting procedure to a family-owned company

Team presentations have the obvious advantages of shared responsibility, more expertise during the presentation and the question–answer period, and an impressive appearance. But team presentations are difficult to coordinate, time-consuming, and fairly expensive.

Successful team presentations have smooth-flowing content, professional visual aids, and dynamic team performance. *(Courtesy of Hewlett-Packard)*

Effective Team Presentations[77]

Successful team presentations have three characteristics:

- Well-organized, well-supported, smooth-flowing content
- Creative, professional, and well-used visual aids
- Smooth, polished, and dynamic team performance

Content ■ Team presentations can be either informative or persuasive and should follow the basic steps discussed in Chapters 11 and 13. Preparing storyboards can be especially helpful to team members because they can view one another's ideas. We suggest that you tape each person's storyboards to the wall for ease of viewing by other members. While you read them, imagine that you are an audience member. Is each presentation completely clear? Are the main points obvious? Would you doubt any of the main points? What additional information or visual aids would ease those doubts? Does each member's presentation flow smoothly into the next? Finding and correcting problems early in the planning process is very important. Otherwise, you may be forced to make last-minute changes requiring new visuals. Then, instead of a relaxed dry run of the entire presentation, you'll have a tense, frantic session.

Visual Aids ■ Visual aids should be consistent in appearance throughout the presentation. If one member has professional-looking transparencies

Figure 13.6 Moving agenda charts.

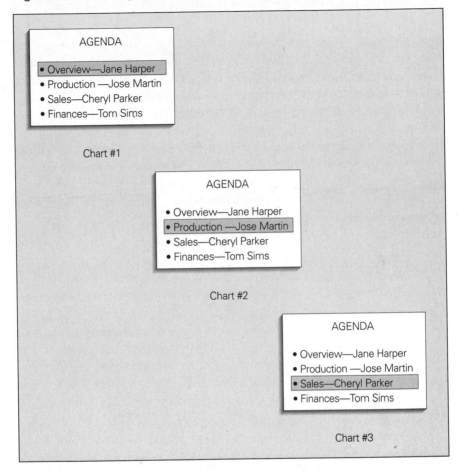

and another has handwritten ones, the overall impact is diminished. We suggest that all the team's visuals be prepared by one group member or by the graphic arts department in your organization. Review Chapter 12 for specific suggestions on preparing effective visual aids.

Moving agenda posters, flipcharts, or transparencies helps unify the team's presentation and clarify the overall organization for the audience (see Figure 13.6).

Team members should practice using their visual aids in front of at least one other team member, who can offer suggestions if needed. Awkward handling of visuals can ruin the effect of a well-organized presentation.

You can estimate the length of the team presentation by the number of visuals you plan to use. Most people spend 1 to 2 minutes per visual.

Twenty visual aids at 2 minutes per visual would make at least a 40-minute presentation. Stay within the time prearranged with your audience.

Performance ■ A smooth, polished, and dynamic team performance requires practice, revision, and more practice. Each member should practice alone, and then the team should have one or more dry runs of the entire presentation. Videotape the practice sessions if possible.

One team member needs to be the coordinator—preferably a member with past team experience or speaking experience and leadership abilities. If the team consists of more than four or five members, select a coordinator who is not one of the presenters. This person will be more objective in critiquing and directing the presenters. During the actual presentation, the coordinator presents the introduction and conclusion, provides transitions, and directs the question-and-answer session.

Adapting Team Presentations to the Media

Mass media, especially television and teleconferencing, are now used by businesses and organizations of all sizes to advertise products, project company image, answer criticisms, educate employees on company policy and procedures, and train employees in job skills. As your career advances, you will probably be asked to tape a team presentation for closed-circuit viewing or even to participate in a local talk show or news interview. You will feel much more relaxed and will help the process work more smoothly if you are aware of the following tips:[78]

- Do not wear white, unless you check with the producer ahead of time. Even a white shirt or blouse, white trim on clothes, or a white handkerchief in your suit pocket can give the camera technicians problems.
- Avoid stripes, polka dots, or patterns because they tend to bleed together. Solid colors are best.
- Avoid warm or hot colors such as red, pink, or orange. Cool colors (blues and greens) are preferred.
- Avoid clothing with sharp color contrast or clothes made of shiny material. A slight contrast is desirable, however. For example, a light-blue blouse or shirt would look good with a medium-blue suit. Men can add a darker blue tie. Men and women with blond hair should wear a darker blouse or shirt to give a slight contrast. Men and women with dark complexions should select colors that are either darker or lighter than their complexions.

- The camera will make you look heavier, so wear slenderizing clothes. Women usually prefer dresses or suits that are fitted or belted at the waist; men look slimmer in suits that are fairly tight at the waist.
- Avoid shiny jewelry (rings, necklaces, tie clasps, and so on).
- Men generally do not need makeup. If you have a heavy beard or a shiny forehead, the producer may want you to apply some powder. Women should wear regular makeup (eyeliner is suggested).
- Studio lights are hot, so you may wish to wear lightweight fabrics. If the lights are so bright that you are squinting, tell the floor manager so they can be adjusted.

Adapting your team presentation to the media is not difficult once the team members have become familiar with the technical equipment and environment used. Follow the advice just described and your team presentations will be as effective as your individual presentations to coworkers, managers, employees, and customers.

Summary

Persuasive presentations are formal or informal presentations designed to influence the audience's choices. Successful persuasion depends on the evidence and logic of the message, the credibility of the persuader, the psychological needs of the listeners, and the opinions held by key audience members.

Preparing a persuasive presentation begins with analyzing your listeners and their needs, writing your purpose, and planning ways to increase your credibility, if necessary. Following that, you must research your topic and decide on the best method of presenting the evidence, decide how to organize your presentation, plan the verbal and visual supports, ensure that your presentation is ethical, and practice the presentation.

Persuasive presentations are sometimes given as a team; such presentations are effective if the team presents well-organized, well-supported content, uses visual aids that are consistent in appearance and unify the overall presentation, and practices its performance. If your team presentation must be adapted to the media, you and your team members will need to become familiar with the media equipment and environment to be used and, as always, practice the presentation.

Dan Peoples, senior writer for Wicks Companies, Inc., tells how he and the chairman of a Fortune 500 corporation used persuasive presentations to convince Congress that the Environmental Protection Agency's "zero discharge" regulation was unnecessary and extremely expensive:

We decided to take our case directly to Congress. Having spent billions, and convinced that we were meeting the goal of the law, which was to "assure swimmable and fishable waters," we were going to try to convince Congress to take the "zero discharge" provision out of the law.

We began the effort on three fronts—lining up influential people who would listen to our pitch; preparing a top-notch presentation with snappy visuals; and putting together a media plan to guarantee some press coverage for the speech and take our case "to the people."

Beginning with a first draft that read like a treatise on industrial chemistry, I simplified and further simplified until we had five charts and four recommendations that even a congressman could understand.

I met with the company chairman. He made a few changes and added a great anecdote about the time he and Senator So-and-so went trout fishing a few miles downstream from one of our factories. Then we began to practice. We ran through the speech twice, reading from the text and making notes. We edited further, and we gave it once again.

Every presentation went beautifully. Our advance staff had set up the meeting rooms to give him favorable position, sound projection, and presence. The press was there, and we made sure there was plenty of opportunity afterward for photos of the chairman posing with his charts. We recorded the speech for later use in reprints and news releases.

In the end our position of reasonable enforcement and "swimmable and fishable waters" won out over more jobs for regulators and higher prices for consumers. The speech itself didn't turn the Congress around. But the effectiveness of the presentation, and the many uses we made of it, gave us the visibility we needed to gain some momentum on the issue.

Our victory saved the industry—and the U.S. consumers—billions, money that can now be invested to create jobs. We still call it the 15-billion-dollar speech.[79]

We hope we have not only convinced you that speaking skills are necessary for successful business and professional people but also have included enough specific information in this chapter to enable you to prepare an effective persuasive presentation. Speaking skill is not learned overnight—it takes practice. Rather than trying to avoid speaking assignments, *volunteer* for them if you are serious about improving your speaking skills. With careful planning and practice, you can become a successful speaker.

CHECKPOINT

Check your understanding of Chapter 13 by completing the following exercises:

1. Select a topic suitable for a persuasive presentation and decide on a hypothetical audience. What method of presenting evidence would work

best for this group? Get feedback on your decision from an experienced speaker.

2. Ask several businesspeople you know what persuades them most: evidence, speaker credibility, personal or departmental needs, or other listeners' opinions? Do their responses agree with this chapter?

3. Take a tour through a television recording studio. Familiarize yourself with the camera lights and microphones. Ask questions. If possible, observe a team presentation of some type.

4. Prepare a 10-minute persuasive presentation on a topic you deal with regularly. Videotape yourself if possible. How do you sound? Did you notice any nonverbal problems? Why not volunteer to give this presentation to a real audience? After all, by now you are a professional speaker, right? Even professional speakers need to practice.

5. Read and analyze a persuasive presentation from Appendix D. If you had been the presenter, how would you have made it more persuasive?

NOTES

1. John E. Baird, Jr., "How to Overcome Errors in Public Speaking," *Personnel Journal* 59 (March 1980), p. 206.
2. T. W. Harrell and M. S. Harrell, *Stanford MBA Careers: A 20 Year Longitudinal Study* (Stanford Graduate School of Business Research Paper No. 723, 1984).
3. K. E. Kendall, "Do Real People Ever Give Speeches?" *Central States Speech Journal* 25 (1974), p. 233.
4. William S. Howell and Ernest G. Bormann, *Presentational Speaking for Business and the Professions* (New York: Harper & Row, 1979), p. 92.
5. Used by Winston L. Brembeck and William S. Howell in their short course, "Teaching the College Level Course in Persuasion," presented at the Speech Communication Association's 61st Annual Convention in Houston, December 30, 1975.
6. Wallace C. Fotheringham, *Perspectives on Persuasion* (Boston: Allyn & Bacon, 1966), p. 32.
7. James C. McCroskey, "A Summary of Experimental Research on the Effect of Evidence in Persuasive Communication," *Quarterly Journal of Speech* 55 (April 1969), pp. 169–176.
8. Kathleen Bell, *Developing Arguments: Strategies for Reaching Audiences* (Belmont, CA: Wadsworth, 1990), p. 262.
9. Erwin P. Bettinghaus and Michael J. Cody, *Persuasive Communication*, 4th ed. (New York: Holt, Rinehart & Winston, 1987), pp. 150–151; R. C. Ruechelle, "An Experimental Study of Audience Recognition of Emotional and Intellectual Appeals in Persuasion," *Speech Monographs* 25 (1958), p. 58; W. R. Dresser, "Effects of 'Satisfactory' and 'Unsatisfactory' Evidence in a Speech of Advocacy," *Speech Monographs* 30 (August 1963), pp. 302–306; James C. McCroskey, "The Effects of Evidence in Persuasive Communication," *Western Speech* 3 (1967), pp. 189–199.
10. R. E. Petty and J. T. Cacioppo, "The Effects of Involvement on Response to Argument Quantity and Quality: Central and Peripheral Routes to Persuasion," *Journal of Personality and Social Psychology* 46 (1984), pp. 69–81.
11. Donald D. Morley and K. B. Walker, "The Role of Importance, Novelty, and Plausibility in Producing Belief Change," *Communication Monographs* 54 (1987), pp. 436–442, and Donald D. Morley, "Subjective Message Constructs: A Theory of Persuasion," *Communication Monographs* 54 (June 1987), pp. 183–203.
12. Bettinghaus and Cody, p. 151.
13. Robert S. Cathcart, "An Experimental Study of the Relative Effectiveness of Four Methods of Presenting Evidence," *Speech Monographs* 22 (August 1955), pp. 227–233; Dresser, pp. 302–306.
14. James C. McCroskey, "The Effects of Evidence as an Inhibitor of Counter-Persuasion," *Speech Monographs* 37 (August 1970), pp. 188–194.

15. H. Gilkinson, S. F. Paulson, and D. E. Sikkink, "Effects of Order and Authority in an Argumentative Speech," *Quarterly Journal of Speech* 40 (1954), pp. 183–192; Cathcart, pp. 227–233; Robert N. Bostrom and Raymond K. Tucker, "Evidence, Personality, and Attitude Change," *Speech Monographs* 36 (March 1969), pp. 22–27; T. H. Ostermeier, "Effects of Type and Frequency of Reference upon Perceived Source Credibility and Attitude Change," *Speech Monographs* 34 (June 1967), pp. 137–144.

16. A. R. Cohen, *Attitude Change and Social Interaction* (New York: Basic, 1964), pp. 6–7.

17. Z. Ginossar and Y. Trope, "The Effects of Base Rates and Individuating Information on Judgements About Another Person," *Journal of Experimental Social Psychology* 16 (1980), pp. 228–242; J. Reinard, "The Empirical Study of the Persuasive Effects of Evidence," *Human Communication Research* 15 (1988), pp. 3–59; T. R. Koballa, Jr., "Persuading Teachers to Reexamine the Innovative Elementary Science Programs of Yesterday: The Effect of Anecdotal Versus Data-Summary Communications, *Journal of Research in Science Teaching* 23 (1989), pp. 437–449.

18. Dean C. Kazoleas, "A Comparison of the Persuasive Effectiveness of Qualitative Versus Quantitative Evidence: A Test of Explanatory Hypotheses," *Communication Quarterly* 41 (Winter 1993), pp. 40–50.

19. Ostermeier, pp. 137–144; D. Papageogis, "Bartlett Effect and the Persistence of Induced Opinion," *Journal of Abnormal and Social Psychology* 67 (1963), pp. 61–67.

20. McCroskey, "The Effects of Evidence as an Inhibitor of Counter-Persuasion," pp. 188–194.

21. M. A. Kamins and L. J. Marks, "Advertising Puffery: The Impact of Using Two-Sided Claims on Product Attitude and Purchase Intention," *Journal of Advertising* 16 (1987), pp. 6–15; A. Lumsdaine and I. Janis, "Resistance to 'Counter-Propaganda' Produced by a One-Sided Versus a Two-Sided 'Propaganda' Presentation," *Public Opinion Quarterly* 17 (1943), pp. 311–318; C. I. Hovland, A. A. Lumsdaine, and F. D. Sheffield, *Experiments on Mass Communication* (Princeton, NJ: Princeton University Press, 1949); C. I. Hovland, A. A. Lumsdaine, and F. D. Sheffield, "The Effects of Presenting 'One-Side' vs. 'Both Sides' in Changing Opinions on a Controversial Subject," in *Experiments in Persuasion*, Ralph L. Rosnow and Edward J. Robinson, eds. (New York: Academic, 1967), pp. 201–225; E. McGinnies, "Studies in Persuasion: III. Reactions of Japanese Students to One-Sided and Two-Sided Communications," *Journal of Social Psychology* 70 (1966), pp. 91–93; J. R. Weston, "Argumentative Message Structure and Message Sidedness and Prior Familiarity as Predictors of Source Credibility," Ph.D. dissertation, Michigan State University, 1967.

22. For a detailed discussion of inoculation theory, see Daniel J. O'Keefe, *Persuasion: Theory and Research* (Newbury Park, CA: Sage, 1990), pp. 179–182; for a review of his work on inoculation theory, see William J. McGuire, "Attitudes and Attitude Change," in *The Handbook of Social Psychology*, 3rd ed., Vol. 2, G. Lindzey and E. Aronson, eds. (New York: Random House, 1985), pp. 233–346.

23. B. Pryor and T. M. Steinfatt, "The Effects of Initial Belief Level on Inoculation Theory and Its Proposed Mechanisms," *Human Communication Research* 4 (1978), pp. 217–230; see also D. Papageogis and William McGuire, "The Generality of Immunity to Persuasion Produced by Pre-Exposure to Weakened Counterarguments," *Journal of Abnormal and Social Psychology* 62 (1961), pp. 475–481.

24. R. G. Hass and D. E. Linder, "Counterargument Availability and the Effects of Message Structure on Persuasion," *Journal of Personality and Social Psychology* 23 (1972), p. 227.

25. For an excellent review of source credibility research, see O'Keefe, pp. 130–140; S. Zagona and M. Harter, "Credibility of Source and Recipient's Attitude: Factors in the Perception and Retention of Information on Smoking Behavior," *Perceptual and Motor Skills* 23 (1966), pp. 155–168; C. Hovland and W. Weiss, "The Influence of Source Credibility on Communication Effectiveness," *Public Opinion Quarterly* 15 (1951), pp. 635–650.

26. Roger P. Wilcox, *Communication at Work: Writing and Speaking*, 3rd ed. (Boston: Houghton Mifflin, 1987), pp. 301–302.

27. R. E. Petty and J. T. Cacioppo, "The Elaboration Likelihood Model of Persuasion," in *Advances in Experimental Social Psychology*, Vol. 19, L. Berkowitz, ed. (San Diego: Academic, 1986), pp. 123–205; for more recent research, see A. Tesser and D. R. Shaffer, "Attitudes and Attitude Change," *Annual Review of Psychology* 41 (1990), pp. 479–523, and S. Ratneshwar and S. Chaiken, "Comprehension's Role in Persuasion: The Case of Its Moderating Effect on the Persuasive Impact of Source Cues," *Journal of Consumer Research* 18 (1991), pp. 52–62.

28. This explanation is suggested by research following the Elaboration Likelihood Model (ELM) developed by R. E. Petty and J. T. Cacioppo, *Attitudes and Persuasion: Classic and*

Contemporary Approaches (Dubuque, IA: Wm. C. Brown, 1981). For an explanation, see Alice H. Eagly and Shelly Chaiken, *The Psychology of Attitudes* (Fort Worth: Harcourt Brace Jovanovich, 1993), pp. 305–325, or Kathleen K. Reardon, *Persuasion in Practice* (Newbury Park, CA: Sage, 1991), pp. 68–70.

29. Steve Booth-Butterfield and Christine Gutowski, "Message Modality and Source Credibility Can Interact to Affect Argument Processing," *Communication Quarterly* 41 (Winter 1993), pp. 77–89.

30. S. Chaiken and A. Eagly, "Communication Modality as a Determinant of Persuasion: The Role of Communicator Salience," *Journal of Personality and Social Psychology* 45 (1983), pp. 241–256.

31. For a detailed analysis of research on similarity, see O'Keefe, pp. 148–151.

32. E. Berscheid, "Interpersonal Attraction," in *The Handbook of Social Psychology*, pp. 413–484; R. L. Applbaum and K. W. Anatol, "The Factor Structure of Source Credibility as a Function of the Speaking Situation," *Speech Monographs* 39 (1972), pp. 216–222.

33. O'Keefe, p. 150.

34. Raymond G. Smith, "Source Credibility Context Effects," *Speech Monographs* 40 (1973), pp. 303–309; Jack R. Whitehead, "Factors of Source Credibility," *Quarterly Journal of Speech* 54 (1968), pp. 61–63.

35. Smith, p. 309.

36. David W. Addington, "The Effects of Vocal Variations on Ratings of Source Credibility," *Speech Monographs* 38 (1971), pp. 242–247.

37. S. Chaiken, "Physical Appearance and Social Influence," in *Physical Appearance, Stigma, and Social Behavior: The Ontario Symposium*, Vol. 3, C. P. Herman, M. P. Zanna, and E. T. Higgins, eds. (Hillsdale, NJ: Erlbaum, 1986), pp. 143–177.

38. James C. McCroskey and R. S. Mehrley, "The Effects of Disorganization and Nonfluency on Attitude Change and Source Credibility," *Speech Monographs* 36 (1969), pp. 13–21; James C. McCroskey and T. J. Young, "Ethos and Credibility: The Construct and Its Measurement After Three Decades," *Central States Speech Journal* 32 (1981), pp. 24–34.

39. W. Barnett Pearce and Forrest Conklin, "Nonverbal Vocalic Communication and Perceptions of a Speaker," *Speech Monographs* 38 (1971), p. 241.

40. Howell and Bormann, p. 29.

41. R. Norman, "When What Is Said Is Important: A Comparison of Expert and Attractive Sources," *Journal of Experimental Social Psychology* 12 (1976), pp. 83–91.

42. McCroskey, "Summary of Experimental Research," pp. 169–176; R. Rosnow and E. Robinson, eds., *Experiments in Persuasion* (New York: Academic, 1967), pp. 2–5; Albert Mehrabian and Martin Williams, "Nonverbal Concomitants of Perceived and Intended Persuasiveness," *Journal of Personality and Social Psychology* 13 (1969), pp. 37–58.

43. J. Miles and J. Jellison, "Effect on Opinion Change of Similarity Between the Communicator and the Audience He Addresses," *Journal of Personality and Social Psychology* 9 (1968), pp. 153–156.

44. Howell and Bormann, p. 30.

45. For a detailed discussion of motivation, see Thomas E. Harris, *Applied Organizational Communication: Perspectives, Principles, and Pragmatics* (Hillsdale, NJ: Erlbaum, 1993), pp. 425–459.

46. Abraham Maslow, *Motivation and Personality* (New York: Harper & Brothers, 1954).

47. Adapted from Robert E. Lefton, V. R. Buzzotta, Manuel Sherberg, and Dean L. Karraker, *Effective Motivation Through Performance Appraisal* (Cambridge, MA: Ballinger, 1980), p. 77.

48. Lefton, Buzzotta, Sherberg, and Karraker, p. 77.

49. Adapted from Dan R. Costley and Ralph Todd, *Human Relations in Organizations* (St. Paul: West, 1978), pp. 169–170.

50. Wilcox, pp. 38–60.

51. For a more complete discussion of the need for achievement, see David McClelland, *The Achieving Society* (Princeton, NJ: Van Nostrand, 1961).

52. Wilcox, pp. 44–48.

53. Bettinghaus and Cody, pp. 96–97.

54. Harriet Buckman Stephenson, "The Most Critical Problem for the Fledgling Small Business: Getting Sales," *American Journal of Small Business* 9 (Summer 1984), p. 27.

55. Stephenson, p. 31.

56. Bert Decker, *You've Got to Be Believed to Be Heard* (New York: St. Martin's, 1991), p. 9.

57. Cheryl Hamilton, *Successful Public Speaking* (Belmont, CA: Wadsworth, 1993), pp. 393–398.

58. Information taken from Robert James Bidinotto, "Must Our Prisons Be Resorts?" *Reader's Digest* 145 (November 1994), pp. 65–71.
59. Jeff Davidson, "Overworked Americans or Overwhelmed Americans? You Cannot Handle Everything," *Vital Speeches* 59 (May 15, 1993), pp. 470–473.
60. Nevin S. Scrimshaw, "The Consequences of Hidden Hunger: The Effect on Individuals and Societies," *Vital Speeches* 58 (December 15, 1991), pp. 138–144.
61. Lawrence M. Lesser, "Aid to Russia: Barter Transactions," *Vital Speeches* 59 (August 15, 1993), pp. 651–653.
62. Farah M. Walters, "If It's Broke, Fix It: The Significance of Health Care Reform in America," *Vital Speeches* 59 (September 1, 1993), pp. 687–691.
63. Hamilton, pp. 406–407.
64. Bruce E. Gronbeck, Raymie E. McKerrow, Douglas Ehninger, and Alan H. Monroe, *Principles and Types of Speech Communication*, 12th ed. (New York: HarperCollins, 1994), p. 196.
65. Gronbeck, McKerrow, Ehninger, and Monroe, p. 209.
66. Gronbeck, McKerrow, Ehninger, and Monroe, p. 211.
67. Hamilton, pp. 399–401.
68. Information from Bill Moyers, "There Is So Much We Can Do," *Parade Magazine*, January 8, 1995, pp. 4–6.
69. Based on information in a speech given by Carl Wayne Hensley, "Divorce—The Sensible Approach," *Vital Speeches* 60 (March 1, 1994), pp. 317–319.
70. Based on information in Randy Fitzgerald, "A Hand Up—Not a Handout," *Reader's Digest* 145 (November 1994), pp. 161–165, 168.
71. Pamela Shockley-Zalabak, *Fundamentals of Organizational Communication* (New York: Longman, 1988), p. 326.
72. Joseph A. De Vito, *The Interpersonal Communication Book*, 5th ed. (New York: Harper & Row, 1989), p. 80.
73. De Vito, p. 80.
74. *Facts on File* 52 (November 26, 1992), p. 893, and *Fort Worth Star-Telegram*, September 24, 1992, Section A, pp. 1, 10, 17.
75. *Fort Worth Star-Telegram*, September 25, 1992, Section A, pp. 1, 5, 26.
76. The Associated Press, "Excerpts from Guerrero's Announcement," *Fort Worth Star-Telegram*, September 25, 1992, Section A, p. 4.
77. The information in this section is adapted from Thomas Leech, *How to Prepare, Stage, and Deliver Winning Presentations* (New York: AMACOM, 1982), pp. 333–347.
78. Evan Blythin and Larry A. Samovar, *Communicating Effectively on Television* (Belmont, CA: Wadsworth, 1985).
79. Prepared especially for this book by Dan Peoples, senior writer for Wicks Companies, Inc.

A

Survey of Communication Styles

The Survey of Communication Styles includes two parts: (1) the Manager Tendency Indicator (MTI) and (2) the Employee Tendency Indicator (ETI). Each part is designed to give you an indication of the style you tend to use when communicating with others.

Everyone should take both the MTI and the ETI. If you are, or have been, a manager (at any level), take the MTI first and the ETI second. If you have never been a manager, take the ETI first; then, when you take the MTI, assume that you are a manager and answer the questions the way you would most likely respond as a manager.

SURVEY OF COMMUNICATION STYLES*

Directions

Read each question carefully: First put an 8 in the answer box in front of the answer that *most closely* represents your feelings and the way you would react in the situation described. Next, put a 1 in front of the answer that *least closely* represents your feelings or the way you would react to the situation. Finally, for the two remaining answers, select the one that is most like what you would do and place a 4 in its answer box; put a 2 in the answer box for the last answer. In other words:

8 means that the answer to the question is most like you

4 is moderately like you

2 is barely like you

1 is least or not at all like you

You may not like any of the answers, or you may like all the answers. Regardless, you may *not* assign any question all 8s, all 4s, all 2s, or all 1s. *Only these four numbers may be used and all four must be used one time for each question.*

Be careful not to answer what you *wish* you would do or what *most people* would do. Instead, select the answers that most clearly represent what *you* would likely do in the situation described.

Manager Tendency Indicator

1. A new procedure is implemented by upper management. All supervisors are requested to monitor the success of the procedure and to let management know if any problems result. Your response:

---

*The Survey of Communication Styles was developed by Cheryl Hamilton in 1981 and revised in 1986.

_____ a.　Wait until a direct order for information is received before making any response. The wise person never volunteers information upward—it isn't safe. What is said is often distorted in some way.

_____ b.　If the new procedure is working well, don't wait for a direct request—send the report now. Promptness makes you look efficient. If the procedure isn't working, be very careful how the message is worded. There is no sense in upsetting the big bosses. Edit and word the report in such a way that any negative aspects are minimized.

_____ c.　If the procedure works, there would be no reason to report. However, if the procedure doesn't work, tell them about it. After all, they were the ones who suggested the idea. If it doesn't work, it should be dropped and replaced with something better.

_____ d.　It is best to send regular reports to upper management regardless of the success of the new procedure. Reports should include successes, failures, and attempts to solve problems. Even when a report contains information that may disappoint management, be complete and truthful.

2.　Your employees have become lax on a few of the company's minor restrictions. Your response:

_____ a.　No regulation or rule should be inflexible. Discuss the problem with the employees to see if they have valid reasons for their disapproval. If so, work with the group to determine an alternative. However, until the change is implemented, request the employees to abide by the regulation.

_____ b.　Strict rules and regulations are essential in well-run organizations. If employees are allowed to ignore some regulations, they may also begin to ignore others. No exceptions should be allowed.

_____ c.　Informality and harmony among employees is more important than a few minor regulations. If necessary to keep employees satisfied, overlook their behavior as long as possible.

_____ d.　It is necessary to follow all the organization's policies and procedures to keep supervisors and their departments out of trouble. Therefore, insist that employees abide by the regulation under discussion. If they complain, simply tell them the truth—the company made the rule, not you. Neither you nor they have any choice in the matter if you all want to keep your jobs.

3. The company has asked for your suggestions on how to motivate employees. Your response:

_____ a. People respond better to praise and rewards than they do to criticism or punishment. However, it is important to praise and reward all employees alike (even though some may be more capable than others). Praising only a few employees serves to decrease the motivation of others and creates bad feelings.

_____ b. Praise usually makes people think they are better than they really are. Therefore, the best way to motivate employees is through criticism. The best criticism occurs immediately after an employee makes a mistake.

_____ c. Praise and reward are good motivators only when they are given to an employee who has performed in an excellent manner. Other employees are then inspired to strive for similar rewards. There are times, however, when criticism and punishment are the best motivators.

_____ d. Actually, very little that a manager does really has any effect on employees (at least no lasting effect). Employees rarely change no matter what the boss does or what motivational techniques are used. Try to hire good people in the beginning.

4. A serious conflict has arisen among several employees in your department. Your response:

_____ a. Because conflict among employees disrupts work and decreases productivity, immediate action is necessary. Listen carefully to all sides and then tell them how you have decided the problem will be solved.

_____ b. Conflict can be productive when handled correctly. Therefore, if the problem doesn't solve itself fairly quickly, gather those involved in the dispute and encourage them to express their complaints openly. When conflicts are examined openly, a workable solution can usually be found. If not, you may have to arbitrate a solution.

_____ c. First of all, try to make sure that serious conflicts between employees never occur. Such conflicts only draw unwanted attention to the department. However, when conflict does occur, try to stay out of it. After all, it's their problem so they should solve it.

_____ d. Because conflict can permanently damage the friendly working environment of a department, try to ease the situation as soon as possible by showing its members how worthless conflict is.

5. One of your colleagues feels that managers not only should relate to employees in a friendly manner but also should share personal information with them. Your response:

_____ a. I disagree. Smart managers keep their distance from employees. All employees should be treated in the same general manner. No employee should be given special consideration.

_____ b. I disagree. The best way to handle employees is to be firm yet impersonal with them. They will respect you more that way.

_____ c. I agree. Employees react best when managers share experiences and feelings with them. People who are friendly work together better. Being friendly with employees doesn't have to harm the boss–employee relationship.

_____ d. I agree in part. Managers should be friends with their employees. Employees will produce more if they think you like them. Ask them about their families and so on, but keep fairly quiet about yourself. Personal information could be used against you in some way.

6. It is time for your company's annual performance appraisals of all employees. Your method of handling employee evaluations:

_____ a. Unfortunately, many managers have found that performance appraisals are usually a waste of time. Even when employees are open to what a manager has to say, they never seem to change. Therefore, keep the sessions short and fairly general. It is also a good idea to keep as few records as possible.

_____ b. Performance appraisals are an excellent time for evaluating the employee's past performance and setting new goals for the future. Both strengths and weaknesses should be considered. Get the employee actively involved in the evaluation so that the final appraisal will be agreeable to both of you.

_____ c. Criticism only serves to hurt people's feelings, and few people can be objective when discussing their weaknesses. Therefore, unless there is a serious problem, concentrate on the employee's strengths.

_____ d. Employee appraisals are quite valuable when used to instruct the employee on how to improve. Although some managers tend to beat around the bush, the direct approach works best. If they have done something wrong, tell them.

7. How much individual responsibility for decision making should employees be given? Your response:

_____ a. After careful training, employees should be given as much individual responsibility as they can handle and want. To be effective, they must be free to implement their decisions and must be accountable for any decisions made. The manager serves in an advisory capacity.

___ b. Many employees have enough training to take responsibility and make decisions. However, when given a free hand, they often make decisions for their personal gain rather than for the good of the company. A manager who gives individual responsibilities must watch for abuse of those freedoms.

___ c. Employees should be responsible for tasks assigned to them. However, since managers know more about employee jobs than employees do, any decisions made must receive manager approval. Really important decisions are usually made by managers.

___ d. Actually very little. Employee responsibility only increases the manager's responsibility of monitoring employees to make sure no decisions bring criticism to the department or its leadership.

8. Which approach to management actually works best? Your response:

___ a. Firm control at all times is the best approach to management. Getting suggestions from employees usually results in a needless waste of time. It is the manager's responsibility to make the necessary decisions.

___ b. Teamwork is the best approach to management. When managers and employees work together as a team and when all members make suggestions and feel free to agree or disagree, better solutions are reached.

___ c. The best approach to management is to keep a low profile and let employees work on their own as often as possible. When managers try to get involved with everything, they only disturb the smooth flow of things.

___ d. One of the most important things a manager can do is keep harmony in the office. Employees turn out more work when they feel friendly with each other.

9. As a manager, how do you view the company grapevine? Your response:

___ a. The grapevine is an excellent way to discover what employees are up to and what they are hiding from their manager.

___ b. Listening to the grapevine allows managers to determine areas of misunderstanding that need to be corrected, and leaking information into the grapevine is a good way to test ideas by judging employee response.

_____ c. Spying on employees and other managers through the grape-vine is necessary for survival.

_____ d. Listening to the grapevine helps managers maintain control over their employees.

10. One of your employees is having a personal problem that is beginning to interfere with the employee's quality of work. Your response:

_____ a. When managers try to get involved in the personal problems of employees, new (and sometimes worse) problems result. Therefore, ignore the situation as long as possible; hopefully, it will resolve itself.

_____ b. Let the employee know that regardless of the reason for the lack of productivity, certain standards must be met. If immediate improvement does not occur, the employee should be terminated.

_____ c. The employee may be taking advantage of the situation to get out of work. Therefore, have a private talk with the employee to discover the real reason for the behavior.

_____ d. As much as possible, managers need to meet the needs of employees. Discuss the problem with the employee, and see if either you or the company can do anything to help solve the employee's problem.

11. During a meeting with your employees, you are explaining each person's role in a forthcoming departmental task. Several employees express unhappiness with their assignments. Your response:

_____ a. To avoid conflict, blame upper management for the assignments and tell the employees that the department's standing depends on how well they complete their tasks.

_____ b. Tell the employees that the assignments have been given and that no changes will be made.

_____ c. Listen to all the arguments and then make whatever changes are necessary to keep group harmony.

_____ d. Listen to all the arguments and work with the group in determining what, if any, changes should be made.

12. Your department is assigned an important task. Unintentionally, you give your people the wrong instructions. Work is well underway when you discover the error. Your response:

_____ a. Admit the mistake and request their best efforts to complete the new assignment on schedule.

_____ b. At the next meeting, revise the instructions and make a joke of the mistake.

_____ c. Explain that upper management has issued new guidelines that will require a change in previous instructions.

_____ d. Tell the employees that they apparently misunderstood the previous instructions. Ask them to listen more closely this time.

Employee Tendency Indicator

1. From your experience, what is the only realistic way to deal with fellow workers?

_____ a. To get ahead, you must actively compete with other employees. Try to stay one step ahead of everyone.

_____ b. You can't be too careful. The chances are that even your friends will try to take over your job if it means advancement for them.

_____ c. A friendly approach is best even if your personal opinions make it necessary for you to pretend friendship.

_____ d. A friendly but truthful approach works best. However, when a misunderstanding occurs, it is important to express your true feelings.

2. While your boss is giving you instructions on how to complete a particular task, you realize that the instructions are wrong. What would you do?

_____ a. Question the boss to make sure you didn't misunderstand the instructions. Then, explain the problem as you see it.

_____ b. Errors such as this are typical, because a good employee usually knows twice as much as the boss. Press your advantage by pointing out the error.

_____ c. Pointing out an error to the boss is a good way to lose your job. Do whatever the boss tells you, regardless of what it is.

_____ d. If you point out the error, it could make the boss feel uncomfortable and even ruin your standing with the boss. Therefore, complete the task correctly, but say nothing.

3. During your employee appraisal, your boss criticizes you for something you feel is unfair. How would you respond?

_____ a. Accept the criticism quietly. Any comment on your part will only prolong the interview.

_____ b. Unless it is a big issue, keep quiet about it. Otherwise, briefly disagree in a good-natured way; then drop it.

_____ c. Defend yourself. Let the boss know you think you are being treated unfairly. Insist that a different evaluation be submitted.

Supervisors respect you more when you stand up for what you believe.

_____ d.   Discuss the boss' view until it is completely clear. Then offer your own opinion supported with facts and data. Debate the issue if necessary.

4.   After receiving a detailed explanation of a new job from your supervisor, you still aren't clear on some of the instructions. What would you do?

_____ a.   If you are good at your job, you should be able to figure out what to do as you go along. There's probably a better way to complete the task anyway.

_____ b.   Never ask questions. You only look stupid. If necessary, get help from a coworker.

_____ c.   Ask questions of your boss any time you aren't completely sure about an assignment.

_____ d.   If your boss believes that asking questions shows employee interest, ask for clarification. If not, pretend you understand and find out the missing information some other way.

5.   Your supervisor calls a meeting to evaluate the success of a new procedure and asks for everyone's opinion. How would you respond?

_____ a.   Listen carefully to everyone's comments. Openly agree with people when possible. However, if your experiences with the procedure differ from those being expressed, keep them to yourself.

_____ b.   Inform those present about the success you've had in implementing the procedure and recommend that your method be adopted by the group.

_____ c.   Don't volunteer any comments. Let the others do the talking. If the supervisor specifically asks for your opinion, keep your answer general so you won't have any reason to regret what you have said.

_____ d.   Participate actively in the discussion. Don't hesitate to express your experiences (both positive and negative) even if they differ from the experiences of the other employees.

6.   Almost by accident, you discover an easier and faster way to perform one of your daily tasks. As a result, you can finish the other duties of the day in a more relaxed manner. Would you tell anyone else of your discovery?

_____ a.   Employees who can perform their duties better than others are the ones who get the raises and promotions. Therefore, the only way to get ahead is to keep such discoveries to yourself.

_____ b.   If the boss knew that a task could be completed in less time, you and your fellow employees would be given an additional job to do, and the smooth pattern of office life would be disrupted. Therefore, say nothing.

_____ c.   Because it is everyone's responsibility to share job-related discoveries with one another, offer to do so. Then, if they are interested, tell them about the discovery.

_____ d.   A discovery such as this gives you the perfect opportunity to prove that you are more capable than your fellow workers. If you can impress your boss during a departmental meeting by presenting your discovery, then do so.

7.   In a last-minute check of a rush job that is due immediately in the boss' office, you discover a minor mistake that you have made. How would you handle it?

_____ a.   If the error is small enough to pass by without notice, keep the problem to yourself. However, if the error is sure to be noticed and could hurt your relationship with the boss, mention the error in a joking manner and ask for extra time to correct it.

_____ b.   Immediately phone or go see the boss and explain that you have discovered an error in your work and will need to postpone delivery of the project a few hours.

_____ c.   The best defense is a good offense. Because you did what the boss told you to do, the mistake is obviously the result of the boss' instructions. Point this out when you deliver the project.

_____ d.   Keep quiet about the error and hope it passes unnoticed. Even if it doesn't, the decision to delay the project is now the boss' responsibility.

8.   You are aware of a situation that has the potential for creating a serious problem for your department or even for the company. What would you do?

_____ a.   It is management's responsibility to be aware of potential problems. As an employee, it is not your responsibility to report on such things. Unless you could benefit by discussing your observations, keep quiet.

_____ b.   Meddling in things that are none of your business is a good way to lose your job.

_____ c.   Because management depends on and should appreciate the input and observations of employees, don't hesitate to mention your observations to your boss.

_____ d.   No one wants to hear negative things. Pointing out the problem to management will only cause trouble and make people unhappy. Also, if your observation is wrong, you will look like a fool. Therefore, just keep the information to yourself.

9. A serious conflict has arisen between you and another worker in your department. How would you handle it?

_____ a. If you give in, the other person will lose respect for you, so try to win the argument. If no decision can be reached, select a person (such as your boss) to serve as an arbitrator.

_____ b. Discuss the conflict in detail, making sure both of you get a chance to express your feelings. Honest discussion usually leads to a mutual agreement and an end to hostilities. In some cases, it may be necessary to compromise.

_____ c. Continuing the conflict will only bring you unwanted attention from other employees and even the boss. If necessary to end the conflict, give in.

_____ d. Continuing the conflict could permanently damage your friendship with this employee. Do your best to smooth over the argument and regain a friendly footing with the person.

10. Your immediate work group has failed to complete its assignment on time in three out of the last four projects. The boss is starting to put pressure on your group and wants to know who's causing the slowdown. You know who the person is. What would you do?

_____ a. Suggest that all members of the group meet to discuss the problem. If you find that the problem is caused by an unfair load distribution or some other group-related cause, try to find a workable answer.

_____ b. Blaming the individual either personally or in front of others only creates a strain on the relationships in the group. The best thing to do is to blame circumstances, such as the instructions weren't clear, there wasn't enough time, or someone outside the group was slow in supplying information.

_____ c. Nothing is gained by keeping quiet. A single individual is making you and the entire group look bad. Put pressure on the person to admit causing the delays. If that doesn't work, tell the boss yourself.

_____ d. Do nothing. It is not wise to volunteer this type of information.

11. While working on a project, a highly unusual problem arises that is not covered in your department's procedures manual. Even your boss is uncertain about it. What would you do?

_____ a. Postpone making a decision. If you put the decision off long enough, someone else will probably make it and any mistakes will be their responsibility.

_____ b.   Discuss the problem with your boss, your coworkers, and even knowledgeable people outside your department. Okay your final decision with your boss before making it official.

_____ c.   Ask your boss and your fellow workers to see what they would do. Base your decision on the majority opinion. That way no one can put the blame on you.

_____ d.   This is a chance to prove your ability. You don't need anyone else's opinion if you are a good employee. Make the decision yourself.

12.   How important is your boss to your individual success?

_____ a.   Except for a few years, you are as knowledgeable as or more knowledgeable than the boss. Therefore, the boss plays only a minor role in your success.

_____ b.   Extremely important. Without the boss to tell you what to do, there could be no success.

_____ c.   Success depends on how happy the boss is with what you do and how well the boss likes you. If the boss is satisfied, you will be successful.

_____ d.   You and the boss work as a team. Both are equally necessary for success.

Survey of Communication Styles Score Sheets

Directions: Copy the scores you selected for answers _a_, _b_, _c_, and _d_ for each of the twelve questions onto the score sheets on the next page. Notice that each score sheet puts your answers in an order different from the way you answered them on the surveys. Total the numbers in each column; plot your totals on the following graph.

The two highest scores on either the MTI or the ETI are probably the most descriptive of your communication behavior. The highest score represents the communication style you typically use when things are going well. The next highest score (or perhaps two scores that are very close in size) represents the style you use under stress. Remember that these tests are not infallible and should be considered only indicators of _tendencies_ in your communication behavior. Each communication style is explained in detail in Chapter 3.

**Manager Tendency Indicator
Score Sheet:**

	I	II	III	IV
1.	d[ ]	c[ ]	b[ ]	a[ ]
2.	a[ ]	b[ ]	c[ ]	d[ ]
3.	c[ ]	b[ ]	a[ ]	d[ ]
4.	b[ ]	a[ ]	d[ ]	c[ ]
5.	c[ ]	b[ ]	d[ ]	a[ ]
6.	b[ ]	d[ ]	c[ ]	d[ ]
7.	a[ ]	c[ ]	b[ ]	d[ ]
8.	b[ ]	a[ ]	d[ ]	c[ ]
9.	b[ ]	d[ ]	a[ ]	c[ ]
10.	d[ ]	b[ ]	c[ ]	a[ ]
11.	d[ ]	b[ ]	c[ ]	a[ ]
12.	a[ ]	d[ ]	b[ ]	c[ ]
Totals	[ ]	[ ]	[ ]	[ ]
	OPEN	BLIND	HIDDEN	CLOSED

**Employee Tendency Indicator
Score Sheet:**

	I	II	III	IV
1.	d[ ]	a[ ]	c[ ]	b[ ]
2.	a[ ]	b[ ]	d[ ]	c[ ]
3.	d[ ]	c[ ]	b[ ]	a[ ]
4.	c[ ]	a[ ]	d[ ]	b[ ]
5.	d[ ]	b[ ]	a[ ]	c[ ]
6.	c[ ]	d[ ]	a[ ]	b[ ]
7.	b[ ]	c[ ]	a[ ]	d[ ]
8.	c[ ]	a[ ]	d[ ]	b[ ]
9.	b[ ]	a[ ]	d[ ]	c[ ]
10.	a[ ]	c[ ]	b[ ]	d[ ]
11.	b[ ]	d[ ]	c[ ]	a[ ]
12.	d[ ]	a[ ]	c[ ]	b[ ]
Totals	[ ]	[ ]	[ ]	[ ]
	OPEN	BLIND	HIDDEN	CLOSED

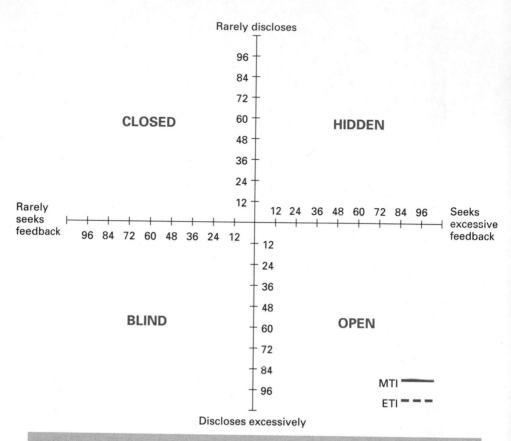

Instructions: To plot your MTI and ETI scores, draw your MTI scores using a solid line arc; your ETI scores using a dashed line arc. Read Chapter 3 to interpret the meaning of your scores.

B Questions Asked of Job Applicants Seeking Nonsupervisory Positions

KNOWLEDGE OF ORGANIZATION

1. Why do you think you might like to work for our company, organization, office?
2. What interests you about our product or service?
3. Tell me what you know about our company.
4. Compare our company with others in this field.

CAREER PLANS OR GOALS

1. What job in our company do you want to work toward?
2. What job in our company would you choose if you were entirely free to do so?
3. What are your future career plans?
4. In what type of position are you most interested?
5. Why did you choose your particular field of work?
6. What do you know about opportunities in the field in which you are trained?
7. What type of work interests you?
8. What are the disadvantages of your chosen field?
9. Are you interested in research?
10. What personal characteristics are necessary for success in your field?
11. What do you see as the major trends in your field today? major problems in your field today?
12. Describe for me the ideal boss.
13. Do you prefer a large, medium, or small company? Why?

WORK EXPERIENCE

1. What qualifications do you have that make you feel that you will be successful in your field?
2. What jobs have you held? How were they obtained and why did you leave?
3. How did previous employers treat you?
4. What have you learned from some of the jobs you have held?
5. Can you get recommendations from previous employers?
6. What jobs have you enjoyed the most? the least? Why?
7. What have you done that shows initiative and willingness to work?
8. Have you saved any money for previous employers?
9. Why are you leaving your current position?
10. What would make you leave us?
11. Why should I hire you?
12. Why do you think you would like this particular type of job?
13. Do you prefer working with others or by yourself? Why?
14. Do you like routine work?

15. Do you like regular hours?
16. What are your own special abilities?
17. How would your coworkers describe you? your supervisors describe you?
18. Describe your greatest accomplishment so far.

JOB PERFORMANCE

1. What do you think determines a person's progress in a good company?
2. What type of performance appraisal system was used by your last (or current) company? Was it fair?
3. What criteria should be used to evaluate employees in this field?
4. How many days were you absent last year?
5. Describe a good attendance record.
6. What was your evaluation on your last performance appraisal?

SALARY AND BENEFITS

1. What are your ideas on salary?
2. How much money do you hope to earn at age 30? 40?
3. Do you expect to be paid for overtime work?
4. What salary would you need to join us?
5. What fringe benefits are the most important to you? the least important?

EDUCATION AND TRAINING

1. Describe your educational background.
2. What school (college) course did you like best? least? Why?
3. What percentage of your school courses did you pay for?
4. How did you spend your vacations in school?
5. Do you feel you have received a good general training?
6. If you were starting college all over again, what courses would you take?
7. Have you ever changed your major field of interest while in college? Why?
8. When did you choose your college major? Why?
9. Do you feel you have done the best scholastic work of which you are capable?
10. Which of your college years was the most difficult?
11. Did you enjoy your college years?
12. Have you plans for graduate work?
13. Have you ever tutored an undergraduate?

PERSONALITY AND GENERAL QUESTIONS

1. What offices have you held?
2. What activities do you enjoy the most?
3. What type of boss do you prefer?
4. Are you primarily interested in making money or do you feel that service to humanity is your prime concern?
5. Can you take instructions without feeling upset?
6. Tell me a story!
7. What size of city do you prefer?
8. What are your major strengths? weaknesses?
9. Do you demand attention?
10. Do you have an analytical mind or a creative mind?
11. Are you eager to please?
12. What type of books have you read?
13. What type of people seem to rub you the wrong way?
14. Do you like to travel?

From *Making the Most of Your Job Interview* (New York: New York Life Insurance Company, n.d.). Originally in a report by Frank S. Endicott, "Trends in the Employment of University and College Graduates in Business and Industry," and Charles J. Stewart and William B. Cash, Jr., 6th ed., *Interviewing: Principles and Practices* (Dubuque, IA: Wm. C. Brown, 1991). Reprinted by permission.

C

Questions Asked of Job Applicants Seeking Management Positions

1. Beginning with your move into your first supervisor job, would you tell me, briefly, *why each change was made*.

ACCOMPLISHMENTS—CURRENT JOB

2. (Refer to most recent position.) What would you say are some of your more important accomplishments? I'd be interested in operating results and any other accomplishments you consider important. (Probe for four or five accomplishments. Get specific data.)
3. Considering these accomplishments, what are some of the reasons for your success?
4. Were there any unusual difficulties you had to overcome in getting these accomplishments?
5. What two or three things do you feel you have learned on this job?
6. What did you particularly like about this position?
7. There are always a few negatives about a position. What would you say you liked least about the position?
8. What responsibilities or results have not come up to your expectations? I'd be interested in things you had hoped and planned to accomplish that were not done. I sometimes call them disappointments. (Push for several, specific answers.)
9. What are some of the reasons for this?

ACCOMPLISHMENTS—SECOND POSITION

I'd like to talk with you about your experience as _____.

(Mention title of second most recent position.)

10. What would you say were some of the more important things you accomplished on this job?
11. What were some of the factors that would account for the accomplishments you have just mentioned?
12. What responsibilities or results didn't come up to your expectations on this job?
13. What were some of the reasons for this?
14. What would you say you learned on this job?
15. What did you like about it?
16. What didn't you like about it?

ADDITIONAL POSITIONS

(Repeat questions 10 through 16 if there was a significant period as a manager in a third position.)

PLANNING DECISIONS

17. I'm interested in how you do your planning. What planning processes have you found useful and how do you go about them?
18. In what ways do you feel you have improved in your planning in the last few years?
19. What are some examples of important types of decisions or recommendations you are called upon to make?
20. Would you describe how you went about making these types of decisions or recommendations? With whom did you talk, and so forth?
21. What decisions are easiest for you to make and which ones are more difficult?
22. Most of us can think of an important decision that we would make quite differently if we made it again. Any examples from your experience? (Probe) What's the biggest mistake you can recall?
23. Most of us improve in our decision-making ability as we get greater experience. In what respects do you feel you have improved in your decision making?

ORGANIZATION (STRUCTURE, DELEGATION, STAFFING, DESELECTION, TRANSITIONS)

24. What has been your experience with expansion or reduction of force? (Explore for details.)
25. How many immediate subordinates have you selected in the last two years? How did you go about it? Any surprises or disappointments?
26. How many immediate subordinates have you removed from their jobs in the last few years? Any contemplated? One example of how you went about it.
27. How do you feel your subordinates would describe you as a delegator? Any deliberate tactics you use?

CONTROLLING

28. Some managers keep a very close check on their organization. Others use a loose rein. What pattern do you follow? How has it changed in the last few years?
29. What has been the most important surprise you have received from something getting out of control? Why did it happen?
30. Let's talk about standards of performance. How would you describe your own? What would your subordinates say? What would your boss say?
31. Sometimes it is necessary to issue an edict to an individual or the entire staff. Do you have any recent examples of edicts you have issued? (Probe) Reasons? Results?

SUPERVISION

32. What things do you think contribute to your effectiveness as a supervisor?
33. From an opposite viewpoint, what do you think might interfere with your effectiveness as a supervisor?
34. In what respects do you feel you have improved most as a supervisor during the last few years?
35. What type of supervisor gets the best performance out of you?
36. Some managers are quite deliberate about such things as communications, development, and motivation. Do you have any examples of how you do this?
37. What have you done about your own development in the last few years?

OTHER

38. Would you describe your relationship with your last three supervisors?
39. Considering your relationships both inside and outside the component, would you give me an example of where you have been particularly effective in relating with others?
40. Would you also give me an example of when you might *not* have been particularly effective in relating with others?
41. Some people are short-fused and impatient in their reactions. How would you describe yourself?
42. Have you encountered any health problems? What do you do about your health?
43. Most of us can look back upon a new idea, a new project, or an innovation we feel proud of introducing. Would you describe one or two such innovations that you are particularly proud of?

FUTURE

44. How do you feel about your career progress to date?
45. What are your aspirations for the future? Have these changed?
46. We sometimes compare the assets and limitations of our products with competition. Let's do a related thing with your career. Thinking of your competition for jobs to which you aspire, what would you say are your main assets, your strengths, and what would you say are your limitations? (Get three or more assets and three or more limitations.)
47. Are there any conditions of personal business, health, or family that would limit your flexibility for taking on a new assignment?

From Walter Mahler, *How Effective Executives Interview* (Homewood, IL: Dow Jones-Irwin, 1976), pp. 91–95. Reprinted by permission of Mahler Assoc.

D Presentations to Enjoy and Evaluate

PLUTONIUM 238

NASA's Fuel of Choice

BY JENNY CLANTON, *a student at Southeastern Illinois College at Harrisburg. Delivered at the Interstate Oratorical Association speech contest in Salem, Oregon, on May 6–7, 1988. Clanton was awarded first place out of thirty-seven contestants.*

On January 28, 1986, the American Space Program suffered the worst disaster in its more than 30-year history. The entire world was shocked when the space shuttle *Challenger* exploded seconds after lift-off, claiming the lives of seven brave astronauts and crippling our entire space agenda. I
5 suppose the oldest cliché in our culture, spoken on battlegrounds and indeed virtually anywhere Americans die, is "We must press forward, so we can say they did not die in vain." Rest assured. They didn't. The deaths of our seven astronauts probably saved the lives of untold thousands of Americans.

10   For, you see, if the O-rings had not failed on January 28, 1986, but rather on May 20, 1987, the next scheduled shuttle launch, in the words of Dr. John Gofman, Professor Emeritus at the University of California at Berkeley, you could have "kissed Florida goodbye."

        Because the next shuttle, the one that was to have explored the atmo-
15 sphere of Jupiter was to carry 47 lbs. of Plutonium 238, which, is again, according to Dr. Gofman, the most toxic substance on the face of the earth. Dr. Helen Caldicott corroborates Dr. Gofman's claim in her book, *Nuclear Madness,* when she cites studies estimating one ounce of widely dispersed Plutonium 238 particles as having the toxicity to induce lung
20 cancer in every person on earth.

        Today, when you leave this room, I want you to fully understand just what impact NASA's plans could have on this planet. I want you to become cynical. I want you to be a little scared. I want you to become angry. But most of all, I want you to begin to demand some answers.

25   To move you in this direction I would first like to explore with you just what plutonium is and what could happen if it were released in our atmosphere. Second, let's consider NASA's argument for the safety of the plutonium as used in the shuttle program. And finally, I want to convince you that NASA's conclusions are flawed.

30   So now, let's turn our attention to the nature of plutonium. Plutonium is a man-made radioactive element which is produced in large quantities in nuclear reactors from uranium. Plutonium is a chemically reactive metal

From *Winning Orations,* 1988, pp. 24–27. Reprinted by permission of the Interstate Oratorical Association.

which, if exposed to air, ignites spontaneously and produces fine particles of plutonium dioxide. These particles, when dispersed by wind and inhaled
35 by living organisms, lodge in the lungs. Lung cancer will follow—sooner or later. Once inside the human body, plutonium rests in bone tissue, causing bone cancer. Plutonium 238 is so poisonous that less than one *millionth* of a gram is a carcinogenic dose.

Last July, *Common Cause* magazine contacted Dr. Gofman at Berkeley
40 and asked him to place Plutonium 238 in perspective. Before I share Dr. Gofman's assessment, please understand he's no poster-carrying "anti-nuke." Dr. Gofman was co-discoverer of Uranium 233, and he isolated the isotope first used in nuclear bombs. Dr. Gofman told Karl Grossman, author of the article "Redtape and Radio-activity" that Plutonium 238 is
45 300 times more radioactive than Plutonium 239, which is the isotope used in atomic bombs.

Dr. Richard Webb, a Nuclear Physicist and author of *The Accident Hazards of Nuclear Power Plants*, said in a similar interview that sending 46.7 lbs of Plutonium 238 into space would be the equivalent of sending
50 five nuclear reactors up—and then hoping they wouldn't crash or explode.

Dr. Gofman's final assessment? It's a crazy idea, unless—unless shuttle launches are 100 percent perfect. Which is just about what NASA would have liked us to believe, and at first glance NASA's guarantees are pretty convincing.
55 NASA estimates the chance of releasing Plutonium into the environment, because of the possibility of a malfunction of the space shuttle, at .002%—that's not quite 100% perfect, but it's awfully close. NASA and the Department of Energy base their reliability figures on three factors: (1) the Titan 34D launch vehicle and its high success rate, (2) Energy
60 Department officials in the March 10th *Aviation Week and Space Technology* magazine explain that the Plutonium would be safely contained in an un-breakable, quarter-inch thick iridium canister which would withstand pressures of over 2,000 pounds per square inch, and (3) in that same article, NASA explains there is "little public danger" because the Plutonium on
65 board would be in the form of oxide pellets, each one-inch in diameter. If you'll remember, the danger of Plutonium is in fine particles.

Now, let's take a second glance. One month later, the April 28th issue of *Aviation Week and Space Technology* reported that two of the last nine Titans launched have blown-up. Two failures in nine trips is great in base-
70 ball, but not when we're dealing with nuclear payloads. That same article estimates loss of orbiter and crew, not at .002% but at 1 in 25.

With odds on the launch vehicle reduced to 1 in 25, the dual questions arise: just how breach-proof is that canister and, in a worst case scenario, what could happen if the pellets of 238 were released? For the answers to

75 those questions we go to Dr. Gary Bennett, former Director of Safety and Nuclear Operations, who not only answers those questions, but also explains why NASA is so insistent on using Plutonium.

Last July, Dr. Bennett told *Common Cause* that there is concern within NASA and the Department of Energy that an explosion aboard the *Galileo* 80 spacecraft, a *Titan* or other rocket, would, in turn, set off an explosion of the booster rockets. Bennett admitted that government tests in 1984 and 1985 determined that if the shuttle exploded, and then the booster rockets exploded, there would be a likelihood of breaching the iridium canister. The Plutonium would then be vaporized and released into the environ- 85 ment; and there goes Florida.

But why would NASA take such a risk? It's really quite simple. On the one hand, Plutonium 238 is the one fuel that would enable space exploration beyond the limit of Mars. Without it, distant space exploration must wait for research to develop an equally effective, safe fuel. On the other 90 hand, a worst case scenario would create the worst nuclear accident in history. In short, NASA weighed exploration now against the chances for disaster and opted to take the risk. The only problem is, I really don't like the idea of someone risking my life without consulting me—and I hope you don't either. By the way, there is evidence that NASA and the Depart- 95 ment of Energy have projected some pretty horrible figures. Under the Freedom of Information Act rules, Karl Grossman was able to obtain agencies' estimates for the number of lives lost in a major accident. The only problem there is, every reference to the number of people affected is blanketed out with liquid paper and the term Exempt #1 is written over 100 the deletion. James Lombardo of the Energy Department explains the white-outs were necessary for—you've got it—national security reasons. I would contend the national security would be threatened by mass anger over the callousness of the Energy Department, and justifiably so. Representative Edward Markey agrees, and when he was head of the House sub- 105 committee on Energy, Conservation and Power, he uncovered most of the information I share with you today.

In a telephone interview last August, I asked Congressman Markey three questions: Why hasn't Congress done anything? What should be done? What can we do to help?

110 His answer to the first question was quite interesting. You may remember that shortly after the shuttle exploded and just when Congress was showing some interest in a thorough investigation of the space program, another larger, even more dramatic accident occurred—Chernobyl. The attention to Chernobyl as it related to our own power industry cap- 115 tured not only the attention of most Americans, but of Congress as well. Consequently, most of our nuclear experts are involved in working with Congress and the nuclear power industry.

And while Congress is focusing on one facet of the nuclear question, NASA and the Department of Energy are receiving much less attention.
120 Which is why Congressman Markey helped found Space Watch.

Representative Markey is of the opinion that hysteria accomplishes nothing, but that all space [exploration] should be halted until either Plutonium 238 can be made safe, which is highly unlikely, or until an alternative fuel can be found. The burden of proof should be on NASA to
125 prove a fuel safe, and not on the public to prove it dangerous.

This is where you and I come in. First, if by now you are sufficiently scared or angry, contact Space Watch through Representative Markey's office. Then, keep abreast of developments and exert pressure through your elected officials if Congress does nothing to interfere with NASA's
130 plans. Send your objections not only to your own legislators, but to Representative Markey as well. Allow him to walk into the House with mailbag after mailbag of letters in opposition to NASA's unbridled desire to go to Jupiter. We have a friend in Congress who solicits help. The least we can do is give it to him.
135 One last thought: as of November, Plutonium 238 is *still* NASA's and the Department of Energy's fuel of choice. Dr. Bennett's last words in that July interview were, "I think you should understand there's a degree of risk with any kind of launch vehicle." But isn't that the point?

THE RIGHT WAY

A Matter of Principle

BY JAMES E. PERRELLA, *Executive Vice President, Ingersoll-Rand Company. Delivered at the University of Illinois, Chicago, January 19, 1989.*

Good afternoon. Professor McLimore's invitation to participate in this course with you today stirred a great deal of reflection as to the best subject for discussion. The number and variety of possible subjects seemed endless.

5 Among the candidates were:

—international business in times of changing currency values;

—product liability and increasing insurance costs;

—business as a societal problem-solver;

—the fact that profit is not a dirty word;

From *Vital Speeches* (April 1, 1989), pp. 375–376. By permission.

10 —the South Africa questions, ranging from business-inspired social improvements to complete disinvestment (now, that's a 20th-century word for you).

The list continued. Many subjects. Many ideas. Many possible
15 directions.

In this sea of subjects, one topic surfaced.

It is a topic that touches on every other subject mentioned, a topic much in the news, a topic that affects our attitudes, a topic that touches our lives:

20 Business ethics.

Think about it for a minute. If you approach the subject, business ethics, in terms of Ivan Boesky or *Dallas*'s J. R. Ewing, you may believe that "business ethics" is an oxymoron, or, as an article in *The Wall Street Journal* suggested, that "business" and "ethics" are mutually-
25 exclusive.

Today, we need to ask:

Are they?

Certainly, in fact and fiction, there is much that says business is not ethical, and stories that even suggest that businessmen cannot operate
30 ethically.

Consider the case of Daniel Drew, a New York cattleman of the early 19th century: Stuart Holbrook tells the story in *The Age of the Moguls:* Mr. Drew

"seems never to have denied his most celebrated piece of knavery, which
35 he used for many years in his cattle business.

"As a big herd of anywhere from six hundred to a thousand head of Ohio beef approached New York City, Drew had his drovers salt them well.

"Then, just before reaching the marketplace, he let them drink their
40 fill.

"Cattle were sold live-weight. Drew's processing with salt and water added many tons to the average herd. 'Watered stock' soon became a term in Wall Street."

Mr. Drew seemed a follower of a 19th-century parody of the Golden
45 Rule:

"do unto the other feller the way he'd like to do unto you, an' do it fust."

Mr. Drew's motives and actions can fit well with motives and actions prevalent in today's business world, or should I say, in today's world.

We seem to put ourselves first. Or try to. At almost any cost.

50 The extreme of this "me-first' attitude is the drug addict who will take advantage of anyone and anything to satisfy his insatiable craving.

Think, for a moment, about every-day situations as well:

The driver who tries to move ahead of other cars at every traffic light.

The greengrocer who puts the reddest strawberries on the top of the
55 basket.

The person who insists always on having the last word in any domestic argument.

The doctor who prescribes more and more tests, not necessarily for the patient's benefit, but for protection against a possible malpractice
60 claim.

The salesman who thinks more of his commission than of his customer's needs.

The student—certainly not anyone here—who cheats on an exam to gain a higher grade or rank.
65 The politician who steals another's speech to make himself sound better or wiser.

The individual who pays a tip to the maitre d' to get preferred seating.

In every case, the action is a me-first action.

Me first. A likely, or as many would say, the source of ethics problems.
70 In your career development, as you become our nation's business leaders, you will face the question:

May business people use any means, fair or foul, to make a sale, to insure success, to take advantage of a customer, or to do a competitor in?

In other words, to put themselves first.
75 In business, the Ivan Boesky/Drexel Burnham Lambert shenanigans keep reappearing in the nation's headlines.

A recent lawsuit charges that Boeing used bogus misbranded bearings in commercial and military aircraft.

While all sorts of special situations of this type have arisen, many
80 people, I am pleased to say, still do things the old-fashioned way.

In fact, many people still depend on a handshake to seal an agreement. A man's word is his bond. In many negotiations people trust each other completely. Even in complex business transactions.

In today's business world, handshake deals have not disappeared. They
85 are fewer, however, as people depend on written warranties and guarantees and exclusions and warnings in the most confusing language and in the tiniest type.

In fact, "put it in writing" is a common request, accompanying the purchase of anything—from a baby buggy to a used car.
90 Lawyers love it. They sue people and companies. They defend. They challenge. They appeal. They seem to relish new opportunities in every business transaction. They try to put their clients, and themselves, first.

At the same time, they pose a new question for businessmen. They replace the question about business activity: "Is it right?" with "Is it legal?"

95   This trend, developing over years, as attorneys try to protect their clients in an ever more complex business world, has created a division between morality and legality, weakening, if not dissipating, the strength and significance of once-prevalent handshake agreements.

In our Western civilization, laws and morals have strengthened each
100 other since the time of Moses. Until now.

Our question of today should be, what's the right thing to do? The right way to behave? The right way to conduct business? Don't just ask, Is it legal?

Several states have passed laws declaring that companies with invest-
105 ments in South Africa are not acceptable bidders on state purchases and not acceptable as an investment by state pension funds.

My company has investments in South Africa and we provide both our white and black employees with working conditions very close to those in the U.S. and we provide our black employees with financial and growth
110 opportunities not otherwise available.

I personally have sat with our black employees to determine their desires.

We are committed to stay even if we lose some business in the U.S. and our stock is affected by the reduced buying by pension plans.
115   The law is trying to be detrimental to our South African employees, and that isn't right.

Apartheid itself is another example of a law that isn't right, moral or ethical, and we break that law in our South African factory every day.

Let me be the first to admit that the choice is not always easy.
120   Consider, for instance, these questions from Scruples, a Milton Bradley game:

—The garage forgets to charge you for a six-dollar oil filter. You think the labor charge is too high, anyway. Do you mention the undercharge?

—In a parking lot you accidentally dent a car. Do you leave a note?
125   —You are applying for a job requiring experience you don't have. Do you claim you do?

Questions of this sort reach beyond legality.

They raise the question of right versus wrong, not legal versus illegal.

The answers require no legal knowledge. They require only common
130 sense and the sense of fair play that we all learned as youngsters.

You remember. I remember. Don't cheat. Don't steal. Don't lie. Don't take advantage of anyone's weakness. The Golden Rule.

Do unto others the way you would have them do unto you.

In other words, treat the other guy fair. That's the way to solve all
135 ethics problems.

You would think that business behavior would reflect that basic groundwork in ethics; that business actions would reflect our generally sound sense of rightness.

You would think that rightness would be an automatic choice—sort of
140 like driving on the right side of the road—for our own benefit.

Have you ever considered what business would be like if we all did it? If every businessman (and businesswoman) followed the Golden Rule?

Ripe, red strawberries would fill a box from top to bottom.

145 Barrels would not contain a single rotten apple.

My company would not have to file a lawsuit alleging that counterfeit bearings were sold to Boeing Company by a California-based bearing supplier.

My company would not have to file a complaint with the Federal
150 Trade Commission charging dumping of other bearings in United States markets.

Congress would not have to tighten curbs on insider trading.

Companies would not have to require employees to sign codes of conduct or establish strict guidelines for purchasing agents to follow.

155 The Harvard Business School would not have to require that each entering student take a three-week course on business ethics.

Drexel Burnham Lambert would not have to pay a $650 million fine.

Many people, including many business leaders, would argue that such an application of ethics to business would adversely affect bottom-line
160 performance.

I say nay.

The ideas we are considering today go far beyond the bottom line.

If we do things right, because that's the way to do things, just imagine the effect we will have on customers.

165 Mr. Iacocca showed the beginnings of the possibilities when he led Chrysler in new directions.

Johnson and Johnson set a solid example when it pulled Tylenol off the shelves immediately during the crisis of a few years ago.

H. J. Heinz and Squibb established a high standard of ethical excel-
170 lence when they supported our nation's pure food and drug laws early in this century.

In these situations, the businesses and their leaders put the public and their customers first.

I ask you to imagine the effect on the bottom lines of tomorrow if
175 business were to follow these examples today.

Good ethics, simply, is good business.

Good ethics will attract investors.

Good ethics will attract good employees.

Moreover, good ethics will attract and retain customers, employees,
180 investors, and build a quality reputation.

As you begin your careers, please remember that you set your own standards.

Your actions can lead to a Chrysler turnaround or to a Wedtech.

In a real sense, the future is up to you. You can change the way things are done. You can make the critical choice.

You can do what's right. Not because of conduct codes. Not because of rules or laws. But because you know what's right.

I will applaud your decision.

HOW TO EARN AN MBWA DEGREE

BY JAMES H. LAVENSON. *Delivered for the Kings Dominion Management Group, Pinehurst, North Carolina, March 12, 1976.*

The last time I was in Chicago, I was making a speech before the Executives Club. I don't know if you're familiar with that organization, but it's impressive for a couple reasons. First, they have over 3000 paid up members. Second, they get anywhere from five hundred to a thousand of the members to come to a luncheon speech every Friday. The week before my speech, they'd had Senator Charles Percy. The week after me, they had Nelson Rockefeller. I felt good about the company I was in until I was introduced with the polite explanation to the audience by the club's president that a "change of pace" was desirable.

Anyway, the point of my telling you about this organization is that before each luncheon, they ask the speaker to meet with a half dozen high school kids whom they've invited as guests. When I met with them, they took one look at me, looked at each other, and almost in one voice wanted to know what kind of education you needed to be in management. Was there a major course of study, a *degree* in management which they could pursue in college?

Naturally, I refused to answer a stupid question like that.

But if you know kids, you know they don't let go, especially if they smell a phoney. They'd been told I had been president of the Plaza Hotel and had had no previous hotel experience, no hotel schooling and they seemed skeptical about what the B.S. degree I'd gotten in college really stood for.

"Mr. Lavenson," one particularly obnoxious little smart alec asked me, "If you had no experience running a hotel and you started at the top, how did you know what to do? Just what did you do?"

From *Vital Speeches* (April 15, 1976), pp. 410–412. By permission.

"I ran the place, that's what! Next question?" I snapped back and figured I'd won. I hadn't.

"Come now, Mr. Lavenson, these students won't accept that answer." It was their teacher who interrupted this time, a guy with a beard and a
30 pipe and a very high forehead and I hated him on sight. "What about an MBA degree? Wouldn't you say that a master's degree in business from a school like Harvard or The Wharton School would qualify a man or woman for management?"

I didn't have an MBA degree and it was painfully obvious this teacher
35 did. If I let him win that point, I knew I was lost, so I resorted to a trick I'd learned through years of experience: I lied.

"Not an MBA degree," I said very calmly. "It takes an MB*W*A degree to qualify as a manager." With that one, I'd stopped the beard and pipe dead in his tracks. But he recovered and just before someone came in and
40 announced lunch was starting, he growled a last question "Just exactly what *is* an MBWA degree?"

I gave him my most generous smile, and gave him a pearl of wisdom in one sentence that I'm going to stretch out into a full speech today. You see, I'd never really thought about it before and my glib answer to that
45 poor teacher and his group of kids was the lucky, accidental, off-the-cuff, wise-guy response of a cornered rat. On my way home from Chicago, I thought a lot about the questions those kids were asking and my answer. The longer I thought about it, the more I realized that MBWA *is* the qualification for management, and it's one I'd unwittingly been using
50 in every job I'd been in. And when I'd started each of the management jobs I've had over the past twenty years—in advertising, in toy products, in luggage, in publishing, in food processing, in sunglasses, T-shirts, dresses . . . There's one thing you can say about me without fear of contradiction from anyone with whom I ever worked. I didn't know from
55 beans about any of those businesses. I don't really mean I didn't know *anything*. . . . But what I didn't know about any of the businesses when I started in them was how to *run* them. And I certainly didn't have any of the technical experience necessary to mold a doll, sew leather into a suitcase which would come out the other end of the production line as Hart-
60 man luggage, or how to dig clams out of the Atlantic Ocean, clean them, vacuum pack them into cans labeled Doxsee. . . .

A long time ago, and this is hindsight, I remember a man I admired a great deal during World War II being quoted and what he said must have made a subconscious impression on me. Today I repeat it to myself every
65 morning. The man was General Sommerville, and he'd spent his entire life in the army. Then came the end of the war, he was retired as a multi-starred general and suddenly it was announced he wasn't really retiring at all. He was made the chairman of the Koppers Company, a gigantic

corporation which had nothing to do with the army, war, tanks, guns,
70 airplanes or VD training films. Some wise guy reporter asked General
Sommerville at the press conference announcing his election to the chair-
manship of Koppers—he must have been related to that young teacher in
Chicago—just why the general thought he was qualified to be the chief
executive officer of a large corporation in the business world, when all his
75 experience had been in the army. Not business, just the army. The general's reply was a classic and if I had my way would replace all those think
signs you see in offices all over this country wherever an IBM man has
been able to get his foot in the door.

What the general replied to the reporter's questioning his qualifica-
80 tions for a job in business was this: "You don't have to be a chicken to smell
a rotten egg." Here it comes again: "You don't have to be a chicken to
smell a rotten egg."

Isn't that nifty? Aside from the fact that it gives every idiot like me an
open season license to take on a management job in any field, it happens,
85 also, to be true. Think about it a little longer than we're going to be
together here today. Think about it tonight, and tomorrow. Think about
it for a week. I believe you'll come up with your own examples and experiences, either yours or a manager you admire, and you'll agree that what
General Sommerville was saying is that he had an MBWA degree.
90 Maybe the president of International Harvester, that gigantic farm
equipment company, was saying the same thing when he was asked what
he looked for in men he hired to help him run the company. "More than
an agricultural degree or courses in business management, I look for men
who know what manure smells like at five o'clock on a frosty morning." I
95 submit that he, too, like General Sommerville, was talking about an
MBWA degree.

Oh my, that's right! I still haven't told you what MBWA stands for,
have I? MBWA stands for *Management by Walking Around.* Just walking
around with your eyes and ears open, asking questions like crazy and trying
100 to understand what the guys working for you are doing. A good place to
start is to see if *they* understand what they're doing.

But, of course, to start you have to get up off that big over-stuffed
leather throne in your paneled office, and actually *walk* around by yourself.
Granted it's hard exercise, particularly because most of us bosses are used
105 to being carried and guided by well-meaning subordinates. Don't take
your secretary with you and have her scribbling notes of your observations,
don't take a portable dictation machine and mumble into it in front of the
guy you're talking to, either. Have you ever had that happen to you? A guy
comes up, asks you a question, then pulls a little machine out of his pocket
110 and starts talking, or rather whispering, into it like he was right out of

1984? Make you nervous? It scares the hell out of me! I figure he's calling in a hit man.

A couple years ago, I was asked to consult with the management of the Tour Hassan Hotel in Rabat, Morocco. They had service problems and
115 profit problems and they wanted me to help fix them. This was really funny because, at that time, I'd not yet been in the hotel business. In addition, in Morocco they only speak French and Arabic. I spoke little of one and none of the other. Unwittingly in Morocco, I got a degree in MBWA, and it was in a language I didn't even understand. I flew to Mo-
120 rocco not having the remotest idea how to start and just checked into the hotel like any other guest. The first morning I wanted my breakfast in the room and walked around trying to figure out how to order it. There were two buttons over the bed with a single sign over both saying "Service" in English. I pushed one button, waited five minutes and then pushed the
125 other one. Nothing happened, so I got dressed and went downstairs for breakfast. The hotel's manager was there and again, like any guest, I was quick to tell him his buttons didn't work. He wasn't the least bit upset. "They've never worked since I've been here and that's five years. You have to call for room service on the phone," he said casually.
130   "Can't you get them fixed?" I asked.

"Cost too much," was his answer, which I've learned to expect from management in almost any business.

"How much?" I wanted to know.

"A lot" was his enlightening answer.
135   Not satisfied, I went to the Controller and asked if he'd seen a bid on repairing the buzzer system from the rooms. He hadn't, but he knew it would cost too much. I went to the chief engineer and asked him if he knew how much it would cost. Do you know what he said? He told me it wouldn't cost anything because there was nothing wrong with the system.
140 It was just turned off. All that was required to make it work was to throw a switch. So why was it turned off? Because, since the two buttons were never identified as to which was which—food or maid—guests batting an even 500 would push the wrong button every other time. The maids got exasperated, the room service waiters were sick of people crying "Wolf,
145 Wolf," or rather, "food, food," when what they really wanted was a clean towel. So the housekeeper persuaded the chief engineer to throw the switch. Nobody had told the manager, and he never asked to find out. Believe it or not, I got a citation from the king of Morocco for a stroke of sheer genius . . . putting labels over each of the two buttons, marking one
150 "food" and one "maid" and asking the engineer to throw the switch.

One day about ten years ago, I suddenly found myself chairman of the Hartman Luggage Company. Like you, I'd known the name for years and before I'd seen the figures, I would have guessed Hartman was at least a

ten or twenty million dollar company. I was shocked to learn its sales
155 volume was under two million, so I started by walking around the territory
with a couple salesmen to see why they weren't selling more. They all told
me the same thing—Hartman was a prestige name without a truly prestige
product—a real top of the line, expensive piece of luggage which by its
very price, had the snob appeal to get it into stores like Saks Fifth Avenue
160 and Neiman Marcus. I brought that story back to the president who pooh-
poohed the idea, but reached into a secret compartment in his office safe
and produced the loveliest, richest looking attache case made of belting
leather and brass trim that I'd ever dreamed of. "Why isn't that in the
line?" I wanted to know.

165 "Too expensive. It would never sell. We'd have to retail this thing for
close to two hundred bucks."

I walked around again, taking the sample attache case with me and
asking the salesmen if this was the kind of thing they had in mind. "Yeah,
man!" was their reaction.

170 "How much should it sell for?" I wanted to know from the guys who
had to sell it. The consensus was three hundred bucks. That MBWA attache case went into the Hartman line along with overnighters and two-
suiters all made of belting leather with price tags that would shock the
Shah of Iran. Today Hartman is stocked by Saks and Neiman Marcus and
175 doing one helluva lot more than two million dollars in sales.

Probably the most important principle of MBWA is really a
philosophy—a philosophy which says that the boss' job is to make sure of
three things: first, that his staff understands what they are doing: second,
that his staff has the tools *they* think they need to do the job: and last, that
180 the boss lets the staff know he has an *appreciation* of what the employee is
doing.

You hear a lot of management types talk sanctimoniously about their
"open door" policy. Their door is "always open to the staff," they tell you.
In my book, the best reason for a boss' open door is so he can go *out* the
185 door and walk around.

On the wall of the office of Eddie Carlson, chairman of United Airlines, is a sign with the word Netma printed on it. He told me that represents the most serious deterrent to success in managing an organization.
Netma stands for "nobody ever tells me anything." Just because you told
190 the vice president doesn't mean he told his subordinates. Get up, walk out
of your office and ask if they know what they are doing? And why? And
does it make sense to them? The question is the single most powerful tool
of management. You'd be amazed, even in a business you know nothing
about, how you can smell the answer. You don't have to be a chicken to
195 smell a rotten egg. You can kill the Netma in any business with an MBWA
degree.